CONGRESS

Stephen E. Frantzich
U.S. Naval Academy
Steven E. Schier
Carleton College

CONGRESS
Games and Strategies

Brown & Benchmark
PUBLISHERS
Madison Dubuque, IA Guilford, CT Chicago Toronto London
Caracas Mexico City Buenos Aires Madrid Bogota Sydney

Book Team

Executive Editor *Irv Rockwood*
Production Editor *Jane C. Morgan*
Art Editor *Jodi Banowetz*
Photo Editor *Rose Deluhery*
Permissions Coordinator *Gail I. Wheatly*
Visuals/Design Developmental Specialist *Janice M. Roerig-Blong*
Production Manager *Beth Kundert*
Visuals/Design Freelance Specialist *Mary L. Christianson*
Marketing Manager *Kirk Moen*

Brown & Benchmark PUBLISHERS
A Division of Wm. C. Brown Communications, Inc.

Executive Vice President/General Manager *Thomas E. Doran*
Vice President/Editor in Chief *Edgar J. Laube*
Vice President/Production *Vickie Putman*
National Sales Manager *Bob McLaughlin*

Wm. C. Brown Communications, Inc.

President and Chief Executive Officer *G. Franklin Lewis*
Senior Vice President, Operations *James H. Higby*
Corporate Senior Vice President and President of Manufacturing *Roger Meyer*
Corporate Senior Vice President and Chief Financial Officer *Robert Chesterman*

The credits section for this book begins on page 303 and is considered an extension of the copyright page.

Cover and interior designs by Lesiak/Crampton Design Inc.

Cover image by © S. Barrow Inc/Superstock

Copyedited by Jo Retzler

A Times Mirror Company

Library of Congress Catalog Card Number: 94–70434

ISBN 0–697–14633–2

Printed in the United States of America by Wm. C. Brown Communications, Inc., 2460 Kerper Boulevard, Dubuque, IA 52001

10 9 8 7 6 5 4 3 2 1

To our mothers,
Winifred K. Frantzich and Marjorie I. Schier,
who gave us so much.

CONTENTS

A PREFACE FOR TEACHERS

Authoring this book revealed to us the many ways instructors teach about the subject of Congress and their differing preferences about the appropriate topical coverage of the subject. Many who field undergraduate courses on our national legislature also teach several other American politics classes as well. Our text incorporates thorough references to the recent literature that will satisfy congressional specialists, but also includes a number of features that will appeal to nonspecialists, such as annotated paper topics and teaching ancillaries.

Explaining Congress to undergraduates can be a difficult task, so we want to support instructors in every way possible. Accordingly, our text supplies more instructional aids than its competitors. Our "In Depth" sections at the end of each chapter provide a battery of possible paper topics and class projects. The computer simulations included with this volume have many class applications. We also believe our text is the first to include an instructor's manual with lecture, exam and assignment suggestions.

We decided to organize our analysis around the game concept for three reasons. First, many participants in congressional politics use the analogy frequently to explain their own calculations and actions. Second, concepts from game theory have proven useful in explaining the behavior of the institution. Third, the analogy makes the subject matter more accessible to undergraduates who grew up contesting Nintendo, basketball, and other games. They will find the concepts of rules, strategies, winners, and losers to be a useful set of tools for making sense of Congress and its components.

Instructors teach about Congress in a variety of formats. Some conduct semester-long courses on the topic; others are limited to a trimester. Some combine coverage of Congress with other topics, such as the presidency or public policy; others do not. We designed this book to fit each of these needs. Those who focus solely on Congress will find this text allows them to include more advanced readings and supplementary books on their syllabus. Teachers combining Congress with other topics will find our book coordinates flexibly with additional readings and assignments on those topics.

We learned much while writing this book and would like to hear from those who adopt it. Please let us know where you think there is room for improvement.

Stephen E. Frantzich
Steven E. Schier

ACKNOWLEDGMENTS

The Publisher wishes to thank the following people who reviewed various versions of this text:

Gayle Berardi
Stephen F. Austin University

Jon Bond
Texas A&M University

Mary Anne Borrelli
Connecticut College

Diane Schmidt
Southern Illinois University

Cheryl Young
University of North Florida

Dale A. Neuman
University of Missouri–Kansas City

INTRODUCTION
The Congressional Games

One of the most frequent analogies [is] between baseball and . . . legislatures. . . . Baseball and legislatures share the notion of a season. . . . The best and most memorable plays occur at the last. . . . In baseball, as in legislative life, the rules frequently determine strategy. (Kurtz 1992, 11)

Analogies serve as powerful mechanisms by which we understand the world. We did not have to directly experience the first night's bombing of Baghdad during the Persian Gulf War to develop a feeling for its eery nature as U.S. pilots told us it was like the biggest Fourth of July fireworks display they had ever seen. A useful analogy allows us to compare something with which we are familiar to that with which we are not as familiar. Analogies fall into the intellectual process of categorizing events and phenomena by looking for relevant similarities. The fact that no two events or phenomena are absolutely identical, however, warns us not to completely trust analogies. Different analogies may be used to describe the same phenomenon. For the residents of Baghdad the air raid was more *like* "being at the center of Hell." Despite their restrictions, analogies can help us better understand phenomena if we remain aware of their limitations.

Useful analogies encourage us to build on our existing knowledge to expand our understanding of unfamiliar realms. This book will compare the political intricacies of Congress with a subject with which we are all familiar—games. One aspect of games, however, their frivolity, is not the aspect of the analogy we wish to emphasize. Congress comprises a set of serious games. The game results regularly decide what resources and programs will be available to the American government, in which life and death matters may be involved. Unlike many contests, Congress is involved in a **continuous game** series,[1] which lacks distinct beginnings and ends.

[1]Continuous games are not won once and for all, while discrete games have a clear beginning and end. The battle over a particular piece of legislation in a congressional conference commitee may be viewed as a discrete game that ends when the final votes are counted and the committee disbands. The game of passing legislation on the floor of either house, though, goes on round after round with the same players, rules, and strategies.

Winners in one round attempt to maintain their advantage, while losers attempt to change the rules, revise their strategies and/or pursue the game in another institutional arena.

We are not proposing to view Congress as one grand integrated game, nor apply a sophisticated and formal game theory.[2] On the other hand, we do not plan to simply take the journalistic approach and use the aspects of games as literary techniques designed to add some color to our writing.[3] Rather, we see the game analogy as a tool for understanding complex phenomena.

Why do we even mention the game analogy if it doesn't fit perfectly? First it is an analogy members of Congress use regularly themselves (see box I.1). Secondly, it provides a checklist of aspects we need to examine when analyzing either Congress or any of its components. Third, the game analogy invites us to ask important questions we might not have otherwise raised when looking at Congress from a different perspective.

KEY ASPECTS OF GAMES: A CHECKLIST FOR ANALYSIS

When attempting to analyze an institution or process, one needs a starting point. The game analogy offers a checklist of factors to look for. This checklist ignores some aspects, but more importantly assures that the analyst at least considers other factors. All games share a set of general characteristics:

Environment: Games are not played in isolation. They are affected by the general societal and historical context.

Players: There would be no game if there were no players. Few games are free-for-alls allowing anyone to play. Determining *who* is allowed to play goes a long way in determining *how* the game will be played.

Rules: Games are defined by the rules which players either voluntarily or are coerced to accept. They define legitimate players and strategies, as well as affect the likely outcome.

Strategies: Players design a set of moves in hopes of gaining advantage and winning the game. Different game rules and the skills of players determine effective strategies.

Winners and Losers: Entire games or individual rounds usually end with one set of players seen as winners and one set as having lost.

---

[2] Game theory in political science involves building formal—often mathematical—models of political strategy. See Steven Brams, 1975, *Game Theory and Politics,* New York: The Free Press.

[3] For one of the better journalistic efforts to apply the game analogy to American politics, see Hedrick Smith, 1988, *The Power Game: How Washington Works,* New York: Random House.

BOX I.1 THE MEMBERS SPEAK ABOUT THE LEGISLATIVE GAME

Members of the House improve their physical fitness and reduce stress through regular basketball games. A number of them see direct parallels between the game on the court and the game in the legislative arena.

Members of Congress play hard both on the legislative and the athletic field.

> Sports is a metaphor for life. . . . People play basketball like they legislate. . . . I try to make the game move along. . . . I try to include people in legislation. My game is much more inclusive. . . . Norm [Norman Dicks, D-WA] plays the complete game because he plays coach, player, referee. This comes from being on appropriations. He believes he can control the whole world, . . . Tom [Tom Downey, former D-NY] is always pushing for a basket, hunting and pecking for the next point, looking for an opening. . . . It's the same way he legislates. He pushes on the margins on issues. (Representative George Miller, D-CA)

Representative George Miller (D-CA) as an inside player (Chairman of the Natural Resources Committee) observes the strengths and weaknesses of other players on a daily basis.

Continued on next page

BOX I.1 Continued

> No politician feels he can't score from any given point on the court once he has his hands on the ball. . . . There is virtually no passing. (Representative Byron L. Dorgan, D-ND)

Representative Byron Dorgan (D-ND) in action, articulating a policy problem related to television violence.

> Democrats try to control the [member basketball] games the same way they control the House: through the rules. . . . Republicans play by the rules. Republicans believe in fundamentals: discipline, homework. Democrats say, "Why do the basic homework, we'll just ram it down their throats. . . . As long as we control the rules, why worry?" (Representative Carl Pursell, R-MI)

[Authors' Note: While we as authors find the above quotes useful, we are sensitive to the fact that the references to some contact sports may resonate with male more than female readers. Although some women enjoy and excel at contact sports such as basketball, a larger percentage of contemporary male students have intensively participated in such activities. While we want to emphasize that we are using a **game** analogy as opposed to a **sports** analogy, we must point out that the current male domination of Congress leads its Members to think in more male sports terms. Throughout the remainder of the book, we attempt to use a broad range of games as examples, but when using the words and perceptions of members of Congress, the possibilities are limited.]

SOURCE: Quoted in Maralee Schwartz, 1991, "The Gym Rats of the House," *Washington Post,* June 26, 1991, pp. A1, A7.

Whether one is looking at congressional campaigns, committee deliberation, debate on the floor, or any other set of activities in Congress, we feel it is useful to ask a series of basic game-inspired questions:

1. What aspects of the general **environment** affect this particular game?
2. Who are the legitimate **players?** What are their motivations and skills?
3. What are the **rules** under which this game must be played?
4. What **strategies** work in this particular setting or process?
5. What is the pattern of **winning and losing** in this game?

ENVIRONMENTS OF GAMES

Congressional games are played within the broad context of American society. Unlike many games where the environment is composed primarily of physical characteristics such as a diamond, court, or board, the more important aspects of the congressional environment lie in the minds of the public, other players, and members of Congress. Congress is subject to a series of cultural **norms** defining acceptable behavior, a variety of **expectations** concerning the role of the Congress and its Members, and a set of societal **resources** affecting Congress' capabilities. Not all aspects of the environment are important for a particular game. Just as indoor tennis players do not care much about the weather outside, only some aspects of Congress' environment affect its games. On the other hand, as the environmental factors change, Congress and its Members are often forced to react.

Norms

Norms relate to informal rules defining acceptable behavior. Broad societal norms are supplemented by a narrower set of constraints applicable to a particular institution. Norms may be enforced through the threat of social sanctions or encoded into formal rules.

General societal norms underlying democratic decision making, such as "fair play," majority rule, protection of minority rights, and free speech, shape the way in which Congress functions. For example, the view that public officials should not use public office for private gain undergirds public hesitation to raise congressional pay. It also serves as the basis for laws against bribery and affects the strategies accepted in the game. Norms of personal interaction, such as honesty and courtesy, frame the ways in which members of Congress relate to their colleagues.

As a continuing social institution, Congress has developed its own set of internal norms guiding the interactions among Members. As we will discuss in more detail in chapter 3, norms have varied over time and the norms in the Senate are somewhat different from those in the House. A general loosening of societal restrictions of norms is also reflected in the modern Congress.

Expectations

The framers of the Constitution created Congress as the center of government and as a counterpoint to the other branches. They intentionally designed a set of intersecting playing fields with imprecise boundaries, differing norms, unique rules, and clashing goals. Congress, as a forum for relatively equal participants struggling to find agreement among competing ideas, differs significantly from expectations of the executive or judicial branches with their clearer hierarchy of participants and their goals of decisive action. The founders not only expected conflict between the branches, but encouraged it by establishing overlapping responsibilities requiring players in each branch to find ways to compromise despite their differing methods of playing the games.

Congress is expected not only to make decisions, but also to serve as an information conduit to and from the spectators (the public). Members of Congress inform other congressional and non-congressional players about the desires of spectators, and inform spectators about the current and impending public policies under which they are expected to live.

On the individual level, the expectation that members of Congress have the responsibility to look out for the narrow **parochial** interests of their constituents while also paying attention to the needs of the country as a whole increases the challenge of the game. The accepted **parochialism** of Congress establishes an environment significantly different from the expectations of the executive branch or the courts where national and universal standards are expected to reign.

Resources

To carry out their expected tasks, Congress and its Members exercise the powers granted by the Constitution by drawing on a series of resources. The Constitution grants Congress and its Members identifiable legal resources. For example, no statutory public policy can be enacted without congressional approval. Taxation proposals must begin their journey into legislation in the House of Representatives. Many presidential appointments and all treaties are subject to approval by the Senate.

Information processing is the "core technology" of Congress. Members **receive** information from their constituents about their needs and desires. They **seek** information to define problems and outline alternative solutions. They **converse** with other players in their attempt to create a supportive coalition enacting a solution. Members **communicate** with spectators in the hopes of educating them about the process and justifying their mode of play. To increase the effectiveness of information processing, Members seek staff support and make use of new technologies such as radio, television, and computers. Since information processing is such a key element of the congressional task, changes in the technological aspects of the playing field are likely to have a significant impact on Congress and its Members.

Some Questions Triggered by the Environment Concept

Thinking about the environment of congressional games invites a series of questions for discussion later in the book:

1. How does the nature of the congressional environment determine the kinds of public policies Congress enacts?
2. Does the environment foster or hinder fair fields of play? Are all interested or affected groups and individuals able to have a say in the policy process?
3. How do changes in the broader American society affect how Congress and its Members perform their tasks?

PLAYERS

All games have **players,** those individuals or groups whose involvement in the game determines its outcome. Not everyone can play in congressional games directly, and each individual game has a different set of players. In fact, the primary goal of establishing Congress as a **republican**[4] institution was to establish a representative government by providing a link between most citizens who are largely **spectators,** except on election day, and the various policy-making games.

The Selection and Recruitment of Individual Players

The possibility of becoming a player depends on personal motivation, individual skill, available resources, a bit of luck, and a set of rules which encourages some potential players and disqualifies others. Players bring to the game different goals and skills. A game of bridge in the dorm among amateurs who are playing more for enjoyment than victory operates differently than a group of experts vying for master's points in a tournament. The mix of players allowed in the congressional games affects both the way in which they are played and their ultimate outcomes. A Congress dominated by experienced career politicians will behave quite differently than one populated by short term amateurs who came to Washington to pursue a specific policy or to use service in Congress as a stepping stone for another position.

Members of Congress are expected to "re-present" (present a second time) the opinions and interests of those who elected them. **Representation** (or re-presentation), is the **process** of speaking and/or acting for the interests of others. The process of re-presentation is often facilitated by selecting players who share many social and political characteristics with those whose interests and opinions they are supposed to represent. It is assumed that individuals will find it easier to represent the opinions and interests of people like themselves. A Congress which mirrors the social and political characteristics of the national population would rank high on **representativeness.** A key question in a representative democracy lies in determining the degree to

---

[4]The framers of the Constitution desired a "small r" **republican** form of government. This type of governing has little to do with the "capital R" Republican Party. The concept of republicanism refers to a form of government in which the interests of citizens are represented by intermediaries.

which the congressional selection process results in a set of players capable of representing the constituents who elected them. As we will discuss in more detail in chapter 3, even a cursory look at the members of Congress indicates that they rank relatively low on representativeness, yet expend considerable effort on the process of representation.

The absolute number and range of congressional players has expanded in recent years through the growth of staff. At the same time, the number of important players was expanded by dispersing power among more individuals. Within Congress, players specialize in terms of the arena in which they get involved. A key player in one committee may be relatively insignificant in a policy arena in which his or her committee plays no role. Recent reforms of Congress have equalized the power of various players and limited the number of arenas in which any one player dominates.

Players arrive with varying resources. Previous experience in state or local arenas increases one's knowledge of the rules and strategies. Members of Congress with strong electoral margins have more flexibility in the strategies and positions they pursue than Members who must watch every step for fear of getting thrown out of the game.

The Joining Together of Players

Congressional players often join together with others in **teams,** competing for power and policy outcomes. Some of the teams are temporary coalitions formed to pursue a particular policy outcome, while others involve permanent alliances. Political party caucuses, state delegations, and interest groupings (i.e., the Black Caucus, Women's Caucus, and the Arts Caucus) serve as relatively permanent rallying points. More temporary **coalition** teams form around specific policy alternatives and often dissolve after the immediate objective has been reached. Congressional teams often find support from their counterparts both within government and among interest groups in the society as a whole. At times, Congress binds together as a team in its attempt to maintain its strategic position relative to competing teams in the executive branch and/or the judiciary.

The numerous congressional teams vary in the resources available to pursue their goals. In an institution based on majority rule, "numbers count" and the larger team usually wins. Occasions arise when the skills and the effective choice of strategy allow small teams to overcome larger, more diverse ones. Since many of the resources members of Congress need to stay in office are not limited to the congressional arena, external teams with access to money, information, and/or loyal supporters receive favorable treatment by Congress. Some questions triggered by the concept of players are:

1. What factors determine which potential players can join the various congressional games?
2. Who are the players? What motivations and skills do they bring to the playing field?
3. How would congressional games differ if the type of players varied?
4. How do congressional teams develop and what determines their success or failure?

RULES

The chief distinguishing characteristic of a game is its **rules,** the legally enforceable set of standards specifying who can play, outlining the acceptable strategies, and defining the winners and the losers.

Congressional rules include a combination of broad written standards from the Constitution, a set of specific written rules applicable to each chamber, and informal rules which although unwritten are enforced by tradition. Congressional rules require the creation of majorities at each of the many stages in the policy-making process. Along with the emphasis on majority rule, however, is an attempt to protect the interests of players numerically in the minority. At numerous points in the congressional process, minorities are given the opportunity to stop or impede a decision until a larger coalition is created. Since the rules of Congress are unique and complex, power devolves to individuals with extraordinary knowledge of the rules.

Rules grant **legitimacy** to specific actions. Policy battles in Congress are often fought as much on how a legislative goal is accomplished as on the substance of the legislation. Some questions triggered by the concept of rules are:

1. Who makes the rules and how are they enforced?
2. To what degree do the rules make playing the game more fair?
3. To what degree do they exacerbate unequal opportunities to affect the games?
4. What is the relationship between following the rules and the legitimacy of congressional action?

STRATEGIES

A **strategy** is a plan of action designed to help a player win a game. Viable political strategies emerge from recognizing the **power** resources of an institution and its members and must be consistent with the norms and rules of each game. Congress and/or its Members' power is in evidence when they get their way despite resistance from other players. Formal rules grant Congress the legitimate **authority** to take on particular tasks or declare themselves the winner. For example, no one questions the Senate's right to approve treaties or Congress' right to override a president's veto if two-thirds of the Members of each house agree. The ability to **persuade** other players that what you want them to do is really what they want to do stems from the skill of the persuader and the availability of relevant information. Personal trust in a fellow player allows them to use **leadership** that can change behavior. When these resources fail, explicit promises of **rewards** or threats of **punishment** are available to players who can reasonably be expected to deliver on their promises or threats.

The nature of a game defines the strategies likely to produce success. Members of Congress employ strategies on a number of different levels. The primary strategy in Congress is coalition building. A **coalition** is a temporary group of often diverse Members who agree to support a particular course of action. Coalition managers, such as party leaders or the president, attempt to secure the votes of individuals whose personal ideology or constituency interests would be favorably affected (the **natural coalition**) and, if necessary for victory, to broaden the support level through bargaining (the **bought coalition**).

Effective coalition building often requires **compromise** in the substance of legislation. Compromise is often difficult since seemingly minor changes may garner additional support, but at the same time drive some Members from the coalition. If compromise is not enough, coalition managers often use inducements unrelated to the issue at hand (**side payments**). Since compromises and inducements are costly in terms of time and other resources, wise players seek to create **minimum winning coalitions** in order to reserve their resources for the next round of battles (see discussion in chapter 7).

Beyond individual votes, members of Congress realize that they are playing in a series of **continuous games** with numerous rounds. Success at one stage does not guarantee victory, while one failure does not deny ultimate satisfaction. Staying in the various games for the long haul is absolutely necessary to protect one's victories or guard against additional losses.

The effectiveness of various strategies varies depending on the specific congressional decision-making arena. Mastering the technical aspects of a policy proposal is often more important at the subcommittee stage, while attempting to drum up public support or opposition might serve a player better during the more public stages of policy making. Players both inside and outside of Congress tailor their strategies and focus their efforts on the arenas in which they have the highest likelihood of winning.

In the broader political game, members of Congress understand that they are part of a set of larger games, competing with players from other institutions who would like nothing better than to limit their options and powers. Encroachments from the presidency, the executive branch, and the judiciary are carefully watched. Members often consider the implications of their actions in light of their long term effect on the Congress as viable players. A strategy of **institutional protection** permeates congressional action. Some questions triggered by the concept of strategies are:

1. What general political strategies work in Congress? What strategies work for particular congressional games?
2. Which strategies are available to which players?
3. What factors change the potential effectiveness of different strategies?
4. How has the strategic environment of Congress changed?

WINNERS AND LOSERS

Congress and its Members determine individual and collective winners in American politics through the passage or blockage of public policy. Congress as an institution is involved in a larger set of political games in which its role, power and viability are at stake.

Some Types of Winning and Losing

All games do not result in the same type of winning or losing. Most often we think in terms of **zero-sum games,** such as a specific congressional election where there is one winner. In such games there is an identifiable and nondivisible benefit to the winner and the loser gets nothing. Other games allow different types of outcomes. The process of compromising and amending a piece of legislation on the floor of Congress may result in a **positive-sum game** in which each player gains a bit more than they had at the beginning, or in a **negative-sum game** in which everyone loses in the process. The ultimate positive-sum game occurs when budgets are expanding and everyone gets to include some of what they want. When budgets are shrinking, negative-sum games prevail as everyone knows their causes will lose something and they make a valiant effort to lose less than others.

Individual Winners and Losers

Members of Congress look out for the interests of individual constituents by attempting to mediate with other players, especially the bureaucracy. Constituents who know what to ask and how to frame their request are most likely to come out winners. Members of Congress vary in their motivation, skill and resources to satisfy individual constituent needs. An individual's success may therefore be based more on who his or her representative is than on the merits of the request.

Individual members of Congress vary in personal goals and their success in reaching them.[5] For some Members, re-election is an important goal in and of itself, while other Members are driven more by the desire to enact specific types of policy, or the goal of enhancing their personal power within the chamber. During most of this century, initial election to Congress almost guaranteed a career to those wishing to pursue it, while the most recent elections have seen some devaluation of the advantages of incumbency. Policy making within Congress has become more complex, and power has become more widely distributed. Reaching one's personal goals requires considerable effort in an institution such as Congress.

Public Policy Determination: Collective Winners and Losers

Because the congressional games are largely based on **compromise** and are **continuous,** there are few absolute winners or absolute losers. Winning and losing tends to be **noncumulative** in the sense that few groups are consistent winners and others continuous losers. Congress attempts to pass legislation giving everyone something

[5]For discussions of Member goals, see Douglas R. Arnold, 1990, *The Logic of Congressional Action,* New Haven: Yale University Press; David Mayhew, 1974, *Congress: The Electoral Connection,* New Haven: Yale University Press; and Richard Fenno, 1973, *Congressmen in Committees,* Boston: Little, Brown.

of what they want, for members of Congress know that losers in one round will simply try again by changing the rules, attempting to remove the opposing players, or revising their strategies.

Congress tends to reflect the dominant goals and values of American society at any one point in time. At times Congress tends to lead public opinion and at times it lags slightly behind, but it is seldom completely out of touch. Individuals holding beliefs outside of the mainstream of American political attitudes are unlikely to look to Congress as a source of their political victories.

The Institutional Power Game

The Separation of Powers doctrine, which divides power between the executive and legislative branches, and the vagueness of Congress' constitutional mandate require Congress and its members to continually battle for their place in American politics. During much of this century, conventional wisdom asserted that this was an age of "executive ascendency," and that changes in societal needs and conditions had passed Congress by. Like Mark Twain, however, who objected that a premature obituary "grossly exaggerated" reports of his death, Congress refused to "roll over and play dead." Thus, a resurgence of congressional "initiative" or "interference" (depending on one's perspective and policy preferences) has marked the last two decades. The games have become much more interesting since we cannot assume whether Congress or the president will be the customary winner. Some questions triggered by the concepts of winners and losers are:

1. Who wins and who loses as a result of congressional activity?
2. How has the pattern of winning and losing changed over time?
3. What is the relationship between various political resources and whether one wins or loses in the congressional arena?
4. To what degree is winning and losing cumulative?
5. What aspects of congressional games (the environment, the playing field, the players, the rules, or the strategies) best explain the patterns of winning and losing?

CONCLUSION

As you read the remainder of this text, keep in mind the game analogy and the questions it brings to mind. We will attempt to give you a full understanding of the modern Congress through a judicious use of the game analogy. We are neither apologists nor unmitigated critics of Congress, but rather hope to give you a balanced view of its strengths and weaknesses. After giving us a chance to present Congress as it is known through the best of contemporary research, we challenge you to make your own judgment on the institution and its members.

This text has a few unique characteristics which we hope will help you get a more realistic feel for Congress. A number of "The Members Speak" boxes throughout the text will allow you to hear what members of Congress say about the institution. In order to encourage you to become less of a spectator and more of a player of the various congressional games, we have included a number of "action oriented" boxes which outline specific methods of joining the game. The "In Depth" sections at the end of each chapter provide ideas for research projects designed to help you better understand Congress. We encourage you to use these resources and take an active role in your learning.

One newly elected member of Congress told us he wrote home saying, "I am embarking on a great adventure which will enlighten and educate me—perhaps it will even change me." We could hope for no less for you as you seek to understand the congressional games.

CHAPTER ONE

THE CONSTITUTION
Establishing General Rules

No doubt the goals of the constitutional elite [of 1787] were subversive to the existing political order, but it is overlooked that their subversion could only have succeeded if the people of the United States endorsed it by regularized procedures. . . . On a fundamental procedural level, the Constitutionalists had to work according to the prevailing rules of the game. (Roche 1961, 800)

When the American power game was organized two centuries ago, the founders deliberately spread the chips around so widely that no single political force could drive the others out of the game. (Smith 1988, 713)

The American political order involves many forms of political competition, each featuring rules, players, winners and losers. Power in government is a common goal in political competition because it shapes the capacity to make public policy. In these respects, American politics is host to a variety of games. The United States Congress provides one of the world's gaudiest environments for the struggle over power. Daily, 535 legislators converge on each other in order to make rules that will govern American society. In the games they play, lawmakers confront limits set by popular opinion, presidential power and the language of the Constitution itself.

The founders who created our constitutional order viewed the legislature as the first and most important institution of national government. This chapter introduces the role of Congress in the constitutional order, beginning with an examination of the game environment, players, rules and strategies at the constitutional convention. The thirty-nine men who signed the proposed Constitution in Philadelphia on September 17, 1787, shared many views on the nature of politics. They attempted to create a "political architecture" that would remain stable through long years of turbulent politics—a structure of rules for subsequent political games.

THE TASK OF RULEMAKING

Creating a stable power structure for any society is no small feat. A sound Constitution only develops from a clear, logical and accurate understanding of the game environment in which the new rules operate. This required three tasks of the founders. First, they needed an accurate assessment of player motivations, a sound comprehension of human nature in politics. Second, they needed a justification of the government goals, a definition of the purpose of political games. Third, they had to set rules creating the proper series of continuous games—a defensible means of making the behavior of humans support the legitimate goals of government. The last requirement constituted the most difficult challenge in 1787. The Articles of Confederation had proven unworkable (see box 1.1). Few historical examples of feasible forms of government applied to the American situation in 1787. The founders, as we will see, largely agreed on human nature and what the goals of government should be. Accordingly, they spent most of their time in Philadelphia working on means to secure their goals.

The convention itself involved aspiring politicians in a game of influence over the contents of the new constitution. Competition among the delegates grew from the intense interests of the individual states they represented. Most adopted the strategy of creating a stronger national government that would also best serve the interests of their home state. They also agreed to majority rule procedures and a method of state ratification of their new rules.

Signing the Constitution. Setting stable rules for the dangerous game of politics was the founders' chief task.

BOX 1.1 The Old Rule Book: Congress under the Articles of Confederation

Under the Articles of Confederation, Congress functioned within a structure and set of powers that greatly limited its effectiveness. The Articles made the states the dominant players in power competition with the national government. Each state retained all powers, freedoms, and rights not granted clearly and expressly to the confederated government—those being national defense, foreign affairs, and interstate trade. State delegations comprised the unicameral Congress; each state cast one vote. Congress had no power of taxation, instead each state received a taxation quota to fund the national government. The Articles did not provide for a national executive or judiciary, but Congress did set up a Committee of the States, composed of one representative from each state, to oversee daily administration in government. Amendment of the Articles required unanimous agreement of the states. The pressure for positive-sum games under such an arrangement doomed the process to inaction.

The states proved to be obstreperous in this game environment. With no strong national referee, states battled among themselves and fought national regulation. States refused to enforce national laws with which they disagreed. Not all met their tax quotas. A proposed amendment to the Articles providing Congress with the power to tax individuals fell directly one vote short of the necessary unanimity in 1784, when Rhode Island objected. Interstate trade was a persistent source of negative-sum conflict. States set up their own tariffs and trade barriers, constricting commerce. By 1787, the delegates to the constitutional convention were anxious to strengthen the national rules.

THE POLITICAL ENVIRONMENT

Attributes of the game environment shaped the contest over the new Constitution. Political resources were dispersed among the delegates because the success of any proposed changes required a broad consensus at the convention. Most delegates had governmental experience and accepted the norm of compromise, increasing the likelihood of consensus. Shared expectations about the nature of politics and the convention's task proved essential to their success.

The Importance of Human Nature

A careful understanding of any game requires an accurate appreciation of the environment shaping the players' motives. That way you can anticipate their likely actions and design the game to take account of them. This is exactly the sort of project that concerned the founders in Philadelphia. First, what did they expect from politics? James Madison put it this way in his *Federalist #10*:

> As long as the reason of man continues fallible, and he is at liberty to exercise it, differing opinions will be formed. As long as the connection subsists between his reason and his self-love, his opinions and his passions will have a reciprocal influence on each other, and the former will be objects to which the latter will attach themselves. (Hamilton, Madison, and Jay 1961, first published in 1789)

In other words, we need to be very cautious about the raw materials of politics. People will naturally disagree and passion can triumph over reason. Zero- and negative-sum competition is common in politics, causing liberty to suffer. Madison, in particular, worried about the presence of **factions,** which he defined as groups of people motivated by a passion or interest "adverse to the rights of other citizens or to the permanent and aggregate interests of the community" (Hamilton, Madison, and Jay 1961, 78). **Tyranny** could be a commonplace strategy in political competition. Democratic governments—those led by direct rule by popular majorities—were to the founders a form of tyranny, because they permitted majority factions to operate without restraint. Elbridge Gerry of Massachusetts stated at the convention that "the evils we experience flow from an excess of democracy" (Farrand 1966, 1:48), a sentiment voiced by other delegates as well. The point of maximum danger lay in the legislature, where majority rule in lawmaking could serve as a very effective means of oppression. In such a forum, according to Madison, situations could arise in which "ignorance will be the dupe of cunning, and passion the slave of sophistry and declamation" (Hamilton, Madison, and Jay 1961, 360). Dangerous games abounded in politics.

The Goals of Governmental Rules

The founders' apprehension about the nature of politics arose from their goals for the governmental system. Individual rights to life, liberty, and the pursuit of happiness constituted the primary ends of government, as stated in the Declaration of Independence. In this view, familiar to students of American government, "people are endowed by their creator with certain inalienable rights," that is, rights that are theirs by nature and nature's God. Accordingly, Constitutional rules aimed to prevent government from violating the rights of citizens of the society. The Constitution, as Madison put it, was "a charter of power granted by liberty, not a charter of liberty granted by power" (Wood 1969, 601).

THE MEANS TO THE GOALS: A GAME OF POLITICAL ARCHITECTURE

To those gathered at Philadelphia in 1787, the political games played under the Articles had cost the nation dearly. Without effective government, how could personal liberty be secure? Madison's study of political history yielded him no examples of a long-lasting and successful confederation. The solution lay in a stronger national government.

The Importance of Representation

The Philadelphia convention based its deliberations on assumptions greatly different from those guiding government under the Articles. The new rules had to be based upon a principle of representation heretofore not seen in the national government of America or Britain. That principle held that sovereignty resided neither in the states as it had in the Articles, nor among the separate ranks of society in differing degrees as it did then in Britain. Instead, sovereignty resided in the citizens of

America *as a whole.* Founder James Wilson of Pennsylvania put it this way: "There is no supreme power but what the people themselves hold. The supreme power is with them; and in them, even when a constitution is formed, and the government is in operation, the supreme power still remains" (Wood 1969, 600). All citizens had to be viewed as players.

Proclaiming a desire for a representative government hardly solves the problem of arranging actual procedures for representation. Direct democracy gave way to mob rule, so a scheme of electing officeholders was necessary. Madison defined the desirable alternative as a "representative republic" that must be "derived from the great body of society." This required that "the persons administering it be appointed, either directly or indirectly, by the people," and "the tenure of highest offices [be] extended to a definite period" (Hamilton, Madison, and Jay 1961, 241). Since the legislature would be the center of power under the new rules, an "impetuous vortex" as Madison termed it, the design of its representative character required careful attention (Hamilton, Madison, and Jay 1961, 318).

Congress reigned as the preeminent topic in the deliberations in Philadelphia and during the ensuing ratification debates. The founders drew upon their knowledge of English parliamentary development and the experience of colonial assemblies in creating the legislative branch. Part of the discussion concerned how to properly represent opinions in the legislature. From the founders' time to ours, the debate has lain between two strategies of representation. One holds that the representative should be an **instructed delegate,** with the duty of replicating the opinions of his or her constituents as accurately as possible. As one member of the House of Representatives put it: "My first duty is to get reelected. I'm here to represent my district. . . . This is part of my actual belief as to the function of the congressman. . . . What is good for a majority of districts is good for the country" (Dexter 1971, 5–6).

A second view maintains that a representative should act as a **trustee,** utilizing his or her best judgment regardless of constituency wishes. English politician Edmund Burke's speech to the electors of Bristol in 1774 is the foremost exposition of this view:

> Your representative owes you, not his industry only, but his judgment; and he betrays, instead of serving you, if he sacrifices it to your opinion. . . . Parliament is a deliberative assembly of one nation, with one interest, that of the whole—where not local purposes, not local prejudices, ought to guide, but the general good, resulting from the general reason of the whole. You choose a member, indeed; but when you have chosen him, he is not a member of Bristol, but he is a member of Parliament. (Burke 1866, 95–6)

Burke's high-intentioned theory of representation did not prove politically helpful, however. Shortly after he gave this speech, the electors of Bristol turned him out of office.

The controversy over representation began at the Philadelphia convention when discussion turned to the length of terms for the House of Representatives. Madison claimed that longer terms would be appropriate, because lawmakers needed time to learn on the job and really could not consult regularly with their

Edmund Burke in 1774 articulated well the arguments for a trusteeship theory of representation.

constituents for instructions. Elbridge Gerry of Massachusetts sharply disagreed with Madison's espousal of trusteeship, arguing that "it was necessary to consider what the people would approve. That had been the policy of all legislators" (Farrand 1966, 1:214–215).

The issue remains unresolved. The rules initially encouraged House members to pursue the delegate strategy more than Senators, who were chosen by state legislatures for six-year terms. Today, lawmakers frequently find little conflict between the roles on most floor votes. Their opinions and those of their supporting electoral coalitions seldom clash even on controversial issues (Kingdon 1989, 242–261). One can be a trustee and delegate at the same time.

Given that strategies of representation might vary among lawmakers, the founders organized the Congress so that the worst aspects of popular politics would be less likely to flourish. In a low version of the delegate strategy, some power-hungry politicians would inflame their constituents' passions in ways threatening the liberties of others. The founders assumed such behavior was likely under the new constitutional rules, for they had seen more of it than they wished in the legislatures of their home states. How could government control itself in order to protect liberty?

Separation of Powers

The concept of separation of powers among the branches of national government constituted a partial response to the problem (Montesquieu 1964). Separating power on paper, though, did not necessarily mean dividing power in practice. Though state constitutions separated power formally, they did not adequately take into account the ambitions of the players, and inadvertently encouraged destructive political games involving the branches of government. One sad result was the steady growth of legislative authority in many states as power-hungry lawmakers exploited popular sentiment. The fact that many states had unicameral lawmaking bodies made the expansion of legislative power that much easier. The "excesses of democracy" complained of at the Philadelphia convention largely were those of the state legislatures.

What was lacking in the states was a system of checks and balances among governmental institutions. As historian M. J. C. Vile puts it:

> In 1776 the doctrine of separation of powers remained the only coherent principle of constitutional government upon which to build a constitution which rejected monarchy and aristocracy. The rationale of an American system of checks and balances had yet to be formulated. (Vile 1967, 141)

The great achievement of the Philadelphia convention was creating such a system of checks and balances. It constituted a stunning innovation that fundamentally shapes the operation of our national legislature and government.

Checks and Balances

Madison, in *Federalist #51*, explained the general logic of the founders' approach:

> The great security against a gradual concentration of the several powers in the same department consists in giving to those who administer each department the necessary constitutional means and personal motives to resist encroachments of the others. . . . Ambition must be made to counteract ambition. (Hamilton, Madison, and Jay 1961, 321–322)

Establishing effective constitutional rules for high-stakes, continuous games required careful deliberation at the Philadelphia convention.

The results are familiar. Congress became a bicameral structure to impede its ability to act resolutely. The president gained the veto power, the power to negate congressional laws; a veto override by Congress required a two-thirds vote of each chamber. Approval of presidential appointments and treaties rested with the Senate. The Constitution denied the branches certain powers over each other. No member of Congress could simultaneously serve in the executive branch, nor could Congress cut any currently serving federal judge's salary. The Supreme Court in the 1803 decision in *Marbury v. Madison* (1 Cranch 137 [1803]) asserted the doctrine of judicial review, under which it claimed final authority to determine the constitutionality of actions by other branches of government. Many of the founders, most notably Alexander Hamilton in *Federalist #78,* endorsed such power for the court. These elaborate rules meant players would have to cooperate and compromise to win any gains, making tyranny less likely.

THE NEW CONGRESS: RULES AND PLAYERS

Out of the protracted discussions at Philadelphia came a legislature unlike any seen in the world before. The "Great Compromise" between large and small states created a bicameral legislature: a popularly elected House with representatives allocated among the states on the basis of population, and a Senate composed of two senators from each state, selected by state legislatures.

The delegates opted for this particular arrangement in the hope it would effectively divide power. James Wilson claimed that "a division of power in the legislative body itself is the most useful restraint on the legislature, because it operates constantly" (Wood 1969, 559). Madison, in *Federalist #63,* argued that the danger of representatives betraying the people's interest was "evidently greater where the whole legislative trust is lodged in the hands of one body and is required in every public act" (Hamilton, Madison, and Jay 1961, 386). In a complex game in which power is widely dispersed, it is quite difficult for oppressive combinations to form.

This new structural wrinkle would be profoundly effective at achieving its goal. The contemporary House and Senate have their own separate and distinctive internal rules and procedures, styles of behavior and pace of action. Each chamber remains suspicious of the other, expecting its members to refer to the rival body during floor proceedings as "the other chamber." Bicameralism greatly slows the pace of legislation, but increases the level of scrutiny devoted to potential laws. The two chambers differ on most major pieces of legislation, requiring extensive negotiations in order to arrive at a final legislative product. Each chamber jealously guards its prerogatives from encroachment by the other. The rules ensure a game of power competition between House and Senate.

THE PEOPLE'S CHAMBER

The House of Representatives serves as the cornerstone of popular government in the Constitution. George Mason of Virginia argued the House "was to be the grand depository of the democratic principle of the government. . . . It ought to know and sympathize with every part of the community" (Farrand 1966, 1:48–49). A powerful, directly elected House meant that the ability of state legislatures to dominate proceedings correspondingly was reduced. Because "no taxation without representation" was a cry of the Revolution, the founders required that all revenue legislation originate in the House. Opponents of popular rule, such as Elbridge Gerry, believed that good government could not come from such a source. A Senate chosen by state legislatures served to blunt that objection. A large majority at the convention endorsed the principle of popular election.

Though agreeing on popular control, the founders did not go on to define the proper electorate for House elections. The game environment sharply limited the number of electoral players. At the time, each state set its own franchise requirements. Social norms and formal rules prescribed property requirements for voting and an electorate drawn only from the population of white males. After 1787, expansion of the congressional electorate proceeded slowly, and in the face of much resistance. Property requirements for voting persisted in some states until 1840. The Fifteenth Amendment, ratified in 1869, supposedly prohibited race discrimination in enforcing the right to vote. In reality, African Americans and other people of color had to wait until the Voting Rights Act of 1965 finally guaranteed their access to the vote. Women did not gain the franchise nationally until the Nineteenth Amendment of 1920.

The ugly institution of slavery had a role in the debate over how to elect the House. Northern states objected to counting slaves for purposes of allocating House seats among the states—if counted, nonvoting slaves would still be an important resource in electoral competition. Southern delegates accepted a compromise that allowed three-fifths of slaves to be counted, because this would roughly equalize the population totals of slave and nonslave states. Southerners accepted these limits on the mistaken assumption that their region would soon outpace the north in population anyway.

The Constitution did not specify other electoral rules for the House. No provision exists in the document requiring each House district to elect one representative, or that House districts be of equal population. These issues were left to future Congresses, as was the question of the overall size of the House. The first Congress required a decennial census that would be the basis for allocating House seats to each state. In 1842 Congress enacted legislation mandating that each House district elect only one representative. Congress fixed the present size of the chamber at 435 in 1911. For nearly two-hundred years, the national legislature failed to require equal populations in House districts. In *Wesberry v. Sanders* (376 U.S. I [1964]), the Supreme Court finally asserted the principle that the Fourteenth Amendment guarantee of "equal protection of the laws" required that House districts in each state be drawn to equal population size. The Constitution also did not set a particular date for House elections. Most states individually decided to hold them on the first Tuesday after the first Monday in November, but the date did not become uniform until this century.

All this indicates that the House slowly evolved into the popularly elected legislature we know today. The founders' version of a constitutional republic does not comport well with the norms of democracy in late twentieth century America. Their suspicion of popular majorities is particularly evident in the original design of the other chamber of Congress, the Senate.

THE COOLING SAUCER

Thomas Jefferson served as ambassador to France in 1787 and did not attend the constitutional convention. When he returned to America, he sought an explanation of various features of the new Constitution from George Washington. "Why," asked Washington, "did you pour that coffee into your saucer?" "To cool it," said Jefferson. "Even so," Washington supposedly replied, "we pour legislation into the senatorial saucer to cool it" (Farrand 1966, 3:359). The composition and powers of the Senate proved to be a particularly controversial topic at the convention. Only gradually did the outlines of the chamber's role crystallize. The game environment for the founders required them to protect state interests in the new, stronger, national government. That task meshed well with their fear of concentrated governmental power.

Many delegates came to accept the need for a smaller second chamber more responsive to state interests and removed from the "turbulence of democracy." Edmund Randolph argued that the Senate would be "so small [so as] to be exempt from the passionate proceedings to which numerous assemblies are liable," and its size would "provide a cure for the evils under which the United States labored." Further, "in tracing those evils to their origin every man had found it in the turbulence and follies of democracy and some check therefore was to be sought for against this tendency . . . and a good Senate seemed most likely to answer the purpose" (Farrand 1966, 1:51). George Mason of Virginia argued for equal state representation by claiming that the "state legislatures ought to have some means of defending themselves from the encroachments of the national government" (Farrand 1966, 1:155–156). Madison eventually endorsed these arguments in *Federalist #62* and *#63*. The adoption of the Seventeenth Amendment in 1913, providing for direct election of senators, constituted a formal abandonment of his rationale.

Since the Senate was to take a "cooler" view of affairs of state than the impetuous House, senators received longer terms and a higher age requirement for election. House members must be twenty-five years of age and serve two-year terms, but senators must be thirty and serve six-year terms. Madison argued at the convention that longer terms were essential to the duties of the Senate: "These [terms] are to protect the people against their rulers; secondly, to protect the people against the transient impressions into which they themselves might be led" (Farrand 1966, 1:421).

The Senate also gained some important exclusive powers: ratification of treaties negotiated by the president (by two-thirds of those present and voting) and approval of presidential appointments of federal judges, "ambassadors, other public ministers and consuls and all other officers of the United States." Convention politics produced these features. As W. R. Davie, a signer of the document, stated at the North Carolina ratification convention: "The small states would not agree that the House of Representatives should have a voice [in treaties and appointments] and the extreme jealousy of all the states would not give it to the president alone" (Farrand 1966, 3:348–349).

Fear of the venal games legislators might play was widespread among the Philadelphia delegates. As a further means of restricting the expansion of legislative power, the founders prohibited members of the House and Senate from holding any additional offices in the federal government. The delegates did, however, vote to allow legislators authority over their own salaries, to be paid by the national government. The alternative was to have the states pay them, but that might unduly threaten national power. Both the House and Senate also received unimpeded power over their internal operations. Each chamber, according to the Constitution, was to be "the judge of the elections, returns, and qualifications of its own members" and to "determine the rules of its proceedings, punish members for disorderly behavior, and, with the concurrence of two-thirds, expel a member."

GENERAL POWERS: THE KEY RULES

Article I Section 8 of the Constitution lists eighteen specific powers of Congress in an attempt to limit both the number and scale of games lawmakers could play. These are the **enumerated powers** of Congress. Some of these powers form sweeping grants of authority, creating new power games for the national legislature to play to victory against the states. Article I, Section 8 phrases the new revenue powers of Congress expansively: "The Congress shall have power to lay and collect taxes, duties, imposts and excises, to pay the debts and provide for the common defense and general welfare of the United States." The suspicion of states about the discriminatory use of this new national power, however, produced some limits on this authority in Section 9. Duties were prohibited on goods moving between the states, taxes had to be uniform nationally and no "capitation . . . or other direct" taxes were permissible unless levied according to population. In 1892, the Supreme Court held that this provision applied to an attempted national income tax, beginning an eighteen-year battle over amending the Constitution to allow for direct income taxes. The Sixteenth Amendment provided for this in 1913.

Congress became the central player in the battle over national spending. Article I, Section 9 states that "No money may be drawn from the Treasury, but in consequence of appropriations made by law." This gives Congress great authority over the operations of all aspects of national government, and produces regular battles with the president over budget priorities. The Constitution further gives Congress the authority to create lower federal courts, and to specify the size of the Supreme Court. Article II distinctly creates only the Supreme Court, and even then its appellate jurisdiction is subject to "such exceptions" and "such regulations as the Congress shall make" according to Article II, Section 2.

The Constitution does, however, spell out specific limits to congressional power. Article I, Section 9 prohibits certain legislative actions, such as bills of attainder—ordering persons held without formal charges placed against them—and ex post facto laws—punishing people for acts that were not against the law at the time they were committed. The Bill of Rights, the first ten amendments to the Constitution adopted in 1791, contains additional restrictions on legislative power. The First Amendment begins "Congress shall make no law. . . ." The Tenth Amendment holds that "powers not delegated to the United States by the Constitution . . . are reserved to the states."

Unforeseeable future circumstances did compel the founders to include language in Article I Section 8 that would give Congress some latitude in the use of its powers. This famous clause allows Congress "to make all laws which shall be necessary and proper for carrying into execution the foregoing powers, and all other powers vested by this Constitution in the government of the United States, or in any department thereof." The necessary and proper clause gives the legislature some latitude in the exercise of its powers. How much?

In 1819 the Supreme Court settled this issue. Chief Justice John Marshall, a former Federalist politician, promulgated the doctrine of implied powers in his decision in *McCollough v. Maryland* (4 Wheaton 316 [1819]): "Let the end be legitimate, let it be within the scope of the Constitution, and all means which are appropriate, which are plainly adapted to that end, which are not prohibited, but consist with the letter and spirit of the Constitution, are constitutional." This expansive interpretation gave Congress the constitutional means to expand its legislative authority over the last 150 years as political fashions dictated. The looser rules allowed lawmaking games with greater potential prizes for the legislative winners.

THE EVOLUTION OF CONGRESSIONAL GAMES

Any game in existence for a long time evolves beyond the intent of its original rules. So it is with the many games played in Congress. Since the first Congress convened in 1789, its internal procedures have altered a great deal. The founders did not discuss the specific operations of the legislature. Most assumed what would result was a Congress made up of part-time legislators in which a committee system would develop and factions would evolve among the membership. A cauldron of popular sentiment would boil in the House, but the more detached Senate would consider the national interest more calmly.

The first House did elect a presiding officer, a Speaker, as provided for in the Constitution, who set up a temporary committee of Members to assist him with specialized legislation. The first permanent committee of the House, on Ways and Means, originated in 1794. A much smaller and "clubbier" Senate initially adopted few rules. Leading politicians of the day sought membership in the House, making it the politically preeminent chamber.

Congress today appears far different from that of 1789. Now senators usually command more public attention and prestige than do representatives. The national legislature has dozens of **standing committees** that receive legislation for consideration before it can be brought to the floor. Standing committees are further divided into **subcommittees** that examine and develop legislation in greater detail. Party organizations are well-entrenched in both House and Senate and Congress employs thousands of staff people to assist individual legislators and committees with their work.

Since its founding, the national legislature has undergone a process of **institutionalization** (Polsby 1968, 144) that transformed ways games are played in Congress. This process produced an institution that has (1) become more well-bounded from its environment, meaning that it provides lasting career paths for its Members; (2) developed a more complex internal organization; and (3) tended over time to use more automatic than discretionary methods for conducting internal business.

Institutionalization has altered many attributes of congressional games. First, the traits of the players have changed. Clearer boundaries mean that the legislature has more professional and stable membership and leadership. Lawmaking is now a distinct career, not an amateur avocation. Second, internal rules are much more elaborate, as evident in the growth and differentiation of the committee system. More subtle aspects of the internal game environment have altered as well. The growth of **norms,** or commonly held expectations among the Members about "how to proceed" in allocating power, led to more automatic methods for internal business. We discuss internal operations further in chapters 3 through 5, but two major norms deserve mention now. One is **partisanship,** the expectation that members of the same party will work closely together. The second is **seniority,** the practice of awarding senior Members greater positions of power on committees, subcommittees, and in each chamber as a whole. An important component of the broader seniority norm is the awarding of standing committee chairs to the Member of the majority party having the longest continuous service on that committee.

The stable membership of the present Congress contrasts starkly with the high turnover during the eighteenth and nineteenth centuries. In the House during that era, at least 40 percent of its Members were in their first terms and the average length of their service was under three years. In recent Congresses, the number of new House members remained well below 40 percent, and usually under 10 percent, though newcomers made up 25 percent of the House in 1993. The average length of service in recent decades has exceeded ten years.

Increasing legislative complexity in the twentieth century led to the landmark Legislative Reorganization Act of 1946. The act established the sizes of House and Senate committees, specified their jurisdictions for the first time, and required public disclosure of lobbying activities. Today the House has twenty-two standing committees and the Senate has sixteen. Underneath them are 115 House and eighty-six Senate subcommittees, producing an elaborate legislative organization in each chamber.

Alongside growing complexity, procedures within each chamber are now more orderly. In the nineteenth century, each chamber was much more raucous than it is today. Representative Balie Peterson in 1837 threatened to shoot a committee witness whose testimony he found intolerable. In 1856, Representative Preston Brooks, Democrat from South Carolina, tracked down Republican Senator Charles Sumner of Massachusetts on the Senate floor and beat him senseless with a cane. Duels between quarreling legislators were not uncommon before the Civil War; one legislator during that era populated the House floor with his hunting dogs. The rules today are numerous and quite difficult to alter. Particularly in the House, floor proceedings are tightly governed. Hunting dogs and canings are less in vogue and banned in both chambers.

RIVAL ARENAS: THE CONTEMPORARY HOUSE AND SENATE

Though we often talk about Congress today as a single entity "doing" something, most of the action attributed to Congress actually involves actions taken by its sub-units. Congress consists of two different arenas—settings in which a game takes place. At minimum, the House and Senate arenas set the context for action by their Members. The two chambers look similar on the surface, but in reality have competing perspectives, procedures and roles. As one House staff person told us, "The House and Senate are not only playing their games on different sides of the Capitol building, they might as well be playing different games in different parts of the world."

Congress is unique among national legislative bodies in that it is composed of two powerful and independent bodies. Most national legislatures feature one powerful

Bicameralism produces frequent disputes between the House and Senate, as suggested by this seeming debate between House Speaker Newt Gingrich (R-GA) and Senator Carol Moseley-Braun (D-IL). In fact, Senators and Representatives never meet each other in floor debate.

chamber, and a second chamber that can do little more than delay action.[1] **Bicameralism,** a two-house legislative system, reflects both the political philosophy and practical political strategy of the founders. Dividing power lessened the chance of tyranny and also facilitated a compromise over representation between the large and small states.

STRUCTURAL DIFFERENCES BETWEEN HOUSE AND SENATE

Several influences emanating from the structure of government and the electoral process assure that House members and Senators will differ in their actions.

Size: The Number of Players

With 100 players, as opposed to 435 in the House, the Senate can be more flexible with rules and procedures. While the House must manage its schedule carefully, the Senate allows almost unlimited debate (**filibuster**) and the inclusion of

[1]In Britain, for example, the House of Commons is the center of parliamentary power, choosing the prime minister and passing legislation. The House of Lords can deliberate and delay legislation for up to one year. Bills dealing entirely with expenditure or taxation can become law immediately without the approval of the House of Lords. In Germany, the Bundestag chooses the prime minister (known as the chancellor) and handles most legislation. The Bundesrat represents the state governments and has special responsibility over tax policy.

non-germane topics in debate and amendments to legislation. Senators tend to know each other personally and accommodate each other's needs and interests (see Baker 1989a, 55–57).

Virtually all senators are "names" when they arrive in Washington, while few House members receive similar recognition until they have attained a degree of seniority and reached a formal leadership position. House members react to many of their colleagues in terms of "team" affiliations ("Democrats," "Member of the Rules Committee," "Member of the Black Caucus," etc.) as opposed to knowing them personally.

Districts: The Fields of Play

Because senators are elected statewide, their constituencies are larger and more heterogeneous than districts of House members. Thus senators must usually accommodate more diverse interests. Senators generally tend to favor legislation aiding minorities and urban areas, since most senators have large urban areas back home. The establishment of relatively homogeneous majority-minority districts in the House (see chapter 2) created a set of districts quite different from the typical senatorial constituency.

Terms of Office: The Length of Rounds

The founders intentionally established two-year House terms in order to keep representatives close to the people. State legislatures until 1926 selected senators, removing them one step from popular passions. The six-year term for senators serves the same purpose today, giving them more freedom to use their own judgement.

Traditions: Informal Rules

The Senate views itself as the "upper" body and likes to be considered "the world's greatest deliberative institution." As evidence of the Senate's presumed authority, in the heat of conflict with the House, one senator blurted out, "No sitting member of the Senate ever ran for election to the House of Representatives" (quoted in Baker 1989a, 28). He recognized the unspoken truth that many House members aspire to the "upper" chamber.

With only one-third of its membership up for reelection each year, the Senate is a "continuing institution," which welcomes new members to an organization with enduring formal rules and fixed traditions. Each new House of Representatives must start afresh, approving or revising old rules and adapting a bit more to the influx of new members.

Constitutional Mandate: Special Arenas for Different Tasks

The constitutional rules grant the House and Senate arenas different tasks. With its proximity to the people, the House was granted the right to initiate bills dealing with the sensitive issue of taxes. The Senate, on the other hand, has the right to approve key presidential appointees to the executive branch and the courts, and must approve treaties negotiated by the president. This advise and consent power forces presidents to take the Senate into account concerning appointments and treaties. Presidents wisely consult key senators prior to making appointments, and keep them informed throughout treaty negotiations. As one key staff member put it,

> The Senate is being brought into the game of treaty negotiation much earlier. Rather than dropping a "done deal" on our doorstep, wise presidents informally request Senate input. If we are involved in the strategy for the game and kick-off, we are much more likely to be with the president as he tries to cross the goal line. (Author's interview)

The House and Senate also play different roles in evaluating other government officials. A majority of the House can **impeach** (bring charges against) executive and judicial branch officials for "high crimes and misdemeanors." The power to try impeachment cases belongs to the Senate, where conviction requires a two-thirds vote. The House has impeached one president (Andrew Johnson), and was about to impeach Richard Nixon before he resigned. Andrew Johnson survived his trial by the Senate by one vote. A few federal judges have been impeached (thirteen) with only seven being convicted.[2]

THE FOUNDERS AND TODAY

The delegates at Philadelphia in 1787 would not recognize the Congress of today. Contemporary national politics involves more numerous and complex games than they ever imagined. The founders could not foresee the large growth of the public sector in the twentieth century and the robust competition between national institutions that it spawned. Most feared the growth of legislative authority above all, but the president, bureaucracy, and Supreme Court are all much stronger institutions than the Constitution originally provided. Judicial review, administrative discretion and presidential popularity all serve to curb congressional power in the 1990s.

The Senate is less of a "cooling saucer" removed from the passions of popular opinion. Debate in the Senate does operate at a much more deliberative pace than in the House, and individual Senators can obstruct the flow of Senate business. But popular election of Senators has made the chamber more concerned with public sentiment (Ornstein 1981, 364–371). Popular responsiveness now supersedes deliberation in the contemporary Congress. Lawmakers today are full-time congressional careerists constantly playing the survival game of reelection, not the part-time "citizen legislators" envisioned by the founders. Turnover tends to be low, in large part because many senators and most representatives do not confront competitive elections. The standing committee system allows particular interests to have "their people" populating strategic committees, promoting responsiveness to particular lobbies. This hinders the deliberation over the common good that the founders

---

[2]One senator (William Blount of Tennessee) was impeached in 1799. William Belknap, secretary of war, was impeached in 1876. Both were acquitted by the Senate. The removal of federal Judge Alcee Hastings in 1989 is under appeal because the entire Senate failed to try him. Perhaps in the ultimate case of "don't get mad, get even," Judge Hastings ran and won a seat in the House in 1992 as a Democrat from Florida.

BOX 1.2 Constitutional Strategies in Congressional Games

Some of the games played in Congress employ the Constitution itself, a marvelous political resource for the pursuit of power. The following are four strategies by which legislators use the Constitution to attain their objectives in competition with fellow lawmakers or other national institutions.

(1) Go to court: When another branch of government challenges congressional authority, an appeal to the Supreme Court on constitutional grounds can work as a strategy for prevailing against the attack. In 1972, President Richard Nixon claimed to have "pocket vetoed" several bills during the Christmas recess of Congress. A pocket veto occurs if a president takes no action on a bill at the end of his ten-day constitutional decision period and meanwhile Congress has adjourned. Instead of the bill becoming law without his signature, the bill dies. However, in this instance Nixon claimed a pocket veto during a temporary recess, not a permanent adjournment. Senator Ted Kennedy took this to federal court and won the case, effectively nullifying the vetoes (*Kennedy v. Sampson* 511 F. 2d 430, 437, [D.C. Cir. 1974]).

(2) Claim institutional prerogative: A savvy lawmaker can secure passage of legislation by developing an argument in defense of the constitutional integrity of Congress. In 1972, Senator Warren Magnuson (D-WA) sought to block the movement of nerve gas from an American base on Okinawa to the United States proper. Though he was concerned primarily about shipment to his home state of Washington, arguing purely on regional grounds would not corral the needed votes. Instead, he used an argument certain to touch the institutional loyalty of many senators: that the president was challenging the constitutional powers of Congress. Magnuson claimed that the nerve gas operation was a presidential device to "avoid consultation with the Senate about Okinawa and the peace treaty with Japan, and thus was also a violation . . . of the Constitution itself" (Riker 1986, 109). This convinced enough senators to object to the shipments, and Magnuson won, 52–40.

(3) Shield yourself from your own actions: Lawmakers can make a law contingent on the proper Supreme Court interpretation of the Constitution. In 1985, Congress considered the Gramm-Rudman-Hollings bill. The measure required future Congresses to cut spending and/or raise taxes to meet federal deficit targets or else incur automatic, across-the-board budget cuts that would meet the targets. Democratic leaders in the House did not like this mechanism, but found their members anxious to vote for some version of it. What particularly concerned the leadership was the possibility that parts of the law might be found unconstitutional, giving the president greater responsibility over the across-the-board cuts. In the House version of the bill, they included an "unseverability" clause providing that if the court ruled any part of the law unconstitutional, the entire act would then be invalid. The prospect of giving more power over spending to Ronald Reagan did not alarm the Republican Senate. Senators forced deletion of the severability clause in the conference committee held to reconcile differences between the House and Senate versions.

(4) Defend your chamber: The House and Senate at times wrangle over alleged violations of each other's constitutional authority. In 1982, the Senate Finance (taxation) Committee took a small-scale revenue measure that had passed the House and tacked on the largest tax increase to that point in American history, totaling $98 billion over three years. The House assented to this, with a few modifications. Conservative House members, however, saw a constitutional means to derail this hated tax hike. They filed suit in federal court, arguing that the procedure had violated the constitutional provision that all revenue measures originate in the House. The federal court, however, dismissed the suit. A tax mouse can become a revenue elephant, as long as the mouse comes from the House.

hoped for. Much of the life on Capitol Hill is organized and segregated by party label. Entrenched partisan factions now run the institution—but they have not sought to destroy personal liberty, as Madison feared they might.

Another major feature of contemporary congressional life that the founders could not foresee is the prevalence of **divided government,** in which no single party has control of Congress and the presidency. Divided government existed for twenty of the twenty-four years, from 1968 to 1992. Usually, Republicans have held the presidency and Democrats the Congress. Scholars differ on the policy effects of this arrangement (Sundquist 1988, 629–30; Mayhew 1991, chap. 7), but it clearly serves to complicate games and strategies on Capitol Hill. The 1994 election guarantees at least two years of divided government with a Democratic President and Republican Congress.

Powerful party factions, careerism and interest-dominated policymaking are phenomena that the founders probably would lament. Ambitious political individualists, who work aggressively with parties and interest groups to get their way, now populate the national legislature. Congress generally, however, has not proven to be quite the power centrifuge that Madison had feared. The Philadelphia delegates may well have viewed divided government as useful for delaying lawmaking and fostering deliberation. Modern congressional games are not as destructive to individual liberty as the delegates of 1787 feared.

CONCLUSION

To the founders, political competition spawned all sorts of dangerous legislative games. They designed checks and balances, bicameralism and enumerated legislative powers to limit the power of Congress. The House would serve as a volatile center of popular sentiment, while the Senate would slow the legislative process and promote deliberation. Two-hundred years later, the Congress is more democratic and less constrained by enumerated powers, but it is also less powerful than the Philadelphia delegates expected. Particular interests do dominate congressional action at times, and partisan factions lie at the center of legislative life. Nevertheless, basic checks and balances, combined with the evolution of strong judicial and executive branches, keep legislative supremacy from becoming a reality. The Constitution continues to structure and limit the games played in Congress.

IN DEPTH

1. How did the adoption of new rules alter the behavior of Congress? You might examine how the national legislature operated under the Articles of Confederation and contrast that with the record of the early years of Congress under the Constitution. A number of questions deserve investigation. How did the differing methods of voting under the two systems alter the way Congress did business? Did the adoption of the Senate slow down the legislative process and produce more careful deliberation, as the founders intended? Did the addition of the institution of the presidency help or hurt the ability of the legislature to function effectively?

REFERENCES

Bell, Rudolph M., 1973. *Party and Faction in American Politics: The House of Representatives 1789–1801.* Westport, Conn.: Greenwood Press.

Dry, Murray, 1984. "Congress." In *Founding Principles of American Government,* George J. Graham, Jr., and Scarlett G. Graham. Chatham, N.J.: Chatham House.

Hoadley, John F., 1986. *Origins of American Political Parties 1789–1803.* Lexington, K.Y.: University Press of Kentucky.

McDonald, Forrest, 1985. *E Pluribus Unum: The Formation of the American Republic 1776–1790.* Boston: Houghton Mifflin.

Wood, Gordon, 1969. *The Creation of the American Republic.* Chapel Hill: University of North Carolina Press.

2. The concepts of "delegate" and "trustee" stimulated much research by political scientists concerning the roles legislators play. Some scholars also posited a third role, that of "politico," in which a lawmaker shifts from delegate to trustee, depending on the situation. Are roles a useful concept in exploring legislative behavior? Is one role superior to any of the others? Should we define roles as resulting from lawmakers' self-descriptions of their activities, their actual behavior, or the expectations of legislative colleagues and the public concerning the proper legislative role?

REFERENCES

Davidson, Roger, 1969. *The Role of the Congressman.* New York: Pegasus.

Kuklinski, James H., and Richard E. Elling, 1977. "Representational Role, Constituency Opinion, and Legislative Roll-Call Behavior." *American Journal of Political Science* 21: 135–147.

McCrone, Donald J., and James H. Kuklinski, 1979. "The Delegate Theory of Representation." *American Journal of Political Science* 23: 278–300.

Prewitt, Kenneth, Heinz Eulau, and Betty H. Zisk, 1966. "Political Socialization and Political Roles." *Public Opinion Quarterly* 30: 569–582.

Wahlke, John C., Heinz Eulau, William Buchanan, and LeRoy C. Furgeson, 1962. *The Legislative System.* New York: John Wiley.

3. Some of the world's legislatures are unicameral—composed of only one chamber—including the state legislature of Nebraska. It is clear that the founders created a bicameral legislature to slow down the course of lawmaking and force a "due deliberation" over policy. Is this "auxiliary precaution" necessary to American government in the late twentieth century? What might be the advantages and disadvantages of switching to unicameral rules for our national legislature?

REFERENCES

Pole, J. R., 1966. *Political Representation in England and the Origins of the American Republic.* New York: St. Martin's.

Richardson, James, 1991. "The Unicameral Legislature: New Look at an Old Idea." *California Journal* 22:5 (May): 211–213.

Riker, William H., 1992. "The Justification of Bicameralism." *International Political Science Review* 13:1 (January): 101–116.

Riley, W., 1973. "Nonpartisan Unicameral—Benefits, Defects Reexamined." *Nebraska Law Review* 52: 377–403.

Wood, Gordon, 1969. *The Creation of the American Republic.* Chapel Hill: University of North Carolina Press.

4. The founders did not intend divided government, because they did not foresee the establishment of a lasting two-party system in American politics. This topic has sparked much recent debate and writing by political scientists, some denouncing divided government and its effects while others dispute such claims. Is divided government a scourge for our country, or are criticisms of it greatly overstated? Does divided government have any redeeming features?

REFERENCES

Cox, Gary W., and Samuel Kernell, ed. 1991. *The Politics of Divided Government.* Boulder, Colo.: Westview Press.

Fiorina, Morris, 1991. *Divided Government.* New York: Macmillan.

Jones, Charles O., 1994. *The Presidency in a Separated System.* Washington, D.C.: Brookings Institution.

Mayhew, David, 1991. *Divided We Govern.* New Haven: Yale University Press.

Sundquist, James L., 1988. "Needed: A Political Theory for the New Era of Coalition Government in the U.S." *Political Science Quarterly* 103: 614–630.

Thurber, James, ed. 1991. *Divided Democracy.* Washington, D.C.: Congressional Quarterly.

CHAPTER TWO

THE ELECTORAL GAME

Elections are the big game in politics. Election night is one of the few times in politics when it is absolutely clear who knows how to play the game and who does not. Little kids used to reach for the brass ring on the merry-go-round; grown up political kids replace the brass ring with a campaign victory. (Author's interview)

Early in January after the previous November's election, all members of the House of Representatives and all new members of the Senate assemble in their respective chambers to take their oath of office surrounded by family and supporters. These members, who are about to guide the public policies of the nation, vary considerably in their political outlook, capabilities and political experience, yet they share three things in common. Each has entered an election contest, emerged triumphant, and obtained a certificate of election signed by the appropriate state official. While each chamber serves as the final judge of its own membership, the chambers only

Hispanic candidate Nydia Velazquez used her personal skills and a carefully drawn majority-minority district to beat nine-term congressman Stephen Solarz in the Democratic primary to represent a New York district in Congress. She went on to win the general election with ease.

rarely second guess the winner's legal right to serve.[1] In those relatively few close races contested by the loser (on the basis of irregularity in the counting of votes or campaign tactics) the House and Senate profess a desire to discover the true choice of the voters, but often end up voting along party lines.[2]

Taking the oath of congressional office remains the privilege of relatively few Americans. It results from many career and strategy decisions. The vast majority of Americans never even consider making the initial decisions which would start them on the route to congressional office. In earlier periods of American history, playing in the congressional arena was seen largely as a short-term commitment. These congresses met for only a few months each year and most Members served a few terms before moving on to other pursuits in the public or private sector. Up through the nineteenth century, Members often resigned without completing their terms (see Kernell 1977). In recent years, service in Congress has become a full-time profession favoring extended tenure (see tables 2.1 and 2.2).

The development of careerism in Congress raises the electoral stakes for both candidates and the voters. Modern congressional candidates realize that they are pursuing a full-time job and that power and influence are closely related to long-term service. The part-time, short-term, legislator is largely the victim of an expanding congressional workload, increasingly complex policy decisions, and a leadership selection process which favors long tenure. The growing power of Congress and the potential for a career assures that congressional contests will be fought with more vigor and require a greater commitment. Potential candidates think twice before entering the congressional game and many voters recognize that today's election has long-term implications. As we will see in chapter 3, once in office, Members have learned how to structure the chamber and their own behavior in ways that allow them to maintain the position they fought so hard to obtain (see Mayhew 1974b).

Understanding why individuals choose to serve in Congress, how they get there, and the degree to which they want to stay, provides a number of important clues as to how Members will behave in office. Congressional elections not only determine *who* will serve, but have a significant impact on the individual and the collective decisions of the Members chosen to serve.

---

[1]Such challenges are not unheard of. In 1984, Republican challenger Richard McIntyre was certified as the winner over Democratic incumbent Frank McCloskey by 418 votes after a recount in Indiana's 8th district. The Democratically controlled House Administration Committee questioned the state procedures which had thrown out more than 4,800 ballots for technical reasons. The committee carried out its own recount, declaring McCloskey the winner by four votes. The Republicans called the result "nothing short of a rape," but did not have the votes to back it up (see Ehrenhalt 1987, 511).

[2]Of the more than 500 contested election controversies, the controlling party in Congress awarded the seat to a member of the minority party in less than 10 percent of the cases. See *Congressional Quarterly's Guide to Congress, 1991,* Washington D.C.: Congressional Quarterly Inc., p. 827.

TABLE 2.1 The Length of Congressional Sessions, 80th–100th Congresses

In the 1960s, the length of congressional sessions stabilized at about 300 days per year. Since that time, the number of hours the House and Senate are in session has generally increased.

	Number of Hours in Session	
	Senate	**House**
80th Congress (1947–48)	1,462	1,224
85th Congress	1,876	1,147
90th Congress	1,961	1,595
95th Congress	2,510	1,898
100th Congress (1987–88)	2,342	1,659
102nd Congress	2,291	1,794

SOURCE: Norman J. Ornstein, Thomas E. Mann and Michael J. Malbin. *Vital Statistics on Congress, 1993–1994*, pp. 151–153, Congressional Quarterly, Inc., 1994.

TABLE 2.2 The Growth of Careerism in the U.S. Congress

	Senate *(% serving more than two terms)*	**House** *(% serving more than seven terms)*
55th Congress (1897–98)	6%	5%
60th Congress (1907–08)	12%	6%
65th Congress (1917–18)	6%	11%
70th Congress (1927–28)	19%	12%
75th Congress (1937–38)	21%	15%
80th Congress (1947–48)	18%	16%
85th Congress (1957–58)	23%	33%
90th Congress (1967–68)	38%	32%
95th Congress (1977–78)	33%	31%
100th Congress (1987–88)	30%	30%
103rd Congress (1993–94)	53%	24%

SOURCES: Norman J. Ornstein, Thomas E. Mann and Michael J. Malbin. *Vital Statistics on Congress, 1991–1992*, pp. 20–21, Congressional Quarterly, Inc., 1992; *Congressional Directory*, for pre 85th Congress data, Government Printing Office, Washington D.C.

RULES OF THE ELECTORAL GAME

The rules of the electoral game determine who can play and how they can pursue victory. Like most sets of rules, they favor some players and diminish the chances of others.

DIRECT VERSUS INDIRECT ELECTION

Until 1913, House and Senate members were selected in different arenas. The House of Representatives, long viewed as the "chamber of the people," was elected from the beginning directly by the people. The founders desired a Senate responsible for protecting state interests and more removed from popular passions. Indirect election of senators by state legislatures worked well until the early 1900s when increasing corruption in state legislatures, more numerous deadlocks in the choice of senators, and pressure from progressive reformers wishing to control undemocratic special interests led to the passage of the Seventeenth Amendment mandating direct election of senators (see Baker 1988, 69).

STATE VERSUS NATIONAL ELECTION LAWS

The specifics of election law in the United States are largely determined on the state level. Congressional elections have not always been held on the same date in all states and some states chose not to select their congressional delegation on the same day as the presidential election. Discrimination against specific groups and the desire to include new groups of eligible voters (such as women and eighteen- to twenty-one-year-olds) led to a series of legislative enactments and constitutional amendments expanding the electorate and guaranteeing voting rights. Over the years, eligibility requirements and election mechanics have become more consistent across the states.

WINNER-TAKE-ALL DETERMINATON OF VICTORIES

Congressional elections are winner-take-all contests. Victory cannot be shared. Unlike **proportional representation (P.R.)** systems in which political parties receive a number of seats based on their percentage of the vote, each congressional election has only one winner. Winning most congressional elections is based on receiving a **plurality,** more votes than any other candidate. Ten southern states require that primary election winners receive a **majority** (50 percent plus one). If no one receives a majority, a run-off primary is required. Such a rule works against minority candidates. (See later discussion of primary elections.)

FIXED TERMS OF OFFICE AND FIXED ELECTIONS

The six-year term of office for senators and two-year term for House members with the right of unlimited re-election, was a compromise between those founders desiring frequent rotation in office and those placing a higher value on continuity (Baker 1988, 7). The six-year Senate term was designed to relieve them of having to respond to the parochial concerns of the public (Wright 1993, 14). Contemporary attempts to limit the number of terms Members can serve have roots in the Articles of Confederation which included such limits (Congressional Quarterly 1976, 43) and reflect a judgement that the infusion of new blood in Congress is more important than continuity.

BOX 2.1 Parliamentary Terms of Office: Controlling the Length of the Game

The United States' presidential system with a separation of powers between the legislative and executive branches is relatively unique among world governments. Most nations use a parliamentary system in which the legislative and executive branches are considerably more interdependent. Members of parliament are more than legislators. If they are members of the majority party or majority coalition, they establish the executive branch of government by choosing one of their members as prime minister. The prime minister forms a government by choosing other members of Parliament as the chief executive officers of governmental departments who then become part of his or her cabinet.

Most parliaments place an upper limit (often five years) on how long a government can serve, but most governments "call an election" before the statutory limit is reached. Prime ministers must call an election when they lose a vote of confidence on a major policy issue in the parliament. Prime ministers often try to gain a strategic advantage by calling an election when their popularity is high or to surprise the opposition. When an election is called, *all* members of Parliament wanting to remain in office must face the electorate again. Since their tenure in office is directly affected by the calling of an election, members of Parliament think twice about opposing the prime minister on an issue which could lead to the dissolution of the sitting government.

For a further discussion of parliamentary systems see the following:

Vernon Bogdanor, ed., 1985. *Representatives of the People? Parliamentarians and their Constituents in Western Democracies.* Brookfield, Vt: Gower.

Ivor Jennings. 1969. *Parliament.* London: Cambridge University Press.

Unlike parliamentary systems, in which legislators serve until the prime minister dissolves the government due to lack of legislative support or for strategic purposes (see box 2.1), congressional candidates know exactly when the next election will occur. Incumbents and challengers alike can prepare for the upcoming contest.

STAGES IN THE ELECTORAL PROCESS

Winning a congressional seat involves filing for office, securing a place on the general election ballot and winning a plurality of the general election votes.

Filing for Office

To file for office one needs only to meet the legal requirements for service in Congress and to pay a small filing fee. House candidates must be twenty-five years of age, United States citizens for at least seven years, and eligible voters in the **state** (not necessarily the district) from which they choose to run. Senate candidates must be thirty years of age, citizens for nine years and eligible voters of their state.

Getting on the General Election Ballot

During the first century of congressional elections, political parties had the right to hold conventions and place candidates directly on the ballot. Beginning around 1900, concern over the unrepresentative nature of party activists and the potential for corruption led to the spread of the **direct primary** for selecting each party's nominee for the general election. A primary is a preliminary election in which party supporters are given the opportunity to choose among aspiring party candidates. Most states (75 percent), use **closed primaries** in which individuals may vote only in the primary election of the party for which they are registered.[3] Other states make it easier for voters to choose the primary in which to participate on election day. Minor party candidates can get on the general election ballot either by holding conventions or via signed petitions, but this process takes a great deal of money and effort. Access to the printed ballot is very important, since write-in candidates seldom win.[4]

General Election Victory

Most congressional elections involve one candidate from each of the major parties. Even when there are more than two candidates, winning a congressional election in most states requires gaining a plurality (as opposed to a majority) of the votes cast.[5]

DRAWING DISTRICT LINES

Members of Congress run **for** office, by running **from** within a particular geographically defined district. We have chosen to use a **single-member-district system** for House elections, in which each district has one designated representative. With two senators for each state, the U.S. has in effect a dual-member-district system, but with staggered six-year terms, the two senators never oppose each other. By associating each Member with a particular district, the founders hoped to assure representatives would feel a responsibility for the interests of their districts and could be held accountable by those they were chosen to serve.

---

[3]Other states use *open* primaries where voters choose the party contest in which they wish to participate, or more rarely, *blanket* primaries where voters can participate in the primaries of different offices for different parties.

[4]Memories of write-in victories remain for a long time on Capitol Hill due to their uniqueness. Members and staff still talk about how long term Louisiana Democratic Representative Brooks Hayes was defeated by a write-in candidate in the late 1950s for refusing to oppose school desegregation.

[5]Democratic Senator Wyche Fowler of Georgia clearly knows the importance of election rules. Georgia law requires congressional candidates to win with a majority. Although Fowler won a plurality in the 1992 election, a third-party candidate siphoned off enough votes to deny him a majority. In the two-candidate run-off a few weeks later, Republican Paul Coverdell won by 2 percent.

During the debates on the Constitution, large population states wanted membership in the legislative branch to reflect population, while small population states wanted equal representation of states. Allowing each state two senators regardless of population was one of the key compromises proposed by the small population states during the constitutional convention.

While Senate district lines are fixed, drawing the lines for House districts is both more complex and contentious. The Constitution provides for a national census every ten years after which seats in Congress are **reapportioned** among the states based on the new population distribution. Once assigned the appropriate number of seats, the state legislature is responsible for **redistricting** the state.

Reapportionment

By all rights, reapportionment should be a relatively straightforward process of fulfilling the constitutional guarantee of at least one district per state, dividing the new population by the number of seats available to establish the ideal population of a district, and then determining how many seats each state receives based on its population. The stakes of this game are so high, though, that a variety of players vie for competitive advantage. Out of fear of losing power, states battled to expand the original sixty-five seats in the House each time a new state was added or the population shifted. The size of the House was permanently set at 435 after the 1910 census, and first applied to the election of 1912. With population growth, fixing the size of the House led to much more populous districts. Whereas Members of the First Congress represented less than 30,000 constituents, Members of the 103rd Congress (1993–1994) represent over 580,000. This makes the member-to-constituent ratio in the U.S. House greater than most other national legislatures.[6]

With the fixing of the size of the House, reapportionment became a **zero-sum game** in which a gain of seats for one state automatically meant a loss for another state. While some controversy existed about the formula for allotting seats when the mathematical division did not work out perfectly, significant controversy did not arise until 1990, when several states seriously questioned the accuracy of the census. Census officials have long known that despite their best efforts, the census fails to count many minorities and physically mobile individuals who are difficult to contact and less likely to cooperate (Vobejda 1991, A17). Such individuals most often live in and use the services of urban areas. After considerable discussion and a series of court challenges by public officials representing urban jurisdictions, the secretary of commerce decided against an adjustment of the 1990 census figures since there was no agreement as to the appropriate adjustment to make. The proposed adjustment would have shifted only four seats between states, but more importantly would also have shifted seats within many states from rural to urban areas (Elving 1991, 1690–91). Some urban Democrats argued that the Republican administration which controlled

[6] The 650 Members of the British House of Commons represent approximately 87,000 constituents; the 577 Members of the French Assembly represent 97,000 constituents, and the 662 Members of the German Bundestag represent 119,000 constituents. See Donald Devine, 1992, "A Growing Plan for the U.S. House," *Insight,* (April 20): 17–18.

the Commerce Department recognized the limited support for Republican candidates in urban areas and was playing politics for their own partisan gain. Republicans questioned the accuracy of the adjusted figures, asserted that such adjustments have never been used, and pointed out the partisan motivations of the Democrats.

Overall, population shifts in recent years have meant a significant number of seats moved from the "rust belt" states of the Northeast and the Midwest, to the "sun belt" states of the South and West (see figure 2.1).

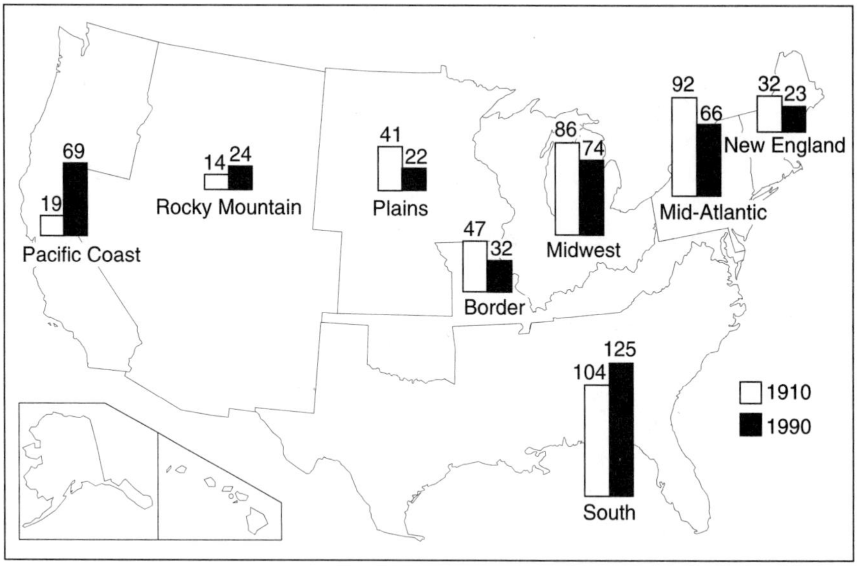

THE WINNERS (1980–1990)

	*Number of Seats Gained**
California	7
Florida	4
Texas	3
Arizona, Georgia, North Carolina, Virginia, Washington	1

THE LOSERS (1980–1990)

	Number of Seats Lost
New York	3
Illinois, Michigan, Ohio, Pennsylvania	2
Iowa, Kansas, Kentucky, Louisiana, Massachusetts, Montana, New Jersey, West Virginia	1

FIGURE 2.1

Regional Shifts in Congressional Seats from 1910 to 1990, Shifts between States from 1980–1990

***SOURCE:** Ronald Elving, 1991, "Bureau Releases New Estimates, Remains Wary of Adjustment", *Congressional Quarterly Weekly Report,* June 15, p.1606.

Redistricting

> Redistricting is the purest of blood sports, largely stripped of pretensions about good government. . . . The game's boundaries are set by the Census Bureau and the Voting Rights Act, and its outcome is driven by power, partisanship, friendship and money. (Sack 1991a, A1)

Congressional districts are drawn by state legislatures and must generally be approved by the governor.[7] For more than 150 years, state politicians controlled the game. When it suited the interests of the legislative and gubernatorial power holders, they redrew the lines after each census. Most often it did not, since population shifts were toward urban areas, and state legislatures—based on the old population distributions—over-represented rural areas. The unwillingness to redraw lines unless the state lost or gained seats meant the number of voters in each district varied considerably.

CHANGING THE RULES AND PLAYERS IN THE REDISTRICTING GAME Until 1962, the Supreme Court refused to enter this political thicket[8] and left redistricting decisions to elected officials. After several appeals based on the unfairness of the current system, especially to individuals residing in large population districts whose voting power was diluted, the Court ruled in *Baker v. Carr (369 U.S. 186* [*1972*]*)* that the equal protection clause of the Fourteenth Amendment gave the courts jurisdiction over cases involving state legislative redistricting. Two additional cases (*Reynolds v. Sims 377 U.S. 53* [*1964*] and *Wesberry v. Sanders U.S. 1* [*1964*]) solidified the principle of **one person, one vote**,[9] guaranteeing that state legislative and congressional districts must be of equal population.

In a series of cases, the courts continually redefined the criteria for fair districts, reducing the leeway of state legislatures. Three basic criteria have guided the definition of "ideal" districts. The "one person, one vote" Supreme Court decisions of the 1960s emphasized the importance of **population equality,** asserting that persons living in large population districts were denied equal protection of the laws, since their individual votes had less of an impact than individuals living in less populous districts. Two additional and potentially competing criteria emphasize the ease of representation and campaigning by favoring districts which are **compact** and composed of **contiguous** rather than physically separated components. It is assumed that compact and contiguous districts are both easier for maintaining political contact and more likely to combine individuals from identifiable communities

---

[7] In North Carolina there is no gubernatorial veto and in New York it cannot be applied to redistricting. Three other states, Idaho, Tennessee and West Virginia, vitiate the veto's power by requiring only a simple majority to override it (Butler and Cain 1992, 94).

[8] Justice Felix Frankfurter warned that the court should not get into the "political thicket" of redistricting in his majority decision in the 1946 case of *Colgrove v. Green (328 U.S. 549).*

[9] The actual court decision read "one man, one vote," but in an era when sexist language was not a major concern, the justices obviously meant the term to include women.

sharing common interests and outlooks (see Niemi and Brace 1993). In the last three decades of court involvement in redistricting, the "judicial fixation with precise mathematical equality requires remappers to give short shrift to [these other] reasonable and important objectives" (Duncan 1990c, 3462). The courts have found it easier to focus on zero mathematical deviation than the other criteria.

Not only did the courts establish criteria, but they also stood on the sidelines as potential players willing to get in the game if the elected officials could not make up their minds. A number of states had their districts drawn by the courts. The Republicans, whose success in winning the presidency has given them control over judicial appointments, have increasingly turned to the courts to enforce standards and draw lines more to their benefit than if the Democratically controlled state legislatures and democratic governors had their way (Edsall 1992, A16 and Duncan 1992, 682). After the courts redrew the California lines in 1992, one Republican activist was excited about the "level playing field" which would help them "recruiting a team and winning the game" (Cannon 1992, A9). A Democratic spokesman looked at the same map and asserted that "this is a Republican reapportionment conducted by a Republican court appointed by Republican governors" (Cannon 1992, A9). Partisan accusations and sanctimonious statements notwithstanding, both parties take advantage of the redistricting process for their own partisan benefit.

THE CONTINUING ROLE OF POLITICS IN THE REDISTRICTING PROCESS Taking away the ability to create districts with different sized populations hampered, but did not eliminate, the role of politics in the process of redistricting. **Gerrymandering**[10] (see box 2.2), the process of drawing district lines for partisan or group advantage, continued despite becoming more difficult. The importance of gerrymandering lies in its ability to tilt the playing field in favor of candidates from a particular party or interest group. Creative districting for political advantage often means that elections are won or lost before the official campaign commences.

Within the constraints of population equality three basic strategies of gerrymandering remain. "Packing" involves concentrating opposition voters into one or a few districts, guaranteeing them a wasteful margin of victory (see box 2.3), and allowing your group just enough votes to comfortably win in a majority of districts. "Cracking," on the other hand, involves dividing up a potentially cohesive group and spreading their votes across a number of districts, denying them enough of a presence to win in any one of them (see box 2.3). A variety of forms of redistricting "mischief" involves drawing the lines so incumbents of the opposing party are either thrown into the same district and must oppose each other or are given a district having little in common with the district from which they were elected in the past

---

[10] During the early 1800s, Governor Elbridge Gerry of Massachusetts gave his name to the process of partisan districting. He approved a districting plan which heavily favored his party. The political cartoonist Tinsdale drew the district like a salamander and dubbed it a "gerrymander" and the name stuck.

BOX 2.2 The Gerrymander Lives

The Original Gerrymander—Massachusetts 1812

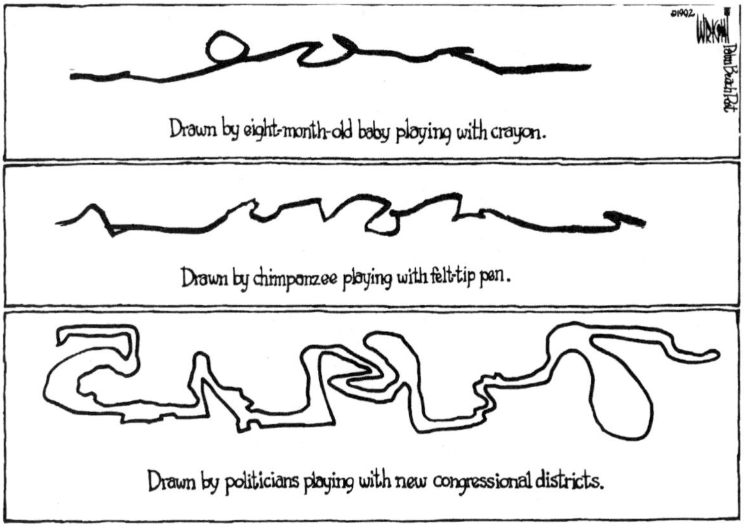
Drawn by eight-month-old baby playing with crayon.
Drawn by chimpanzee playing with felt-tip pen.
Drawn by politicians playing with new congressional districts.

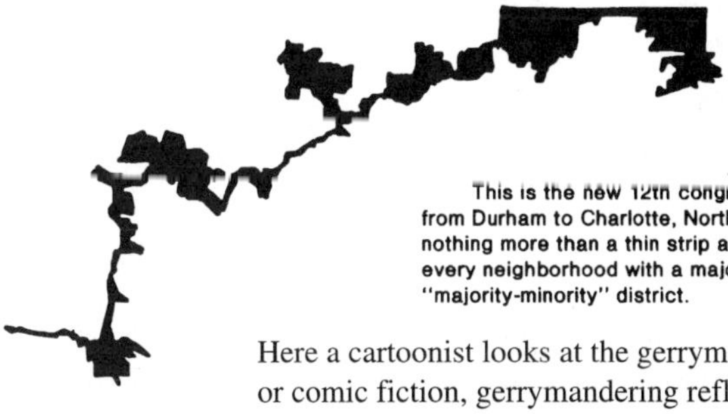

This is the new 12th congressional district of North Carolina. It snakes 175 miles, from Durham to Charlotte, North Carolina, along Interstate 85, and at certain points is nothing more than a thin strip along the highway. The mapmakers drew it to include nearly every neighborhood with a majority of blacks between the two cities to fashion a "majority-minority" district.

Here a cartoonist looks at the gerrymander and its real-life equivalent. Whether in fact or comic fiction, gerrymandering reflects creative artistry.

(see box 2.3). Sitting members of Congress often view redistricting as "an unsettling game of musical chairs [and] 'nobody has any confidence about when the music will stop and who will be it.' " (The late Congressman Ted Weiss [D-NY] quoted in Sack 1992, A1)

NEW CRITERIA, EMERGING STRATEGIES, AND THE CONTINUATION OF THE REDISTRICTING GAME

> Redistricting in the 1990's will not be just a donkey vs. elephant game of partisan checkers. It will be an intricate contest of multidimensional political chess in which party interests are by no means paramount. (Duncan 1990b, 3902)

BOX 2.3 Packing, Cracking and General Redistricting Mischief

a. "Packing" for Partisan Advantage (Democratic packing to win three out of four districts)

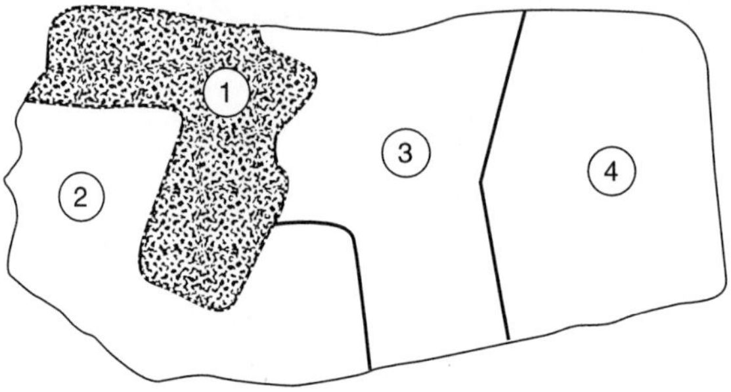

Partisan Distribution
= Republican areas

b. "Cracking" to Dissipate Republican Party Power ("Wheel and spoke" cracking)

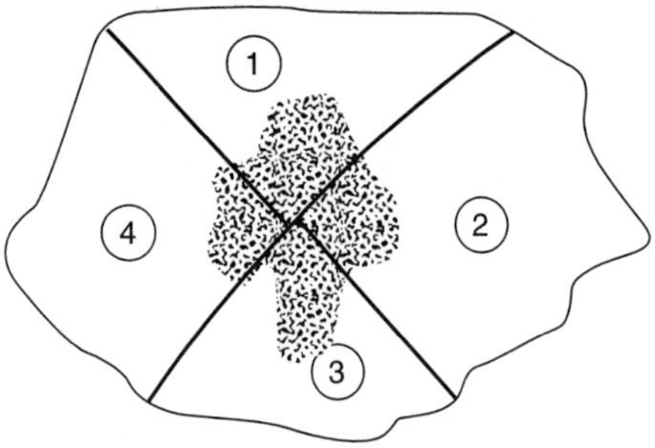

Partisan Distribution
= Republican areas

c. Partisan "Mischief"

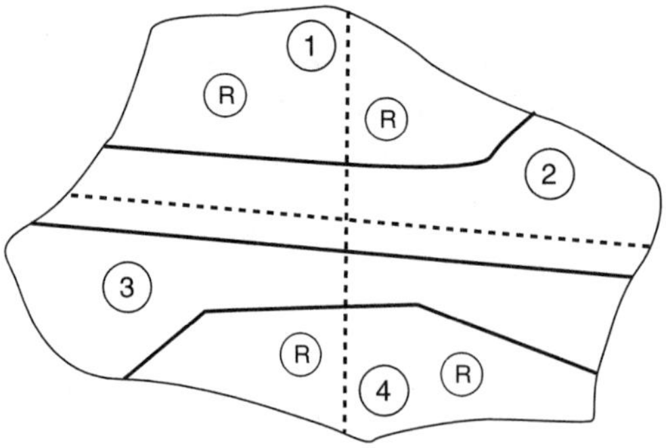

------ = Existing districts

(R) = Republican incumbents' residences

—— = New districts (Disadvantaging the Republican incumbents by making them run against each other in the same district)

Those involved in the redistricting that took place after the 1990 census saw the expanding use of new technology, one major new offensive strategy, and a reinvigorated defensive strategy enter the game.

Harnessing new technology. Drawing possible redistricting plans was once a laborious process of calculation and "guesstimation." The extensive effort required to design even one plan discouraged the development of alternatives. The arrival of the computer and machine-readable census data has changed the chemistry of the process. It is now possible to display the census data associated with a proposed district, shift a boundary, and observe the impact on the quantitative data (Anderson and Dahlstrom 1990, 76). A sequence of plans can be developed and compared in a matter of moments. Using computers increases the temptation to rely on population equality alone. Savvy legislators have

> come to realize that the court could be led to accept partisan gerrymanders no matter how blatantly the lines fractured community boundaries, as long as the districts were equal in population. . . . The looming duels to zero deviation that could pit one party's computer against another will not be a productive use of legislator's time . . . there will be an unprecedented and calculated chase of politicians and interest groups spending millions of dollars and months of time to produce serpentine maps with partisan spins and decimal-point deviations (Duncan 1990c, 3462).

To some degree computer power has replaced voting power in the state legislature. As one Republican party strategist put it:

> In the past, only the majority in the legislature has really had the tools to play the game. . . . If we [the minority] can help somehow in providing technological capabilities for groups, that goes to our goal of creating a fair and open process (quoted in Bragdon 1990, 1741).

After the 1990 census, the Republican Party saw the advantage of making its computer technology available to minority groups who wanted to create strong minority districts, as the following discussion indicates.

Minority rights and an offensive "assist" from another team. A series of court cases and the Justice Department's interpretation of the 1982 amendments to the 1965 Voting Rights Act established a new mandate to, wherever feasible, create districts in which a minority group enjoys majority status (Merry 1991, 2346). Such intentional packing had the support of many African Americans and Hispanics who hope to guarantee "winnable" districts for members of their ethnic groups. Democrats were much more hesitant, fearing the siphoning of traditional Democratic voters into wasteful victories.[11] Republican leaders supported the idea of ethnic packing, thus creating an alliance with minority groups. Arguing that "strict enforcement of the Voting Rights Act is going to lead to fairer redistricting," (Republican Party Chief Counsel Ben Ginsberg quoted in Donovan 1991, 2295), Republicans were also aware

[11]The partisan and ethnic consequences of majority-minority districts were borne out in 1992. Of the thirty-two black-majority districts, most elected African Americans and all elected Democrats. Only four of the twenty Hispanic-majority districts elected Republicans to Congress (*Congressional Quarterly Weekly Report,* 1993, [10 July]: 1829.)

that wasting Democratic votes would bolster Republican chances of victory in the remaining districts. Republican National Committee Chairman Richard Bond openly made the state-of-the-art redistricting software available to minority groups in 1991 (Yeutter 1991, A21). He asserted that this action had made eighty previously Democratic sets "competitive for the 90's," [and] resulting in substantially increased minority representation (Gugliotta 1992, A4).

Due to the ethnic packing, a record number of minority Members were elected to the 103rd Congress in 1992 (see chapter 4). A number of individual careers were affected as well. Nine-term incumbent Stephen Solarz was one of the casualties when his district was redrawn to be 55 percent Hispanic. Solarz' experience, institutional power and campaign funding advantage could not compete with the twelfth district voters' desire to have someone from their ethnic group in Congress and he lost to Nydia Velazquez (D-NY) in the Democratic primary.

After the 1990 census, the number of majority-minority districts doubled from twenty-six to fifty-two, with thirty-eight of them electing minority candidates. The legal right to draw congressional districts to boost minority representation is not a settled issue. A series of challenges are currently in the courts. In 1993 in *Shaw v Reno,* the Supreme Court questioned the North Carolina racially based redistricting plan and sent it back to the state courts.

An enhanced defensive strategy—the incumbents fight back. As one New Jersey politician put it, "You have 120 guys down there [in the state legislature], all of whom figure they should be congressmen. Sometimes party interests or the interests of incumbent congressmen fall by the wayside" (quoted in Jacobson 1992, 14). Members of Congress have long been uncomfortable as pawns in a political game played by state level politicians who do not necessarily have their national counterparts' best interests in mind.

After the 1990 census, several states, (see figure 2.1), lost seats in the House of Representatives. The fear of being forced to run against another incumbent or have significant changes in one's district encouraged many Members from these states to strengthen their political ties with the state legislators charged with redrawing the lines. As one headline put it, "Incumbents court state legislative leaders who control a game of musical chairs" (Hook 1991b, 1035). Given the high stakes in the politics of redistricting, members of Congress attempted to produce a more favorable outcome by contributing millions of dollars to state legislators (Alston 1991b, 1343). For example, Representative L. William Paxon, an aggressive Republican from western New York who was in danger of losing his seat, met with each of New York's thirty-five Republicans and

> . . . proposed a redistricting plan to the Senate majority leader, Ralph J. Marino. He has also contributed $30,000 from his campaign treasury to the Senate Republican Campaign Committee and has raised an additional $23,000 for the Committee. He said he promised Mr. Marino that he would contribute $10,000 a year to the Senate Republicans if he keeps his seat. (Sack 1991a, A1)

Representative Paxon went on to win in his new district with more than 60 percent of the vote.

While state legislators claim that money does not have a major impact on redistricting, staying on the good side of those who hold your political fate in their hands cannot hurt. As Representative Norman Lent (R-NY) sees it, a significant contribution "gets their attention" (Sack 1991a, A1 and Sack 1992, A1).

While the district lines determine the playing field, the game cannot go on without available and capable players. A number of important considerations go into the decision to seek a seat in Congress.

DECIDING TO PLAY THE ELECTORAL GAME: MOTIVATION AND OPPORTUNITY

After losing his reelection bid to the Senate in 1950, Florida's Claude Pepper expressed his frustrated ambition in these words: "I felt like an athlete benched when he was at the peak of his game. I had to watch the players on the field, knowing I could do better than many of them if only I could get back in the game" (Fessler 1989, 1298). When the opportunity arose, Pepper won election to the House in 1962 and spent more than twenty-five years there.

Contemplating entry into the congressional arena requires both **motivation** and **opportunity.** The motivation generally precedes the opportunity by several years. Running for Congress is seldom an individual's first political experience. Potential congressional candidates generally have considerable political experience before they run. Much earlier in their careers, most have weighed the benefits and costs of political activity.

MOTIVATION

> The men and women who run for Congress have one thing in common: an intense desire to serve. . . . At a minimum, a bona fide congressional aspirant is someone interested in local and national affairs, who tolerates living simultaneously in sharply different worlds and who navigates through life without intimate personal connections (or lives in a family that can withstand great stress and long separations). A viable congressional candidate also feels a strong sense of public approval and is confident that the voters see him or her as qualified and competent. . . . (Fowler and McClure 1989, 225)

People seldom enter politics on a whim. Despite its relatively low pay compared to their previous occupations and large sacrifices of time and privacy, politics is dominated by those who love some aspect of this raucous game and begin to play it early.

> These are the people who, as teenagers, begin passing out brochures and learning to read voter target lists; as college students, start organizing campaigns; as graduates, take up work as aides to other office holders. In their late twenties and early thirties, they surface as city council members and state legislators. Not all of them make it as far as they would like to go. But to an increasing extent, these are the people who dominate American politics at every level. As politics turns into full-time work, in a congressional district, or a state legislature, or a city hall, it attracts people for whom political life itself is the reward. (Ehrenhalt 1991a, C3)[12]

---

[12]Ehrenhalt's analysis of the development of political "junkies" applies more to white, middle-class males. Other demographic groups may follow different patterns. For a more complete discussion of his argument, see Alan Ehrenhalt, 1991, *The United States of Ambition: Politicians, Power and the Pursuit of Office,* New York: Times Books.

Benefits of Political Involvement

The rewards of political life are numerous. Political involvement can help satisfy some basic human needs and few players are dragged kicking and screaming into the political arena. Most find some combination of significant rewards for their actions. Renowned psychologist Abraham Maslow[13] said that individuals proceed through a hierarchy of needs, with the satisfaction of each lower level need paving the way for the desire to make life more meaningful by the satisfaction of higher level needs. The necessity of **physical security** must be satisfied before an individual seeks **social acceptance and affection.** The individual comfortable with his or her social support is freed to pursue a sense of **personal accomplishment**—striving to "be the most one can be."

PHYSICAL SECURITY Political involvement in modern liberal democratic societies seldom stems from a raw need to protect one's physical security. Being the member of the "right" political party, or backing the "right" candidate is not necessary for survival. More indirectly, some individuals see political involvement as a way to **secure employment** and improve their socio-economic level. Volunteering in that first campaign is only the first step in gaining the credentials for more remunerative positions. Moving up the political career path has provided opportunities for many minorities and women in America who found other careers less accepting. Immigrants such as the Irish and Italians used politics to secure the future for themselves and their descendants.

Some relatively well established individuals are drawn into politics when the economic status quo is challenged. Congress is filled with individuals who got their start in politics by protesting local legislation that proved harmful to their business or profession. The experience of participating in the local political game often whets their appetite for further involvement, while the visibility they gain makes other players aware of their interests and skills.

SOCIAL BENEFITS

> Politics [is] an outlet for the ambitions of bright young people who [are] rightly suspicious of how far merit might alone carry them in a prejudiced private realm. (Ehrenhalt 1991b, 50)

Politics in America is relatively "inclusive," embracing almost anyone who helps maintain a political party organization or support a campaign. Politics becomes the **social outlet** for many individuals, including those rejected by or uninterested in traditional social activities such as religious and hobby groups. Since many do not find a sense of belonging in their own family due to physical separation and divorce, some people may satisfy their need for affection and acceptance in other realms. The "hand shaking . . . back slapping or the camaraderie of a campaign headquarters," (Ehrenhalt 1991a, C3) may be superficial, but it certainly beats isolation.

---

[13]Abraham Maslow, 1954, *Motivation and Personality,* New York: Harper and Row. For an application of Maslow's theories to political behavior, see Stanley Renshon, 1974, *Psychological Needs and Political Behavior,* New York: Free Press.

Senator Tom Harkin (D-IA) has played the political game on both the state and national level. He knows what it is like to compete as a team member in Congress and one-on-one for the presidency.

ACCOMPLISHMENT

> The game of politics allows [you] to draw upon your abilities and your background. It's different than team sports. It's like individual sports. It's like a boxing match. (Senator Tom Harkin [D-IA] quoted in Grove 1992, B1)

Political involvement can satisfy one's need for **accomplishment.** Involvement in a winning election campaign or the passage of a piece of legislation provides validation of one's worth (Ehrenhalt 1991a, C3 and 1991b, 250). Running for office is not just a selfish endeavor. Many candidates see the potential for improving public policy, upgrading a constituency's representation in Congress and/or enhancing the performance of Congress as a whole (Baker and Bennett 1991, 8–10 and Kazee, *passim*). While it is particularly rewarding to have an unambiguous victory, political games often have many perceived winners, thus increasing the likelihood for claiming accomplishment. Even a losing campaign can be justified as "having done better than anyone expected," or "having raised the level of political discourse." The policy process provides numerous opportunities for small victories in the form of amendments or delays, even if the overall outcome is less than desired.

One explanation for Democratic domination of Congress rests on the assertion that Democrats seem to get more satisfaction out of governmental service. As the majority leader of the Wisconsin State Senate argued

> The Republicans hate government. Why be here if you hate government? So they let us [Democrats] run it for them. (Ehrenhalt 1991b, 126)

It may well be that the Democrats are more likely to field ambitious legislative candidates who are willing to make the sacrifices necessary to win (Ehrenhalt 1991b, 224–225).

Costs of Political Involvement

Running for office involves costs and risks which dampen motivation. Few first time candidates are assured victory. The campaign, and especially one leading to electoral victory, tampers with one's financial well being and impacts on one's personal and professional life.

DIRECT COSTS Potential candidates must either give up their jobs or take a leave of absence. Reentry into a job or profession might well be difficult if not impossible. Above and beyond the **opportunity costs**[14] of diminished or lost income, candidates must often financially underwrite a significant portion of their own campaigns, especially for lower level offices or when they are not front runners.

The financial impact of running for political office is not evenly distributed. Poor people often lack the resources to run. While Democrats often have fewer personal resources to contribute to their own campaigns, it has been argued that they also find it less of a financial sacrifice to make the transition from lower paying jobs such as teaching and private legal practice than would be the case for a Republican businessman or corporate lawyer (Ehrenhalt 1991b, 126).

Time and effort are precious commodities, and running for Congress involves a full-time commitment to often undesirable tasks for several months. The toll taken on family life and other personal pursuits means that not everyone is willing to absorb these costs. Campaigning can be a demeaning activity. After following a freshman Member's campaign, one journalist observed the following:

> If Hoagland didn't want to win, he wouldn't have tolerated the thousand indignities he had borne this far. He wouldn't have had the stomach to panhandle for campaign money from almost everyone he knew from old law school classmates [to] those legions of anonymous voices on hundreds of cadging phone calls. (Cwiklik 1992, 23)

SOCIAL AND PSYCHOLOGICAL COSTS

> When people run for office, not only do they think they're the smartest people in the district, but they're also confident enough to put it up for a vote. (David Jennings, Speaker of the Minnesota House, author's interview)

Politics stimulates significant passions. Friendships are often strained when political viewpoints fail to coincide. Individual candidates place themselves in a precarious psychological position when facing the electorate. It takes a strong sense of self worth (ego) to play the electoral game, especially in the modern era when

[14] "Opportunity costs" refer to those foregone options a person bypasses by committing his or her time and resources to politics.

voters focus more on individual candidates than party or ideological labels. Not only do candidates become subjects of scrutiny for the most personal aspects of their public and private lives, but the election results are hard to interpret in any way other than as a public judgment on the candidate's worth and capabilities.

Despite the personal costs, candidates appear eager to join the fray. Few elections go uncontested. Primary elections have become necessary to limit the number of contenders. The potential benefits clearly outweigh the costs for a significant number of players.

OPPORTUNITY

The opportunity to run for office is both offered and sought. Being in the "right place at the right time" accounts for a great deal in politics.

> Every opportunity to run for Congress comes wrapped in context—those few undeniable realities of time and place that provide a modicum of order to an otherwise topsy-turvy political world. . . . [Context] is the product of a district's party registration figures, election results, political geography and media markets. (Fowler and McClure 1989, 25)

Opportunity is also the result of the fit between a potential candidate's personal characteristics and the expectations of other political players. Opportunity factors are not absolutely fixed. Ambitious candidates have the uncanny ability to assure that they are in the right place at the right time. For example, when 1992 became characterized as the political "year of the woman," viable female candidates, who had once waited in the background (see Fowler and McClure 1989, 101) began coming out of the woodwork in increasing numbers.

Recruitment of Congressional Candidates

Congressional candidates emerge in a number of ways. Some are encouraged to seek public office by others, while many become candidates largely due to their own efforts.

THE ROLE OF EXTERNAL RECRUITERS In an earlier era, when political party organizations were much stronger, party leaders often formally recruited candidates to run for Congress and controlled their opportunities to run. Prior to 1900, political parties had the legal right to place candidates on the ballot after nominating conventions which were limited to party activists. The introduction of the direct primary, allowed candidates to circumvent party activists and appeal directly to the voters for a place on the ballot. Contemporary political parties show considerable hesitancy to get involved in the candidate selection process prior to the primary. If the candidate favored by the party loses in the primary, it is an embarrassment and causes considerable hard feelings. State and national party organizations do encourage individuals to run when no candidates seem to be emerging, and at times, will quietly discourage candidates in order to avoid a divisive primary (Herrnson 1988, 54).

Candidates often hear the voice of the people somewhat differently than others.

Reprinted by permission: Tribune Media Services.

With the weakening of the parties, other entities have begun playing more significant roles in the recruitment process. Candidates are seldom forced onto the campaign trail. Most decide to run for office after receiving some sign of support from politically active individuals or organizations. Local interest groups often serve to provide valuable experience for potential candidates to gain experience in public affairs and to encourage members to seek elective office. The media serves as the "mentioner" of potentially viable candidates, sparking the interest in persons mentioned and planting the notion to run for office in the minds of local political activists (Fowler and McClure 1989, 140).

THE RISE OF THE SELF-RECRUITED CANDIDATE Despite the contemporary mythology of the modest candidate reluctantly running for office, most modern candidates are self recruited. They assiduously pursue opportunities to be heard and seen so that they will show up on the lists of people mentioned by the press and local opinion leaders. If their subtle attempts to emerge do not succeed, potential candidates often simply set modesty aside and announce their intention to pursue office.

The concept of "candidate emergence" rather than direct "recruitment" reflects the broadened process by which individuals consider running for office and eventually make the decisive step of "throwing their hat in the ring."[15]

PREVIOUS POLITICAL EXPERIENCE Unlike many occupations where one follows a prescribed set of steps on a career ladder, there is no approved or required set of positions from which to launch a bid for congressional office. Most viable candidates have proven themselves in lower level electoral offices such as the state legislature or local government, or as congressional staff members (see Hammond 1989, 277).

[15]The phrase "throwing one's hat in the ring" is one of the abiding game analogies in American politics. Teddy Roosevelt first adapted the phrase to politics from boxing in which a challenger willing to take on all comers threw his hat in the ring (see William Safire, 1978, *Safire's Political Dictionary,* New York: Random House, p. 293).

BOX 2.4 The Ultimate Political Game

Getting started on the early rungs of the political jungle gym may be as much luck as ability. Many members of Congress began their careers as members of state legislatures. When Richard Kyle and John Galord tied in their Republican primary for a seat in the Arizona state House of Representatives, they used a game of poker to determine the outcome. State law requires a drawing of lots or an equal game of chance to decide an election tie. By drawing a pair of sevens in a stud poker game, Kyle became the nominee, and went on to win in the general election.

SOURCE: Associated Press. 1992. "Poker Hand Ends Election Tie." (1 October), LEXIS-NEXIS database.

Not all candidates have extensive political experience. A relatively long list of actors, athletes, astronauts, and other public figures who gained visibility and experience in other realms, now walk the halls of Congress. David Canon points out that during this century over 6 percent of U.S. senators and over 25 percent of House members held no political office prior to service in Congress, with the percentages increasing in recent years (Canon 1990, 5). Two factors have contributed to the increasing number of amateurs. Political parties have lost the ability to control the recruitment process, and media such as television have given individual candidates the opportunity to make themselves known in ways other than serving in lower level offices.

Rather than viewing the race for Congress as part of a career **ladder,** it is more of a **jungle gym** in which there is relatively open recruitment at the bottom with options becoming more limited as one approaches the top (see box 2.4). House members come from much more diverse political backgrounds than do Senators. The House serves as the primary "bench" from which senatorial candidates are chosen, with more than one-third of the Senators having served in the House (Canon 1990, 51).

THE DAMPENING IMPACT OF INCUMBENTS AND HOPELESS RACES

> In politics, it is not how you play the game, but whether you win or lose. If you lose, you get known as a loser. You have to choose your playing field carefully. (author's interview with potential candidate)

Few individuals contest congressional elections when they see no chance of success. While some candidates find the reward in "running rather than winning" (Huckshorn and Spencer 1971, 83), most harbor a "syndrome of maybe" (Kazee 1980, 83) in which they hope against hope that they can pull off an upset. The presence of an incumbent member of Congress on the ticket, especially from one's party, keeps all but the most foolhardy potential candidates from the race. Over 90 percent of House incumbents and about 80 percent of Senate incumbents running for re-election have been successful in recent years.[16] In 1992, after a series of scandals, an obvious anti-incumbent mood, and a large number of retirements, 93 percent of House members and 88 percent of senators running for re-election still were victorious. Even when a challenge to an incumbent arises, the typical pattern is that "incumbents win re-election more or less by default against invisible opposition. . . . voters lack enough information and tilt toward incumbents because they have no reason to be against them" (T. Cook 1989, 172).

"Open" seats in which there is no incumbent running, increase the opportunity to win and draw more contenders. Open seat races are not as rare as the incumbent re-election figures might indicate. Since the 1960s, each year an average of 7 percent of the House members and 5 percent of the senators have voluntarily retired or have run for another office.[17] In 1992, the combination of redistricting, a variety of scandals (see chapter 3) and an anti-incumbent mood led to a modern day record of 15 percent (sixty-five) of House members and 24 percent (eight) of senators deciding not to run.

Although contemporary voters are less likely to choose among candidates solely on the basis of their party label, party still plays an important role in congressional elections. During the 1980s, less than 6 percent of the House seats changed parties per election. Lacking other information, voters rely on party as a useful predictor as to how a member of Congress will serve in office. Districts dominated by one party draw relatively few challengers from the minority party, but are known for spirited contests to win the party nomination, especially when no incumbent is running.

THE PERSONAL SIDE OF OPPORTUNITY

> Engaging, witty and casually irreverent, he is as natural a politician in the House as he is on the streets of Philadelphia. He moves through the floor as smoothly as he glides through pickup basketball games in the gym—always in motion, using others to block for him, throwing an elbow now and then. He does not give up the ball, and he loves to win. (Description of former congressman William H. Gray III [D-PA] quoted in Calmes 1989, 1381)

Certain occupations and personal characteristics increase one's opportunity to run. Politics appeals little to introverts and those without passion for conflict. Individuals with flexible job schedules and/or personal wealth experience less risk in their run for office. Lawyers are often encouraged by their firms to pursue political

---

[16] The figures vary considerably for the Senate ranging from a 55 percent re-election rate in 1980 to 96.9 percent in 1990. During the 1970s, the re-election rate averaged 72 percent, and during the 1980s, 80 percent. Re-election rates for the House have been more consistent, averaging 93 percent during the 1970s and 94.5 percent during the 1980s.

[17] Again the figures vary considerably from year to year. Retirements were up in both the House and Senate during the 1970s. For a discussion of the reasons for voluntary retirements, see Stephen Frantzich, 1978, "Opting Out: Retirement from the House of Representatives," *American Politics Quarterly* (July): 251–273; and John R. Hibbing, 1982, "Voluntary Retirement from the U.S. House of Representatives: Who Quits?", *American Journal of Political Science,* 26, no. 3 (August): 467–484.

activity as a natural expansion of their professional skills, and in some cases as a way to expand business. Lawyers, in particular, have less of a job reentry problem either after service in electoral office or even electoral defeat.

Voters, local political activists, and the media have expectations about the kind of person who would make a good member of Congress. Verbal skills, organizational ability, a well known name, and often personal appearance grant some individuals opportunities denied others. Women and minorities are just beginning on career paths that lead to congressional office. The dramatic increase in women serving in state legislatures and local offices bodes well for expanded opportunities in the future.

Physical ties to the district benefit some potential candidates and hinder others. Congress is still seen as a place for hometown candidates. Individuals without credible ties to the district through birth or long-time residence invite charges of "carpetbagging," a derisive term for a self-seeking outsider. The impact of localism can be seen by looking at the senators in the 103rd Congress. Sixty-two were born in the state they now represent. Of the remaining thirty-eight, two were born in Washington, D.C. where their fathers were serving in Congress and twelve went to college in the state they represent. Atypical of our physically mobile society, 76 percent of the senators in the 103rd Congress were born or spent the bulk of their adult lives primarily as residents of the states they came to represent.

Candidates lacking the necessary depth of motivation and/or the conditions and skills which enhance their opportunity seldom enter the electoral arena, and those few who slip in are almost always doomed to failure in the actual campaign.

CAMPAIGN STRATEGY: THE COMPETITION FOR VOTES

> You're dealt a hand to play. If the two sides play perfectly, yes, there is a limit on what you can do. But both sides don't always play perfectly. Campaigns do matter. (John Petrocik quoted in Morin 1992c, C4)

GATHERING THE NECESSARY RESOURCES

A viable congressional candidate needs money, campaign expertise and campaign workers. Once provided by the political parties, contemporary candidates act largely on their own to find and pay for these resources.

Campaign Money: The Price of Admission

> Competition—the lifeblood of democracy—is drying up, because challengers have been almost shut out of the fund raising game. (Senator Robert Dole [R-KS], *Congressional Record,* 1991, [6 June]: S-7246)

Modern campaigns, with their reliance on new technology and purchased services, are expensive. In 1992 the average House candidate spent more than $280,000 and the average Senate candidate more than $1.7 million in his or her general election campaigns (Federal Elections Commission press releases). Such

TABLE 2.3 Average Expenditures of Winning Congressional Candidates in 1992

HOUSE		
Safe* House Incumbents Winning Re-election		
	Democrats (138)**	$494,885
	Republicans (95)	$485,010
Marginal House Incumbents Winning Re-election		
	Democrats (57)	$835,238
	Republicans (34)	$698,112
Challengers Defeating Incumbents		
	Democrats (6)	$351,898
	Republicans (13)	$487,033
Open Seat Winners		
	Democrats (57)	$506,158
	Republicans (34)	$577,588
SENATE		
Safe* Senate Incumbents Winning Re-election		
	Democrats (9)	$2,662,706
	Republicans (4)	$2.781,370
Marginal Senate Incumbents Winning Re-election		
	Democrats (4)	$2,829,340
	Republicans (6)	$5,307,257
Challengers Defeating Incumbents		
	Democrats (2)	$5,022,338
	Republicans (2)	$3,076,938
Open Seat Winners		
	Democrats (5)	$4,237,290
	Republicans (3)	$2,279,956

*Winner received over 60 percent of the vote

**Numbers in parentheses reflect the number of candidates

SOURCE: Norman J. Ornstein, Thomas E. Mann and Michael J. Malbin, *Vital Statistics on Congress, 1993–1994,* pp. 82–86, Congressional Quarterly, Inc., 1994.

averages are misleading, because they do not indicate the cost of winning. The average House winners spent $535,000 and the average Senate winner spent $3.5 million in 1992 (see table 2.3). Even these figures underestimate the actual cost, since some candidates coasted to victory with little or no opposition.

In general, incumbents in tough races and challengers in open seats can raise the most money. Incumbents are almost always able to raise more money than challengers. Democratic incumbents capitalize on their control of Congress to raise more money than Republicans, while Republicans shine in their ability to raise money for open seat races. "Challengers need not spend more than an incumbent. They must, however, be able to spend a **sufficient** amount of money to get their message across" (Alston 1990, 1623). This is a hurdle that many challengers cannot overcome.

WHERE THE MONEY COMES FROM Unlike most democracies, American legislative candidates must depend almost exclusively[18] on private campaign funding (see Levush 1991 for procedures in other countries). Options such as direct government funding and indirect subsidization of services (transportation, printing, broadcasting, etc.) typical in other countries have been discussed but not enacted for congressional elections.

Political parties: Political parties, once the mainstay of direct candidate campaign sources, now account for less than 5 percent of total receipts, down from over 15 percent in the early 1970s and considerably more in earlier periods. Each party in each chamber has established a party campaign committee to raise and distribute funds. Their top priority is to protect their incumbents. They next focus on winnable open seats, and only take on incumbents of the opposing party when there is a unique chance to win. Ideally, party campaign committees should be tools of party discipline, but they tend to "focus on candidates who are electable regardless of their commitment to the principles of the party" (Baker 1989b, 12). Despite recent attempts to dramatically increase national party congressional campaign committee resources, they pale in comparison to the amounts needed to mount a credible campaign. The limited percentage contributed by the parties overall is misleading, since in close races, the parties tend to give money at strategic points in the campaign (usually very early and quite late) when it is most needed (Sorauf 1988, 140 and Herrnson 1988, 69). The parties have also multiplied the effect of their resources by providing services such as public relations and advertising to candidates at a less than market rate and/or in a way which does not show up as a direct contribution (see Frantzich, 1989 on the rise of the "service-vendor" party and Herrnson, 1988, 67).

Individual contributions and political action committees: Individual contributions to candidates from friends and relatives account for close to 50 percent of receipts for House candidates and more than 70 percent of receipts for Senate candidates, with challengers depending considerably more on individual contributions than incumbents. The major shift in campaign funding of congressional candidates has been the growing importance of political action committees (PACs):

> The game of raising PAC [Political Action Committee] money here in Washington will make the difference. Understand how the game is played. It's crucial to your being one of the few that will win. (Consultant Frank Greer quoted in Sovern 1991, C4)

> To be best understood, a PAC should be considered a political mutual fund. As the investor relies on a mutual-fund manager to invest his or her money in a variety of companies . . . the PAC director donate[s] the fund to a variety of candidates. (Baker 1989b, 9)

---

[18] In 1990, Minnesota became the first state permitting public financing of congressional campaigns. Candidates accepting spending limitations can offer their contributors state tax credits. If only one candidate in a race accepts the limitations, the state will provide that candidate up to 25 percent of the allowable funds. (See "At a Glance-Politics—Minnesota's Public Campaign Funds," 1990, *National Journal* [5 May]: 1099.)

Percentage of Total Campaign Funds That Came from PACs

	House	Senate
1982	30	17
1984	36	18
1986	36	21
1988	40	22
1990	41	21
1992	36	21

Percentage of Incumbents' Campaign Funds That Came from PACs, House and Senate, 1982–1992

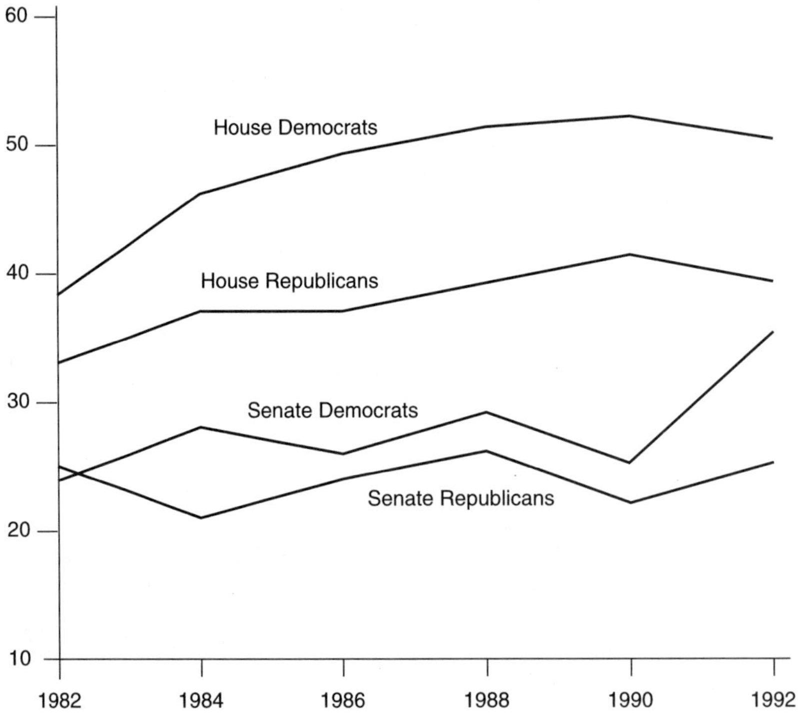

FIGURE 2.2

The Increasing Role of PACs in Congressional Campaigns

SOURCE: Norman J. Ornstein, Thomas E. Mann and Michael J. Malbin, *Vital Statistics on Congress, 1991–1992,* p. 87–93, Congressional Quarterly, Inc., 1994.

The Federal Election Campaign Act (FECA) of 1972 and its subsequent amendments encouraged interest groups to create separate organizations to combine small contributions and make them directly to candidates. By 1992, the number of these PACs had grown to more than 4,000. Political action committees have developed around occupational interests, business concerns, ideological outlooks, partisan affinity, and personal motivations (see box 2.5). Each PAC is allowed to give up to $5,000 to each candidate in each election (primary and general). Political action committees tend to be strategic in their giving, focusing on incumbents and open seat races. As figure 2.2 indicates, PACs are responsible for about 40 percent of incumbent House candidate's receipts and 20 percent of incumbent senator's receipts.

BOX 2.5 Friends Don't Let Teammates Campaign without Money

Beginning in the late 1970s, some individual members of Congress began using their excess campaign funds to support less endowed colleagues or potential colleagues. Money from these leadership PACs is both given and received with full awareness that the contributor hopes to "gain votes from members they have supported to further their own legislative ends and leadership aspirations" (Baker 1989b, 1).

Virtually all the current and aspiring party leaders have an active PAC. Creating a PAC allows the individual to bypass the $1,000 limit on individual contributions and fall under the $5,000 PAC limit. After initially criticizing leadership PACs, Representative David Obey (D-WI) with a certain amount of resignation created his own and explained, "You can't play touch while the other guy is playing tackle [football]" (Baker 1989b, 2).

In recent years, PACs have donated a decreasing percentage of their total contributions to challengers. In 1978, 19 percent went to challengers and by 1990, the figure was down to 6 percent (see Ornstein, Mann, and Malbin 1992, 98).

Political action committees are also allowed to make "independent" expenditures, as long as they do not coordinate their efforts with the candidate. They don't support candidates as their unbiased contribution to better informing voters and supporting democracy, but rather they hope to increase the likelihood that candidates agreeing with their position will win, and once in office, the winners they supported will listen to their concerns. As George Gould, a letter-carriers union official put it, "When you take PAC money, you are saying that you're their friend" (quoted in Sovern 1991, C4).

Political action committees have found creative ways to get around election law restrictions. By using the process of "bundling," PACs accept contributions for candidates, and send the original checks en masse to selected candidates. By using the original checks, they are not restricted in how much they pass through. One of the most successful bundling strategies is carried out by EMILY's List ("Early Money Is Like Yeast") which backs female Democratic candidates for Congress. In 1992, they became the biggest single campaign contributor, giving $4.6 million and playing a significant role in the election of many women in Congress (Schwartz and Cooper 1992, A38).

Campaign fund raising has become an unending task for both potential candidates and incumbents. "[The candidate's] mission is to raise his credibility so he can raise money so he can raise more credibility and raise more money" (campaign consultant quoted in Sack 1991b, A1). The average senator must raise $2,000 per day, six days a week for his or her full six-year term to run a credible campaign (Anderson 1993, C7). Incumbents often engage in "preemptive spending." By raising significant amounts of money early in the game they scare off challengers (see Ragsdale 1989, 30). Early fund raising and spending also builds credibility and attracts more money, and adequate funding assures that the candidate's message will get out. Large amounts of money will not necessarily assure victory, but limited funds almost always assure defeat. In raising these funds, Members become more and more dependent on interest groups (see box 2.6). On the average, incumbent House

BOX 2.6 The Members Speak About Fund Raising

The views of members of Congress about campaign financing, and especially the role of PACs vary.

> In a sense, we politicians have lost faith in ourselves. We are afraid to let go of the slick ads and the high-priced consultants—afraid to let go of the PAC money and the polls—unsure we want to change the rules of the game that we all understand and know so well. But the people understand the game, too. . . . I have long felt that once the people really understood how much time we spend on fund raising and away from our committees and away from the floor and away from our families, and how this affects the perceptions of this institution, and how it undermines the trust in the institution—I have long felt that the people would rise up and demand that we clean up our act. . . . (Senator Robert Byrd [D-WV], *Congressional Record,* 1991, [15 January]: S534)

Senator Robert Byrd (D-WV) entered national office in 1958. As former majority leader in the Senate and past chairman of the Appropriations Committee, he carries with him considerable political experience and power.

BOX 2.6 continued

I am not saying that all political action committees are evil. I am not saying that it is wrong for people to get together for the sake of joining to serve a common political purpose. That has always been a part of the American tradition. (Senator David Boren [D-OK], *Congressional Record,* 1988, [17 February]: S786)

Senator David Boren (D-OK) has been a tireless crusader for campaign financing reform.

It is axiomatic that he who writes the rules can control the game . . . the majority has crafted here both for the House and for the Senate the perfect set of rules to perpetuate the majority in power . . . [the majority will] write the rules in a way that benefits them. I do not blame them for trying, but it is not going to work. (Senator Mitch McConnell [R-KY] debating the Congressional Campaign Spending Limit and Election Reform Act of 1992, *Congressional Record,* 1992, [29 April]: S-5681, 5693)

Senator Mitch McConnell (R-KY) (left) arrived in the Senate recognizing the importance of rules in the political game.

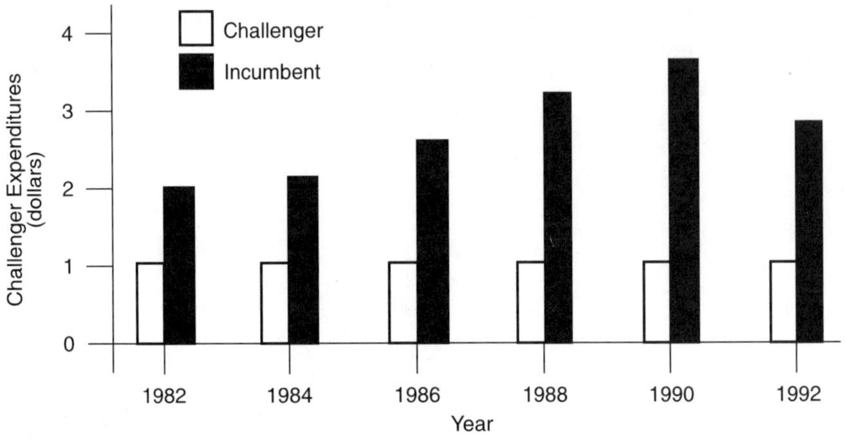

FIGURE 2.3
Incumbent Advantage in Campaign Fund Raising. For every $1 expended by a challenger in 1982, the incumbent was able to expend $2.025.

SOURCES: Federal Elections Commission data for 1982–1990 reported in Maura Keefe, "Political Business Cut by Incumbent Security" in *Campaign,* Vol. V, No. 8 (August), p. 18, 1991; 1992 data, Federal Elections Commission. Later the ratio was over three to one.

members are able to raise over three and one-half times the amounts challengers are able to raise, an advantage which has been increasing in recent years (see figure 2.3).

There has been considerable discussion about the role of PACs and the possibility of publicly financing congressional elections, but real reform has run afoul of partisan bickering for political advantage. Proponents of public financing argue that it is "a way of getting people into the game so that they can begin to compete" (Representative Vic Fazio [D-CA]). The cost and partisan implications of public financing have thwarted enactment. Many Republicans see federal funding as a raid on the treasury and fear that low expenditure limits would lock in Democratic incumbents even more. Democratic incumbents, who receive the lion's share of PAC contributions, are not terribly unhappy with the current situation and fight proposals which would undermine the right of PACs to play a role in the game.

WHERE THE MONEY GOES The largest single expenditure for most congressional campaigns is for electronic media. Incumbent House candidates spend about 20 percent of their funds for electronic media, and senators with their large districts expend about one-third of their money for radio and television (Fritz and Morris 1991, 5–6). Other large cost areas are staging fund raising events, staff salaries and targeting mailings. About half of the average candidate's expenditures goes to hiring campaign consultants who produce electronic media, raise funds, and facilitate voter contact using the mail (Stencel 1993, 15).

The Human Resources

Money is a crucial transferable resource, but campaigns also require expertise and human effort. Block workers, envelope stuffers and volunteer managers were once provided by the party organization and served as the repositories of effort and expertise for campaigning. The pool of volunteers is shrinking, partly due to the increasing percentage of women working, and the new technologies of campaigning. The use of computerized lists and electronic communications are well beyond the skill level of most volunteers. Congressional candidates, especially in Senate races, have turned to paid campaign consultants and paid staffs (Salmore and Salmore 1989, 78). Consultants bring in expert advice on polling, advertising, and fund raising, but what often escapes analysis is the fact that consultants can walk away from the victorious candidate after the election. With their goal of improving their campaign "batting average," consultants can push candidates into irresponsible policy stands and strategies. While consultants enjoy the challenge and gamesmanship of campaigns, they do so without any responsibility for governing (Rosenbloom 1973, 156–161).

IDENTIFYING THE PLAYERS IN THE ELECTION ARENA

Voters ultimately determine election outcomes. A simple, but often overlooked fact is that it does little good for a candidate to be immensely popular among people who cannot, or who fail to vote. During presidential election years, the congressional electorate expands to include 50 to 55 percent of the eligible voters excited by the high information presidential campaign. Even in presidential election years, about 5 percent of the presidential election voters fail to cast a ballot for a congressional candidate. The drop off in **off-year** elections is even more dramatic, with only 35 to 40 percent of the eligible voters casting a congressional ballot (Jacobson 1992, 104). Candidates who can get traditional nonvoters to the polls through registration drives, effective campaigning, and get-out-the vote initiatives increase their likelihood of electoral victory.

COMMUNICATING WITH THE VOTERS

Effective communication involves a skillful communicator engaging in the interests of a receptive audience. Candidates must take on the task of developing their messages and knowing their audiences.

Voter Motivations

Individuals approach the voting booth with a variety of motivations that could trigger a specific choice between candidates. Some voters use their vote to promote particular **policy** preferences and support the candidate who implied promises to help them reach that goal. Some policy voters show concern for broad national issues, while others are more interested in what the candidate can do for the constituency or for them personally. These policy voters assess campaign promises and the past performance of a candidate and his or her party to make their choice. Other voters are driven by a more **psychological affinity** toward some symbolic label associated with a particular candidate, such as party identification or ethnic origin. Supporting the candidate linked to the preferred symbol allows such a voter to verify his or her own self image as a loyal supporter of that symbolic label. **Social** voters take their voting cues from friends and/or neighbors, following the crowd and using their vote to identify themselves with the people they want to impress. Individual voters may be motivated by a combination of the above factors. Facing voters with such a mix of motivations requires candidates to communicate a variety of different messages to different sets of voters.

Candidate Strategies for Activating Voters

The goal of a campaign is more than developing a positive feeling for the candidate. Candidates must get voters to act on their feelings in the voting booth.

THE DECLINING UTILITY OF PARTY IDENTIFICATION Political party identification once served as almost a determinative symbol for psychological voters who would vote the straight party line out of loyalty. For policy voters, the party label served as a short hand cue as to the types of policies each candidate would likely support. Since most voters supported their party, the party loyalty of social voters was reinforced by friends and neighbors. While almost 75 percent of the voting public still stick with their party in congressional elections, an increasing percentage of voters are willing to cross party lines (see Jacobson 1992, 111) on the basis of specific issues and psychological symbols.

THE DECLINE OF THE TEAM APPROACH Congressional candidates, like most candidates, once campaigned as members of a partisan team. Campaign advertisements emphasized supporting the party ticket. Candidates on various levels publicly endorsed each other. Presidents were known for their "coattails"—the candidates of their party which they pulled into office. As voters decreasingly linked their presidential vote to their congressional vote, candidates began campaigning on their own. When the top of the ticket was in trouble, congressional candidates began to ignore it and look out for their own fortunes. As it became more and more clear that George Bush was more of a liability than a benefit in 1992, Republican congressional candidates began to disassociate themselves with him. The traditional campaign picture session with the president drew only about two dozen of the more than 400 Republican congressional candidates invited. Even Senate minority leader Robert Dole [R-KN] ran as an "independent voice" (Devroy 1992, A1).

THE IMPORTANCE OF BECOMING KNOWN The decline of political party identification as a voting cue forced candidates both to expand the voter motivations they attempt to activate and to develop innovative ways to provide voters with the information needed to make a decision. The first goal of any candidate is to become known among voters. Voters are much more likely to support a candidate whose name they can recognize than an unknown quantity. House challengers as compared to incumbents, face a particular problem when it comes to becoming known. Evaluating the level of constituent information and contact with congressional candidates depends on the measures one chooses to use. Only about half of the voters can **recall** the name of their congressional incumbent during the campaign, and challengers are even more invisible, with an average recall of less than 20 percent. On the other hand, more than 90 percent of voters **recognize** the name of their incumbent and only about 50 percent recognize the name of the challenger (See Jacobson 1992, 118 and table 2.4). The level of voter contact with congressional candidates is quite significant given the size of U.S. congressional districts. As table 2.4 shows, a sizeable portion of the electorate remembers receiving mail from the candidate, seeing the candidate on television, and reading about him or her in the newspaper. A surprising portion of the electorate even recalls meeting either the incumbent or the

TABLE 2.4 Voter Awareness and Contact with House Candidates in 1988

	Incumbents	*Challengers*
Recognized name	93%	53%
Recalled name	46%	16%
Received mail from candidate	73%	15%
Read about candidate in newspaper	66%	28%
Saw candidate on television	53%	18%
Met candidate in person	17%	4%

SOURCE: American National Election Studies, reported in Gary Jacobson, *The Politics of Congressional Elections,* (New York: HarperCollins, 1993), p. 123.

challenger in person. Challengers are clearly disadvantaged in terms of visibility and contact (see Arnold 1990, 30; and Mann and Wolfinger 1980, 621–622).

Visibility varies for the Senate and for different types of races. Almost all voters recognize the name of their incumbent senator, while about 80 percent recognize the challenger. Open seat races, with their higher level of competitiveness, lead to an almost 80 percent recognition level for House candidates and more than 90 percent for Senate candidates (see Jacobson 1992, 118). As we will see in chapter 3, incumbents expend considerable effort keeping their names in front of the public in order to retain the recognition gap. The media tend to heavily favor coverage of House incumbents, but treat incumbents and challengers in competitive Senate races almost equally (Kahn 1990, 6). Challengers rely both on their past reputations and on attention grabbing gimmicks such as flooding the district with advertising, taking controversial stands, walking door to door and/or working in typical district jobs for a day.

COMMUNICATING THE "RIGHT" MESSAGE The "rightness" of the message depends on the voters to which a candidate is appealing. Policy voters evaluate candidates both on the basis of the positions they take and on their perceived competency for accomplishing their promises. Incumbents with powerful positions in Congress, or challengers with impressive accomplishments in a previous office tout their competency. Personal characteristics relating to performance such as honesty, perseverance, integrity, and general moral character loom quite large in the evaluation of a candidate (see box 2.7). Increasingly, single issue concerns such as abortion, gun control, homosexual rights, and cutting taxes have become "litmus tests" by which policy voters judge candidates. The single-mindedness of many of these blocs of single-issue voters frighten many candidates into refusing to take a stand on such issues and make it difficult to create the compromises necessary to enact policy.

The most important message for psychological voters lies in linking the candidate with the preferred symbol. Democratic candidates in districts with a Democratic majority emphasize their party identification, while Republican candidates urge people in those districts to "Vote for the person, not the party." Other symbols such as ideology, race, family background, and ties to the district allow the candidate to assert that he or she is "one of us."

BOX 2.7 Negative Strategy

Although democratic theory glorifies positive announcements on issues and candidates modestly touting their abilities and experience, candidates are now aware that negative advertising which takes their opponent to task often works. In 1990, Representative John Murtha (D-PA) almost lost when his opponent likened his performance to the television game show "Wheel of Fortune." Using a spinning roulette wheel with sections labelled "pay raises," "junkets," and "money laundering," his opponent asserted that "with every spin . . . Murtha continues to line his pockets—and you pay for the fabulous prizes" (Cook 1990c, 1584). By outspending his challenger ten to one, Murtha was able to eke out a slim victory.

In 1992, a hard fought senate race in Oregon between incumbent Republican Bob Packwood and Democratic challenger Les AuCoin brought out a similar negative game analogy. One Packwood commercial featured a mock game show called "Hypocrisy" in which contestants win cash prizes for identifying AuCoin with vote-skipping, congressional pay raises, and overdrafts on his House bank account (Kosterlitz 1992, 2434).

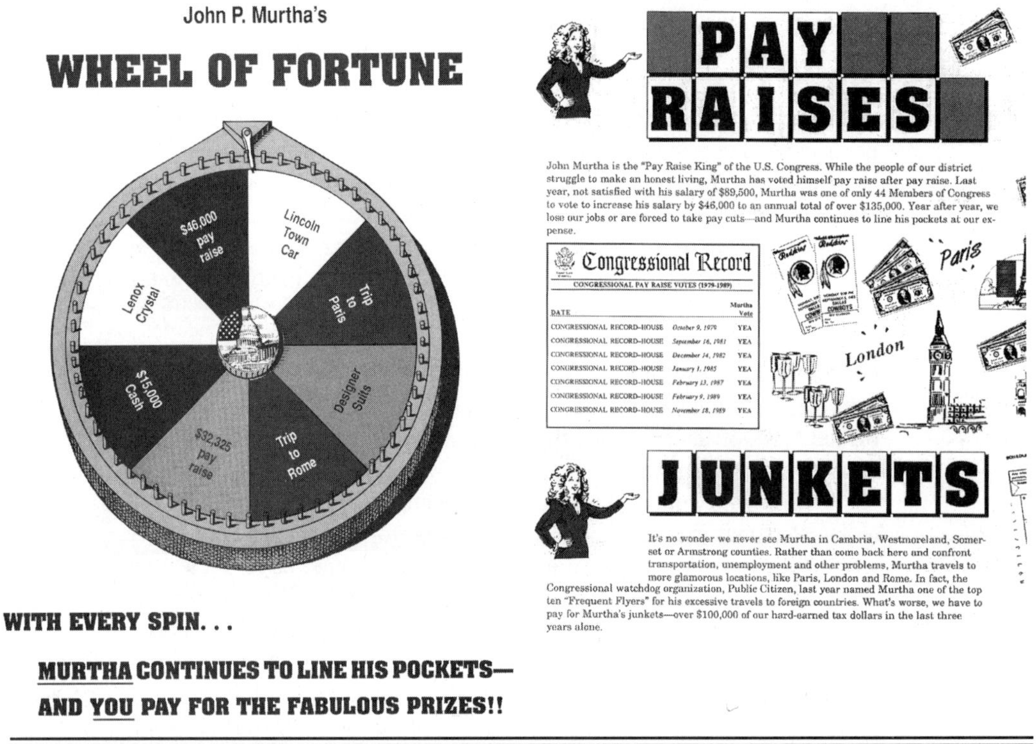

Candidates relying of the forces of social voting attempt to create a "band wagon" effect through one-sided public opinion poll results, massive turnouts at rallies and/or blanketing the district with lawn signs to show the breadth of their support. Endorsements by popular politicians, civic leaders, and entertainment figures help reinforce the message that "everyone who is anyone" backs them.

BOX 2.7 Continued

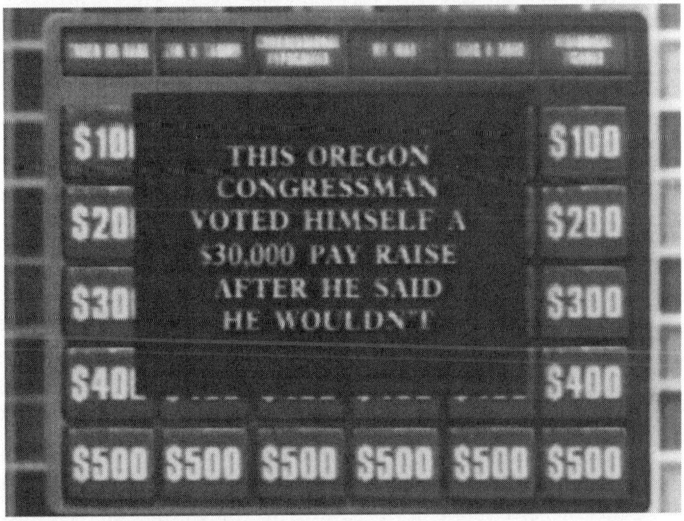

COMMUNICATING IN THE "RIGHT" WAY

> Ninety percent of all the information we attempt to give to voters is wasted. The problem is that we do not know which of our efforts fall in the 90 percent realm and which in the 10 percent realm. (author's interview with a congressional candidate)

Congressional candidates must compete with a cacophony of other voices attempting to sell, convince, and motivate individuals. Paying close attention to congressional election campaigns falls far down the list of priorities for most individuals requiring expanded efforts to reach voters. Traditional voter contact methods are often not sufficient. Well-organized squadrons of party bloc workers going door to door are seldom available any more. The news media often covers congressional campaigns, but its messages cannot be controlled by the candidate and often focus more on the "horse race" aspect of who is ahead and who is behind rather than on the factors which might help voters make a more informed choice. While continuing with the traditional campaign rallies, debates, buttons, lawn signs, and speeches, modern congressional candidates have reacted to these new realities by using new technologies to control both the messages and who receives them.

Purchased television advertising, especially short spot advertisements, dominate Senate campaigns. As Senator Hollings (D-SC) put it,

> Television advertising is the name of the game in modern American politics. In warfare, if you control the air, you control the battlefield. In politics, if you control the airwaves, you control the tenor and focus of a campaign. (*Congressional Record,* 1993, [21 January]: 618)

In 1988, 60 percent of the campaign budgets of Senate candidates went to paid media advertising, with more than three-quarters of that used for television advertising. House candidates have a somewhat more difficult time using television, since media markets often "do not recognize electoral boundaries, and commercials are seen by many voters who aren't part of the candidate's constituency" (Barnes 1989, 2882). Even so, almost one-third of House candidate expenditures in competitive races was used for television advertising (Cantor and Coleman 1990, summary).

Since impersonalized messages are less potent than personalized ones, modern campaigns use computer-generated mailing lists to send specific messages to particular groups of voters. While the farm family might get the candidate's "personal" message on farm price supports, the business person gets a discussion of the capital gains tax, and the long time party contributor gets a message about how the candidate upholds the traditions of the party. Although not as precise as targeted mailing lists, the choice of radio stations and television programs with specific audiences allows some targeting. The emergence of cable television, fax machines, computer bulletin boards, and satellite television opens up a new horizon for candidates desiring to "narrow cast" their message to a more identifiable bloc of voters.

GETTING ONE'S SUPPORTERS INTO THE ARENA Each candidate is engaged in the delicate task of consolidating his or her support base while making enough inroads into his or her opponent's base to win. But as one party activist summarized it, it does little to simply convince voters of your worth, you have to get them to the polls, because "the name of the game is turnout" (Jenkins 1988, B1). This is not a new strategy. Abraham Lincoln pointed out that the job of the campaign is to identify one's supporters and get them to the polls.[19] It has as much validity today as it did more

---

[19] In his detailed advice to campaign workers in 1840, Lincoln charged precinct captains with identifying each party supporter and procure his pledge to not "stay away from the polls on the first Monday in November, and that he will record his vote as early on that day as possible." (*Abraham Lincoln: Speeches and Writings: 1832–1858,* 1989, The Library of America, p. 66)

than 150 years ago. Congressional campaigns, especially for Democrats whose party supporters are less likely to vote, commit a significant amount of their effort and resources to getting out the vote. The winner in an election is the person with the most **votes,** not the person with the best message or the most supporters.

DETERMINING THE PLAYERS: WINNING AND LOSING CONGRESSIONAL ELECTIONS

A number of factors determine who wins and who loses congressional elections. Resources and partisanship play the largest role.

RESOURCES

There are few hard and fast rules about winning elections. While winners almost always outspend losers, it is too simple to say that money determines the outcome. Likely winners are able to raise more money, which probably increases their chances of winning, but does not determine their victory. Winners tend to be experienced politicians, better known and organized—factors that are both a cause and effect of campaign resources.

THE INSIDE TRACK FOR INCUMBENTS

Incumbents **who choose to run for reelection** are almost guaranteed victory in the House and are much better than even bets in the Senate (see figure 2.4), but a relatively significant number of members of Congress anticipate electoral difficulties and decide not to run. As we will see in chapter 3, incumbents have found a number of ways to parlay their inherent advantages into electoral success.

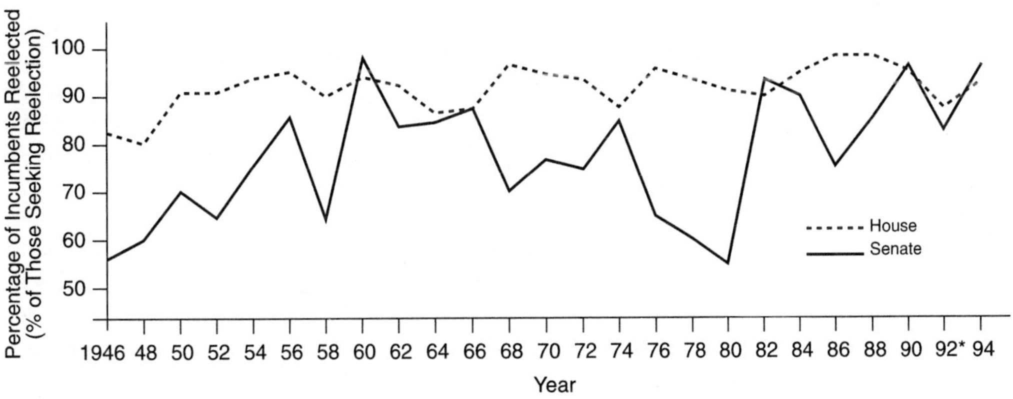

*A larger than normal number of House incubents (19) lost in the primaries in 1992. Ninety-three percent of the 1992 House incumbents who survived the primaries won the general election.

FIGURE 2.4

Incumbents' Success in House and Senate Elections, 1946–1994

SOURCE: Norman J. Ornstein, Thomas E. Mann and Michael J. Malbin, *Vital Statistics on Congress, 1993–1994,* p. 58–59, Congressional Quarterly, Inc., 1994.

THE PERFORMANCE OF PARTY TEAMS

The partisan nature of a congressional district still means a great deal for congressional candidates. **Ticket-splitting,** the voting for candidates from one party for some offices and candidates from the opposing party for other offices, has increased in recent years. Voters tend to split **away** from their party in the presidential race and return to their normal party for the congressional race. This has been especially true in the South where Republican presidential candidates tend to win while voters at the same time think of themselves as Democrats and return Democrats to Congress. While the loosening of party ties and the availability of new campaign technologies create more opportunities for candidates to overcome traditional party-line voting, only a few candidates win in districts predominantly populated by partisans of the opposing party. In the aggregate, the willingness to split one's vote between the parties allows the development of divided government in which one party wins the presidency and the other controls one or more houses of Congress.

Congress has largely been a Democratic bailiwick for almost four decades while at the same time Republican presidents are elected on a regular basis. Unlike earlier eras when concepts such as **presidential coattails** helped explain congressional elections, more and more, contemporary presidential and congressional elections are independent of each other (Arnold 1990, 39). While former Speaker Tip O'Neill's assertion that "all politics is local," is a bit of an overstatement, congressional elections tend to be won or lost on the basis of local conditions and issues more than on partisan considerations. Sweeping tides of partisan shifts and public opinion are seldom translated into significant shifts in congressional election outcomes.

In recent years overwhelming Republican presidential victories have had only marginal impact on congressional outcomes. Even elections such as 1980, in which Ronald Reagan won the presidency and the Republicans took over the Senate by winning twelve additional seats, the Republican Senate victories could be explained more by local factors than by the appeal of Ronald Reagan's campaign. The traditional view of a president's **coattails** sweeping fellow partisans into office belies the fact that in presidential elections since 1980, the winning Republican presidential candidate ran ahead of his winning Republican congressional candidates in less than one-quarter of the districts (Ornstein et al., 1992, 65). The president's party usually loses a few seats in the subsequent midterm elections as the expanded presidential electorate reverts to its more normal size and composition. In recent years the impact has meant a loss of less than ten seats (see Ornstein et al., 1992, 53). In 1990, the anti-incumbent mood, most closely associated with the national movement to limit congressional terms, was reflected in a general decrease in incumbents' electoral margins and the actual loss of seats was minimal. By 1992, the anti-incumbency mood had deepened, yet the result was more one of increasing voluntary retirement and a weeding out of weaker candidates more than a wholesale "throwing the rascals out." Most losses are caused by strategic errors on the part of the individual candidates rather than on a national mood swing. In general, members of Congress succeed or fail at the ballot box more on the basis of their own performance in office and on the campaign trail than on the basis of overall trends.

Republicans turned the 1994 election into a referendum on the Clinton presidency and offered a unified alternative. Their "Contract with America," signed in a public ceremony by most Republican candidates, was not read in detail by most voters, but left the impression that Republicans were ready to act on publicly approved initiatives such as cutting the deficit, reducing government and imposing term limitations. Not one Republican incumbent was defeated and the Democrats lost far more seats than is usual in an off-year election.

Congressional Elections and Divided Government

Ticket splitting and the lack of presidential coattails allow for **divided government.** Numerous analysts have attempted to determine the origin of the pattern of divided government exemplified by a Republican presidency and a Democratic Congress. One school of thought argues that until 1994 the Democrats were able to maintain themselves in office by expanding and using the numerous incumbent advantages. Incumbents develop a personal following based on service to constituents (see chapter 3) as opposed to running on the basis of policy alternatives or partisan linkages (see Cain, Ferejohn, and Fiorina 1987, 9). Another view gives the voter more credit and asserts that voters intentionally divide power and responsibility between the parties. Voters seem to prefer to have one branch of government committed to low taxes, reduced government, and a strong national defense, and the other branch promising expanded government benefits (see Jacobson 1991, 6; see Minton and Scarrow 1993 for competing views). The 1994 elections, with the defeat of over thirty incumbent Democrats, indicates some weakening of the incumbency advantage explanation.

CONCLUSION

The electoral process determines the prime players in the congressional arena. Many congressional elections are determined before the formal campaign begins on the basis of partisan preferences of the voters, the presence or absence of an incumbent, and the high stakes political game of drawing the congressional district lines. Deciding to contest a congressional election requires evaluating the significant costs and benefits of such political involvement, and relatively few individuals have both the motivation and opportunities to take the step. An effective campaign strategy involves gathering the adequate financial and human resources so one can communicate the right campaign message to the right people in the right way. The complex mix of voter motivations complicates the necessary strategic decisions and requires campaigns with a multi-faceted approach. While most congressional elections are determined by local factors, the overall outcome tends to reflect a pattern which favors incumbents, candidates from the majority party in the district, and those rare challengers who can expand the relatively limited congressional electorate with a disproportionate number of their supporters. The electoral process not only determines the individual players, but also establishes many of the ground rules which effect how they will behave once in office.

IN DEPTH

1. Money plays an important part in congressional campaigns. The Federal Elections Commission (FEC) gathers information on fund raising and expenditures by candidates for federal office and provides its information free to the public. Contact the FEC (see directions below) and get a summary of the two candidates for the House or Senate in your state or district for the last election (ask for a "schedule E" index). This computer printout will summarize the total campaign receipts and expenditures, and indicate the amount of contributions given by individual PACs. Compare the two candidates and attempt to determine the basis for the differences. For contextual information on your district or state, see the *Almanac of American Politics* or *Politics in America.* You can contact the FEC toll free at 800–424–9530 or by writing:

Public Records Office
Federal Elections Commission
999 E. Street N.W.
Washington, D.C. 20463

2. Design a detailed campaign strategy for your congressional district or state. Develop a political profile of the district, outlining past voting records, key issues and likely opponents. (See the *Almanac of American Politics* and *Politics in America* for district information.) Specify the issues you would emphasize and the details of your media strategy. Outline the rationale for your plan and compare it to the political science literature on campaign strategy.

CHAPTER THREE

THE SURVIVAL GAME
Keeping the Elected Players in Place

Congress does not mirror the U.S. population. In fact [for me] serving in Congress is more like **looking** in a mirror, since most of the Members I see every day look a lot like myself. (Author's interview with a white, male, middle-class, middle-aged House member)

As the new members of Congress assemble to take their oaths of office in the House and Senate, a quick look around the chamber will verify that neither chamber is a random sample of the American population. The nature of individual motivation, career opportunity, and the selection criteria used by voters assure that new Members will confront a sea of white, male, middle-aged, and middle-class faces. Virtually all Members are college-educated lawyers and/or businessmen (see figures 3.1–3.4). Few new Members look around in total awe at the political process, since more than 75 percent have served in state and/or local legislative office (Canon 1990, 54). In general, the Senate is more atypical of the population than is the House.

THE ELECTED PLAYERS

The social background mix of members of Congress is neither fixed by law nor tradition. Change does occur, but it tends to be glacial rather than dramatic. In recent years (see figures 3.1–3.4), the number of women and African Americans has increased, while the mix of occupations has broadened and the number of lawyers declined. In a country where the average age is less than thirty-three (U.S. Bureau of the Census, *Statistical Abstract* 1992, 14–15) and the average age of eligible voters is somewhere in the forties (U.S. Bureau of the Census, *Statistical Abstract* 1992, 269), the Congress remains more than a decade older. House members average close to fifty years old and Senators average closer to sixty. Despite some shifts in background characteristics, the major under-represented groups still have a long way to go before their numbers in Congress match those in the population.

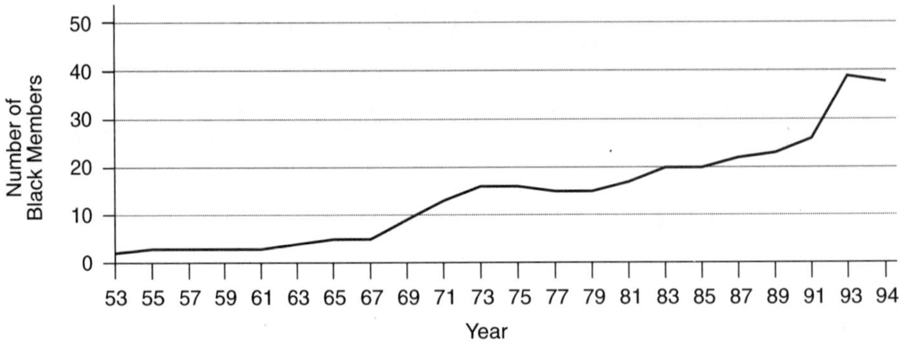

FIGURE 3.1

Number of Black Members of the House, 1953–1996

SOURCE: *Congressional Quarterly Almanac, 1953–1993,* (Washington, D.C.: Congressional Quarterly, Inc.).

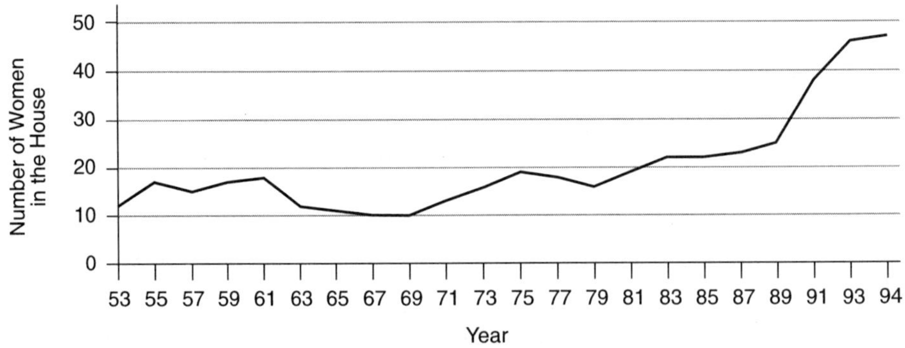

Comparative Percentages of Women in the Lower Houses of Selected National Legislatures

Denmark	59%	Canada	13%
Finland	39	Italy	13
Norway	37	Mexico	12
Sweden	38	United States	11
Netherlands	25	United Kingdom	9
China	21	Israel	7
Germany	20	Australia	7
Spain	15	France	2
		Japan	2

FIGURE 3.2

Number of Women in the House, 1953–1996 (graph)

SOURCE: Holly Teeters and Jody Neathery, *APSA Legislative Studies Section Newsletter,* Vol. 16, No. 1 (November 1992).

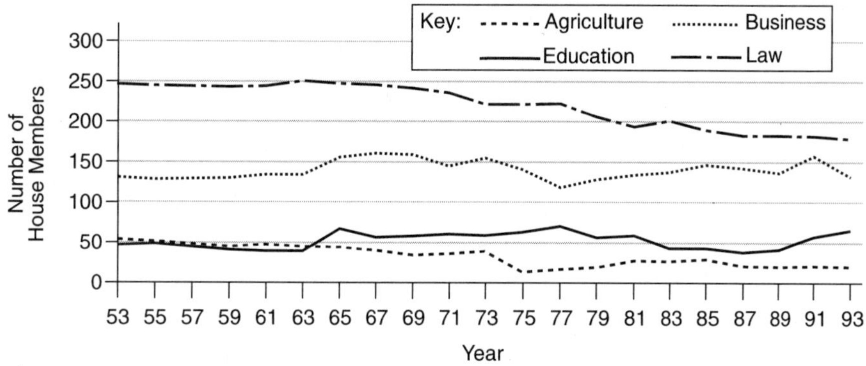

FIGURE 3.3
Prior Occupations of House Members, 1953–1993
SOURCE: *Congressional Quarterly Almanac, 1953–1993,* (Washington, D.C.: Congressional Quarterly, Inc.).

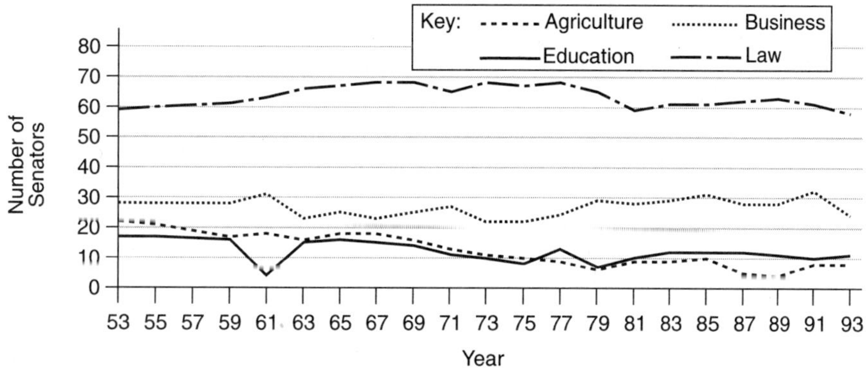

FIGURE 3.4
Prior Occupations of Senators, 1953–1993
SOURCE: *Congressional Quarterly Almanac, 1953–1993,* (Washington, D.C.: Congressional Quarterly, Inc.).

EXPLAINING THE DEMOGRAPHIC MIX

It is difficult to fully disassociate the interaction of motivation and opportunity factors which affect population groups in varying ways. The perceived lack of opportunity of certain demographic groups to win congressional elections dampens the motivation to run, while the lack of motivated candidates from some demographic groups almost assures less electoral success and reinforces the original stifling of motivation.

Even with adequate motivation, members of certain groups often lack key resources helpful for victory. Personal financial resources, verbal skills, organizational experience, public visibility, personal ties to local political leaders and other useful campaign resources are not randomly distributed throughout the population. Despite public opinion polls in which individuals claim they would not vote against a person solely on the basis of race, ethnic background, or gender,[1] in the privacy of the voting booth such biases are much more likely to prevail.

Gender

> You can look at the Congress and . . . play the game, "what's wrong with this picture?" It is 95 percent white. It is 95 percent men . . . what it means is that women are simply not represented at the highest levels of policy making in this country, that our voices, our needs, our experience, our perspective is simply missing when the rules of the game are set. (Patricia Ireland, president, National Organization for Women, Reuter's Transcript, 4 August 1992)

A strictly representative House of Representatives would have more than 225 women, almost five times as many as now serve, while the Senate would have to multiply its female membership by over seven times to match the 51 percent of the population which is female. The U.S. lags well behind most foreign parliaments in the percentage of women (see Rule 1992, 309 and figure 3.2).

Until the last few decades, the majority of women in Congress followed a "widow's succession" route, replacing a departed husband or father, while contemporary female Members tend to have made it on their own (Gertzog 1984, chapter 2 and 3, passim). While female candidates were once relegated to running as sacrificial lambs in hopeless districts, they now have more opportunities. The lack of female Members results from the relative lack of female **candidates** (see Darcy, Welch, and Clark 1987, 67–68) which in turn reflects the relative lack of women in the lower offices from which congressional candidates are typically drawn.

Women as compared with men still seem to lack the same level of political motivation that it takes to make it in politics (Bernstein 1986, 163).

> To the extent that it can be said that politics has been a man's game, presumably this is at least in part because women have chosen not to play. The ambition gender gap helps explain the persistent pattern of sex differences with respect to public office holding. (Costantini 1990, 765)

When confronted with conflict between desire for political power and family responsibilities, women "choose in favor of their family [while] men in favor of political ambition" (Shapiro 1983, 274). The situation is not static, though. The ambition

[1]While we have little data on the impact of race and gender on congressional voting choices, more than 80 percent of voters indicate that they would vote for a qualified woman or black for **president** (Gallup Poll, 1987; and CBS/*New York Times* Poll, 1991; from the POLL database). On the other hand, less than 50 percent of voters believe that most white Americans would vote for a qualified black presidential candidate (CBS/*New York Times* Poll, 1991; POLL database). Polls during the 1992 campaign indicate that female candidates were uniquely positioned to capitalize on the anti-incumbent mood and the desire for an outsider, especially when they emphasized domestic issues (Compton 1992, 17).

gender gap is closing substantially (Costantini 1990, 765). An increasing number of women are now waiting on the "bench" in state and local office and are "poised to move up to the federal level" (Arkel 1988, 1). After the 1992 election, women constituted 20 percent of the state legislatures, four times as many as two decades earlier (*Washington Post* A4).

The confrontation over the 1992 nomination of Clarence Thomas to the Supreme Court with the high drama of sexual harassment charges by Anita Hill galvanized a number of female candidates. While 1992 as the political "year of the woman" turned out to be an overstatement, significant gains were made. In 1992, EMILY's List, which strategically channels funds to pro-choice female Democratic candidates became a major player in the fund raising process.[2] The mid-term election of 1994 did not lead to significant gains for women. One additional woman, Olympia Snow (R-ME), entered the Senate, while the total number of women in the House remained constant. In 1994, it was not enough to be a qualified woman, most new female winners also had to be Republicans.

Family pressures, lack of campaign resources,[3] and remaining voter biases assure that equal representation of women in Congress may remain an illusive goal. Once in Congress the difficulties remain. Senator Barbara Boxer's (D-CA) assertion that "There still isn't true equality [in Congress] when decisions are made," (Romano 1990, C1) may temper the motivation of potential female candidates. It also may well reinforce some of the biases of voters who rationalize not supporting a woman because they are of the opinion that "Congress is a man's world anyway."

Racial and Ethnic Background

African Americans and many ethnic minorities tend to be concentrated in the lower economic groups, which often lack both the political motivation and resources to seek elective office. More than 13 percent of the electorate is black.[4] On that basis, the House should include more than fifty-five African Americans as compared to the thirty-eight who now serve. Voter biases have made it difficult for minorities to be elected from districts in which they are not the majority, which helps explain the support of minority leaders for legislative redistricting plans which concentrate minorities into winnable districts. African Americans find it more difficult to raise campaign funds, even in races with no white incumbent (Public Citizen 1992).

---

[2] The name "EMILY" stands for "Early Money Is Like Yeast," emphasizing the importance of seed money in a campaign. EMILY's List is unlike a typical political action committee in that it does not give its own money directly to candidates. It selects female candidates with a good chance of winning, and serves as conduit for funds by "bundling" together checks made out to those candidates. In 1992, EMILY's List was responsible for more than $4.6 million in contributions (Schwartz and Cooper 1992, A38). On the Republican side, the much smaller WISH List (Women in the Senate and House) uses the same tactics to support pro-choice Republican women candidates.

[3] It is not so much that women candidates cannot raise as much money *because they are women,* but rather they lack the non-gender based criteria such as experience and incumbency which facilitates fund raising (see Uhlaner and Schlozman 1986, 30–50 passim).

[4] Population figures for this and the next section come from the U.S. Census Bureau projections reported in the *Washington Post,* 18 February 1992, p. A15.

Other ethnic minority groups are only beginning to find their way into Congress. Their numbers are so small that generalizations are hard to make. Like women, the "bench" of potential minority candidates is growing at the state and local level, but their ability to translate this strength into congressional seats is a slow process.

Age

Legal requirements assure that the average age of Congress will remain considerably higher than the population as a whole. Congress fails to match the age distribution in the population. While people twenty-five to thirty-nine years of age make up over 30 percent of all Americans and more than 40 percent of eligible voters, only about 9 percent of House members in the 103rd Congress fell into this age bracket. Potential younger candidates often have not had the time to establish themselves politically and to acquire the necessary resources for victory. On the other end of the scale, about 13 percent of Americans are more than sixty-five years of age compared to about 9 percent of House members. Older individuals often lack the motivation and/or physical stamina to stay in office. Congress is clearly the bastion of middle-aged individuals.

Occupation

The over representation of law and business reflects both the increased motivation and the expanded opportunities these professions have for contesting political office. Many occupational groups find political activity disruptive to their careers, and/or are unable to provide the resources necessary to become a viable candidate. On the other hand, some occupational choices lead naturally to success in congressional elections. Although former congressional staff members account for only 5 percent of non-incumbent candidates, they account for more than 16 percent of the winners, "a tribute to the value of staff experience" (Herrnson 1991, 8).

Other Characteristics

Despite the geographical mobility in American society, members of Congress tend to be "locals," representing states and regions where they were born, educated and began their careers. In the 103rd Congress, 64 percent of the senators were born in the states they now represent and 12 percent of the remaining senators were educated in the state of their current residence. Thus 76 percent of the senators have spent the bulk of their adult lives in the states they now represent. On the House side, 67 percent of the Members were born in the states they now represent. Among the 110 new Members of the 103rd Congress, there was less localism, with 63 percent having been born in a different state ("The Carpetbagging Caucus" 1993, 1).

Despite 1992 being characterized as the "year of the outsider," we saw the election bring in a class of congressional members somewhat more experienced than the average class. Of the 110 new House members, 72 percent had previously held public office, and only one of the fourteen new senators (Robert Bennett, R-UT[5]) had no political personal experience (Canon 1993, 4). In general, service in Congress is reserved for individuals who have "paid their dues" by working their way up through the political process.

While few of the victors in 1994 were political neophytes, incumbency in Congress emerged as a detriment to overcome. Winning incumbents often did so in very close races. Almost half of the losing incumbents were first term Democrats elected in 1992. Most of the senior Members who lost, such as Jack Brooks (D-TX) with 42 years of service and former Speaker Tom Foley (D-WA) with 30 years, were criticized as having had their chance and for losing touch with their districts.

The fact that members of Congress are well educated[6] and come from more upper-middle class religious groups,[7] reflects their financial resources more than any inherent characteristics of education or religion. Comparing the average member with the population as a whole, it is not surprising that voters could reasonably assert that "we have an aristocracy, not a Congress 'of' the people" (Duncan 1991a, 3166).

The relatively unrepresentative nature of the elected players has implications both for the decision-making process and the way Congress as an institution is perceived.

UNDERSTANDING THE IMPORTANCE OF THE DEMOGRAPHIC MIX

Concern with the social background of members of Congress revolves around the issues of performance, representation and legitimacy. Performance is concerned with the ability of individual Members and the Congress as a whole to competently carry out their duties. The various congressional duties require particular perspectives, motivations, and skills. Well-spoken individuals with analytical minds, a desire to aggressively serve the public good, and possessing a perceptiveness about the problems facing society are an asset to Congress. A Congress which perfectly mirrored the population might not include the necessary mix of performance characteristics to carry out its duties.

One of the critical duties of Congress is **representation,** the **process** by which the wishes and interests of citizens are **re-presented** (presented a second time) to policy-makers. While virtually anyone can serve as an "honest broker" transmitting the wishes of another, individuals who share the characteristics of those they must represent have a better feel for the needs and desires of those people. An individual is **representative** when he or she shares the basic characteristics of the people to be represented. A Congress rated high on **representativeness** would closely mirror the social background characteristics of the population it is charged with representing. Representation is not the only goal of the selection process. The relatively narrow range of people elected to Congress does facilitate compromise and more comfortable

---

[5]Classifying Bennett as a political neophyte stretches the definition a bit. Although he had no personal elective or appointed experience when elected, his father served as U.S. Senator for Utah from 1951 to 1974 (Canon 1993, 4).

[6]Seventy percent of the House members in the 103rd Congress had graduate degrees, while only 6 percent had not earned a college degree (*Roll Call,* 31 May 1993).

[7]Members of Congress are more likely to be Episcopalians and Presbyterians and less likely to be Catholics or Baptists than is the population as a whole.

interpersonal relationships than would be the case in a more diverse institution. It often does so, however, at the expense of being portrayed as an institution to which all segments of the population can not realistically aspire.

Political institutions with **legitimacy** are viewed as having both the legal and perceived right to make binding decisions. In a society that, at least rhetorically, aspires to "government **of** the people and **by** the people" (Abraham Lincoln's phrase in the *Gettysburg Address),* frustrations with an institution's performance are exacerbated when it is viewed as unrepresentative. The declining public respect for Congress (see chapter 6) and the move during the early 1990s to "throw the rascals out" by imposing term limitations imply a lessening of legitimacy and that "voters may be catching on that the demographic characteristics of Congress do indeed shape the policy debate (Duncan 1991a, 3166).

The current mix of social background characteristics is not likely to change dramatically in the future, both because it stems from real differences in ambition, opportunity and voter selection criteria, and because once in office individual Members expend considerable effort to remain.

Specific background characteristics are at times linked with clear behavior patterns. Members of categoric groups (women, African Americans, Hispanics, Catholics, etc.) can generally be counted on to support legislation clearly favoring that group. Women in Congress stand out as a "cohesive group and . . . the dimensions of voting behavior are significantly different from their male counterparts" (Frankovic 1977, 329). While women in Congress are not a monolithic bloc, gender does play a significant role in the type of legislation supported and typical patterns of voting. Female legislators on the state and national level tend to more regularly pursue and more heavily support issues with particular relevance to women, children, and the family (Durst and Rusek 1993, 300; Thomas 1991, 958). As the number of women increase, it is assumed that the difference *between* women will also increase (Kelly, St. Germain, and Horn 1991, 77).

African Americans almost universally support civil rights legislation and display a liberal voting pattern. Contemporary African American office-holders have an expanded agenda. "The Black politicians of years ago were basically advocates of the Black agenda, and that's all they did . . . [today] they need another issue to appeal to white voters" (Cooper and Dewar 1992, A16). With increased numbers of African Americans and Hispanics, their influence as individuals and as a group has increased. In 1993, the Black Caucus stood firm against cuts in welfare programs and forced President Clinton to change his budget plan (see chapter 4).

It is difficult to determine whether social background or the type of districts these members represent serves as the driving force for their uniqueness. Candidates with little experience in elective office tend to be more extreme in their behavior, less willing to compromise and more willing to cut their careers short than the more experienced politicians (see Canon 1990, 115, 121). Other background may have a positive effect. Political commentator Michael Barone observed that former professional athletes such as Wilmer "Vinegar Bend" Mizell (R-NC), Bob Mathias (R-CA), and Jack Kemp (R-NY) showed themselves to be "team players" in Congress as well as on the athletic field (quoted in Canon 1990, 114).

The creation of a more representative Congress may well have implications beyond the behavior of individual Members. In dealing with major issues, Congress has often been hampered by the limited perspectives of its Members.

> Congress, a club traditionally dominated by white men, lawyers and businessmen, has long debated the most difficult issues of the day with only minimal participation from those with relevant firsthand experience. (Brown 1993, 2246)

In 1993, the nature of debate on the renewal of a patent including the Confederate flag took a different twist when Carol Mosely-Braun took the floor to point out that as the only Senator descended from slaves, she was not talking theory but from personal experience. Senator Ben Nighthorse Campbell (D-CO) adds a new dimension of issues of American Indian rights that stem from his personal background. Republican Gary Franks (R-CT) forces many Members to confront their stereotypes and assess their views of representation when he outlines how an African American can support Republican policies. When the House debates welfare, it now has a former welfare mother (Representative Lynn Woolsey, [D-CA]) in its midst. Far from abstract pontificating, a more representative Congress will provide more opportunities for "genuine, from-the-heart exchanges that call on useful person experience [that] lend a whole new credibility to congressional debate and decision making" (Brown 1993, 2246).

THE DESIRABILITY OF STAYING IN OFFICE

While it is simplistic to assert that all members of Congress are "single-minded seekers of re-election," the reality that one cannot remain a statesman without being re-elected looms high in the consciousness of most Members. Congress has become an institution in which most elected Members want to stay, and those planning to leave for other pursuits clearly do not want to be pushed out on the heels of electoral defeat. The desire to stay in office is not evenly distributed throughout the chamber. Suffering under minority status and often frustrated with the unfairness and inefficiency of Congress, Republicans tend to retire at higher rates than Democrats (Frantzich 1978; Gilmour and Rothstein 1993, 345).

THE GROWTH OF THE CONGRESSIONAL CAREER

Since the 1950s, the typical member of the House has served more than five terms in office. The growing importance of the seniority system during the early part of this century, which linked the acquisition of leadership positions with continuous service, encouraged Members to stay around and voters to keep them in office (Hibbing 1991, 22). The development of Congress as a powerful player in American politics increased the appeal of long-term service (Hibbing 1991, 3). The more appealing serving in Congress became as a career, the more interested Members became in surviving from one election to the next.

THE IMPORTANCE OF ELECTORAL MARGINS

While winning or losing remains the ultimate test of one's performance, few incumbents receive the ultimate electoral sanction of removal from office by their constituents. The desire to stay in office encourages Members to seek out signs of

relative success or failure. Elections provide signs of political support which allow Members to determine whether they can continue their current patterns of behavior or whether a mid-course correction in strategies is necessary. As Marjorie Hershey put it,

> Campaigns may leave their mark on American politics less by changing the officeholder's face than by influencing the officeholder's thinking—and the perceptions and behavior of challengers, activists, [and] reporters. (1984, 31)

Political support is one of the key factors in a Member's worldview. Most Members seek re-election, not only to accomplish the policy and ideological goals which drew them into politics in the first place, but also to soothe their individual egos and vindicate their performance in office. Electorally secure Members have more freedom in the activities they pursue and the positions they take. Most electorally marginal Members preface each action with the question, "Will this enhance or decrease my support among the voters?"

From the perspective of outside observers, most incumbents "win in a walk" (see Mayhew 1974b, 35–36), with closely contested elections limited almost exclusively to races without incumbents. To incumbents, though, electoral marginality is as much a factor of **perception** as reality. Winning or losing is only the most extreme consequence of an election. Politicians look for a wide variety of signals to gauge their electoral well being. While outside observers look for clearly identifiable measurements of electoral strength, members of Congress evaluate an election result in light of its context. It is common for outsiders to classify Members receiving less than 55 percent of the vote as electorally "marginal," but such a classification misses many of the factors that comprise a perceptual feeling of marginality. A Member winning with 51 percent of the vote after a messy divorce and facing a tough opponent, might perceive a level of electoral security bordering on invincibility. On the other hand, a Member receiving 70 percent of the vote facing an incompetent challenger whose messy personal life dominated the news might wonder how that 30 percent opposition might be expanded in the next election by a more formidable opponent.

While absolute percentages mean relatively little in establishing a Member's perception of electoral security, unexpected changes in those percentages can undermine or build confidence. Incumbents can expect a 2 to 7 percent increase in their voting percentage each time they run as the result of positive publicity and increased name identification generated by serving in office (see Jacobson 1987, 27). A decreased percentage signals potential danger.

The conventional wisdom prior to the 1990 election indicated an increased distrust of incumbents. Incumbents were stuck in Washington trying to hammer out a budget so the government would not shut down, while their opponents used each detour to criticize Congress and encourage voters to "throw the bums out."

The morning after the 1990 election, most incumbents breathed a sigh of relief. Of the 407 House incumbents seeking re-election, 96 percent won, and only one incumbent senator lost (Alston 1990, 3796). The only immediate evidence of voter backlash against incumbents was that three states (California, Colorado, and Oklahoma) passed referenda limiting the number of terms state legislators could serve, fueling the demand for similar moves on the national level. The glow of incumbent victories tarnished when they evaluated the cold reality of their electoral margins. Far from the normal increases, most incumbents lost ground compared with their 1988 electoral showing. The average percentage of the vote declined eight percentage points for House Republicans and three percentage points for Democrats. While clearly not a wholesale rejection of incumbents in terms of turnover, the 1990 election "could be considered an important wake-up call" (Cook 1990c, 3798) for incumbents. Just because the anti-incumbent mood "wasn't sufficient to defeat very many people doesn't mean that it will be discounted by those who survived (Stephen Hess quoted in Wolf 1990, 11a). As Douglas Arnold concluded,

> Legislators are a cautious lot. Even though a legislator may have won the most recent election by a comfortable margin, most of them have had at least one close election, and all of them can recall stories of "safe" congressmen who are no longer congressmen. (Arnold 1990, 61)

In 1992, the second shoe dropped. The combination of redistricting, a scandal over check-bouncing[8] in the House and a general anti-incumbent mood led to a higher than average number of retirements and defeats at the polls primaries.[9] Setting a post-war retirement record, sixty-five House members left voluntarily, nineteen lost in the primaries, and twenty-four lost in the general election, for an overall turnover of 110 Members. Even the 93 percent of the incumbents who won saw a decline in their share of the vote. In the Senate, seven Members retired, one lost in the primaries, and four lost in the general election. Fourteen additional states passed term limitation amendments affecting Congress.[10]

The 1994 election saw voter frustration fueled by extensive negative campaigning leading to Republican control of both houses of Congress for the first time in forty years. While retirements and primary defeats returned to more normal levels, and over 90 percent of the incumbents won (albeit with lower percentages), Republicans swept the open seats and defeated a number of Democratic incumbents to gain eight seats in the Senate and 52 seats in the House. In the 104th Congress, Republicans control the Senate with a 53 to 47 margin and the House with a 231 to 204 partisan advantage.

---

[8] Of the eighteen top "abusers" of House banking privileges, eight retired, six lost in the primaries, and three lost in the general election. Another nine of the primary losers were clearly affected by redistricting (Cooper and Dewar 1992, A16).

[9] Many factors affected the number of House retirements in 1992. While Members bouncing a large number of checks were more likely to retire, 1992 also marked the last year in which incumbents benefited from the "golden parachute," that is, being allowed to take their campaign war chests with them (see Groseclose and Krehbiel, forthcoming, 1994).

[10] The constitutionality of state-imposed term limitations is under question. The proposals that were passed provide for a twelve-year limit for senators and vary from six to twelve years for House members. Provisions vary as to re-eligibility for office after sitting out a term (Gross 1992, A1). Proponents justify term limitations as reinvigorating Congress by bringing in new blood, and returning Congress to the people—although the voters supported the legislation more out of frustration with Congress. Opponents raise both questions of constitutionality and politics, predicting decreased congressional power, reduced effectiveness of individual Members and growing power for staffs and lobbyists (see Benjamin and Malbin 1992, 209–222; Will 1992, 1–10).

STRATEGIES FOR SURVIVAL

> Electoral support is not won once and for all. It requires continual renewal and reinforcement, the more so now that party loyalties are weaker and the incumbent's personal performance more determining. (Jacobson 1987, 5)

> If a group of planners sat down and tried to design a pair of national assemblies with the goal of serving Members' re-election needs year in and year out, they would be hard pressed to improve on what exists. (Mayhew 1974a, 81–82)

Members of Congress are not simply victims of national trends nor helpless bystanders in their political futures. Once elected, they use a number of tried and true strategies designed to help them survive in office.

DEFINING THE CONGRESSIONAL JOB

A key factor in keeping any job lies in proving that one has adequately fulfilled its responsibilities. "The Constitution contains nothing on the duties of individual members of Congress" (Cain, Ferejohn, and Fiorina 1987, 1). The vague nature of the congressional job description is both a curse and a blessing. On the one hand, no one clearly outlines the specifications with an agreed on "bottom line" of performance. Members of Congress cannot be measured on the basis of sales quotas, products produced or number of hours put in. Members are pretty free to define the job as they wish and then wait for the delayed job performance rating handed out by the voters on election day. While the freedom to define the job adds excitement and challenge, it also makes members of Congress subject to a myriad of competing demands. Since the job is not clearly defined, a wide variety of groups and individuals take this as an invitation to "help" Members decide where to put their efforts. David Mayhew (1974b) points out that in their seeking of re-election, Members spend much of their time **taking positions** on issues that please their constituents, **advertising** their efforts, and **claiming credit** for their successes. Who Members try to please and how they go about it varies.

Playing to the Crowd or Impressing Other Players

> Members of Congress have two constituencies, one back at home and one in the chamber. It soon becomes clear that to be successful they must be elected and selected by both. (Former Speaker John McCormack's advice to new Members; author's interview with former Representative Lester Wolff [D-NY])

Members of Congress quickly realize that they are faced with two sets of often competing expectations as to how they should do their job. Constituents back home want a representative who will keep in close touch, represent their interests on proposed legislation and help secure their fair share of government benefits.[11] Party leaders and colleagues, on the other hand, want Members dedicated to work hard

---

[11] A 1978 national poll indicated that 48 percent of the respondents felt that Members should spend most of their time "helping people in the district," 28 percent thought they should "work on bills of national interest," and 21 percent felt both should be given equal weight (CBS/*New York Times* Poll, 30 September 1978). There is no evidence that this balance of constituent desires has changed.

crafting legislation, interested in seeking legislative coalitions through compromise, and committed to making sure that the chamber works effectively. Each set of tasks could well be a full-time job and Members seek an acceptable compromise to satisfy the competing demands.

Members choose a **role,** based on their view as to which of the demands are most feasible and legitimate. A role establishes a preprogrammed behavior pattern which allows the Member to make a series of behavioral choices without having to rethink all the options and possible consequences. The Member choosing to emphasize constituent demands over colleague/chamber demands is more likely to slip out of the chamber before a key vote to catch a plane back home for a scheduled speech, while the colleague/chamber oriented Member is more likely to cancel the speech in order to get the legislative work done. Role choices are not absolutely fixed. Demands change over time and constituents and colleagues react to the behavior patterns stimulated by role choices. If the Member who slipped out of the chamber before a key vote receives significant criticism from colleagues and/or constituents, he or she might well rethink either the role choice and/or how the role should be played. Junior Members with their weaker electoral margins must usually emphasize constituent demands in order to stay in office, while senior Members have both the freedom and the additional burden of leadership positions which force more of a chamber orientation.

DEFINING THE RESPONSIBILITIES The lack of a constitutional or legal job descriptions means that the role of a member of Congress is defined by tradition, trial and error, and the expectations of others. If you ask Members to outline "the major kinds of jobs, duties, or functions you are expected to perform as an individual member of Congress" (U.S. Congress, House Commission on Administrative Review 1977), the answers vary considerably (see table 3.1). The single most common role is that of "legislator." Legislators are the most chamber oriented in their willingness to study and facilitate legislation. Being a legislator does not necessarily mean ignoring constituent legislative interests, but it does take away from other constituency oriented tasks.

A close second in Member priorities is the "constituency-servant" role which involves attempting to solve individual constituent problems with government (casework) and seeking out benefits for the constituency as a whole. Extensive constituency service almost guarantees that the Member will be "better known, more favorably evaluated and more successful electorally" (Cain, Ferejohn, and Fiorina 1987, 213). It is not surprising that junior Members with weak electoral margins are more likely to define their jobs in terms of constituency service than legislative activity (see Johannes 1983, 538). Other roles such as "mentor/communicators" and "representatives" also orient their activities more to the constituency than to the needs of the chamber or their colleagues. Representation may focus on general policy, but also includes activities we might subsume under constituency service. As Cain, Ferejohn, and Fiorina argue,

> Representation is generally viewed as **policy responsiveness**. . . . How faithfully does the representative respond to the wishes of the district in words and deeds. Representation also includes **allocation responsiveness** . . . [working] to assure that his or her district gets a fair share of government projects. (1987, 2, emphasis added)

TABLE 3.1 Defining the Congressional Job

House members' volunteered responses to the question, "What are the major kinds of jobs, duties, or functions that you feel you are expected to perform as an individual member of Congress?" (Multiple responses encouraged)

Legislator	
Expectations: emphasizing legislative work; analyzing issues and committee specialization	
Behavior: carefully studying issues; attending committee and floor sessions	87%
Constituency servant	
Expectations: helping constituents with problems associated with government; making sure the district gets its "fair share" of government funds and programs	
Behavior: emphasizing individual **casework;** helping local government units apply for government grants	79%
Mentor/Communicator	
Expectations: serving as a two-way conduit of information between citizens and government; assessing and communicating constituent interests to colleagues; and educating constituents on the issues	
Behavior: keeping in touch with constituents through numerous trips back to the district; paying careful attention to the mail; and other taking part in "outreach" efforts	43%
Representative	
Expectations: understanding constituency interests and re-presenting them to relevant colleagues	
Behavior: keeping in close touch with constituents; monitoring governmental initiatives with potential impact on the constituency	26%
Other roles	
Politico: seeker of re-election	
Overseer: watchdog over the bureaucracy	
Broker: coalition builder and intermediary between groups competing for government attention	
Office manager: organizer of the congressional office enterprise	33%

SOURCE: U.S. Congress, House, Commission on Administrative Review, *Final Report,* H. Doc. 95-272, 31 December 1977, pp. 874–875.

THE OVERRIDING REPRESENTATIONAL ROLE

> Senators tend to go one of two ways. [Some of them] become elevated and sort of national in their thinking and national in their orientation, and more removed from their states . . . there are other kinds of Senators, whose history and orientation and whose states call for a much more intimate kind of constituent relationship. (Senator Donald Riegle, quoted in Starobin 1991, 58)

While not leading the pack in terms of distinct mentions, the role of representative pervades the consciousness of all Members. The specifics vary as to **who** a Member defines as a constituent and **how** he or she goes about representing him or her.

At first it seems obvious who a Member's constituents are. The single-member-district system assigns each Member a geographical entity, but this legal constituency often bears little resemblance to individuals whose interests the

Member feels responsible for "representing." About one-quarter of the House members perceive their job as looking out for the **national** interest, even if it is not in the best interest of their legal constituents (Davidson 1969, 122). More than 40 percent of House members report choosing **district** interests over national interests when the two come into conflict (Davidson 1969, 122), with the remainder varying their **representational focus** depending on the nature of the issue or level of interest among constituents.

Even Members asserting a willingness to represent constituency interests seldom focus on the entire geographical constituency. Within the legal constituency lie narrower constituencies of supporters (the re-election constituency), loyalists (the primary constituency), and intimates (the personal constituency) whose views and interests have a successively greater impact on the Member's votes and behavior (see Fenno 1978, 8–27). Less politically secure Members are more likely to emphasize constituency interests over national interests. They also attempt to improve their electoral position by looking beyond their past electoral constituency in hopes of broadening their constituency base. Senators, with their six-year terms and responsibility for more national tasks such as approving treaties and nominations, tend to pay somewhat less attention to their geographical constituency, except when clear state interests are involved.

The decision to represent a particular constituency tells us little about **how** the member goes about assessing constituency interests. The choice of a **representational style** has faced legislators since the origin of representative government. About a quarter of House members view themselves as pure "delegates" who subsume their own views and follow the instructions of their most vocal constituents (Davidson 1969, 117). Delegates tend to travel back to their districts regularly to assess constituency opinion, use their newsletters to poll constituents, and look to election results for guidance on policy choices.

Another quarter of House members argue that they were elected to make tough choices **on behalf** of their constituents and to serve as a "trustee" for their interests (Davidson 1969, 117). They see their election as a sign of constituent trust and assert that service in Congress provides them with the expertise and information that allows them to represent constituents' true interests as opposed to uninformed whims. Constituency opinion is only one factor in the trustee's decision. Trustees spend considerable time attempting to educate constituents and explain their decisions which on the surface may seem antagonistic to constituency interests (see Fenno 1978, 157–160; Kingdon 1989, 47–54). The remaining House members, while recognizing the distinction between a delegate and a trustee approach explained that their method of representation varied with the issue at hand. Issues generating considerable constituency interest tend to be dealt with as a delegate, while issues of relatively little interest to the constituency allow a trustee orientation. Although we lack survey data of senators, their six-year terms and more heterogeneous statewide constituencies probably lead to more of a trustee orientation.

MARSHALLING THE AVAILABLE RESOURCES

Members of Congress use their staff and mailing privileges to improve their chance of survival.

Congressional Staff: Bolstering the Members' Supporting Team

> The First Congress . . . had three staff people, not three staff people per Member, but three staff people for the Congress of the United States of America. (Representative Lynn Martin [R-IL], *Congressional Record,* 24 May 1988, p. H3589)

Members of the contemporary Congress cannot meet all their responsibilities by themselves. Growing demands and the desire to stay in office has encouraged Members to expand staff support. Earlier this century, a member of Congress got by with a few clerks. Now congressional offices have been compared to a bustling small business with only one product to "sell"—their member of Congress (see Loomis 1979, 35). In order to work "smart," members of Congress have not only expanded their personal staffs, but bolstered their information gathering with extensive committee and support agency staffs. The current staff of more than 30,000 (see table 3.2) makes Congress the most heavily staffed legislature in the world, surpassing second place Canada by almost tenfold (Goldstein 1991, 13).

PERSONAL STAFFS Congressional personal staffs research issues and manage constituent communications. Members are given allowances (see table 3.3) to manage their offices and assemble their personal staff team. Personal staffs tend to be young, well educated and serve a relatively short tenure—using service on a personal staff as a stepping stone to other positions (see Fox and Hammond 1977, 46). Personal staff members serve at the pleasure of their Members and can be hired or fired at any time. Staff are usually hired on the basis of their loyalty to their bosses' career and policy goals. Members are free to organize their staff team and allocate staff efforts in any way they wish, with a significant amount of staff time spent on answering constituent mail, general public relations, and other non-legislative tasks. While Members once kept their staff teams close at hand in Washington, the increased importance of dealing with constituent problems and the loosening of rules on allowances have led to staff relocation. Over 40 percent of House and one-third of Senate staffs now work out of district offices (Ornstein, Mann, and Malbin 1992, 120). Being sent to the district office was once viewed as banishment from the power center; however, the growing use of new communications technologies such as computer networks and fax machines now make it possible for staff members to interact, secure information, and do their jobs despite decentralized locations (Frantzich 1982, 253; Pincus 1990, A21).

Although personal staffs spend most of their time working on the margins of the policy process, a few key staff serve Members' legislative interests and "become their alter egos . . . [who] learn to anticipate what their bosses need to know and how they will react once they have certain information" (Maisel 1981, 259).

The growth of congressional staff was justified by Congress on the basis of increasing efficiency and improving the legislative process by unburdening Members of more routine information gathering and communications tasks. Some observers argue that congressional staff has become too powerful and has created new burdens while alleviating only some of the old ones. Personal and committee

TABLE 3.2 The Supporting Players: Congressional Staff as of 1991[a]

Personal staffs	
House	7,278
Senate	4,294
Leadership and chamber staff	
House	1,442
Senate	1,187
Committee staff	
House	2,321
Senate	1,154
Joint	145
Support agencies	
General Accounting Office	5,054[b]
Congressional Research Service	831
Congressional Budget Office	226
Office of Technology Assessment	143
Miscellaneous	
architect, police force	3,364
TOTAL	27,439

[a]Congress has proposed a phased staff cut of 18 percent beginning in 1994.
[b]Only 30 percent work directly for Congress.

SOURCE: Norman J. Ornstein, Thomas E. Mann, and Michael J. Malbin, *Vital Statistics on Congress, 1993–1994,* Washington D.C.: Congressional Quarterly, pp. 124–125.

Congressional staffs have expanded in size beyond the expectations of many Members.

TABLE 3.3 Staff and Office Allowances for Each Member of Congress as of 1993

House of Representatives	
Clerk-hire allowance	$557,400
—Up to eighteen full-time staff (up to four additional must be part time)	
Official expenses	$153,128–$306,279[a]
—Travel (thirty-three round trips to district)	
—Postage, district office rental,	
—Supplies	
—Equipment: telephone, computers, etc.	
Senate	
Clerk-hire allowance	$1,540,000–$1,914,000[b]
—No limit on the number of staff, with the average Senator employing more than seventy people	
Legislative assistance (purely legislative staff work)	$374,000
Official expenses[c]	$74,000–$241,000
—Travel (twenty to twenty-two round trips)	
—Postage, supplies, equipment	

[a]Amount varies depending on variations in travel, telecommunications and office space rental costs.
[b]Senate allowances vary depending on the population of the state.
[c]Senators are reimbursed directly for 4,800 to 8,000 square feet of district office space, depending on the population of the state.

SOURCE: Norman J. Ornstein, Thomas E. Mann, and Michael J. Malbin, *Vital Statistics on Congress, 1993–1994,* Washington D.C.: Congressional Quarterly, pp. 142–145.

staffs[12] have become agenda setters, policy initiators and negotiators. Their more activist and entrepreneurial activities lead them to "drum up more business" (Malbin 1980, 24) for both Congress and its Members (see box 3.1). By serving as surrogates for Members in the policy-making process, making compromises and cutting deals, appointed staff members may usurp some powers of elected Members and undermine the representational process by reducing Members' direct involvement with key issues (see Malbin 1980, chapters 1 and 10).

The heavy reliance on the abilities and political discretion of staffs has long been the basis for Members' claims that they alone have the right to determine the employment conditions. Members traditionally have had the unilateral right to hire and fire their staffs. Increasing awareness of alleged improprieties (such as the sexual harassment charges against Senator Packwood, [R-OR]) and the lack

[12]The line between strictly personal staff members and committee staffs is difficult to draw. Key Members, especially committee leaders have "their" key persons on the committee staff whose wages come from committee allowances. At a minimum, most committee staff members are hired by and work for one of the party delegations on the committee. The loyalty and effort of most staff members is directed more to their "patron(s)" on the committee than to the committee as a whole. In chapter 4 we will discuss committee staffs in more detail.

BOX 3.1 The Players Speak: Members Talk About Their Staffs

Congress is bogged down in detail, missing the big picture. . . . It has become so bureaucratic itself that it can't legislate effectively. . . . Staffs have mushroomed. . . . These large staffs tend to push members of Congress to artificially inflate their legislative agendas. Staffers develop their own ideas and agendas, which get introduced as bills, increasing the glut of inconsequential legislation clogging an already sluggish system (Senator David Boren [D-OK] 1991, A15).

Former Senator David Boren (D-OK) may have decried staff influence, but would have been be a much less effective legislator without it.

It is the staff that makes the real quality difference . . . we should recognize that largely anonymous, behind-the-scenes, overwhelmingly unknown staff persons conceive many of the ideas and do most of the work to advance those ideas for what we, as senators, take 100 percent of the credit (Senator William Proxmire [D-WI] *Congressional Record,* 15 June 1988, p. S7818).

Former Senator Proxmire (D-WI) fully recognized that the effectiveness of his public appearances was heavily dependent on the quality of staff work analyzing issues and writing speeches.

Continued on next page

BOX 3.1 Continued

We are now suffering from a staff infection. . . . Our system of democracy through a deliberative legislative process is threatened to the extent that we overwhelm ourselves with staff and delegate to them responsibilities which should be ours (Senator Trent Lott [R-MS] *Congressional Record,* 25 February 1987, p. H822).

Senator Trent Lott (R-MS) may question the growth of staff, but like other Members relies on them quite heavily.

of opportunities for women and minorities, led to people describing Capitol Hill as "the last plantation." Such charges were even more difficult to defend given the fact that Congress has exempted itself from most national laws concerning employment opportunities and conditions. Significant negative publicity has begun to force Congress to reassess its privileged position in terms of staffing.

SUPPORT STAFFS AND RESOURCES Above and beyond personal staffs, Congress relies on a series of research agencies for objective analysis and advice (see box 3.2). Staff agencies prepare reports at the request of Members and their staffs. Key personal staff members combine the objective analysis of the staff agencies with their own political acumen to advise Members on how to reach their more political goals (Thurber 1981, 301; Maisel 1981, 267).

Information is a key resource in the legislative process. Members need help identifying problems, canvassing solutions and monitoring the progress of legislation. Relying on its own resources and commercial databases, the U.S. Congress has become the most technologically supported legislature in the world. With a few computer keystrokes, a Member can acquire the latest trade figures from the executive branch, find the full text of a newspaper article, check the U.S. Code for a particular word, or determine the status of a piece of legislation (Frantzich 1982, 146; Frantzich 1987, 13–14). Information technology cannot make the tough value choices members of Congress are elected to tackle, but can help assure that all the known facts are available before the decision has to be made.

BOX 3.2 The Duties of the Key Congressional Staff Agencies

LIBRARY OF CONGRESS (ESTABLISHED IN 1800, CURRENT STAFF OF APPROXIMATELY 4,800)

Description: The Library of Congress (LOC) is the largest library in the world with more than ninety-eight million items in its collection (twenty-three million books). Thomas Jefferson contributed his personal library to start the collection. One division of the LOC handles all U.S. copyrights, assuring that all books published in the U.S. are considered for inclusion in the library. The LOC is open to the public, but provides special services for members of Congress and their staffs.

Methods of supporting Congress: Aside from housing its research collection and making it available to Congress, the LOC includes the **Congressional Research Service** (see below).

CONGRESSIONAL RESEARCH SERVICE (ESTABLISHED IN 1914, WITH DUTIES EXPANDED IN 1970, CURRENT STAFF OF APPROXIMATELY 860)

Description: The **Congressional Research Service (CRS)** is Congress' in-house research agency. At the request of individual Members and their staffs, CRS carries out short-term research on pending legislative issues and handles thousands of specific inquiries for facts and quotes.

Methods of supporting Congress:
- Reference inquiries (facts and quotes): an average of almost 1000 per day answered
- Individualized research
- Development of "issue briefs"—analyses of policy issues pending in Congress (more than 100 available at any one point in time)
- Serving as expert witnesses at committee hearings

OFFICE OF TECHNOLOGY ASSESSMENT (ESTABLISHED IN 1972, CURRENT STAFF OF APPROXIMATELY 140)

Description: The **Office of Technology Assessment (OTA)** carries out and contracts for medium and long range research requested by committees focusing on the impact of science and technology in a variety of policy realms.

Methods of supporting Congress:
- Publication of research reports
- Serving as expert witnesses at committee hearings

GENERAL ACCOUNTING OFFICE (CREATED IN 1921, CURRENT STAFF OF APPROXIMATELY 5,000 WITH ABOUT 30 PERCENT WORKING EXCLUSIVELY FOR CONGRESS)

Description: The **General Accounting Office (GAO)** audits and evaluates the programs and financial operations of the federal government at the request of committees.

Continued on next page

BOX 3.2 Continued

Methods of supporting Congress:

- Carrying out routine audits of federal programs
- Responding to requests for special studies by congressional committees
- Serving as expert witnesses at committee hearings

CONGRESSIONAL BUDGET OFFICE (CREATED IN 1974, CURRENT STAFF OF APPROXIMATELY 220)

Description: The **Congressional Budget Office (CBO)** analyzes budget options and objectively attempts to forecast their ramifications.

Methods of supporting Congress:

- Providing cost estimates for proposed legislation
- Keeping track of congressional appropriations and revenue bills, and comparing the results to targets established in current legislation
- Analyzing economic projections in light of the president's proposed budget
- Carrying out special studies related to government spending
- Serving as expert witnesses at committee hearings

Congressional Mail: Expanding Congressional Visibility

Americans take seriously their constitutional right to "petition government for the redress of grievances" (1st Amendment) and the dictum "write your congressman" has become a common strategy. Although less than 15 percent of Americans report having written their member of Congress (Congressional Quarterly 1991, 511), they generate over 80 million pieces of incoming mail per year (Ornstein et al. 1992, 161). Individuals write for a variety of reasons. About half the incoming mail involves constituents expressing their opinions on public policy issues before the Congress (Frantzich 1986, 13). Most of the remainder is **casework,** individual constituent requests for information, or help with a governmental problem.

The average House office receives between 250 and 500 constituent letters a week (Kenworthy 1990b, A4) and senators receive many times that. While the flood of incoming mail is a burden, most offices have turned it into an opportunity to show constituents they care and are there to help them. The basic congressional strategy is to respond to all incoming mail from constituents. The question is seldom "should we respond?" but rather "how can we respond most effectively?" At a minimum, all letters receive an acknowledgement of their receipt. Casework requires special attention since the congressional office has been asked to acquire information or intervene with the bureaucracy.

CASEWORK: RESPONDING TO CONSTITUENTS CRIES FOR HELP

> The electorate is most concerned with the things that hit closest to home. By heeding the widespread demand for constituency service, Members can improve their position in the electoral arena. (Cavanaugh 1979, 241)

> Many lawmakers' home offices exist primarily to assist voters through the maze of the federal bureaucracy, and some Members have built their entire careers—and reputations—on playing ombudsman[13] to the people who elect them. (Birnbaum 1991, 28)

Individuals increasingly find themselves entwined with the federal government, responding to government regulation, and seeking government services. "While not malevolent, bureaucracies make mistakes. . . . Members of the U.S. Congress . . . hold an almost unique position vis-à-vis the bureaucracy; congressmen possess the power to expedite bureaucratic activity" (Fiorina 1977a, 68). Members of Congress have been neither victims nor bystanders in this process. They help create the government programs that provide services and/or regulate citizens, and then stand by willingly to become intermediaries when the bureaucracy fails to respond, or responds in a way the constituent feels is inappropriate (see Fiorina 1977b, 48). "People turn to their congressman or senator for help when the rest of the system fails" (Cavanaugh 1981, 66). The cries for help vary:

> "I haven't got a social security check in three months and I can't get anyone to answer my letters."

> "I have lost my passport and am stuck in Athens. Can you get me a replacement before my flight leaves tomorrow?"

> "My family and I will be in Washington in June. Can you get us tickets to the special tour at the White House?"

> "My daughter is going to be thrown out of the Naval Academy and hasn't been given a fair hearing. Could you help her?"

Members of Congress seldom demand a positive response, only that the bureaucrats find their case and/or give it a second look. Cases pursued by congressional offices generally move to the head of the line, since "every administrator moves fast when dealing with a congressman's case" (Gellhorn 1966, 77). Congressional offices are usually allowed to report back on positive results, while the agency sends out bad news. No matter what the outcome, constituents usually appreciate the congressional effort (Frantzich 1986, 55). "The nice thing about casework is that it is mostly profit; one makes many more friends than enemies" (Fiorina 1977a, 68). In the aggregate, it is not clear that extensive casework activity improves electoral security, since Members often emphasize casework as a reaction to past electoral insecurity or in anticipation of future problems (see Johannes

---

[13] The term "ombudsman" originated in the scandinavian countries to describe a special government office reporting to the parliament which helps individuals deal with the bureaucracy. Despite numerous proposals for the creation of such a centralized office, members of Congress prefer to retain this activity solely for themselves.

1984, 187–211; Serra 1992, 231–244; Serra and Cover 1992). Members and their staffs do act as if casework is important and often go out of their way to solicit cases to handle (Yiannakis 1981, 570). Supporters of casework activity point out how it humanizes the government, keeps the bureaucrats on their toes, and provides important first-hand information on how government is working. Opponents question the amount of effort expended, the interference with the orderly operation of the bureaucracy and the potential for favoritism (see box 3.3). (For a further discussion of the arguments, see Frantzich 1986, 57–62; Johannes 1984, passim.)

SEEKING GROUP BENEFITS: PORK AND PREFERMENTS Above and beyond individual cases, members of Congress go to bat for interest groups, businesses, and governmental units in their districts who are seeking relief from government regulations and/or who desire access to government programs, grants, or contracts. Decisions about where to locate a new bulk mail facility, or which military bases to close and which to expand, can seldom be made solely on the basis of objective merits, so **pork barrel politics** often takes over (see box 3.4). Members attempt to assign specific public works projects to their districts, or establish eligibility criteria giving their districts an inside track. "Pork [barrel politics] is spending with a zip code attached to it" (Allen Schick quoted in Kelly 1992, 6). Members often cooperate with each other to get benefits in a process called **"logrolling."**[14] Each Member allows his or her colleague to get district benefits in exchange for similar treatment.

When applications for government benefits are necessary, Members help constituency groups learn about government programs, advise them during the application process, and speak in favor of their application to the appropriate agency. As one Senate staff member argued, Members must constantly make deals and "if you don't play the game, you lose federal dollars for your state" (quoted in Causey 1991, B2). Pork is in the eye of the beholder. Members gaining district benefits justify it as good public policy, while others see it having little rational purpose or justification (see box 3.5).

The political importance of casework and pork barrel politics is not so much the amount of casework and service activity Members undertake, but rather the ability of Members to "credibly present themselves as public servants indispensable to constituent groups" (Dodd and Kelly 1990, 11–12). "Virtually all Congressmen announce with great fanfare the awarding of grants and contracts to groups in their constituencies, and few forget to have their own names mentioned at the same time" (Douglas Arnold quoted in Cain, Ferejohn, and Fiorina 1987, 7). By providing services to constituents, members of Congress build a personal base of support which gives them more electoral security and allows them more freedom when it comes to voting on national policy (see Cain, Ferejohn, and Fiorina 1987, 197).

---

[14] The term comes from the game of skill popular among lumberjacks in which two people must work together to keep their balance on a spinning log.

BOX 3.3 When Some Players Get an Inside Track: The Keating Five Case

> Helping Charles Keating was just like "helping the little lady who didn't get her Social Security Check." (Senator John McCain quoted in Liedl 1990, C4)
>
> This was "just another example of elected officials going to bat for a constituent who appeared to be getting pushed around by bureaucrats." (Senator Dennis DiConcini quoted in Liedl 1990, C4)

Members of Congress are not only allowed, but encouraged to plead the cases of their constituents with the bureaucracy. During the early 1990s, a major ethics investigation raised the question of whether large campaign contributors gained an unfair advantage in having their cases pursued and whether some members of the Senate were being given and/or solicited campaign contributions on the basis of their ability to help campaign contributors.

The five senators investigated by the Ethics Committee (Alan Cranston [D-CA], Dennis DeConcini [D-AZ], John McCain [R-AZ], John Glenn [D-OH], and Donald Riegle [D-MI]) all received significant contributions from Lincoln Savings and Loan owner Charles H. Keating, Jr. In various degrees, each senator intervened on behalf of Mr. Keating's now failed Lincoln Savings and Loan in an attempt to discourage federal regulators. All the senators claimed that they were doing what any senator would do as a part of routine constituent service. Senator Cranston did admit that "A person who makes a contribution has a better chance to get access than someone who does not" (quoted in Cranford 1991, 230), but asserted that the five charged senators were no different than any other senator.

The Senate Ethics Committee divided the senators into three groups. Senators Glenn and McCain were chided for using poor judgement in their intervention but not charged with breaking any rules. Senators DeConcini and Riegle were singled out for using poor judgment and giving the appearance of wrongdoing for pursuing Mr. Keating's interests so vigorously after receiving campaign contributions, but were not charged with breaking any specific rule. Senator Cranston received the most severe treatment for initiating fund-raising activities in exchange for intervention. He announced his intention to not run for re-election and was eventually rebuked, but not formally censured by the Senate (Cranford et al. 1991, 517–527; Berke 1991, 24).

The close link between campaign contributions and constituent intervention struck home for many other senators who began reassessing their own actions. As Senator Cohen (R-ME) put it, "There will be some chilling effect on constituent service, and that's not all bad" (quoted in Kuntz and Hook 1991, 525). Until they could write their own standards, the Senate accepted the standards established by the House in 1970. These standards indicate that it is **proper** for a Member to:

- request information on the status of a case
- urge prompt consideration
- call for reconsideration
- arrange for appointments

In the process, though, the Member should make sure that all constituents are treated equally irrespective of political considerations and that the Member has no right to threaten reprisal against an agency for unsatisfactory handling of the cases he or she refers (Congressional Quarterly *1991, 510*).

BOX 3.4 Winning the Big One for the Home Team

Pork barrel: A political phrase probably derived from the holding tank for salt pork from which slaves would attempt to pick the juiciest cut of meat (Safire 1978, 553). In politics, it has come to mean seeking out and acquiring public works projects for one's district.

"DRAWING A $10 MILLION 'GET OUT OF JAIL FREE' CARD"

Ten million dollars is little more than a "rounding error" on the $271 billion dollar defense spending bill for 1992, but it amounts to one-third of Marywood College's annual budget. One might ask how a small Catholic college ends up in the defense budget with a grant to do unspecified research. Neither the college nor the U.S. Department of Defense asked for the money. The earmarking of these funds on a non-competitive basis makes a little more sense when one realizes that Marywood is in the congressional district of Joseph M. McDade (R-PA), the ranking minority member of the House Appropriations Defense Subcommittee who both initiated the grant idea and inserted it during closed-door negotiations on the bill. Members justify such earmarking as a method of overcoming the unwarranted advantage prestigious universities receive in a competitive process (Congressional Quarterly 1991, 513; Greenberg 1992, A17). The college was of course pleased and outlined its plans to study substance abuse and stress management among military families (see Lancaster 1991, A21). McDade's success in funneling more than $1 billion worth of federal projects into his district insulated him from the electoral repercussions of having been indicted during the campaign on five counts of accepting bribes from lobbyists and military contractors (Hinds 1992, 28L). He won with more than 60 percent of the vote in 1992.

"HEAD 'EM UP, AND MOVE 'EM OUT"

West Virginia may only be west by location, but Senator Robert Byrd (D-WV) was committed to using his position as chairman of the Appropriations Committee to follow the pioneers and move the center of gravity of the federal government "westward ho." Secure in his position and unflappable in his commitment to his constituents, Senator Byrd promised to "bring at least a billion dollars in projects that [he] put in the [appropriations] bill" (Ayres 1991, A16) back to West Virginia. His success in the first year was impressive. More than one-third of the new highway projects funded by Congress was earmarked for West Virginia. He steered more than $750 million in federal government projects and 3,000 federal jobs to West Virginia, including moving the Federal Bureau of Investigation fingerprint center and the Treasury Department's bureau of public debt, lock, stock, and barrel (pork barrel?) to his home state. When the Central Intelligence Agency proposed saving money by moving some of its operations to a lower cost area, a West Virginia site was belatedly added to those under consideration and eventually won agency approval for the 6,000 employee relocation (Jenkins 1992b, A1). Only when the media began talking about Byrd's success in "relocating Washington" did the CIA reconsider (Jenkins 1992b, A1). This was a rare failure for Senator Byrd. He has demonstrated "that he can play the Congressional power game as well as anyone around, especially when it comes to 'pork barrel' politics" (Ayres 1991, A16).

Continued on next page

BOX 3.4 Continued

"TAKING THE LAST TRICK AND SHOWING YOUR CARDS"

Highway "demonstration projects" have a long history as relatively low risk methods for trying out new road building technologies and techniques. In recent years, the number of these projects has increased dramatically (see graph) and "most of the projects demonstrate nothing more than the congressman's ability to get money for his district" (Francis B. Francois, executive director of the American Association of State Highway and Transportation Officials, quoted in Congressional Quarterly 1991, 515). For example, the construction of three parking garages in Chicago was justified with the "innovative" desire to show that such garages would "relieve on-street parking congestions and unsafe parking practices" (Congressional Quarterly 1991, 515). As the following graph indicates, highway demonstration projects have tripled in the last decade.

Highway Demonstration Projects

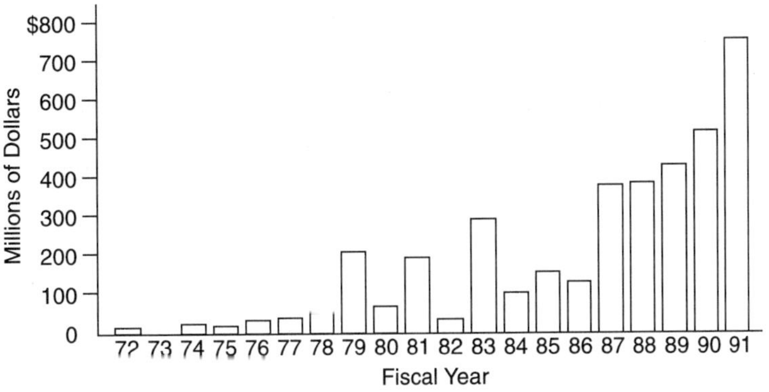

Funds appropriated for highway demonstration projects began to climb in fiscal 1979, when they reached $207.6 million. In fiscal 1991, the projects' price tags more than tripled to $751.4 million.

SOURCE: Mike Mills, "House Travels Favorite Road to Funding Local Highways," *Congressional Quarterly Weekly Report,* 13 July 1991, pp. 1884–1888.

"SUDDEN DEATH OVERTIME"

The annual spring supplemental appropriations bill is designed to take care of "dire emergencies" unanticipated during the passage of the original appropriations bill. Many of the revisions reflect changed conditions or new crises, while others simply reflect Members' desire to use the crises-oriented second chance as a vehicle for funding projects which did not make it in the initial round. Among the 180 changes, the 1990 bill included such "emergencies" as the following:

- building a fish farming experimental laboratory in Stuttgart, Arkansas (promoted by Senator Dale Bumpers [D-AR]).
- $185 million to move the FBI fingerprint facility to West Virginia (pushed by Senator Robert C. Byrd [D-WV]).
- expediting harbor building in Mississippi, building an army ammunition plant in Louisiana that the U.S. Army is not sure it wants, and developing a battery recycling facility in New Jersey (see Morgan 1990, A9).

BOX 3.5 The Members Speak About Pork and Policy

What helps West Virginia, helps the nation. (Senator Robert Byrd [D-WV], the so called "Pontiff of Pork," quoted in Kelly 1992, 45)

This is not what so many of you folks glibly call "pork"; its infrastructure. (Senator Robert Byrd [D-WV] commenting on a $41 million set of research grants for Wheeling Jesuit College—almost three times the college's annual budget, in Jordan 1992, A1)

If that ain't pork, what is? He doesn't want to bring home the bacon; he wants to bring home the whole pig. (Representative Dan Burton [R-IN] opposing one of Senator Robert Byrd's [D-WV] many highway demonstration projects which helped West Virginia with 1 percent of the U.S. population get 50 percent of the demonstration projects; quoted in Mills 1991, 2941. See also Kelly 1992, 44, 234)

"Pork" is an epithet that applies to projects that are not in one's district. . . . I'm trying to represent my area as effectively as I can. (Representative Steny H. Hoyer [D-MD] after acquiring $10 million in military projects for areas added to his district after redistricting; Jenkins 1992b, A1)

For most of his career, [Hoyer] has voted against defense spending. . . . Now he acts like Santa Claus. . . . He is using the powers of incumbency as best he can to buy votes. (Larry Hogan, Steny Hoyer's unsuccessful opponent in the 1992 election; Jenkins 1992b, A14)

ADVERTISING

> They [newsletters] can be sent to every household, hundreds of thousands of them. Any guy with an ounce of sense makes the newsletter a campaign document. (Representative Guy Vander Jagt [R-MI] quoted in Roberts 1987, 65)

Increasingly members of Congress are unwilling to simply respond to constituent inquiries and are embarking on active *outreach* programs using the mail. The **franking privilege**[15] allows Members free use of the mail. Congress sends out five times as much mail as it receives. Only about 4 percent of the outgoing mail involves responses to individual requests from constituents (Kosova 1990, 32). Regular newsletters keep the Member's name and accomplishments before the voters. The inclusion of a questionnaire portrays the impression that the Member cares about constituent opinion and only secondarily may inform the Member of constituent opinion. The return of a questionnaire gives the constituent outreach wheel another spin by leading to a "thank you" letter from most offices, and recording the constituent's name on a new mailing list "of interested voters."

Aside from sending out newsletters to all constituents, most offices develop targeted mailing lists which allow them to send specific messages of interest to segments of the population. Every letter coming into a congressional office is coded on the basis of the issue as well as any information that can be gleaned about the letter

[15] The term "frank" comes from the Latin term "francus," meaning "free." The frank originally applied to mail both *to* and *from* constituents. Currently, members of the House and Senate can send correspondence dealing with their "official duties" free of charge (see U.S. Senate, Committee on Government Affairs 1978; Navasky 1991, 438–439).

writer's occupation, educational level, group memberships, political activity, and/or party identification. These coded lists are augmented with membership lists of organizations, subscription lists of publications, and any other address lists which could identify individuals with common outlooks. Rather than sending a general "Dear Voter" letter, the Member can enhance the chance of having his or her letters read by writing "Dear Politically Independent Environmentally Concerned Small Town Resident Who Reads Sports Magazines" to individuals fitting those characteristics and focusing the letter content on specific issues. Members develop a politically advantageous "pen pal" relationship with those who correspond frequently by putting these correspondents on newsletter and mass mailing lists.

Members of Congress use their franking privilege strategically. The volume of mail goes up considerably during election years. New Members and those who are electorally insecure use the mail more regularly (see Cover 1980, 125). In 1992, House members in tight races spent almost two and one-half times as much on mailings than Members who were retiring (*Washington Post* 1992, A29). Many incumbents spend more on official mailings than their challenger's entire campaign budget (Kosova 1990, 33).

PERKS AND PRIVILEGES Members of Congress receive a number of "perquisites" (**perks**) or benefits of holding office. Most perks are justified for their contribution to making the congressional job easier. Personal benefits such as on-site barber and beauty shops, restaurants, gyms, free medical care, free parking, and a credit union save time for busy Members.[16] As members of the House found out in 1992, when such privileges are afforded at cut rates or without standard controls, the public outcry is vociferous. Although the sloppy way in which the House "bank" was run by allowing uncontrolled overdrafts did not involve any public money, it was the kind of abuse of power that outrages the average voter. After much public outcry, personal perks were trimmed considerably beginning with the 103rd Congress.

Congressional pay has also become an issue in recent years. While a salary of more than $130,000 per year sounds impressive, it is important to point out that many Members would be making more in the private sector, especially considering the financial demands of office holding and the need to maintain two households. The growing cynicism toward Congress led to ratification of the 27th Amendment in 1992[17] denying members of Congress the right to accept a pay raise until they had faced the voters in a subsequent election.

---

[16] Before you immediately dismiss such benefits as illegitimate, remember that your status as student often affords you some of the same privileges. You could be forced to join a health club instead of using the campus gym, be required to go to the U.S. post office rather than the campus mail room, or not be given access to a campus health center. On many campuses, it has been decided that cost and convenience legitimizes student access to such services.

[17] This amendment holds the record for the longest period for state ratification. It was first proposed by James Madison in 1789, but failed to get enough state legislatures to ratify it. Concern over the congressional pay raises in the early 1990s led to a renewed effort. Despite some constitutional question about timely ratification, the anti-Congress mood led to its rapid acceptance.

Other perks, such as travel allowances for district visits, receive less public scrutiny. Currently members of the House and Senate are given allowances providing for almost weekly trips back to their districts on government funds.[18] Junior Members, and those who are more politically insecure, tend to take most advantage of the travel opportunities. District trips are limited to "official purposes," but once back in the district for official functions more political events can be added to the agenda.

Drawing the line between unjustifiable perks and necessary resources for doing the job of a representative or senator is difficult. But it is only one of the challenges new Members face.

ADAPTING TO THE HUMAN ENVIRONMENT: LEARNING THE SOCIAL RULES

Congress is a social institution which welcomes and rewards individuals on the basis of their ability to "fit in." As players in a **continuous game,** Members realize they will repeatedly need each other. Since today's opponent might well be tomorrow's compatriot, it becomes important to establish an extensive set of rules to structure the relationships. These social rules or norms outline expected patterns of behavior.[19] Far from being hollow legalisms, norms have developed to help both the Members and the institution function more smoothly. Over time, some norms change as Congress adapts to a new type of Member and an altered environment. Among the most abiding norms are the following:

> *Courtesy:* Members of Congress must work together day in and day out. The more personal animosities can be harnessed, the more likely policy conflicts can be worked out. Members reduce the sting of personal attack by referring to their colleagues as "the senior Senator from New York," or "my esteemed colleague from California," even when they disagree with them completely. While there is some evidence that comity and courtesy in Congress has declined in recent years with the election of a "new breed" of more aggressive partisans (Uslander 1990, passim), few members of Congress attempt to pick fights.
>
> *Reciprocity:* Far from being a dirty word, compromise is a necessity for survival in Congress. While the "you scratch my back and I'll scratch yours" approach seems self serving, it underlies the ability to forge a compromise. Members are expected to "be reasonable" and give a little on one issue, and then expect a reciprocal flexibility from colleagues on issues they feel are important. Members informally "keep book" on who owes them and whom they owe.
>
> *Reliability:* Reciprocity and accommodation only work to the degree that the subsidiary norm of *keeping true to one's word* can be anticipated. Members accept the fact that colleagues will oppose them on some issues, but rarely forgive a Member who makes a commitment and then breaks it (see box 3.6).

---

[18] Members are given allowances for travel, postage, equipment lease, telecommunications, and stationery. The figures are adjusted for variations in travel and communications costs. The totals averaged $173,500 for House members and $269,000 for Senators in 1991 (Ornstein, Mann, and Malbin 1992, 140–143).

[19] The literature on congressional norms is relatively extensive. The norms of the Senate were first outlined in a detailed fashion by Donald R. Matthews in *U.S. Senators and Their World,* 1964, Chapel Hill: University of North Carolina Press 1964.

Members of Congress often do not see the seeming inconsistency of criticizing Congress and fighting to remain a Member.

Reprinted by permission: Tribune Media Services

> *Institutional loyalty:* Members of both chambers are expected to refrain from criticizing their own chamber and temper their criticism of Congress as a whole. Members such as Joseph McCarthy (D-WI in 1954), Adam Clayton Powell (D-NY in 1967), and Alan Cranston (D-CA in 1991) were rebuked by their colleagues for bringing discredit to their chamber more than for any specific acts. The growing number of Members who have run *for* Congress by running *against* Congress has strained the norm of institutional loyalty. The move to limit congressional terms has encouraged some Members to distance themselves from the institution of which they are a part.

Serving an **apprenticeship** and **specializing** in a limited number of topics are not the requirement anymore (see Schneier 1988, 117; Rohde 1988, 139; Rohde et al., 1985, 179). New Members of both chambers jump into the political battle early, without serving an apprenticeship period. Senators are not looked down upon for taking an interest in a wide variety of policy areas.

BOX 3.6 The Members Speak About Reliability

Voting commitments are considered sacrosanct in Congress. During a heated debate on the Clean-Air Bill, Senator Robert Byrd [D-WV] proposed an amendment to provide job-loss benefits to coal miners. Senator Byrd, normally an assiduous vote counter, thought he had the fifty necessary votes lined up. When he fell one vote short, his temper flared and he said,

> I went to many offices and said, "I need your vote." Two or three who were uncertain went with me . . . [but] three of my votes took wings [at which point he flapped his arms] and went with the boys downtown [in the White House]. (quoted in Kuntz and Hager 1990, 984)

New members of the congressional game learn these norms by observation, at practical orientation sessions given by academic institutions and party organizations,[20] and through trial and error. Members arriving with state legislative experience have a better understanding of the norms and therefore are more effective as legislators (see Asher 1973, 131; Canon 1990, 158). Ideologically extreme Members tend to be more willing to violate the established norms (Asher 1973, 129). There is some evidence that the democratization of power in Congress has lessened the ability of senior leaders to enforce norms through the threat of punishment. The numerous trips back to the district and the mandated "district work periods" which take Members away from Washington and their colleagues also reduce the power of socially enforced rules. When asked what the biggest change in Congress had been since he was first elected, former Senator Russell Long (D-LA) stated,

> Going to Congress used to be like going to camp. We all stayed for the duration. We worked together all week and spent most of our weekends together. Now with the jet airplane you hardly get to know your colleagues and what they expect. (author's interview)

Members who break the norms early in their congressional careers are counselled by senior colleagues, that "We don't do things like that around here." Members who continue to break the rules are labelled as troublemakers and find their effectiveness diminished.

DEALING WITH ISSUES: STRATEGIES FOR SURVIVAL

Constituents are not obsessed with policy congruence between their preferences and the votes of their Members (Cain, Ferejohn, and Fiorina 1987, 51). Limited public awareness of individual votes in Congress gives Members considerable leeway on most votes. The political problem for Members is that they never know which votes will attract enough attention to threaten electoral survival. Legislators regularly anticipate how specific votes might be used against them in the next election and plan ways in which to explain their behavior should questions arise (see Arnold 1990, 9; Kingdon 1989, 47–54). Members of Congress attempt to thwart policy voting by making it difficult for voters to identify their actions. Key decisions are often made behind closed doors, and many votes in Congress are done by voice and with no permanent record kept of how individual Members voted (see chapter 5). **Omnibus legislation** provides a strategy for hiding a variety of proposals in one all-purpose bill. Both the legislator and the voter must take the good with the bad in such legislation (Arnold 1990, 102). The ability to "cover one's tracks" frustrates some of the players. Former Representative (and later Secretary of De-

---

[20] In recent years, Members have been invited to orientation sessions sponsored by the Committee on House Administration, the John F. Kennedy School at Harvard (a policy think tank), the Democratic Study Group (the liberal congressional caucus), the Republican Study Committee (a conservative congressional caucus), the Congressional Management Foundation (a nonpartisan management consulting organization), and the Free Congress Foundation (a conservative think tank).

fense) Richard Cheney (R-WY) argued that "incumbents are re-elected because of the way they can hide their policy decisions. Irresponsibility in turn breeds bad policy" (*Congressional Record,* 24 May 1988, H3591).

Whatever the specific mix of causes, members of Congress tend to survive from one round to the next. Despite public frustration over specific policies and general congressional performance (see chapter 6) each new team of players is likely to include a strong representation from last year's team.

THE CONSEQUENCES OF THE SURVIVAL GAME

Both the growth of careerism and the utility of the various survival techniques come into clear focus when looking at the electoral success of incumbents. Few incumbents lose, and when they do, observers can usually find a personal failing in the form of an ethical transgression or a particularly inept pattern of voting to explain the anomaly.

Throughout history incumbents have always had an advantage when running for re-election. While the advantage is slightly greater today, the major change lies in the percentage of incumbents choosing to parlay their advantages into another term. During the nineteenth century only 60 to 70 percent of incumbents chose to run for reelection, while the percentages during the twentieth century increased to 85 to 95 percent (Huckabee 1989, 1). Since World War II, the desire for re-election has remained relatively constant. The biggest change is associated with the increase in incumbent skills and the set of resources they have to invest in their re-election bid (see Fiorina 1977b, 67). Incumbents do not win simply because they are incumbents, but rather because they have learned to use the resources of incumbency and to keep their public actions within the acceptable realm. Incumbents are not free to thumb their noses at their constituents. As Douglas Arnold points out,

> If the legislators consulted the scholarly literature on congressional elections, they might conclude that they need not worry much about either the position that they take or the effects they produce because they are not the major determinants of electoral outcomes. This would be a dangerous conclusion. It would be equivalent to concluding that one need not file a tax return because the Internal Revenue Service prosecutes only a few thousand individuals each year for tax evasion. The problem is that legislators as a group have not offered congressional scholars much to analyze. No legislators have offered to take positions directly opposite to their electoral interests so that we may measure the full impact of positions on electoral margins. (Arnold 1990, 37)

The American political system is faced with voters who only irregularly get "turned on" by specific issues, and legislators with heterogeneous districts who take perceived constituent interests into account when voting and who harness all the other resources of political office to keep their names in front of their constituents in a positive way. "The incumbency advantage results from the ability of incumbents to focus attention on aspects of their job performance that generate favorable constituent evaluation of their performance" (Parker 1980, 461). Most constituents cast a "personal vote" for congressional candidates based on their actual or anticipated constituent service and attention to the district (Cain, Ferejohn, and Fiorina 1987, 51). Incumbents obviously have the advantage of a proven track record in this realm.

The degree of concern over the uneven playing field of incumbent advantages varies. The desire for continuity and expertise provided by high incumbent reelection rates comes into conflict with the desire for responsiveness and innovation which is stilted by the lack of turnover. In recent years, concern over incumbent reelection rates has focused on the issue of legally limiting the number of terms a Member might serve.

Writing two centuries ago James Madison built a strong case for the advantage of naturally reigning in the ambition of politicians to stay in office. He felt that the public's mandate would be thwarted if politicians were not relatively unfettered in their ability to capture and retain their seats (see Fowler and McClure 1989, 238). In Madison's words,

> Those ties which bind the representative to his constituents are strengthened by motives more selfish in nature. His pride and vanity attach him to a form of government which favors his pretensions and gives him a share in its honors and distinctions. . . . Duty, gratitude, interest, ambition itself are the chords by which they [representatives] will be bound to fidelity and sympathy with the great mass of the people. (*Federalist #57*)

A more recent analysis of performance in office (Hibbing 1991, 179–180) comes to the conclusion that members of Congress become more competent over their careers, and term limitations would strip Congress of some of its most effective Members. George Will points out that "compulsory rotation out of office would bring in 'fresh faces,' but another name for them is 'rookies': people with a lot to learn in a town where there is a lot to learn" (Will 1990, B7).[21] Representative Al Swift (D-WA) questions the conventional wisdom of a "permanent Congress" and asserts that

> a clear majority of the nation's citizens have chosen a new congressman or congresswoman once during the 1980s. . . . We have exactly what we should expect of the "people's house": a regular infusion of new faces reflecting the current mood of the voters they represent." (Swift 1989, A9)

David Broder, on the other hand, laments that "the Constitution envisaged the House as the most sensitive barometer of changes in political mood, but the 'incumbent lock' makes it no barometer at all" (Broder 1988, A21).

Like many political issues, the unevenness of the playing field galls those most disadvantaged. The Democrats, with their large number of congressional incumbents, find virtue in "continuity and consistency instead of having a revolving

[21]To be fair, it must be pointed out that columnist George Will changed his mind. In 1991, he reversed himself and concluded that "more talent is excluded from public service by clotting the system with immovable incumbents—and by the atrophy of the talents of incumbents once interested in things other than job security—than would be lost by term limits" (Will 1991, 102).

door district" (Democratic Congressional Campaign Committee spokesperson quoted in Frazier 1988). Republicans, on the other hand, bemoan what they perceive as an unfair and unrepresentative system favoring incumbents:

> The concern is what has happened in terms of skewing the playing field of politics. Elections are not where one individual suits up on January 1 in an election year, and the other individual suits up on January 1, and they both take the field to play the game. No, incumbents are suited up a year ahead of time because they are using taxpayers money. (Representative William Thomas [R-CA], *Congressional Record,* 26 September 1990, H8062)

CONCLUSION

Each new Congress welcomes a relatively small group of new players, most of whom pretty much resemble the Members they replaced in terms of social background and political experience. Patterns of motivation and opportunity make it significantly easier for middle-aged, well-educated, white men with experience in business or law to successfully vie for election to Congress.

Members of Congress increasingly view service in the legislative branch as a continuous game with numerous rounds and guide their behavior by that expectation. In the desire to stay in office, Members marshall staff resources and expend personal effort to accomplish the tasks voters expect and to make sure that voters know of their efforts. For incumbents desiring to stay, electoral office is something lost by mistakes or inattention rather than won by a challenger.

IN DEPTH

1. The change over time in the social background characteristics of Congress is dramatic. Take two congresses separated by at least fifty years and compare the aggregate distribution of social background characteristics such as age, occupation, and education. Using the biographies in the *Congressional Directory* for the chosen years, sample every fourth member of the House or every second member of the Senate to gather your data. Summarize your data in a chart or graph. In your paper, discuss the key causes and consequences of the patterns you discover.

2. The imposition of term limitations would undermine the survival game discussed in this chapter. Outline the changes you would expect if members of Congress were limited to twelve years in office.

CHAPTER FOUR

ORGANIZING FOR ACTION

Party, Committee, and Policy Teams within the Congressional Arenas

We on this side of the aisle could play the partisan game. We could support this amendment, and we could then have the President and the Secretary of State and the Secretary of Defense out into an embarrassing position, because they know full well they cannot sustain the gentleman's amendment. (Representative Curt Weldon [R-PA], *Congressional Record,* September 9, 1992, H6539)

The Democratic Party is taking responsibility for all of [the policy agenda] today. We have been elected. Our President was elected. We have majorities in the Congress and are about to do things that have been put off so long because of the blame game, and the gridlock and the inability to have a consistent view. (Representative Vic Fazio [D-CA], *Congressional Record,* September 23, 1993, H2980)

I know that sometimes, in conference with the House, we look at this as sort of a little game to see what we can give and we get something in return. Sometimes legislating in conference is not unheard of . . . we get in there and someone brings up something that was not actually passed on the floor of either the House or the Senate and we wind up accepting that in conference. (Senator John Glenn [D-OH], *Congressional Record,* July 14, 1993, S8677)

Most of the action attributed to Congress stems from actions taken by its sub-units. Congress consists of "teams" of players who take on important tasks. The concept of "teams" implies the intentional joining together of players to act as a group. The various teams in Congress make conflicting demands on the time and loyalty of Members. Members of Congress make significant choices concerning the action-oriented teams with which to affiliate and the degree to which they will grant these teams their loyalty. Committees draw together individuals with common policy interests, while political party allegiances frame many policy divisions. Other teams form around common constituency and/or policy concerns.

The team orientation of the modern Congress is somewhat more strained than in the past. Members "run **for** Congress by running **against** Congress." Candidate-centered campaigns emphasize self-reliance as opposed to team loyalty. Changes in American political culture, campaign laws, and accepted political strategies have led to more individualistic Members who use their personal entrepreneurial skills to win office and pursue policy. Congress is, "a group of individuals rather than a collective whole" (Hertzke and Peters 1992, 3). These members of the House and Senate are atomistic, that is, they associate with various teams, using them as a means to reach their more individualistic goals.

A newly elected member of Congress soon finds that he or she is selected by some teams and must decide with which other teams to associate. Different teams not only involve different players, but they also have unique rules, strategies, and patterns of winning and losing. The outcome of the policy process results from the interplay of the various teams and their leading players.

CHAMBER LEADERS

Power within most institutions is not evenly divided. Some individuals have the ability to achieve their goals through personal skills and/or access to rewards or sanctions. Each chamber has a set of leaders who organize action and mediate conflicts.

CHOOSING CHAMBER LEADERS

Individuals holding formal positions of power have proven their skills and are granted the legal authority to take certain actions. Two parallel and often intertwined sets of leadership positions coexist in Congress: formal chamber leaders and party leaders are distinct on paper, but less distinct in action.

Formal Senate Chamber Leaders

The constitutionally mandated presiding officer of the Senate is the vice president of the United States. In reality, vice presidents spend very little time presiding over the Senate, and generally only show up for close votes in which their power to break a tie might make a difference. The **president pro tempore,** or someone he designates presides over the Senate on a daily basis in the absence of the vice president. In recent years, the majority party has nominated its most senior member as president pro tempore (or pro tem), and the Senate has approved its choice. As presiding officer, the president pro tem has, by tradition, been expected to act in a fair and objective manner. While a prestigious position, the president pro tem is clearly overshadowed by the more partisan majority leader.

Formal Leadership in the House

The **Speaker** of the House is more clearly a product of the leadership winnowing process of the majority party than the more seniority based selection process for the Senate's president pro tempore. Party majority leaders generally move up the speakership when a vacancy occurs (Peabody 1976, 31–33). The Speaker is not only the constitutionally mandated presiding officer of the House, but is also clearly seen as the spokesperson for the party. The Speaker presides over significant debates, recognizing Members and ruling on procedural questions.[1] The Speaker also plays a significant role in appointing Members to committees, refers bills to committees, and appoints conference committees which work out compromises between the two chambers. The tradition of strict objectivity and non-partisanship applies less to the Speaker than the president pro tempore of the Senate. The role of the Speaker has changed over time. The autocratic Speakers of earlier this century were replaced by Speakers presiding over an institution dominated by a feudal distribution of power. The contemporary Speaker must manage a more open and democratic institution (see Peters 1990, 207–216 passim).

Within the House and Senate arenas, Members affiliate with colleagues in a variety of teams. The performance of these teams is affected by the context of each arena, but depends more on the size, composition, and loyalty of each team.

THE PARTY TEAMS

Virtually all members of Congress arrive with significant ties to one of the political parties.[2] Candidates get on the ballot by winning their party's nomination in the primaries and often receive important campaign support from the party organization.

ORGANIZING THE PARTIES IN CONGRESS

Shortly after each election, the existing party leaders call their Members together for a **caucus**[3] to decide on party policy and make party and committee leadership selections. The parties in each chamber select a Policy and Steering Committee to establish and coordinate the party's legislative program.[4] The four Congressional

---

[1]Rulings of the chair can be overturned by the House, but this rarely occurs.

[2]The only exception during recent congresses has been Bernie Sanders, the former Socialist Party mayor of Burlington, Vermont. Elected as an independent, Representative Sanders was initially given his committee assignments by the Speaker, but now caucuses with the Democrats.

[3]The Republicans in the House and the Senate prefer to call their party meeting a "conference" as opposed to a caucus.

[4]The Republicans in the House divide the policy coordination and research functions and have a separate Research Committee.

(or Senatorial) Campaign Committees raise funds and provide advice to party candidates. The major work of the policy and campaign committees is done by paid staffs under the direction of a small group of elected senators or representatives (Patterson and Little 1992, 21).

From the day they arrive on Capitol Hill, new Members are constantly reminded that they are part of a party team. The party caucus orients them to the chamber. The route to favorable committee assignments is through recommendation by their party's committee on committees. Seating on the floor of each chamber is by party, with Democrats to the left and Republicans to the right of the aisle as one faces the presiding officer.[5]

When it comes to policy, the party policy organizations are advisory rather than coercive. Party organizations provide relevant information and services to their Members. They often use task forces to study issues and attempt to foster the emergence of a consensus on an issue by involving a larger percentage of the players (Patterson and Little 1992, 10). Individuals who feel part of the policy development team are more likely to put aside their own reservations and show loyalty to the organization (see Sinclair 1983, 172–174). The tradition of binding caucuses in which the minority within a party is required to follow the majority decision, found in some states, is not the pattern in Congress. More recent research (Rohde 1991, 67–69) reveals how the Democratic Caucus in the House was transformed during the 1980s into an effective coordinating mechanism.

THE FUNCTIONS OF PARTY LEADERS

> The principal duty of the leadership is janitorial. (Former Majority Leader Howard Baker [R-TN] quoted in the *Congressional Record,* 98th Congress, 2nd Session, 1984, S4877)

Senator Baker's statement that leaders serve others as much as they are served represents the situation in Congress well. Party leaders have the following responsibilities:

- managing the affairs of the party
- influencing the scheduling of floor debate[6]
- monitoring floor proceedings
- serving as a conduit to the other chamber and the White House
- acting as the public voice of their party to the media (see Davidson 1985, 236).

---

[5]The tradition which gave rise to liberals as "left wing" and conservatives as "right wing" originated in nineteenth century parliaments in which the conservative nobility was given the place of honor to the King's right, and the representatives of the liberal masses relegated to the left.

[6]In the Senate, the majority leader actually does the scheduling, while in the House the Rules Committee formally takes on the task of scheduling. Leaders in the House must negotiate with their colleagues on the Rules Committee for favorable scheduling.

ELECTING TEAM CAPTAINS: CHOOSING PARTY LEADERSHIP

To be freely selected as a leader in an institution rife with policy conflict and filled with strong-willed, highly ambitious individuals is quite a task. Members of Congress are quick to measure a potential leader's abilities, openness, and fairness. Lower level leadership positions are used to test the mettle of would-be leaders. Increasingly the television age has encouraged the parties to choose leaders able to represent party interests effectively on the electronic media (Cook 1989, 101). Former Senate Majority Leader George Mitchell (D-ME) and House Speaker Newt Gingrich (R-GA) both won their leadership positions partly on the basis of their ability to use the media (see Elving 1989, 722 and Hook 1989c, 1376). With the retirement of Minority Leader Robert Michel (R-IL) in 1994, Newt Gingrich's success as a public spokesman for the party placed him in a good position to become Speaker when the Republicans won the majority of seats in 1994.

Lower Level Party Functionaries

Would-be leaders most often start out as party **whips,** tasked with gathering information on voting intentions of party members and getting them to the floor for key votes.[7] The parties in each chamber have a chief whip and a series of assistant whips who are assigned to particular geographic regions. In recent years, the size of the whip organizations has increased with almost 40 percent of members serving as whips (Patterson and Little 1992, 11). Satisfactory performance of the whip task allows one to move up the whip organization and/or into more important party leadership positions. Party leaders have traditionally been expected to forego some of their independence in favor of party loyalty, but not all divergence gets punished (see box 4.1).

Intermediate Party Leaders

Becoming chief whip, chairperson of the caucus, chairperson of the Campaign Committee or chairperson of the policy committee requires being elected by the caucus[8] and indicates that one is clearly on the leadership ladder. These positions are the breeding and training ground for becoming Speaker, majority leader, and/or minority leader (see Kolodny 1991, 2). Selection for these important "stepping stone" positions involves more than presenting one's credentials to his[9] or her colleagues for evaluation. Above and beyond running on abilities and issue positions, potential leaders actively campaign for party office. Favors such as speaking

---

[7]The term "whip" comes from the horseback rider in a fox hunt who serves as the "whipper in," keeping the dogs from straying.

[8]The Democrats in the Senate allow the majority leader to appoint the chairman of the Senatorial Campaign Committee.

[9]So far all major elected party leaders in Congress have been men. With the increase of women elected in 1992, there was growing pressure to select women. Senate Majority Leader George Mitchell appointed Barbara Mikulski (D-MD) Assistant Democratic Floor Leader, making her the highest ranking woman in Congress.

BOX 4.1 Striking Out at the Home Team

Some of the younger House leaders are unwilling to forgo their personal preferences for the sake of the party team. In 1991, Republican Whip Newt Gingrich was diametrically opposed to the tax increases in the budget compromise agreed to by President Bush. He declared that on this vote "the Whip's office is closed," and proceeded to "take a walk" on this tough vote (see Broder 1990, D7). Despite such team disloyalty, there were no apparent repercussions.

In 1993, a similar situation developed within the Democratic Party. Democratic whip David Bonior (D-MI) has a cartoon on his wall of a dejected baseball player with the caption "Babe Ruth struck out 1,330 times" to remind him that "you don't always win in sports or life" (Merida 1993a, C14). Bonior, the master of the "inside game" (Merida 1993a, C14) of passing information and lining up votes for his party, found himself in the uncomfortable position of disagreeing with the North American Free Trade Agreement (NAFTA) which was heavily supported by President Clinton. Fearing massive losses of jobs in his constituency, Bonior became one of the prime organizers against the President, and the normal Democratic whip organization was "sidelined for this legislative battle" (Cooper 1993a, A26). The President went on to win the battle despite Bonior's opposition, and Bonior slipped right back into his supportive role on subsequent votes.

Such breakings of team ranks as outlined previously, receive significant publicity because they are the exception rather than the rule. No team could exist very long if its leaders would not—or could not—lead.

in a colleague's district or helping raise funds have become common. After the 1992 election, House Speaker Tom Foley (D-WA) and other current party leaders traveled around the country to personally congratulate and provide media exposure to several newly elected House members, a tactic designed to endear himself and his leadership team to new members of the caucus (Cooper and Dewar 1992, A18). A number of recent battles have involved the use of leadership PACs, in which aspiring leaders contributed generously to colleagues in need of campaign funds (see Baker 1989b, 1–18 passim; Alston 1991b, 2663). Like most campaigns, incumbent party leaders are difficult to disengage except when major scandals arise.[10] The departure of top leaders and the ascent of intermediate leaders into new positions sets in motion a "game of musical chairs" (White and Brewer 1992, 1) to fill the newly opened positions.

Top Party Team Leaders

The Speaker of the House, and the majority and minority leaders in the House and Senate hold key positions for guiding their parties. The powers of the leaders to speak for the party, help assign colleagues to committees, provide strategic information, schedule legislation, and rule on parliamentary procedure assures that members of the House and Senate will show considerable interest in who leads their team (see box 4.2).

When the party controls the presidency, party leaders take on the task of speaking for the president. House Republican leader Robert Michel (R-IL) called himself "a servant of the president" during the Bush and Reagan years (Hornblower 1981, A1). At the same time, Senate Republican leader Howard Baker (R-TN) expressed similar sentiments when he called himself "the president's spear carrier in the Senate" (Baker 1983, S11029). Senator Bob Dole (R-KN) talked about "carrying water" for the administration and being "part of the team" (quoted in Bates 1987, 106). After the 1992 election, House Speaker Tom Foley revealed his own leadership challenge when he pointed out that "Democrats have a special commitment to seeing that this new administration succeeds" (Duncan 1992, 3656). Journalists talked about the Democratic leadership as the president's "point men" (Krauss 1992, A15). Even junior party Members recognize the need to support one's president. House Freshman Bob Filner (D-CA) responded to Foley's challenge by saying,

> The ball is in our court, and we're going to run with it. We feel the responsibility. We're going to show the American voters that a Democratic president and a Democratic Congress can in fact deal with real issues facing the nation. (quoted in Duncan 1992, 3656)

---

[10] In 1989, two key Democratic leaders were forced to resign. Speaker Jim Wright (D-TX) was charged with technical violations of misusing public funds and taking advantage of his office, charges he might have withstood if he had not made so many enemies because of his partisanship (see Peters 1990, 276–278). A few weeks later, the Democratic Congressional Campaign Committee Chair, Tony Coehlo (D-CA) was forced to resign in 1989 being charged with questionable investment practices (Congressional Quarterly 1989, 41).

BOX 4.2 The Players Speak about Party Leadership

The importance of the top party leadership is not always obvious as party members seek to portray an image of independence and objectivity. When the party leadership process breaks down, its normal importance is highlighted. After Speaker Jim Wright was forced to resign during the 101st Congress (1989) under the cloud of ethics charges, a party colleague said,

> The first year of a Congress is like the first half of a football game. When you change coaches in the middle of the first quarter, you are bound to have trouble putting together a new game plan. (David Obey [D-WI] quoted in Hook 1989a, 2093)

In explaining the early failures of the new set of House Democratic leaders during the 101st Congress, colleagues pointed out the difficulty of their ascension and revealed their optimism about the ability of the leadership to learn. As one party colleague put it,

> A football team improves 100 percent between its first and second game. Win or lose, we learn a lot about the players. (Richard J. Durbin [D-IL], quoted in Hook 1989b, 2529)

Speaker Thomas Foley (D-WA) was quick to point out the difficulty of leading the contemporary Congress made up of independent individuals:

> Things are much more complicated in society, not just in Congress. We are in a more participatory society. . . . The acceptance of hierarchy and authority is much less clear. (quoted in Cohen 1992, 118)

Dan Rostenkowski (D-IL), then-chairman of the powerful tax writing Ways and Means Committee put the relationship between a congressional leader and a president of his party more graphically when he described a meeting with newly elected Bill Clinton:

> I put my hands on his shoulders and I said, "Bill, I'm going to be your quarterback and you're my 600-pound gorilla of a fullback moving these bills." (quoted in Broder 1992, A9)

After regaining the presidency in 1992, Democratic leaders expressed concern over their ability to shift gears from being the loyal opposition to controlling both branches of government. As William Ford (D-MI), a senior committee chairman put it,[11]

> What you're doing is trying to take a football team that only ever played defense and asking them to play offense. I'm telling them, "Let's not launch any great offense and start running our own plays until the coach tells us what he wants us to do." [And when the president calls the wrong play] you go back and talk to the coach. You don't go to the field and say, "We ran that play in the last game and got knocked on our. . . ." (quoted in Cooper 1993b, A8)

[11]The careful reader will note the emphasis on contact sports in these descriptions. This reflects the male domination of Congress in both overall composition and leadership.

When the party is out of power, congressional leaders of the party in Congress take on a more active role as the national spokespersons for the party. Bob Dole (R-KS), Republican party leader, made the best out of the Republican defeat in 1992 when he pointed out that when your party is out of power "you sort of get to pick your shots. . . . But if you're out there for the Administration, every day is a new bucket of water" (quoted in Clymer 1993, B10).

While top leaders are not chosen solely for the longevity in office, modern leaders are some of the most senior members of their respective parties. This generally means that leaders represent safe seats.[12] Top party leaders have tended to be ideological moderates trusted by all segments of their party team. In recent years, both parties have been somewhat more willing to choose more ideologically extreme members. Current Speaker Newt Gingrich (R-GA) is one of the more conservative members of Congress, while Democratic Whip David Bonior (D-MI) votes in a quite liberal manner. The choice as a top party leader is generally the last step on a progressively narrow recruitment ladder. House Speakers almost always ascend from the majority leader position. Majority and minority leaders have generally proven themselves in one of the intermediate party positions. Leadership contests tend to be internal affairs in which colleagues evaluate the personality and skills of their contenders, rather than contests marked by public or external intervention (see Peabody 1976, 470–476; Brown and Peabody 1984, 193).

Although party team leaders share numerous characteristics, their own personalities affect the way they lead their colleagues. Former House Speaker Tom Foley (D-WA) emphasizes cautious conciliation as opposed to the brash and conflictual approach of his predecessor Jim Wright (D-TX) or the back room politics of Tip O'Neill (D-MA), one of the last of the old urban "pols." Previous Senate Majority Leader George Mitchell (D-ME) was certainly less colorful than his predecessor Robert Byrd (D-WV) known for his impassioned rhetoric and detailed discourses on philosophy and Senate history. Neither Mitchell nor Byrd used the repertoire of leadership tactics of Lyndon Johnson (D-TX) known for the "Johnson Treatment," a combination of threats, supplications, factual evidence, emotional cajolery, and physical manipulation depending on the targeted senator (see Evans and Novak 1967, 104 and Shuman 1991, 215).

---

[12]An exception was House Republican Leader and aspiring Speaker Newt Gingrich (R-GA) who survived a very close general election race in 1990 and a stiff primary challenge in 1992. These challenges came *after* his selection to the leadership by one vote, and to some degree were caused by Gingrich's outspoken conservatism and charges that he was spending so much time on his leadership tasks that he had "lost touch" with the district. After all these close calls, one Democratic party leader lamented that watching Gingrich survive is "like losing the pennant by one game two years in a row" (Edsall 1992, A13).

Senate Majority Leader Lyndon B. Johnson gives "The Treatment" to Senator Theodore Francis Green, D-RI.

Reprinted with special permission of King Features Syndicate.

PARTY TEAMS IN ACTION

> When the President says it is a deal, then it is a deal, while at the other end of Pennsylvania Avenue [Congress], it is very difficult for the leadership to deliver on their part of the deal. (James Miller, III, President Reagan's director of the Office of Management and Budget, quoted in Clark 1988, 22)

Although parties play an increasingly diminished, although not insignificant, role in the election process, Members think of themselves as Democrats or Republicans, accept much of their party's ideology, and normally represent typical party districts. A survey of members of the 103rd Congress bears out the differences in party perspectives. Eighty-three percent of Democratic lawmakers thought jobs were one of the most important issues with which to deal compared to 70 percent of Republicans. On the other hand, 78 percent of Republican lawmakers would target the deficit for attention, while only 64 percent of the Democrats would target that issue. Democratic lawmakers were also much more likely to target issues such as health care, education and welfare. Republican lawmakers were more likely to be concerned about high taxes, defense, and foreign policy (Morin 1992a, A21).

The level of party conflict and cohesion in congressional floor voting is quite modest when compared with other national legislatures where most important votes reveal stringent partisan divisions. Only about half of the recorded floor votes in the U.S. Congress find a majority of Republicans opposing a majority of Democrats, with partisan divisions somewhat more likely in the House than in the Senate (see table 4.1). On the individual level, party identification remains a powerful predictor of votes which split the parties (see Bullock and Brady 1983, 29; Patterson and Caldeira 1988, 111). The average Member supports the party more than 75 percent of the time. House members are somewhat more supportive of their party than Senators and the majority party more cohesive than the minority (see figure 4.1).

TABLE 4.1 Party Unity Votes in the House and Senate, 1980–1993

	House	***Senate***
1980	38	46
1981	37	48
1982	36	43
1983	56	44
1984	47	40
1985	61	51
1986	57	52
1987	64	41
1988	47	42
1989	55	35
1990	49	54
1991	55	49
1992	64	53
1993	66	67

Note: Data indicate the percentage of all recorded votes on which a majority of voting Democrats opposed a majority of voting Republicans

SOURCE: Norman J. Ornstein, Thomas E. Mann, and Michael J. Malbin, *Vital Statistics on Congress, 1993–1994,* p. 200, Congressional Quarterly, Inc., 1994; *Congressional Quarterly Weekly Report* (18 December 1993): 3432.

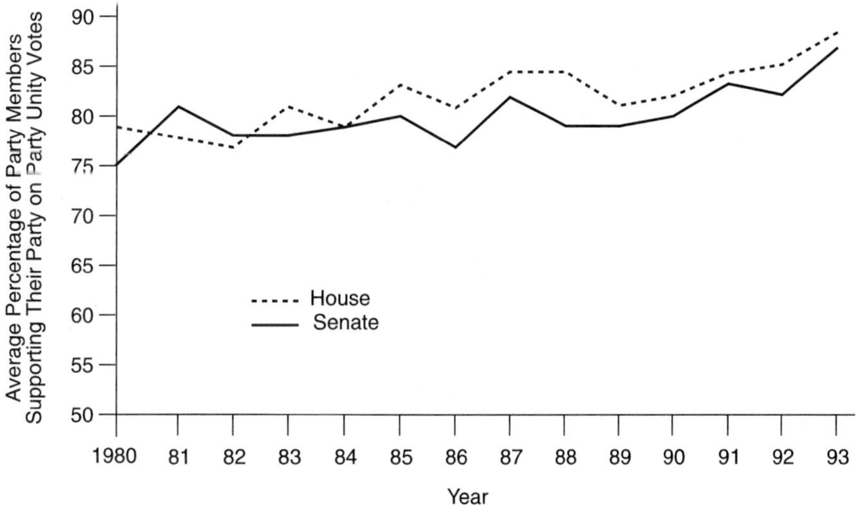

FIGURE 4.1
Party Unity Scores in the House and Senate, 1980–1993. Party unity votes are those recorded votes on which a majority of voting Democrats opposed a majority of voting Republicans. The effects of absences are eliminated.

SOURCE: Norman J. Ornstein, Thomas E. Mann, and Michael J. Malbin, *Vital Statistics on Congress: 1993–1994,* p. 202, Congressional Quarterly, Inc., 1994; *Congressional Quarterly Almanac,* 1993; *Congressional Quarterly Weekly Report* (18 December 1995): 3432.

BOX 4.3 The Members Speak about the Changing Party Team

In an orientation for new Members, Representative Michael Kirwin (D-OH), a senior party leader, warned the new Members about the greatest danger that could befall a new member of Congress. Former Speaker Thomas Foley remembers leaning forward to hear whether this was some ethical trap or other, but heard Kirwin say,

> Thinking for yourselves. That is the single greatest danger. Maybe, if it is a small matter within your own constituency, go ahead. Otherwise, trust the Subcommittee Chair. Trust the Committee Chairman. Trust the Chairman of the Democratic Caucus. Trust the Whip. Trust the majority Leader, and especially pray God, trust the Speaker. (Federal News Service transcript, LEXIS-NEXIS, 6 May 1991)

Speaker Foley told this story, not as a description of the current power of the leadership, but as a representation of how much things had changed. In recent years, party leadership in Congress has "gone from government by junta to a kind of quasi-democratic system" (Greenfield 1992, 72).

Despite the relatively low levels of party division and support, both of these have increased in recent years after hitting bottom in the 1970s. Some of the reforms of the 1970s which limited the powers of committee chairs and enhanced the powers of the Democratic party leaders to affect committee assignments and the assignment of bills to committee have led to a centralization trend (see Rohde 1991, 11–16; Davidson 1988, 345; and Elving 1993, 194).

Political party leaders expend considerable effort hammering out consensus party positions in formal caucuses and informal meetings (see box 4.3). Party whips serve as the "ultimate internal lobbying firm" (Merida 1993a, A1) polling Members to assess their level of support, anticipating potential problem areas, providing information, and assuring that supporters get to the floor to vote. Party leaders often go beyond the use of gentle persuasion. The leaders build "credits" with Members by doing favors and keep track of those who are loyal. The Democratic whip in the House is described as keeping separate

> lists of who's naughty and who's nice—on procedural votes that are considered tests of party loyalty . . . [which] are shared with the president and the Democratic leadership and referred to when it comes to [doling] out perks such as appointments to task forces, overseas trips, and choice committee assignments. (Merida 1993a, A7)

It is impossible to determine the degree to which party members are "led" to support party positions and the degree to which their personal and constituency backgrounds stimulate them to naturally coalesce around particular options. "Now, more than ever, congressional party leaders are reactive consensus-builders more than they are policy innovators" (Patterson and Little 1992, 22). Today, "every member of Congress, no matter his or her party label, judges each vote by the highly personal standard of whether it will help or hurt that particular Member's re-election chances" (Broder 1993, A10). While party voting during the first year of Clinton's presidency was up (Patterson 1993, 7), on high visibility votes such as the Budget Plan and the North American Free Trade Agreement (NAFTA) many Members showed significant independence (see chapter 7).

When support of the party will help them back home, or at least not hurt their re-election chances, most Members will opt for party loyalty. Rather than powerful enforcers of the party line, party leaders are more like cheerleaders, encouraging and cajoling party Members to support party positions despite their lack of perfect match with the legislator's personal preference or constituency ideal. Due to their longer terms, higher visibility (see Serra et al. 1991, 12), more viable personal campaign organizations and more heterogeneous districts, members of the Senate are somewhat freer from party domination than their House colleagues:

> Senators are largely autonomous beings, but sometimes they are led; state ties are frequently more critical than partisanship, but party labels are still the best single indicator of a senator's voting patterns. The center aisle . . . continues to mark an important dividing line in an institution that nevertheless goes out of its way, most of the time, to operate on the basis of muted partisanship. (Peabody 1981, 104–105)

Richard Fenno (1989, 316–317), sees the shift from a communitarian organization based on cooperation and party loyalty to an individualistic body responding to external conditions as one of the major marks of the modern Senate.

Despite the party leadership's limitations, members of Congress go out of their way to please the leadership whenever possible. While the fate of individual Members is not directly tied to party fate, making the party look good generally has benefits for all Members. Leaders can grant loyal followers legislative favors, provide critical information, and negotiate legislative compromises with the White House.

THE COMMITTEE ARENA: TASK-ORIENTED TEAMS

Most policy-making takes place in committees. Committees have become important institutionalized arenas in the modern Congress, but this was not always the case.

ORIGIN OF COMMITTEES

The early congresses worked under the assumption that all Members should be involved in every decision. After discussion on the floor, short term ad hoc committees were used to draft the basic principles of the previous floor debate into detailed legislation (Cooper 1988, 13–14). The House, with its greater responsibility for establishing the legislative agenda covering increasingly complex legislative issues was first to establish permanent committees. The committee format provided a division of labor to carry out tasks assigned by the House. The number of standing committees in the House increased from ten in 1810 to thirty-nine by the Civil War. Although the Senate also created committees during this period, Senate committees played a less significant role (see Smith and Deering 1990, 26–28).

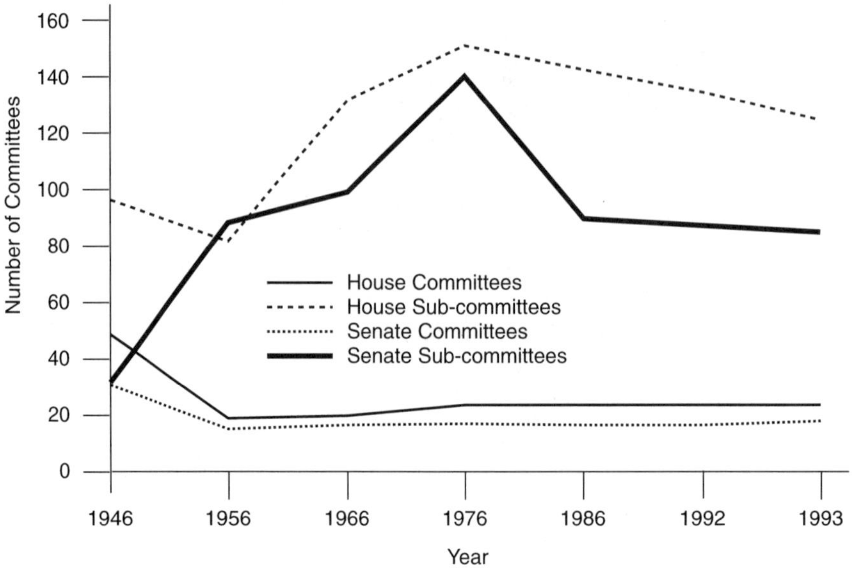

FIGURE 4.2

The Growth of Committees and Sub-Committees

Note: The graph includes standing committees and sub-committees of standing committees and excludes joint committees and select committees and their sub-committees.

SOURCE: Norman J. Ornstein, Thomas E. Mann, and Michael J. Malbin, *Vital Statistics on Congress, 1993–1994,* pp. 114–115, 1994; Robert A. Diamond, (ed.), *The Origins and Development of Congress,* p. 136, Congressional Quarterly Press, 1976; and Steven Smith and Christopher Deering, *Committees in Congress,* p. 43, 1990.

Between the Civil War and the early 1900s, the number of committees grew rapidly, with new committees typically created for each new policy area. While there was some attempt to weed out inactive committees before World War II, pressure grew for more rational committee jurisdictions and reducing the number of committees. The Legislative Reorganization Act of 1946 reduced the number of committees in both chambers and increased committee staff support. Since 1946, few full committees have been added, while dramatic growth has come in the form of sub-committees. Although later reforms reduced the number of sub-committees slightly (see Cooper 1993a, A19), decentralization of activity and power to the sub-committees marks the current era (see figure 4.2). Along with a decentralization of responsibility came a counter attempt to make committees and sub-committees more responsive to the party leadership. The increased role of the party leaders in appointing loyal Members to committees contributed to party cohesion, while the Speaker's right to assign bills to more than one committee for deliberation created the competition that would encourage speedy committee action (see Rohde 1991, 11–12).

Reprinted by permission: Tribune Media Services.

TYPES OF COMMITTEES

Committees are created for different purposes. Most legislative work is done in permanent **standing** committees. **Select** and special committees deal with emerging policy areas, while **conference** committees work out compromises between House and Senate versions of bills.

Standing Committees and Subcommittees

Woodrow Wilson's famous assertion that "Congress in session is Congress on public exhibition, whilst Congress in its committee-rooms is Congress at work" (Wilson 1885, 69), is even more true today than it was 100 years ago. Permanent standing committees with designated substantive jurisdictions screen, analyze, and polish legislation before it gets to the floor of either chamber. Two major types of committees must deal with most legislation. **Authorizing** committees decide whether programs or policies should be enacted, while **appropriating** committees determine whether authorized programs should be funded. The size and breadth of concern of most committees requires them to break into a set of smaller and more substantively narrow subcommittees for the initial handling of a piece of legislation (see table 4.2).

Select and Special Committees

At times legislative tasks are seen as temporary, and needing only the development of an impermanent committee team. **Select or special** committees deal with tasks such as the presidential inaugural ceremony. Emerging issues are frequently handled by creating select committees, often with the hope of those interested that a permanent standing committee will be created (see table 4.2). Select committees have the power to study issues, but do not propose legislation. In 1993, as part of a budget cutting attempt, the select committees on Narcotics Abuse and Control; Children, Youth and Families; and Aging and Hunger were disbanded, leaving only the Select Committee on Intelligence.

Joint Committees

Members of Congress generally accept the redundancy and inefficiency of competing committee entities in each chamber as a protection against inadequate consideration. Some areas of legislative consideration require more coordination or secrecy. Joint

TABLE 4.2 Current Congressional Committees (103rd Congress)

House Standing	***Senate Standing***
Agriculture	Agriculture, Nutrition, and Forestry
Appropriations	Appropriations
Armed Services	Armed Services
Banking, Finance, and Urban Affairs	Banking, Housing and Urban Affairs
Budget	Budget
District of Columbia	Commerce, Science, and Transportation
Education and Labor	Energy and Natural Resources
Energy and Commerce	Environment and Public Works
Foreign Affairs	Finance
Government Operations	Foreign Relations
House Administration	Government Affairs
Judiciary	Judiciary
Merchant Marine and Fisheries	Labor and Human Resources
Natural Resources	Rules and Administration
Post Office and Civil Service	Small Business
Public Works and Transportation	Veterans' Affairs
Rules	
Science, Space, and Technology	***Senate Special***
Small Business	Aging
Standards and Official Conduct	Ethics
Veterans' Affairs	Indian Affairs
Ways and Means	Intelligence
House Select	***Joint***
Intelligence	Economics
	Library
	Organization of Congress
	Printing
	Taxation

committees are an attempt to expedite consideration of legislation, facilitate coordination, and/or reduce the potential for leaking sensitive information (see table 4.2).

Conference Committees

Conference committees are temporary joint committees established to work out the details of legislation passed by both Houses in different forms. While the presiding officers of each chamber name the conferees, they do so on the recommendation of the chairperson and ranking minority member of the committee originating the legislation. Conferees are appointed in rough proportion to the party division in each House. In a conference committee, each chamber has one vote, and conferees are often instructed by their chambers of important components of a bill which they must include. The evidence indicates that the Senate's wishes tend to prevail more often in conference committee (Baker 1989a, 61–63). The causes of Senate dominance are less clear. While one might argue that it is due to the differences in the status and capabilities of House and Senate members, it turns out that the last chamber to deal with a bill usually wins. In most cases, this tends to be the Senate (Longley and Oleszek 1989, 44–45).

JOINING A COMMITTEE TEAM

> The [committee assignment] game is a little like musical chairs; every two years, members of the House of Representatives circle for position as retirements and defeats open spaces on influential committees. . . . The survivors [and new members] try to make sure that when the music stops . . . they have a seat on the Appropriations Committee. (Anderson 1992)

Members realize that much of their influence will stem from committee activity. Getting on the "right" committee can make or break a career.

The Committee Assignment Process

During the early years, House committees developed much more as a tool of the leadership by giving the Speaker the right to appoint chairpersons and members. A series of activist Speakers between the Civil War and 1910—Samuel J. Randall, John G. Carlisle, Thomas B. Reed, and Joseph G. Cannon—assiduously used the appointment power to stack committees and control the chamber (see Cooper 1988, 76; and Smith and Deering 1990, 34). Frustration with autocratic domination of the appointment process and management of the House led to a revolt against the leadership shifting the appointment power to the entire party caucus and diminishing other powers of the Speaker.

The Senate originally selected committee members by secret ballot of the entire chamber, and shifted to appointment by the presiding officer. Eventually the Senate began relying on party committees to make appointments (Baker 1988, 31–32; and Smith and Deering 1990, 28–31).

In the contemporary Congress, each party in each chamber has a Committee on Committees composed of relatively senior members which makes its committee assignments (see box 4.4). The complex process of staffing all the committees and satisfying both party and individual needs has been called a "giant jigsaw puzzle" (Shepsle 1978, passim). Since the 1970s, formal party leaders have played a somewhat more important role on these committees, often serving as chair.[13] In the House, considerable attention is paid to regional representation when constituting

[13]At times the party leadership uses committee assignments as rewards or punishment. After Dave McCurdy (D-OK) publicly criticized Speaker Tom Foley (D-WA) for his handling of the House Bank and Post Office Scandals in 1992, he found himself dropped as chair of the House Select Intelligence Committee when the 103rd Congress convened in 1993 (Elving 1993, 194).

BOX 4.4 Setting up the Committee Team Rosters

The parties in each chamber use slightly different sets of Members to determine their committee roster:

Senate

- ✦ The Senate Democratic Steering Committee serves as the committee on committees. It is appointed by the Democratic majority leader and has twenty-five members (101st Congress).
- ✦ The Senate Republican Committee on Committees is appointed by the conference chair. The fifteen member committee is augmented by top party leaders who serve ex officio.

House

- ✦ The House Democratic Steering and Policy Committee serves as the committee on committees. It is composed of twelve regionally elected members, eight members appointed by the Speaker, and eleven top party leaders serving ex officio.
- ✦ The House Republican Committee on Committees is composed of twenty-one members. Each state with more than five Republican Members elects one representative, with states having smaller delegations electing a regional member. Each of the two most recently elected classes select one member. The floor leader and the whip are automatically on the committee.

SOURCE: Steven Smith and Christopher Deering 1990, *Committees in Congress,* Washington, D.C.: CQ Press, p. 69.

the Committee on Committees. Party leaders attempt to use the assignments to help party members get re-elected, protect state and regional committee positions, reward party loyalty, tap the unique experience of members, and to strategically place members on committees to improve the enactment of key policies (Smith and Deering 1990, 74). The dominant pattern is one of "interest-advocacy-accommodation" in which members express an interest in a particular committee, lobby for selection and are accommodated by the leadership (see Shepsle 1978, 231–237).

Existing Constraints

The committees on committees are not presented a clean roster to fill committee teams at will. Committee sizes are relatively fixed, and the majority party assigns each party positions to fill proportional to the party percentages among the chamber membership.[14] (See box 4.4.) Sitting Members generally have a "property right" (see Bullock and England 1992, 285–308; and Smith and Deering 1990, 69) to remain on a committee as long as they wish. States and regions often have an accepted right to positions on certain committees which have direct impact on their well being. Thus a "California seat" on the Natural Resources Committee will generally be filled by a new Member from California. Both chambers have passed rules

[14]The major exception is in the House, where the Democrats have reserved extraordinary majorities on the Appropriations, Rules, and Ways and Means committees.

TABLE 4.3 The Opportunities for Committee Team Involvement

House		
Congress	**Mean number of standing committee assignments per Representative**	**Mean number of subcommittee assignments**
94th (1971–72)	1.5	3.2
98th (1983–84)	1.7	3.4
102nd (1991–92)	1.9	4.0
103rd (1993–94)	2.0	3.7
Senate		
Congress	**Mean number of standing committee assignments per Senator**	**Mean number of subcommittee assignments**
94th (1971–72)	2.5	9.5
98th (1983–84)	2.9	7.5
102nd (1991–92)	2.9	7.4
103rd (1993–94)	3.2	7.8

SOURCE: Norman J. Ornstein, Thomas E. Mann, and Michael J. Malbin, *Vital Statistics on Congress, 1993–1994,* p. 116, Congressional Quarterly, Inc., 1994.

limiting the number of assignments each Member can have and attempt to spread around the most desirable positions. In the House, assignment to one of the designated "exclusive" committees[15] denies the Member a seat on any other committee. Despite the stated rules, exceptions are often made, especially in the Senate.

Member Goals

Membership on various committees can serve different Member goals. Research indicates that such strategic considerations are most common in the House where Members are more limited in the number of committees on which they can serve, and election alone guarantees them less influence (see Fenno 1973, 1; Smith and Deering 1990, 85–108). Some committees (such as Agriculture, Public Works and Transportation, Science, Space and Technology, and Merchant Marine and Fisheries) primarily serve **constituency interests.** Membership on such committees helps Members serve local needs and reinforce their potential for re-election. Whether it is protecting crop subsidies, securing a new highway, or getting a research grant, such committees help Members "deliver for their districts" (Cooper 1993c, A15). In 1993, more than half of the new House members requested spots on the Public Works, and Science, Space and Technology committees (Cooper 1993c, A15).

Other committees (such as Education and Labor, Judiciary, Foreign Affairs, and Banking and Commerce) draw Members hoping to satisfy broader **policy interests.** Members of such committees often have a policy agenda which they hope to pursue through membership on the appropriate committee.

[15]Committees such as House Rules, Appropriations, and Ways and Means are considered exclusive.

An even smaller group of committees (such as Appropriations, House Rules, Budget, and Ways and Means) have such broad responsibilities that membership helps serve **influence and prestige interests.** Members of these committees find their influence over the entire legislative process enhanced. At the bottom of the heap are **penance** committees (such as the Committee on House Administration or the Committee on the District of Columbia) which deal with relatively insignificant issues or whose policy focus have been placed on the back burner.[16] Members usually only accept appointment to these committees in exchange for another better appointment.

Vying for Position

> [Requesting a committee position] is a little bit like a board game, or like bridge, you always have to know what cards have been played. (Representative Blanche Lambert [D-AR] quoted in Krauss 1992, A11)

> I like to think of this committee jockeying as very much like the game of Monopoly. There are the Baltic Avenue committees (Veterans' Affairs, Post Office and Civil Service); Boardwalk and Park Avenue committees (Appropriations, Ways and Means). . . . Whereas the Boardwalk group are prestigious and highly profitable in the long run, still one can build hotels sooner on Baltic Avenue. The point is that certain clever members do very well with the cheaper properties. (Jones 1982, 206–207)

Directly on the heels of the election campaign **for** Congress, new and old Members alike begin a campaign **within** Congress for desired committee positions (see box 4.5). Unless party electoral fortunes have dramatically altered the party ratio, returning members can almost always be assured of retaining their present positions. Returning Members wishing to improve their assignments and new Members carefully watch for positions that have opened up because of retirements, defeats, and committee switching.

Certain committees such as Ways and Means, House Rules, and Appropriations are highly sought after by returning Members willing to give up seniority on another committee (see Jewell and Chi-Hung 1974, 433–441 passim; and Ray 1982, 609). Newly elected Members are less likely to receive appointments to the most prestigious committees and appeal to party leaders through their state delegation leaders pointing out their experience, loyalty to the party leadership, and constituency needs. Members express their interest and advocate their preferences, while leaders attempt to accommodate those interests (Shepsle 1978, 1–20 passim). In recent years, there is some evidence that leaders are also trying to use committee assignments as a tool for increasing party loyalty (see Rohde 1991, 77–78; and Cox and McCubbins 1993, 188–228). "The more independent, the more of a maverick you are, the worse off you are in this insider process" (Committee on Committee member, quoted in Krauss 1992, A11).

---

[16]After the 1992 election with its emphasis on domestic policy, House leaders had to practically beg Members to consider the Foreign Affairs Committee which had twenty openings (Krauss 1992, A11).

BOX 4.5 The Full Court Press for a Committee Assignment

In the fall of 1992, while most of the subsequently elected freshmen were campaigning for their seats in the 103rd Congress, Carrie Meek (D-FL) embarked on another campaign. After winning her primary with 83 percent of the vote, she faced no opponent in the general election. Representative Meek decided to try for the long shot and win a seat on the Appropriations Committee, a usually unattainable goal for a freshman. She met with the members of the Florida delegation to get their support, reminding them of her experience on the Appropriations Committee in the Florida Senate and pointing out that Florida had lost two seats on Appropriations through retirement. Her next step was to convince the leadership of the Black Caucus that she was the right minority member to serve their interests on this key money dispensing committee. She then personally brought her campaign to the members of the Democratic Steering and Policy Committee which serves the Democrats' committee on committees. After weeks of hard campaigning, her efforts paid off and she got the desired assignment.

SOURCE: *The New Congress,* 1993, p. 70 Washington, D.C.: Congressional Quarterly.

Representative Carrie Meek (D-FL) had learned how to play the game in the Florida legislature and applied that knowledge to her successful bid for a coveted place on the Appropriations Committee.

Several potential consequences flow from the committee assignment process. Far from being simply microcosms of the entire chamber, committee teams are composed of individuals with particular interests. Committees draw "high demanders" who seek a particular committee assignment based on individual or constituency interests and often gain a disproportionate share of benefits from the policy area within the committee's jurisdiction (see Weingast and Marshall 1988, 162). Chamber colleagues allow committee members increased benefits as a "payment" for the costs of specialization in the topics covered by the committee (Krehbiel 1991, chapter 3).

The decision to join a particular committee is constrained by the existence of available openings, the judgments of party leaders, and competing goals—such as the desire to maintain one's seniority on a less desirable committee (see following discussion). Members of Congress realize that committee assignments can often make or break their careers.

CHOOSING COMMITTEE LEADERSHIP

For the first three-quarters of the twentieth century, formal committee leadership devolved to Members outlasting their committee colleagues. The **seniority system,** the process of granting chairmanships to the majority party member of a committee or subcommittee with the longest continuous service,[17] grew from a convenient custom to a virtually unviolated rule.

Desire to increase democratization and enhance the position of the party caucus in the early 1970s led to a significant change in committee leadership selection, especially in the House. Automatic caucus votes on committee chairs, with an option for secret ballots was instituted (see Smith and Deering 1990, 120). While seniority still prevails as the most important factor (see table 4.4), a number of chairs have been unseated due to alleged incompetence or for being out of tune with party goals. Less visibly, the new procedures placed elected chairs on guard and reduced their freedom to run roughshod over party and committee preferences. After the large influx of new Members in 1993, freshman Republicans got the support of their senior Republican party colleagues to upset Democratic chairmanships by placing a three term limit on the number of years any leader could serve. Although a chamber-wide limit failed, the new rule does apply on the Republican side, and ranking minority members of committees will have to surrender their positions after reaching the limit (Krauss 1992, A13).

The minority party establishes a set of "shadow" leaders poised to take over if their party should win a majority, and charged with keeping the majority in check. The **ranking minority members** of committees and subcommittees are elected by their party caucus. The relations between committee chairs and ranking minority members varies from cooperative leadership to hostile conflict.

Contemporary committee chairs have fewer unilateral powers than their predecessors. Complete control over committee agendas and staffs has given way to more collegial agenda setting and staff resources have been more widely distributed

---

[17]The most important seniority in Congress relates to continuous service on a committee. Members who have a gap in congressional service or who switch committees start at the bottom of the seniority ladder.

TABLE 4.4 The Old Timer's League of Leaders (103rd Congress)

Name	Age	Years in Office	Leadership Position
Sidney Yates (D-IL)	83	42	Subcommittee chair, Appropriations Committee
William Natcher (D-KY)	83	39	Former chair, Appropriations Committee
Jamie Whitten (D-MS)	82	51	Former chair, Appropriations Committee
Henry Gonzales (D-TX)	76	31	Chair, Banking, Finance and Urban Affairs Committee
James H. Quillen (R-TN)	76	30	Ranking subcommittee member, Rules Committee
Jack Brooks (D-TX)	70	40	Chair, Judiciary Committee
Robert Michel (R-IL)	69	36	Minority leader
John Dingell (D-MI)	66	37	Chair, Energy and Commerce Committee
Dan Rostenkowski (D-IL)	64	34	Former chair, Ways and Means Committee

NOTE: Members in **bold** have served more than half their lives in Congress.

to subcommittees and the minority party. While party leaders have attempted to regain some of their power over committee leaders, committee and subcommittee chairs remain significant players. Personal skills, hard work, formal power resources for structuring decisions and rewarding supporters, and extraordinary motivation can mean a great deal in terms of effective leadership.

Committee leaders have a stake in monitoring the issues and policy processes within their committees' jurisdictions, which increases the chance that their preferences will prevail. Committee chairs use their information advantage to frame issues into politically viable alternatives. When the legislative process is rife with uncertainty, a committee leader's informational advantage may be the significant factor allowing them to facilitate legislation closer to their own preference (Evans 1991, 170; see also Arnold 1990, 85–87).

Routine control over the committee agenda allows the chair to use scheduling as a "carrot and a stick" (see Evans 1991, 170), rewarding supporters and punishing opponents. Although the full committee can overrule a chair since the acceptance of committee "bills of rights" during the 1970s (Oleszek 1989, 95), the cost of offending the chair limits such challenges. Chairs still control the majority of committee staff and can retard the passage of legislation they oppose by directing the staff to ignore it, or by stacking committee hearings with favorable witnesses. Recalcitrant House committees or committee chairs can be forced to report bills if a **discharge petition** garners the necessary 218 votes, but such challenges are rare.

COMMITTEE LEADERSHIP STRATEGIES

Committee and subcommittee chairs approach their jobs with varying skills, energy, and strategies. Some chairs place themselves at the center of the policy vortex, introducing legislation and attempting to take full credit. Others serve as "coat-holders," observing the battle and waiting for a consensus to emerge. Since the democratizing reforms of the 1970s, committee chairs are less able to be tyrants and are more often facilitators for the will of the majority (see box 4.6).

BOX 4.6 The Players Speak about Committee Leadership

Before the reform of the committee process, committee chairs could be quite arrogant about their powers. When asked about how he stood on a bill in his committee, Emanuel Celler (D-NY), chair of the House Judiciary Committee from 1955–1973, said,

> I don't stand on it. I am sitting on it. It rests four-square under my fanny and will never see the light of day (quoted in Udall 1988, 229).

In the 1920s, Congressman Philip Campbell (R-KY), chairman of the Rules Committee from 1919 to 1923 was even more direct when he told his colleagues,

> You can go to hell; it makes no difference what a majority of you decide; if it meets my disapproval it shall not be done; I am the committee (quoted in Bolling 1966, 39).

Member willingness to acquiesce to party and committee leadership began to wane in the post World War II era. One Senator frustrated with the activity and number of leadership positions of Robert Taft (R-OH) exclaimed in exasperation,

> I don't mind one man calling the signals, taking the ball, throwing the forward pass, running around and catching it, making the touchdown and then marking up the score. But I'm goddamned if I like it when he rushes over after that and leads the cheers (quoted in *Time* 1947, 24).

Modern chairs must be more circumspect. John Dingell (D-MI), powerful chairman of the House Energy and Commerce Committee, often operates through a junior Member, permitting that Member to introduce the bill and providing committee staff to help manage it. As one committee member explained it,

> He finds some young eager beaver who is looking to make a name for himself . . . and who is willing to really work on a bill . . . [He] gave me tremendous latitude and five or six crack staff folks to work with me [on the Superfund]. . . . He had the role of convener and sometimes he was the shotgun behind the door (Representative Dennis Eckart [D-OH] quoted in Stanfield 1988, 792).

SUPPORTING THE COMMITTEE TEAM: COMMITTEE STAFFS

Much of a committee's administrative and investigative work is done by professional staff. They organize hearings, help select witnesses, research policy options, and help frame legislation. During the 1970s, the professionalism of committee staffs increased (see figure 4.3). Committee staff is now much less likely to be simply an extension of the chair's personal staff, and less likely to be the "old timer . . . who got the job by working on the committee chair's last campaign" (Henschen and Sidlow 1986, 701). Current committee staffs arrive with significant policy experience, and often gain significant control over areas of their policy expertise.

While a number of committees have traditions of nonpartisan staffing, most committees apportion their staffs among the majority and minority parties. The battle continues over how many staff members the minority should receive. Despite

Senator Hank Brown (R-CO) leans back for advice from a staff member during a meeting of the Judiciary Committee.

the fact that the minority generally has more than 40 percent of the membership in both chambers, they control a much smaller percentage of the staff (*Congressional Quarterly* 1991, 488).

COMMITTEE TEAMS IN ACTION: PLAYERS, RULES, AND STRATEGIES

Each congressional committee and subcommittee is a different arena with its own unique set of players, rules, traditions, and strategies. To a large degree, the common goals of the players set the tone for the committee. Committee members often see themselves as a team with a task to be done. Team effort and loyalty to the team will increase the ability of the committee to determine the future of its legislative initiatives. Committee teams vary in terms of the effort and loyalty they can generate.

Player Goals and Committee Behavior

Committees, especially in the House, vary in terms of their policy responsibilities and Member goals. The distribution of Member goals affects committee behavior (see Fenno 1973, 46–79). **Constituency oriented committees** (such as Public Works, Agriculture, or Science and Technology) tend to draw Members with relatively narrow policy interests and the desire to enact policies favorable to their geographic area, agricultural crop, or industry. Each Member becomes an advocate for constituency interests in a bidding game about distributing government programs. Each Member's request is viewed as an essentially equal bargaining chip (Fenno 1973, 58). Partisanship is minimal as Members with similar constituencies bind together to form the nucleus of a voting coalition. The desire for action results in a "live and let live attitude," with the committee presenting a united front once a deal has been struck from within (see Parker and Parker 1985, 38–39).

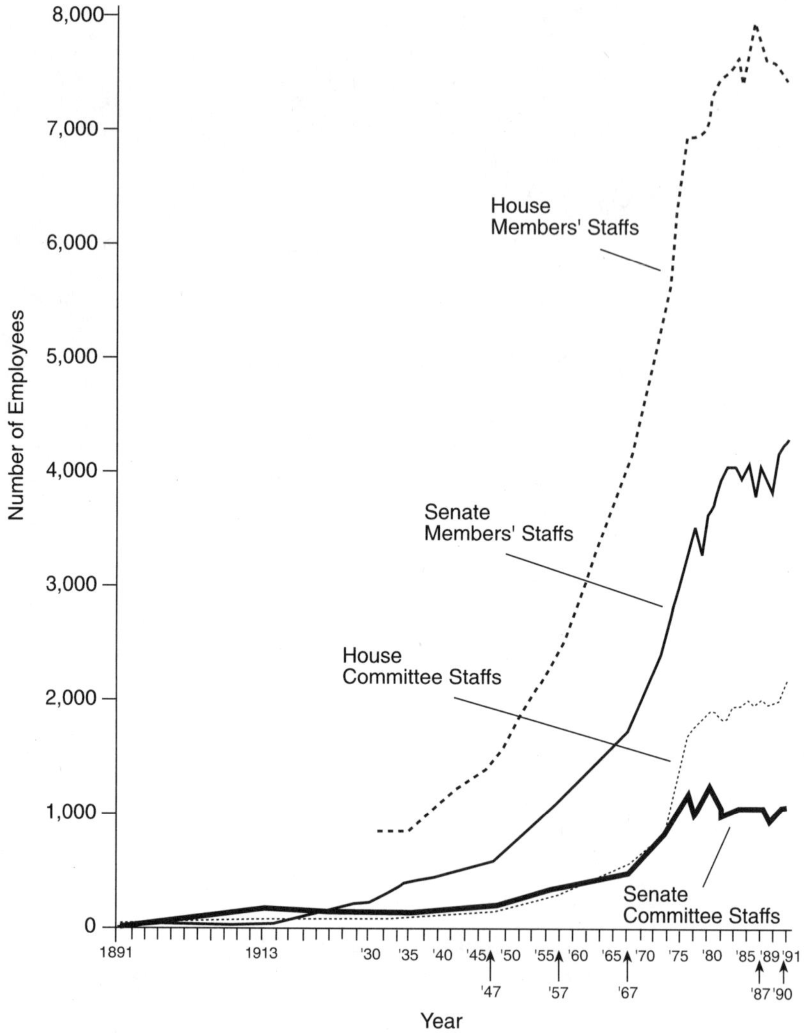

FIGURE 4.3

The Growth of Congressional Staffs

SOURCE: Norman J. Ornstein, Thomas E. Mann, and Michael J. Malbin, *Vital Statistics on Congress, 1993–1994*, p. 129, Congressional Quarterly, Inc., 1994.

Members of **power and prestige committees** (such as Appropriations, Ways and Means, and House Rules) gain much of their influence based on the perceived invincibility of their committees. Their desire is to write bills that will pass the parent chamber and impress their colleagues with the futility of "messing with the big boys." While conflict may reign within the committee rooms, such committees attempt to present a united front on the floor.

Policy Committees (such as Education and Labor, Judiciary, and Foreign Affairs) draw members with deep commitments on inherently divisive issues. The underlying desire to pursue one's policy preferences undermines partisan loyalties and the pursuit of consensus. Individualism tends to reign and teamwork suffers. Such committees often take their battles to the floor rather than presenting a united front.

The Participation Rule: You Can't Win If You Don't Play

> This is a put up or shut up game. . . . The whole system operates on a speak now or forever hold your peace basis. . . . If a senator is on the committee and he has not participated and he goes down to the floor, what's he going to say, "Hey, my colleagues put one over on me"? . . . If you have participated and your view was not adopted, then you have a perfect opportunity to go down on the floor and raise a ruckus (Senate staff member quoted in Evans 1989, 159).

Members of Congress serve on numerous committees with conflicting schedules. They must pick and choose the sessions to attend. Lack of attendance carries with it the assumption of approval of committee actions. In most cases, less than half of a committee's members regularly participate in deliberation, and "on any given bill, the membership of a committee or subcommittee abdicates its considerable legislative authority to some subset of self-selected members" (Hall 1987, 105).

At times, committee and subcommittee chairs schedule meetings when probable opponents have conflicting meetings on issues of higher importance. Members accept the fact that committee sessions are generally where the work is expected to be done. In order to protect their interests, Members often send staff to monitor meetings they can not attend. Many committees allow **proxy** voting in which a trusted colleague is allowed to cast an absent Member's vote.

Committees hold two basic types of meetings, hearings and mark-up sessions. Hearings provide the opportunity to question experts from other parts of government or the private sector. Deciding who to put on the witness list for hearings is often a carefully orchestrated strategy controlled by the committee leadership and influenced by interest groups demands. Hearings can be as important for influencing the public as for educating the members of the committee, especially when an increasing number of committee hearings are broadcast on television.

Mark-up sessions allow Members to go over the legislation line by line and make amendments. Until the early 1970s more than one-third of the committee and subcommittee meetings were closed to the public (Ornstein, Mann, and Malbin 1992, 117). Since the passage of the Legislative Reorganization Act of 1970, virtually all committee sessions are open (see Smith and Deering 1990, 46–47).

The Politics of Deference

Members of Congress generally accept the guidelines "Support the committee because it has studied the issue with care" (Hook 1992, 515). Committees tend to defer to the judgment of their subcommittees, and each chamber tends to defer to the judgment of its committees. Increases in floor amendments threaten the autonomy of

The high visibility of the Clarence Thomas confirmation hearings was heightened by the charges of sexual harassment brought by Anita Hill, a former subordinate of Judge Thomas. The committee, and its staff, attempted to craft hearing procedures which would allow public access without turning the event into a media "circus."

committees, but a good proportion of floor amendments "represent legislative contributions that committee members find acceptable" (Smith and Deering 1990, 181). More than 90 percent of bills passed by committee eventually pass on the House floor (Kubik 1992, table 2). Members of the majority party are especially likely to accept voting cues from party members on the committee, and their numerical majority on the floor helps assure that the majority party coalition in the committee prevails (Kubik 1992, 15). House committees are more important than Senate committees in sending signals since a larger proportion of House members are not on the reporting committee and House floor proceedings do not allow as extensive amendments and debate as the Senate does (see chapter 7). The practice of creating conference committees primarily from members of the reporting committee increases committee dominance since members of the reporting committee can veto any changes made on the floor (Shepsle and Weingast 1987, 95).

COMPETING TEAMS

Chamber, party, and committee interests do not exhaust the allegiances which potentially link members of Congress. Cutting across these major alliances are other interests motivating Members.

SPECIAL INTEREST CAUCUSES: TEAMS WITH A THEME

> I see the Black Caucus as being far more representative and powerful now than it has ever been. First, this is because of sheer numbers. As we all know, getting legislation passed is purely a numbers game." (Representative Cynthia McKinney [D-GA] quoted in Browning 1992, 3732)

In an institution where numbers count, Members increasingly attempt to increase their potential influence by joining together with colleagues. More than 140 congressional membership organizations are currently active (see Richardson 1989 and 1991) (see table 4.5). The growth of caucuses has been dramatic. As late as 1969, only three such organizations existed (Hammond 1991, 278). Regional, ideological, and special concerns serve as motivations to organize. Some organizations are informal and emerge only sporadically, while others are more fully organized with formal membership, regular meetings, clear expectations, and full-time staff members. Caucuses help institutionalize **natural coalitions** (see chapter 7) which serve as the basis for backing the broader coalitions necessary to pass legislation. Approximately thirty special interest and ideological caucuses have been designated as **legislative service organizations (LSOs)** and draw funds from Congress' operating budget (Richardson 1992, 1). While special interest caucuses exist in both the House and Senate, the large size of the House makes them more numerous and powerful in that chamber.

Regional Groupings

The most obvious special interest teams are the state delegations, most of which meet on a regular basis to discuss issues of local interest. Members report on issues emerging from their committees and plan their strategy to protect state interests. States with large delegations tend to meet in separate partisan groups, while smaller states find it more practical to eschew partisanship and bolster their numbers.

Regional groupings bring together Members attempting to promote and protect the unique economic, educational, and environmental interests of their region. For example, the Northeast-Midwest Congressional Coalition is a bipartisan group of more than 200 members in the House and more than thirty senators with particular concern for the location of federal programs and the allocation of federal benefits.[18] This coalition developed out of the concern that federal policies were exacerbating the shift of individuals and corporations to the "sun belt" states and away from the northeast and midwest "rust belt" region.

Ideological Groups

Many issues in Congress split along liberal and conservative lines, causing members to trust the guidance of colleagues with similar ideological perspectives. The largest ideological organization is the Democratic Study Group (DSG), a research and policy organization serving more than 200 liberal and moderate House Democrats.[19] Democratic Study Group staff and members analyze issues, organize policy

---

[18]Information on the various caucuses and study groups comes from the *Congressional Yellow Book* (New York: Monitor Publishing Company), a frequently updated guide to who's who in Congress.

[19]The size and growing importance of the DSG have led it to a special status as an accepted policy arm of the Democratic Party in the House. The chair of the DSG is now treated as part of the party leadership, even though he is selected only by DSG members (see Patterson and Little 1992, 4).

TABLE 4.5 A Sample of Informal Member Organizations in the House and Senate

House:	***House:***
Unofficial Partisan Groups	**Unofficial Bipartisan Groups**
Conservative Democratic Forum (58)*	Animal Welfare Caucus (10)
Conservative Opportunity Society (40)	Army Caucus (70)
Democratic Study Group (255)	Bearing Caucus (40)
House Wednesday Group (36)	Footwear Caucus (104)
House Republican Study Committee (120)	Human Rights Caucus (200)
Mainstream Forum [Democratic] (30)	Mushroom Caucus (60)
Ninety-Two [Republican] Group (35)	Steel Caucus (100)
	Sunbelt Caucus (150)
	Urban Caucus (75)
	Northeast-Midwest Coalition (100)
	Pro-Life Caucus (20)
Senate:	***Bi-cameral:***
Unofficial Bipartisan Groups	**Unofficial Bipartisan Groups**
Concerned Senators for the Arts (68)	Committee for Irish Affairs (122)
Anti-Terrorism Caucus (14)	Arms Control and Foreign Policy Caucus (140)
Children's Caucus (30)	Alcohol Fuels Caucus (100)
Delta Caucus (14)	Black Caucus (26)
Drug Enforcement Caucus (NA)	Clearinghouse on the Future (130)
National Guard Caucus (70)	Coalition on Adoption (90)
Rural Health Caucus (55)	Copper Caucus (35)
Sweetener Caucus (23)	Corn Caucus (51)
Western State Coalition (30)	Ferroalloy Caucus (33)
Wine Caucus (11)	Hispanic Caucus (13)
	Rural Caucus (100)
	International AIDS Study Group (85)
	Military Reform Caucus (135)
	National Security Caucus (200)
	Olympic Caucus (35)
	Tennessee Valley Caucus (38)
	Vietnam Era Veterans (64)

*Indicates the number of members in 1992.

SOURCE: Sula P. Richardson, "Caucuses and Legislative Service Organizations of the 102nd Congress," Congressional Research Service Report No. 92-257 GOV, 1992.

forums, send Members voting guidance and operate its own whip system. On the other side of the ideological spectrum, about fifty conservative House Democrats meet as the Conservative Democratic Forum to promote conservative economic and national defense issues.

The Wednesday Club is a long standing moderate Republican by-invitation-only organization of thirty-six moderate Republicans who meet weekly to discuss issues and facilitate legislation. One of the most publicly active ideological groups is the forty-member Conservative Opportunity Society. It not only meets to promote a conservative agenda, but has aggressively used the "special orders" portion of House debate each day to criticize the Democratic majority and spread its views via television. One of its leaders, Newt Gingrich (R-GA) used his public visibility and the power of the group to gain his position as Republican Whip, the second ranking party Republican leadership spot.

Statistical Artifacts: Team Behavior Without Organization

While the above groups have formal officers, members, and meetings, another type of grouping arises out of the inherent ideological and constituency interests of Members. During much of the last fifty years, the "Conservative Coalition" made up of Republicans and southern Democrats has left its mark on congressional policy making. The statistical monitoring of the Conservative Coalition is a key example of modern political science's attempt to empirically measure political behavior. While each partisan component welcomes support from the other, no formal coordination occurs. Despite its lack of formal organization, the coalition appeared[20] in about 20 percent of House votes between 1960 and 1990, and in a slightly higher percentage of Senate votes (Ornstein, et. al. 1992, 201). When the coalition appears, it tends to win. The frequency and success rates of the Conservative Coalition have varied over time, with less frequency in recent years as the ideological distinctiveness of the southern Democrats has declined.

Special Interest Groupings

The range of other special interest teams is almost endless. Each new freshman class of Members usually creates its own Republican and Democratic caucuses to promote the interests of their class. After a few sessions, the common interests of these caucuses tend to wane and they are phased out. More abiding teams remain. The Congressional Black Caucus, for example, uses its staff to provide information, hold conferences, offer student internships, and prepare an "Alternative Federal Budget." Conflict between special interest caucus goals and those of the Member's political

---

[20]Congressional Quarterly Inc. defines the Conservative Coalition as having appeared any time a majority of Republicans and a majority of southern Democrats vote together.

party have become more common. When the Democratic leadership and President Clinton pushed for a modified line-item veto, it put Representative Bobby Rush (D-IL) into a quandary. As both a party leader (one of the whips) and a member of the Black Caucus, he sided with the Black Caucus's opposition to the change and successfully urged the party to delay consideration of the proposal (Povich 1993, 10). This not only indicated his primary loyalty, but also revealed the power of such caucuses.

With the increasing number of minority Members, the Black Caucus and the Hispanic Caucus now have a critical mass of votes which must be taken into account. Both groups revealed a new aggressiveness during the 103rd Congress. The Black Caucus withheld its thirty-nine votes from President Clinton's economic package until programs of special interest to poor people were reinserted. The twenty Latino members of the Hispanic Caucus refused to support a $1 billion unemployment compensation bill until financing mechanisms which singled out immigrants were removed (Cooper 1993d, A4). With an increase in size, both caucuses now find that diversity reduces the ability to speak with one voice on all issues. The Black Caucus found itself in a difficult political position when it attempted to exclude Gary Franks (R-CT), its one Republican member, from its strategy session.

The Congressional Human Rights Caucus with more than 200 members maintains a computerized tracking system of human rights violations and promotes human rights legislation. Narrower groups such as the Congressional Mushroom Caucus and the Congressional Bearing Caucus promote and protect particular industries.

The Special Interest Teams in Action

Special interest teams vary considerably in size, operation and level of commitment. Some are informal and largely symbolic, while others serve important information functions. Most groups serve as "inside" lobbyists, promoting the interests around which the group was formed. Many groups serve as a contact point and facilitator for external lobbying groups, lending them a sympathetic ear, furnishing them with insider information, and providing an access point for coordinating internal and external strategies. A much smaller set of membership groups offer a significant cohesive voting bloc and have the ability to use their cohesiveness as the basis for building coalitions and striking bargains. Many caucuses have established an "exchange relationship" (see Hammond 1991, 294) with party and committee leadership. In exchange for the leader's responsiveness to their policy concerns, caucuses offer leaders access to blocs of members with expertise and votes. Although many caucuses were created out of frustration with other team leaders, many now serve as the building blocks for leadership coalitions (see chapter 9).

NEW TEAMS FOR TROUBLED TIMES

In recent years, amidst charges of "gridlock" and inefficiency, Congress has increasingly bypassed some traditional teams and attempted to avert stumbling blocks through the creation of short-term study groups and task forces (Sinclair 1992, 98). By creating new teams with specified tasks, congressional leaders hope to control the nature of the participants and assure that the vested interests and intransigence of existing party or committee teams would not prevail. As two staff members put it,

> A goal of our task forces is to give people . . . entry into an arena of interest that they might not otherwise have. You might have someone interested in agriculture, but not on the committee. (quote in Patterson and Little 1992, 17)

> By picking who is on the team and putting a spin on the outcome, leadership can exert more control. (Cohen 1990, 1881)

Members selected for task forces owe a debt of gratitude to the leadership for including them in the decision-making process, and both this debt and their inherent interest in the policy area increases the likelihood that they will be motivated to accomplish something.

Bypassing the established committee process is admitting that on some issues the committee system does not work. This generally occurs when the issues Congress is facing become "more complex, and the solutions don't fit neatly into baskets represented by the committee system" (Cohen 1990, 1876). Such a step has the potential for offending members and leaders of the circumvented committees, but for individual Members, a high visibility agreement on a controversial issue "can provide them with some political cover" (Fessler 1990, 2127). In recent years, a special National Commission on Social Security Reform was used to bypass the congressional process, and budget "summits," including congressional and executive branch players, have become favored strategies (see chapter 9).

Even within Congress, new teams have been developed to handle emerging problems. After a series of scandals over perks, privileges, and procedures rocked Congress in 1992, the Speaker and Senate Majority leader created a special Joint Committee on the Organization of Congress to make recommendations rather than relying on the committees having jurisdiction in this area. By balancing the temporary committee by party, it hoped to guarantee that its conclusions would not fall victim to partisan gridlock.

The increased tendency to use new teams to handle old tasks signals the willingness of party leaders to exert their influence and force policy action, especially when the committees are unwilling or unable to act (Cohen 1990, 1876). In the long run, this could either diminish the role of standing committees or spur them into action out of fear of being superseded.

CONCLUSION

Members of Congress are either selected for or choose to join various teams. Knowing with whom a Member affiliates helps explain his or her behavior on policy. The nature of the players, rules, and strategies differ between the various chambers, parties, committees, and special teams. The teams within each chamber are task oriented, transmitting information, suggesting policy alternatives, and/or coordinating efforts. Team leaders guide party and committee efforts, but increasingly lead through persuasion and accommodation as opposed to authority and power. For the individual Member, participating in a particular party or special interest team defines the key issues on which they will spend their time, while affiliating with a party team or policy team provides guidance as to which policy positions are acceptable to embrace. Increasing Member independence does not vitiate the continuing impact of congressional teams on either the Members or Congress. Some of the most interesting challenges for Members arise when different teams demand conflicting behavior. Loyalty and commitment are more often extended to Congress' team-like sub-units than to the institution as a whole.

IN DEPTH

1. Compare the U.S. Senate with the "upper" legislative chamber in one or more foreign countries. (You might consider looking at the British House of Lords or the German Bundesrat.) Compare how the members are selected, the powers they have to initiate and block legislation, and the role they play in the political process.

REFERENCES

Inter-Parliamentary Union. 1986. *Parliaments of the World.* New York: Facts on File.

HOUSE OF LORDS:

Jones, Bill and Dennis Kavanaugh. 1991. *British Politics Today.* Manchester: Manchester University Press.

Kingdon, John. 1991. *Government and Politics in Britain.* Cambridge: Polity Press.

Pike, Luke Owen. 1964. *A Constitutional History of the House of Lords.* New York: B. Franklin.

BUNDESTRAT:

Smith, Gordon, ed. 1992. *Developments in German Politics.* Durham, NC: Duke University Press.

2. It is said that "exceptions prove the rule." Look at the party cohesion scores for individual members of the House or Senate and identify the eight or ten who are least likely to vote with their partisan colleagues. Research each of these "outliers" to determine the reasons for their isolated partisan stance and relate your findings to the generalizations about party loyalty of legislators.

REFERENCES

The *Congressional Quarterly Weekly Report* lists individual party support for the previous session late each year.

Demographic information on members of Congress can be found in the *Congressional Directory,* Washington, D.C.: Government Printing Office; *The Almanac of American Politics,* Washington, D.C.: National Journal Inc.; and *Politics in America,* Washington, D.C.: Congressional Quarterly Inc.

3. Compare the demographic characteristics of two or three committees and/or subcommittees. Consider such factors as Members' occupations, gender, ethnic background, and type of district. Determine the degree to which the committee is representative of the entire chamber. Discuss the implications of your findings.

REFERENCES

Committee listings and demographics can be found in the *Congressional Directory,* Washington, D.C.: Government Printing Office; *The Almanac of American Politics,* Washington, D.C.: National Journal Inc.; and *Politics in America,* Washington, D.C.: Congressional Quarterly, Inc.

CHAPTER FIVE

BROADCASTING AND INTERPRETING THE LEGISLATIVE GAME

Congress, the Media, and the Public

If you like laws and sausages, you should never watch either one being made. (Attributed to Otto Von Bismarck, first chancellor of Germany, quoted in Platt 1989, 190)

[The] informing function of Congress should be preferred to even its legislative function. Unless [Congress informs], the country must remain in embarrassing, crippling ignorance of the very affairs which it is most important that it should understand and direct. (President Woodrow Wilson, quoted in Mathias 1982, S11332)

The functionaries of every government have propensities to command at will the liberty and property of their constituents. There is no safe deposit for these but with the people themselves; nor can they be safe with them without information. Where the press is free, and every man able to read, all is safe. (Thomas Jefferson, 1799)

Although the historical time periods and political experiences differed, the two quotations from the American statesmen and the quip from Count Bismarck reveal divergent perspectives about an informed citizenry. The relations between Congress, media,[1] and the public are guided by the ideas of the American statesmen resulting in a commitment to broad public information via an unfettered and privately owned set of media.

[1]In this chapter we will use the inclusive term "media" to cover the wide range of print and electronic methods of regularized information dissemination as opposed to the more narrow and increasingly anachronistic concept of the "press."

The game of informing the public involves three separate but interrelated two-player games. The **Congress versus the public game** is based on Congress' desire to persuade the citizenry that Congress and its individual Members are doing a good job. Congress realizes that the public are more than passive spectators; at times they take the floor to determine subsequent players and or affect the subsequent plays.

The **Congress versus the media game** pits the Congress, which sees the media as a vehicle for persuading the public, against the media, who desire to inform the public and in the process turn a financial profit. Both the games involving Congress react to the more general **media versus the public game** which defines what the media need to do to maintain their audience or readership in a profit-making environment. The public depends on the media for political information, while the media depend on the public to legitimize their activities to participants and investors. In order to reach the public through the media, members of Congress must take into account the motivations and needs of various media. The underlying needs of the media will be taken as a given in this analysis. Congress realizes that the media's commercial interests often result in coverage detrimental to Congress' persuasion goals, leading Congress to use a number of strategies for communicating directly with the public.

From the early days of the Republic, Congress has shown a commitment to supporting an informed public through both its own efforts and by encouraging media coverage.[2] Press and public galleries were provided in the House from the beginning, while the Senate did not open its galleries until 1795 (Baker 1988, 25). Until 1812, the official records of congressional debate were secured and published by the private sector media. Congress then contracted out the printing of its official records to commercial printers, often as a patronage payment to newspapers supporting the majority party. Eventually Congress took control of the production of its official records by creating the Government Printing Office in 1861. It followed its commitment to expanded official information by taking over publication of the daily *Congressional Record* in 1873 (Amer and Nickels 1989, 31) and the development of the Federal Depository Library Program in 1913.[3]

The Congress facilitated media coverage by providing press galleries in 1857 (Amer and Nickels 1989, 31). The modern Congress allows its Members to hire press secretaries and use subsidized radio and television studios. Congress has not, however, limited itself to reliance on the media to get its message out. Recognizing the inherent, and at times intentional, biases of the media, Congress has equipped itself with alternative and changing methods of reaching the public directly through

---

[2]The Senate initially followed the practice of the Constitutional Convention and the Continental Congress and met in secret. Senators looked with disdain at the House where occupants of the gallery routinely hissed and cheered, and felt that the publication of a yearly journal of actions and votes was sufficient (Baker 1988, 24).

[3]Currently more than 1,400 depository libraries (with a minimum of two per congressional district) receive free copies of most official documents from both Congress and other agencies. These collections of federal materials are open both to representatives of the media and the general public.

both the mail and television.[4] Most recently, Congress has acquiesced to the contemporary technology by allowing television cameras into the chambers (see later discussion). Congress and its Members work on the premise that "to know us is to love us," and expend more effort on providing than restraining information.

THE CONGRESS VERSUS THE MEDIA GAME

Political scientist David Mayhew (1974) forcefully argued that members of Congress emphasize three tasks, **advertising, position-taking,** and **credit claiming** (see chapter 3). Each of these tasks requires communication with the public. With congressional districts averaging close to 600,000 residents and senators representing states with much larger populations, members of Congress must rely on the media for much of their communications.

THE COMPETING PLAYERS

> The fundamental dilemma is that the good congressman's job is to participate in the building of consensus that leads to serious legislative purpose. The good reporter's job is to tell the story before the consensus has been reached and to inform as many people as he can, even if it prevents consensus-building. (Cater 1987, 4)

Competing Player Backgrounds

In many ways, the reporters and commentators covering Congress are very much like the people they cover. They tend to be well-educated members of the middle class (Hess 1991b, 60). A deep cynicism seems to run through many of the reporters who feel that they could do a better job of governing than most of the members of Congress. The reporters given the task of covering Congress have reached a position of prestige which almost guarantees them the chief measure of professional success, front page stories, or segments on the evening news (Hess 1991a, 65). They see Congress' foibles and machinations as vehicles for defining routine activities into legitimate news.

Competing Player Perspectives

As a news **source,** Congressional players often have very different goals from the news media. Congress and its Members want to communicate information which puts their efforts in the most positive light and/or which facilitates particular policy

---

[4]In this "information age," Congress has found it difficult to keep up with changing technology. A number of commercial firms are now providing computer access to congressional documents, procedural information, and voting records for a fee. The efficiency of searching these records electronically raises significant issues about the equity of access to congressional information. The established information "safety-net" is beginning to reveal some significant holes (see U.S. Congress, Office of Technology Assessment, 1988).

ROB ROGERS reprinted by permission of UFS, Inc.

goals. This generally means wanting to present an image of hard work, thoughtful deliberation, routine competence and reasonable compromise. The news media, on the other hand, has a basic commitment to objectively presenting reality, and a more proximate goal of turning a profit by maintaining an audience. News, by definition, is something out of the ordinary[5] such as inadequate effort, obvious incompetence, and/or sharp conflict. Each set of players attempts to "use" the other for its own purposes.

Congress does not speak with one voice. Individual Members may find it advantageous for their own career or policy goals to speak anonymously against the institution or question the actions of colleagues. News "leaks" are endemic to Congress. "Congress leaks like a sieve, since Members often find it politically advantageous to get a message out with little concern for the institution as a whole" (author's interview with House member). Reporters themselves encourage leaks as an alternative information source. As one reporter put it,

> Leaking has become a Washington parlor game, a secret code that inside players use to send messages and warnings to each other. And reporters (including me) unable to resist a juicy story, are all too willing to serve as a conduit. (Kurtz 1992, 11)

The news media also are not monolithic. The electronic media with their limited "news hole" and reliance on pictures to tell a story, deal with Congress in different ways than the print media. The national media have an audience with an

[5] The word "news" stems from the archaic plural of the word "new." News itself, as reported by the media though, continues to be a collection of "new" things.

interest in more far-reaching stories and a wider range of Members than the local media whose attention is focused on Members from their geographic area and the policies affecting their local well-being. The development of expanded cable television channels and the explosion of special interest publications has increased the number of available media outlets and the variety of media characteristics.

TRADITIONAL AND CHANGING RULES

Two sets of rules frame the relationship between Congress and the media. Formal **rules of access** determine what and where reporters can cover. More informal **canons of good journalism** define the kinds of stories reporters decide to pursue. Neither set of rules is fixed.

Rules of Access

Primary access to Congress comes via official galleries reserved for various types of media (daily press, periodicals, radio and television, and still photographs). Bona fide media representatives are given access to necessary equipment, limited desk space, and the right to take notes in the galleries—a right denied to those visiting the public galleries. Representatives of the electronic media find congressional rules most constraining. They cannot take cameras into the chamber and must get permission to film in the hallways or offices. As NBC correspondent Linda Ellerbee described it,

> Congress was able to enforce a handful of stupid rules it would never have tried with print journalism . . . not only could I not take my camera crew—my equivalent of pen and notebook—into the chamber of the House or Senate, I could not take my camera crew to some places in and around the Capitol that were, at the same time, open to tourists with their cameras. (Ellerbee 1986, 64–65)

Despite the limitations, the number of media personnel requesting official accreditation to the media galleries has grown significantly in both size and diversity (see table 5.1). Although many accredited personnel work the congressional beat only occasionally, interest in having official access to Congress is extensive.

Access to Congress has increased dramatically in recent years. While the official documents and reports of congressional action have long been readily available, most of the key decisions—strategy sessions, mark-ups, and votes—were made behind closed doors. Beginning in the 1950s, the Senate selectively allowed radio and television to cover key committee meetings, but the control remained in the hands of Congress.[6] Government in "sunshine" reforms moved much of the game out of the back rooms and subjected it to increased public scrutiny. These

[6]A number of these hearings drew large audiences, increased public debate over important policies, and made instant media stars of the congressional participants. Congressional careers that were changed dramatically by their television exposure were those of Estes Kefauver (D-TN), who investigated organized crime in 1951; Joseph McCarthy (D-WI), who instigated the witch hunt of communists in 1954; and Sam Ervin (D-SC), who chaired the Watergate investigation in 1973.

TABLE 5.1 Personnel with Official Accreditation to the House and Senate Media Galleries

	Periodicals	*Press*	*Radio and Television*
1950 (82nd Congress)	223	750	109
1960 (87th Congress)	363	859	236
1970 (92nd Congress)	458	1291	492
1980 (97th Congress)	1003	1349	1044
1992 (102nd Congress)	N.A.	1601	2095
1993 (103rd Congress)	1518	1778	2226

SOURCE: U.S. Congress. *Congressional Directory,* Washington, D.C.: Government Printing Office.
N.A. = not available.

reforms opened committee sessions to the public, increased the number of recorded votes, and expanded the access for the media (see Ornstein 1987, 8–11; Cook 1989, 2). Regular televising of congressional proceedings, which began in 1979 for the House and 1986 for the Senate, made it easier for both Washington-based and local reporters to monitor and report on Congress. Watching Congress live became a spectator sport for a small, but politically active group of C-SPAN (Cable Satellite Public Affairs Network) "junkies" (see later discussion).

Canons of Congressional Journalism

> The press always plays the game of "gotcha." I mean, you try to trap the person into saying something that will make news, and news by definition tends to be negative . . . and the process is now so speeded up that . . . the interpretation happens at the same time as the event. (journalist Eleanor Clift on the "McLaughlin Group," 4 December 1993)

At the same time Congress was becoming more open, the media was changing its own coverage rules. The media became "harder, tougher, [and] more cynical" (Robinson 1981, 55). Until the 1970s, most journalists made a distinction between the official public actions of members of Congress, which were fair game for coverage, and their private lives, which were out of bounds. Slowly the traditional boundaries began to change. Once private peculiarities of public official's sex lives or financial dealings became legitimate news. In many cases, allegations of impropriety forced a story onto the front pages or into the evening news. Stories about the personal lives of Members and alleged misuse of public office became easier to explain than the more complex intricacies of public policy battles.

COMMUNICATOR AND SOURCE STRATEGIES

Members of Congress and the media exist in a symbiotic relationship—they each need the other, but have different goals. Each try to reach their goals while maintaining a working relationship with the other. As communicators, the media picks and chooses what to cover and how to present it. As sources, members of Congress seek to structure coverage to present their perspective on the news.

Media Biases and Congressional Coverage

Bias comes in two forms, intentional and structural. **Intentional bias** emerges from the conscious desire of the media to use their power to communicate information selectively. This type of unprofessional activity is relatively rare. **Structural bias,** on the other hand, emerges from unintentional factors such as the subconscious mind set of journalists, the demands of particular media, and/or the economic needs of responding to a particular audience. For example, the social sciences and liberal arts educational backgrounds of Washington journalists tend to result in issues being viewed from a relatively liberal perspective (Hess 1991a, 113). Various media also have unique structural demands. Radio and television need sound bites, while television seldom covers stories without a visual component. The nature of media coverage is also colored by the intended audience. Journalists attempt to tell stories of relevance and interest to their readers or viewers, and in the process develop strategies which ignore some news stories and highlight others. Structural biases affect who is covered and how the news is portrayed.

THE NATURE OF CONGRESSIONAL NEWS In deciding whom to cover, journalists are well aware of the fact that Congress is not the only game in town. Coverage of Congress must compete with other political players, especially the president. During the nineteenth century, Congress dominated press coverage of national politics (Balutis 1976, 509; and Cornwell 1959, 275). Beginning with the twentieth century, presidential domination began to emerge. More powerful and active presidents used the media to get public attention in the hope of persuading the public to their point of view. The media responded to shifts in presidential power by focusing more of their attention on the president. The arrival of the electronic media gave the wheel another spin toward presidential dominance as television found it easier to get good pictures and focus on an individual. While both presidential and congressional coverage are down a bit in recent years, congressional coverage has declined to a greater degree and pales in comparison to presidential coverage (see figure 5.1). "Congress remains largely a print story, and as newspapers lose out to television as the news purveyor of choice for Americans, Congress loses out to the president" (Hess 1991a, 105). In the last decade, both the absolute number of stories about Congress and the coverage of Congress relative to the president has declined on national television (see Rutkus 1991, 25; and Ornstein and Robinson 1986, 4–6). As former Senator Howard Hughes (D-IA) warned,

> The system of checks and balances is, in a point of fact, checkmated, unless the legislature is afforded equivalent opportunity to present its point of view to the American people. (quoted in Barrett and Sklar 1980, 34)

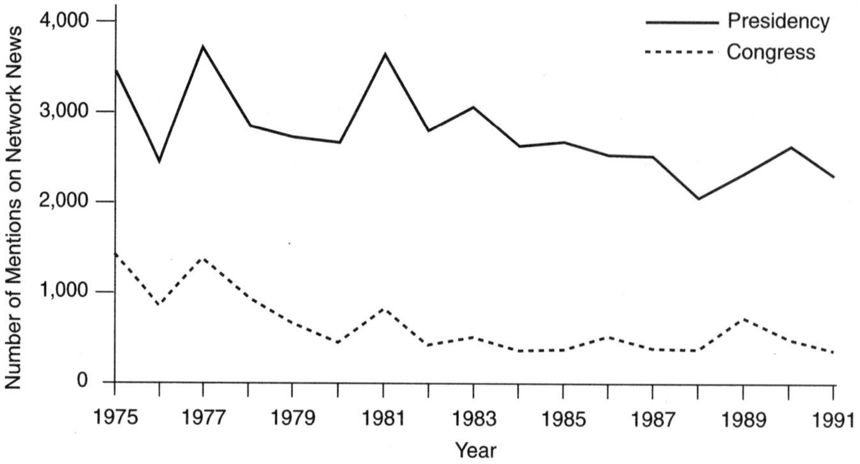

FIGURE 5.1
Presidential Domination of the Evening News
SOURCE: Calculated by the author from *Television News Index,* 1975–1991, Nashville: Vanderbilt University Television News Archives.

Congress is difficult to cover since it is "a process, not an event" (former Representative Bill Frenzel [R-MN] quoted in Wolfson 1985, 35). The complexity of the congressional process and the multiplicity of playing fields make it hard to interpret in the brief time allotted for radio or television stories.

The news "hook" for most stories in the electronic media is an individual whose name and general characteristics are known to the public. The president is of course the most widely recognized news hook and virtually every presidential action could be defined as news. Most members of Congress are not common household names and fail to become news hooks unless involved in some extraordinary activity. With a more limited membership, senators are better news hooks than members of the House, and the Senate tends to receive more extensive coverage. Within each chamber a relatively small cadre of formal leaders and individuals with high media-created name recognition for previous activity garner the bulk of the subsequent coverage (see T. E. Cook 1989, 62–68; and Squire 1988, 139).

Media coverage of Congress is not monolithic. There is considerable variation in the strategies of how national and local media outlets approach congressional reporting.

NATIONAL MEDIA Journalists for nationally oriented newspapers, news magazines, and television networks have considerable flexibility in defining news and choosing whom to cover. Most stories will be of some interest to some members of their broad audience, so they choose the story with the widest level of potential interest. Adversarial journalism has become the norm, as national reporters appear unconcerned about offending a particular source with a tough story. Most sources desire national coverage and cannot afford to "freeze out" a reporter. One offended source can readily be replaced by any number of the other 534 principal congressional sources. Perhaps the clearest evidence that few congressional sources are offended enough to eschew their opportunity for national coverage is the fact that the national television networks seldom have trouble convincing members of Congress to appear. Actually, the networks base their stories on only a small number of Members. More than half the House members are never mentioned on the evening news during a typical year and more than one-third of the senators receive one mention or less (See T. E. Cook 1989, 60; and Hess 1991a, 105).

On the other hand, "pack" journalism often takes over in the coverage of Congress as it does in many realms (Wolfson 1985, 36). Key members of the congressional media corps interact regularly and find it comfortable to be covering the same stories and talking to the same people. Going off on one's own to get a scoop may win some kudos from your editor, but may not compensate for missing the "big" story everyone else has covered. Congressional reporters tend to use a "defensive" strategy, making sure they follow the pack before breaking new ground. The stories coming out of Congress look remarkably similar no matter which national news source one uses. National stories tend to be critical of Congress, emphasizing conflict and/or the inappropriate behavior of a few Members (see Ornstein and Robinson 1986, 4–6; and Ornstein 1987, 7–19).

LOCAL MEDIA The local and regional media face more constraints than their national counterparts. Policies to be covered and relevant interview sources are limited to local issues and members of Congress representing one's audience (see Wolfson 1985, 38; and T. E. Cook 1989, 45). Offending *the* Member one must intensively cover often undermines the journalist's effectiveness. Tough investigative reporting is often replaced with the journalist becoming a conduit for the Member's preferred stories and interpretations. Local coverage tends to emphasize parochial concerns and allows Members "to magnify their role in congressional actions" (Wolfson 1985, 38). Reporters and Members are symbiotic "partners" with differing goals, but tied together by necessity in a cordial, rather than an adversarial relationship (see Robinson 1981, 76–78). In recent years, an increasing number of local media have begun to regularly publicize the official actions of the Members they cover through "how your member voted" boxes and stories. In general, local stories tend to be more descriptive than critical.

None of the players see contemporary media coverage of Congress as ideal (see box 5.1). Part of the problem results from imperfect observers covering an imperfect institution, but to better understand the problems, one must recognize that the players have conflicting goals and must operate under differing constraints.

News Sources and the Manipulation of Coverage

It is often said that the best defense is a good offense. Congress and its Members are not without strategies for turning media coverage to their own advantage.

Members of Congress often recognize the needs of the various media and use those needs to their benefit. Committee deliberations and floor debate are often scheduled with news deadlines in mind (see box 5.2). Hearings are made into news events by inviting high visibility "experts" to testify (see box 5.3).

BOX 5.1 The Players Speak about Media Coverage of Congress

THE MEMBERS OF CONGRESS SPEAK

The man-bites-dog syndrome is a real affliction. What makes news is the exception and not the rule. And, clearly, what makes news is what feeds public suspicions . . . if ten congressmen are misbehaving, the public thinks the condition is epidemic and forgets that there are 425 others who are living with their wives, keeping their hands out of the cookie jar, and probably doing a good job of trying to represent their constituencies. (Barber Conable former [R-NY] quoted in Bates 1987, 23)

The number one problem is superficiality. [The media] emphasize the conflict rather than the true mood of the House on many issues. . . . They [play] to the extremes and [ignore] much of the debate because the main issue at hand was not that visually exciting. (David Obey [D-WI] quoted in Bates 1987, 22)

First, the media deal with scandals, superficialities, faux pas, peccadilloes. . . . Second, the media often deal with the problems that reinforce cynicism and negativism—junketing and that sort of thing—things people "understand." (former Senator John Culver [D-IA] quoted in Bates 1987, 47)

There's a veritable feeding frenzy out there, and the Congress is the first entree on the menu. (Dennis Eckart [D-OH] quoted in Cohen 1992, 120)

MEMBERS OF THE MEDIA SPEAK

It was hard to sell stories [about Congress] unless they were "exciting"—a fierce clash on the Senate floor or some dramatic film from a Senate hearing. . . . Another problem is that certain members of Congress are very adept at using the television medium, and you have to guard against people reaping excessive, unwarranted publicity. (Paul Duke, moderator of "Washington Week in Review," quoted in Bates 1987, 41)

You have to sell a story to the editor, and the editor wants action, not process. . . . And that isn't what Congress is about. Congress is about process. . . . So [we] are constantly beating our heads against the wall, caught in battles both with sources in Congress and the producers in New York. (Jacqueline Adams, Capitol Hill correspondent for CBS, quoted in Bates 1987, 43)

The importance placed by individual Members on relations with the media is evident by the increased number of staff assigned to related tasks. In 1970 only about 12 percent of House offices had a full-time press secretary; today that figure is more than 60 percent (T. E. Cook 1989, 72–73). Virtually every senator has a full-time press secretary and many have a multi-member press office (Hess 1991a, 62–68). Press secretaries respond to media requests, create events designed to get media coverage, communicate the Member's story through press releases and interviews, and develop relationships with relevant journalists—especially those with the local media back in the district (see T. E. Cook 1989, 75, 83).

Unlike a few decades ago, Congress has equipped itself with the technology to serve the needs of the media. Computers and FAX machines allow instant communications with lists of media outlets. Publicly subsidized radio and television

BOX 5.2 Beating the News Media at Its Own Game

THE BATTLE FOR THE AIRWAVES

Newsman David Brinkley once commented that "it is widely believed in Washington that it would take Congress thirty days to make instant coffee," but when action is believed necessary, Congress can move with significant speed (NBC "Nightly News," 3 February 1976). After President Bush committed troops in the Gulf War, many believed that congressional approval was necessary. Over the previous few weeks sentiment in the Senate had been deeply divided over whether economic sanctions or military action should be used. The day after troops were committed, the Democratic Caucus met in an all-day session to develop a compromise which could be supported by all Members. At 5:30 p.m. the Senators rushed over to the floor to officially debate the issue. Unlike its normal pattern of unlimited debate and leisurely roll call votes, the Senate agreed by unanimous consent to a fifteen-minute debate and an immediate vote. With their eyes on the clock and the desire to preempt stories about opposition to the war, Senate leaders shepherded a major decision to completion by 6:05, just in time for the national network news.

THE BATTLE FOR PRIME TIME

Members of Congress not only battle to outsmart other news sources to get on the air, but also battle with each other. Then-Senate Minority Leader Robert Dole (R-KN) openly discussed the strategy of "prime-time amendments":

> These are the ones you offer between 2:30 and 4:30 on a normal day, which is about right for the evening news. Sometimes you have people competing for prime-time amendments. You can't choose among your friends, so you let them each offer a prime-time amendment or a prime-time substitute. Then everybody had a fair shot at the evening news. (quoted in Bates 1987, 104)

studios are available to Members wishing to send audio or video press releases directly to local stations. Given a limited budget and staff, local stations often accept written, audio, and/or video press releases verbatim, allowing the Members to control their content (see Kenworthy 1990a, E5). The utility of such outreach was tested experimentally and showed that placing articles in local newspapers tended to increase constituent support for Members (Larson 1990, 1102).

THE CONGRESS VERSUS THE PUBLIC GAME: CIRCUMVENTING THE MEDIA AND REACHING THE VOTERS DIRECTLY

> I am not only a news maker, but a newsman—perhaps the most widely read journalist in my district. I have a radio show, a television program and a news column with a circulation larger than that of most of the weekly newspapers in my district. (member of the House quoted in Haskell 1982, 50)

Members of Congress are unwilling to have their collective and individual images controlled by the media alone. They constantly look for ways to circumvent the media and present an image they control.

BOX 5.3 Johnny We Hardly Knew You . . . [Were the Expert]

> The "celebrity as moral authority" is part of a larger game Congress plays, stacking the hearing process to produce a desired result. (Dutton 1990, B2)

Star studded congressional committee hearings attract more attention than testimony from scientists and bureaucrats. Individuals from the entertainment and sports fields are used to draw attention to issues and assure that the hearing will get on the evening news. In recent years, the following "experts" have testified on the indicated topics:

- Singer John Denver on the environment (He sang "Ode to Alaskan Forests" to the House Committee on Interior and Insular Affairs.)
- Actress Elizabeth Taylor on AIDS
- Singer Frank Zappa on censorship of rock lyrics
- Talk show hostess Oprah Winfrey on child abuse
- Actor Robin Williams and actress Whoopi Goldberg on homelessness
- Actress Mary Tyler Moore on animal rights
- Actress Meryl Streep on pesticide residues

Drawing on personal experience, talk show host Oprah Winfrey prepares to testify before a Senate Judiciary hearing on child abuse.

CONSTITUENT OUTREACH

As we saw in chapter 3, Members use the mails to communicate directly with their constituents through newsletters and targeted mail. A number of Members are more aggressive in their outreach activities, hosting local radio or television programs and securing speaking invitations where they can communicate with constituents directly (see box 5.4).

RECONSTRUCTING HISTORY

Congress is one of the few places where someone can say, "Gee I wish I had said that"—and then do so. Members end each speech with the request to "revise and

Representative Ron Klink (D-PA), right, hosts Representative Robert Dornan (R-CA), left, and Professor Stephen Frantzich on his cable television program, "The People's House."

extend" their remarks. This allows them to adjust the grammar, syntax, and even content of what appears in the *Congressional Record.* Members have the right to insert entire speeches with only vague indications that they were never delivered.[7] The *Record* serves as the legal statement of legislative intent, but is clearly not a verbatim record of what transpired on the floor (see box 5.5). It represents what Members would have liked to have transpired on the floor. In most cases, the edited debates make both the Members and the chamber look better to the outside world.

TELEVISING CONGRESS

> Borrowing from a theory of political scientist James Q. Wilson—"organizations come to resemble the organizations they are in conflict with"—Senator Daniel Patrick Moynihan invented the Iron Law of Emulation: "Whenever any branch of the government acquires a new technique which enhances its power in relation to the other branches, that technique will soon be adopted by those other branches as well. (Hess 1991a, 103)

Congress reacted to presidential domination of television by facilitating television's access to its own proceedings. As Senator J. William Fulbright (D-AR) framed this issue,

> Television has done more to expand the powers of the president as would a Constitutional amendment formally abolishing the co-equality of the three branches of government. . . . Stories about the executive branch that describe what is actually done are far more memorable than reports about the laborious process of hammering out legislation. (quoted in Graber 1980, 208–209)

---

[7]The House and Senate have used different techniques to indicate speeches that were never given. At times they are printed in a different type face or proceeded with a black dot. The *Congressional Record* includes a note to indicate the current practice.

BOX 5.4 Congress and the Tapping of New Technology

Technology has long been a tool which enhances the political power and effectiveness of individuals who choose to use it. Congress has seldom been on the cutting edge of technology applications, but eventually sees the potential—especially after such tools begin to be used successfully by the president.

Several Members have seen the potential of new technology for improving communications with constituents. The use of FAX machines and electronic computer bulletin boards to send newsletters and press releases is increasing. Some Members have seen the potential for teleconferencing, allowing the Member in Washington and the participants in the other location to both see each other and interact as if they were in the same room. Such use of technology eliminates travel and has the potential for including many groups in physically remote locations. Representative Amo Houghton (R-NY) has used two-way videoconferencing to hold constituent meetings. The potential of videoconferencing for general town meetings, educational link-ups with local schools, gathering information from experts, and crisis coordination is significant. In one staff member's view,

> Ten years from now congressional office use of videoconferencing will have gone the way of other technological applications such as the telephone, television camera, and computer. Its use will not be an issue. We will just wonder how we got along without it. (author's interview, 1992)

Representative Amo Houghton (R-NY) uses teleconferencing to expand his presence among his constituents.

BOX 5.5 You May Not Know the True Plays Even with a Program

The right to "revise and extend" leads to an official record which may lose some of the flavor of what actually went on in Congress. The following two examples indicate the kind of revisions Members make to speeches on the floor.

During a debate on grazing rights, Senator Alan Simpson (R-WY) waxed eloquently using rather pithy terminology. On second thought, he decided that his original words might not look too good in the *Congressional Record.*

THE ORIGINAL STATEMENT

[Those favoring higher fees] don't want those cows on public land. They are ugly and leave poop all over the prairie. (Kamen 1993, A19)

THE OFFICIAL RECORD

[Those favoring higher fees] don't want those cows on public land. They are ugly and leave "cowpies" all over the prairie.[a]

During a particular rancorous budget debate, Senators D'Amato (R-NY) and Byrd (D-WV) got into a shouting match which lost some of its flavor when it was reported in the *Congressional Record.*

The Spoken Record (with variations underlined)[b]

Mr. D'AMATO. But let me refer to the Standing Rules of the Senate, page 19, Senate Manual, ("October" not said), OK:

It is clear, No Senator in debate shall, directly or indirectly, by any form of word, impute to another Senator, or to any other Senators any conduct or motive unworthy or unbecoming of a Senator.

I am just simply going to make a point that this is out of order, and that we are not doing this body any good by this.

Mr. BYRD. Mr. President, I ask for the regular order I know enough about—

Mr. D'AMATO. I raise a point of order—

Mr. BYRD. I know enough about the Senate Rules to know that I have not violated rule XIX.

Mr. D'AMATO. I ask the—

Mr. BYRD. The Senator can just—Would the Senator just shut his own mouth and let the chair rule?

The Official Record[c]

Mr. D'AMATO. But let me refer to the Standing Rules of the Senate, page 18, Senate Manual, October:

No Senator in debate shall, directly or indirectly, by any form of word, impute to another Senator, or to any other Senators any conduct or motive unworthy or unbecoming of a Senator.

I am simply going to make a point that this is out of order, and that we are not doing this body any good by this.

Mr. BYRD. Mr. President, I ask for the regular order. I know enough about—

Mr. D'AMATO. I raise a point of order—

Mr. BYRD. I know enough about the Senate Rules that I have not violated rule XIX.

Mr. D'AMATO. I ask the—

Mr. BYRD. The Senator can just—

[a](*Congressional Record,* 14 September 1993)

[b](Tape of floor debate, Purdue Public Affairs Video Archives)

[c](*Congressional Record,* 26 June 1992, S9043)

The House adopted live television coverage in 1979, while the more traditional Senate feared upsetting its procedures. When it became clear that the existence of video footage increased visibility of the House and especially its leaders (T. E. Cook 1989, 63; and Foote and Davis 1987, passim), the Senate was forced to emulate the House in 1986. As Senator Howard Baker outlined the argument,

> I don't begrudge the House the recognition or public attention [it] gain[s]. . . . But it does mean that if we don't get television in the Senate in a decade or less, the House will be the dominant partner in the Congressional branch. (quoted in Hunter 1984, 11)

Despite pleas from the commercial networks for simply changing the rules to allow videotaping of live congressional proceedings, Congress was unwilling to give the media complete control. Instead, each chamber controls its own cameras and provides a "feed" to outside users. The rules of both chambers emphasize broadcasting official activity, as opposed to panning the chamber or looking for the most interesting shot. The gavel-to-gavel coverage of the House and Senate as well as selected committee hearings is currently distributed to more than 60 million households by C-SPAN (Cable Satellite Public Affairs Network), a private network created by the cable industry.

While it is difficult to prove the full implications of televised coverage (see Frantzich 1990, passim), most of the dire predictions of "grandstanding" Members and disruption of procedures, as well as the optimistic hopes of creating a national dialogue of fully informed citizens on all issues have not been borne out (see box 5.6). More modest impacts such as an increase in the length of congressional sessions, increased Member efficiency due to the ability to monitor floor activity, better prepared speakers, and the expanded potential for some proceedings to enhance the national policy dialogue have become commonly accepted. Issues such as sexual harassment and the hiring of illegal aliens received more public attention because of the Clarence Thomas and Zoe E. Baird confirmation hearings and debate.

THE NEXT WAVE

Until recently much of the attention on informing the public has been on the efforts of the media and Congress itself. The arrival of commercial computer databases of congressional activity[8] puts more pressure on the citizenry to obtain the most complete and up-to-date information. While interest in Congress has always been unequal among the population, increased reliance on efficient, but costly databases could exacerbate the inequality of citizens' access to congressional information. In the new game, resources and skills largely replace interest in determining the "haves" and "have nots" of congressional information (see U.S. Congress, Office of Technology Assessment 1988, 8–9).

[8]A number of commercial databases such as LEXIS-NEXIS, LEGI-SLATE, and WASHINGTON ALERT *(Congressional Quarterly),* allow individuals to do full text searches of congressional floor and committee proceedings, as well as scan congressional documents and perform voting analyses. The Congress is in the process of developing a CD-ROM version of the *Congressional Record* that will be distributed to Federal Depository Libraries. Some congressional documents are now available free on the Internet.

President Clinton's nominee for attorney general, Zoe Baird, began her confirmation hearings before the Senate Judiciary Committee with confidence. Within a few days, serious questioning about her knowingly hiring illegal aliens to work in her household led to the withdrawal of the nomination.

BOX 5.6 Lights! Cameras! Action?

Necessity is often the mother of invention. After many years of frustration with the Democratic Party domination of Congress and congressional news, a group of conservative Republicans decided to take advantage of the new opportunity gavel-to-gavel coverage of Congress provided. House rules allow Members to use time at the end of each legislative day to present "special orders" speeches. After most Members had returned to their offices, members of the Conservative Opportunity Society used these "extra innings" to castigate the Democrats and present their own agenda to a national television audience. House rules provided for narrow angle shots which meant that viewers did not realize that most speeches were being given to an empty chamber. After a particularly vicious attack, then Speaker Thomas P. "Tip" O'Neill had had enough. He surreptitiously had the cameras use wide angle shots to unmask the Republican "fraud." The Republicans took the changing of rules mid-game in stride and used it as "another example of Democratic Party duplicity." The next day, O'Neill took the floor angrily and his intemperate words were eventually struck from the *Congressional Record,* much to his embarrassment. The Democrats initially decided to limit special order speeches, but were charged with limiting public dialogue. They eventually decided that "if you can't beat them, join them." The Democrats now have attempted to present a more consistent and unified front during the special orders period.

For further information, see Stephen E. Frantzich, "Communications in Congress," in Gerald Benjamin, ed., 1983, *The Communications Revolution in Congress,* New York: Academy of Political Science; and Steven S. Smith, 1989, *Call to Order: Floor Politics in the House and Senate,* Washington D.C.: Brookings Institution, 65–67.

THE CONSEQUENCES OF CONGRESSIONAL COVERAGE GAMES: PUBLIC KNOWLEDGE AND EVALUATION OF CONGRESS

Both the media and individual members of Congress expend considerable effort attempting to inform the public about Congress. The results are far from extensive knowledge or a uniform perspective.

KNOWLEDGE ABOUT CONGRESS AND ITS MEMBERS

For all the efforts of the media and congressional offices, knowledge of Congress and its Members is relatively limited. Only about one half of the public can name their House member (*Gallup Poll Monthly,* no. 302, 21), and only about two-thirds recognize the incumbent House member's name from a list of candidates (Bernstein 1989, 15). Senators are somewhat better known than members of the House, but knowledge seldom goes much beyond superficial knowledge. Despite the relatively low level of recognition, media practices and Member efforts assure that incumbents are better known than challengers—another factor that increases incumbents' chances of re-election (see chapter 2).

On the institutional level, despite the importance of political parties in choosing leadership and controlling congressional behavior, only about half of the public knows which party controls Congress (POLL database 1992). The arrival of television coverage of floor proceedings and media emphasis on personalities has increased public knowledge of individual congressional leaders.

THE EVALUATION OF CONGRESS AND ITS MEMBERS

> [Members of Congress] too often behave as if we are playing some game of chicken with the public's trust, the object of which is to come as close to losing the trust we have been given without going over the line. (Senator Mark Hatfield [R-OR] *Congressional Record,* 21 May 1991, S6205)

The public makes a distinction between the Congress as an institution and their individual Member. Members of Congress encourage the distinction, and media strategies exacerbate the seemingly schizophrenic set of evaluations.

Evaluation of Congress

Despite public inattention to much of congressional activity, the popular view of the institution overall is decidedly negative. Pollsters ask a variety of questions about Congress, and their results follow a consistent pattern. Since the early 1970s, less (and often much less) than a majority of the public have had a "great deal" or "quite a lot" of confidence in Congress as an institution. Figure 5.2 illustrates long-term trends in public support for Congress. Public evaluation of Congress is considerably lower than evaluation of other national institutions such as the presidency and the Supreme Court.

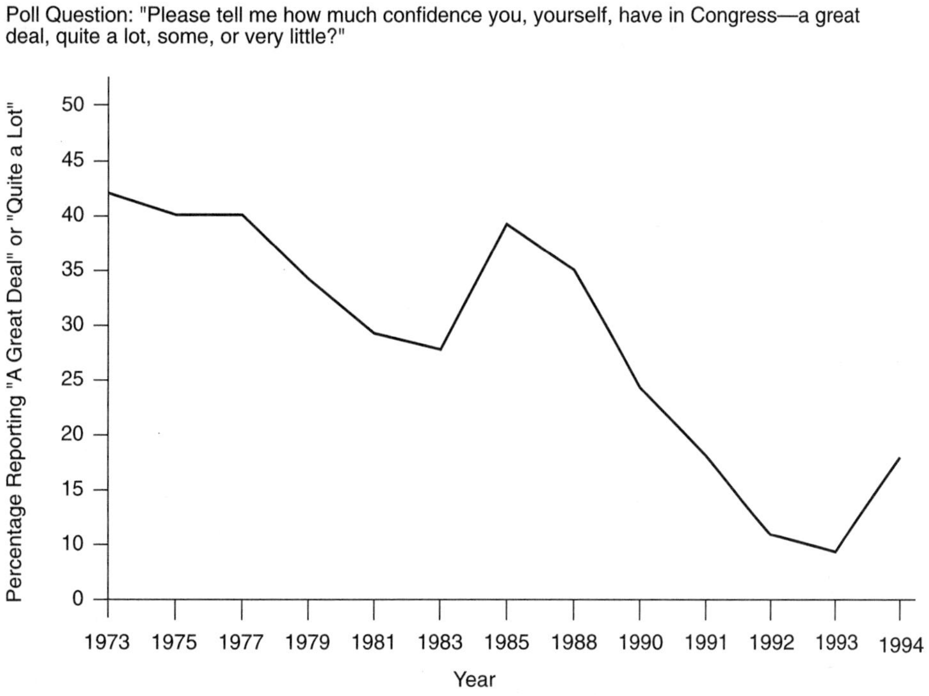

FIGURE 5.2
Evaluation of Congress, 1973–1994
SOURCE: *The Gallup Poll Monthly,* October 1991, No. 313, p. 37, and July 1992, No. 322, p. 3.: LEXIS-NEXIS Rpoll database.

Low evaluations of Congress stem from a variety of sources. Congress has historically been the subject of jokes by humorists (see box 5.7). In recent years, there has been a general trend of increased cynicism toward all national institutions. Congress has been particularly hurt by charges that it preserves a protected position for itself by exempting itself from rules like employment discrimination and freedom of information procedures. As Senator John Glenn (D-OH) put it,

> We make the rules but we do not play the game. We apply those rules to everyone else but we will not apply them to ourselves. . . . It's a little like a doctor prescribing medicine for a patient that he himself would not take. (*Congressional Record,* 10 October 1991, S15502)

Some of Congress' current problems arose from a series of misadventures in 1991, which led to historically low ratings in opinion polls for the institution (see box 5.8).

BOX 5.7 Humorists Take Congress to Task

1897

It probably could be shown by facts and figures that there is no distinctively native American criminal class except for Congress. (Mark Twain)[a]

1890s

Suppose you were an idiot. And suppose you were a member of Congress. But I repeat myself. (Mark Twain)[b]

1935

I'm an amateur, and the thing about my jokes is that they don't hurt anybody. . . . But with Congress—every time they make a joke it's a law. And every time they make a law it's a joke. (Will Rogers)[c]

1947

Congress is so strange. A man gets up to speak and says nothing. Nobody listens—and then everybody disagrees. (Boris Marshalov)[d]

1991

Above the doors [of the House chamber of the Capitol building] are medallions bearing bas-relief profiles of mankind's great and reasonably great lawgivers: Moses, Solomon, Alfonso X, Hammurabi, Pope Innocent III. No U.S. congressmen are included. (P. J. O'Rourke)[e]

1992

(On members of Congress pleading ignorance as a check-bouncing defense) That's not necessary. If there's one thing Congress doesn't have to plead, it's ignorance. (Jay Leno)[f]

1993

How is it that Congress can pass bills on ethics, which they know nothing about, but can't pass a bill on crime, on which they've had tremendous experience. (Jay Leno, the "Tonight Show," April 8, 1993)

[a]*Following the Equator,* vol. 1 (vol. 5 of *The Writings of Mark Twain*), Hartford CT: American Publishing Co., p. 98.

[b]Fred Metcalf, 1987, *Penguin Dictionary of Modern Humorous Quotations,* London: Penguin Books, p. 55.

[c]Quoted in P. J. O'Brien, 1935, *Will Rogers, Ambassador of Good Will, Prince of Wit,* Philadelphia, Chicago: John C. Winston, pp. 156–157.

[d]Quoted in Alexander Wiley, 1947, *Laughing with Congress,* New York: Crown Publishers, p. 58.

[e]P. J. O'Rourke, 1991, *Parliament of Whores,* New York: The Atlantic Monthly Press, p. 50.

[f]"Tonight Show" quoted in the *Washington Times,* 29 March 1992, p. 32.

Evaluating One's Own Member of Congress

Although Congress as an institution suffers from low popularity, individual Members receive more favorable poll ratings (see figure 5.3). How can we explain this seeming contradiction? One reason is that judging an abstract institution is different from evaluating a living, breathing human being. A diverse institution like Congress cannot nimbly field the varying objections of the American electorate. An individual senator or representative, however, does have a greater strategic ability to convince the public of his or her merit.

BOX 5.8 Throwing the Game: Increasing the Public Hostility toward Congress

In recent years, a number of incidents in Washington have stoked public hostility toward Congress and shaved the electoral margins of incumbents.[a] In fall of 1990, a lengthy budget deadlock involving much partisan carping between the Congress and president took place, resulting in a shutdown of all government offices during the Columbus Day weekend. The final budget agreement, reached a mere week before the election, raised taxes for most Americans. One week later, the proportion of the 1990 vote for House incumbents facing major-party opposition dropped by a substantial 5 percent. In January 1991, the House compounded its unpopularity by voting to increase the pay of its Members from $96,600 to $125,100—a 29.5 percent hike. The Senate followed suit with a comparable hike in July. Both chambers attempted to justify the increases by also banning acceptance of honoraria for speeches given to interest groups. This point got lost in the fray. Opinion polls showed strong opposition to the pay hikes. Television and radio talk shows lambasted lawmakers for increasing their pay while the nation was sliding into a recession.

In October of 1991, the Senate Judiciary Hearings on Clarence Thomas produced much public disgust with the Senate. Anita Hill testified that Supreme Court nominee Thomas had sexually harassed her when she worked for him at two federal agencies in the 1980s. Thomas denied all wrongdoing, and eventually won confirmation. Hill's supporters expressed outrage at the inability of a white male Senate to take her charges seriously. Advocates of Thomas argued that he was the victim of a scurrilous partisan witch hunt that no nominee should be forced to endure. None of the players in this drama came out looking good. In particular, "The Senate appeared foolish, if not outright prurient, in the glare of a televised confirmation hearing of a Supreme Court nominee turned into an X-rated national morality play" (Cohen 1992, 118).

Also during the fall of 1991, it was disclosed that the "bank" operated for House members and House employees had routinely covered hundreds of checking account overdrafts by those Members. Speaker Foley ordered the practice terminated immediately, the House bank was soon closed, and the House Ethics Committee began an investigation into the problem (see Gugliotta and Cooper 1992, A1). After much delay, in April of 1992 a list of 355 present and past Members responsible for overdrafts was made public. Public outrage reached a new crescendo, again inflamed by talk show ridicule. More than 80 percent of the public felt that Members who had bounced checks had done something unethical.[b] After public disclosure of the bank scandal, members of Congress dropped from number eighteen to number twenty-two on the list of ethics and honesty among twenty-five major occupations—ending up just above car salesmen, insurance agents, and advertising practitioners.[c] Congress had sunk to a new low in public esteem. By July of 1992, only 11 percent of the public had much confidence in Congress as an institution, down from 24 percent two years earlier (see figure 5.3). The task for incumbents of disassociating themselves from their institution became even more important for electoral survival. Many Members who retired or were defeated in 1992 showed up on the list of the most obvious House Bank abusers.

[a]Rhodes Cook, "Most House Members Survive, But Many Margins Narrow," *Congressional Quarterly,* 10 November 1990, p. 3798.

[b]Richard Morin and Helen Dewar, 1992, "Approval of Congress Hits All-Time Low, Poll Finds," *Washington Post,* (20 March): A16.

[c]Leslie McAnemy, 1992, "Pharmacists Again Top 'Honesty and Ethics' Poll; Ratings for Congress Hit New Low," *Gallup Poll Monthly,* no. 322 (July): 2–4.

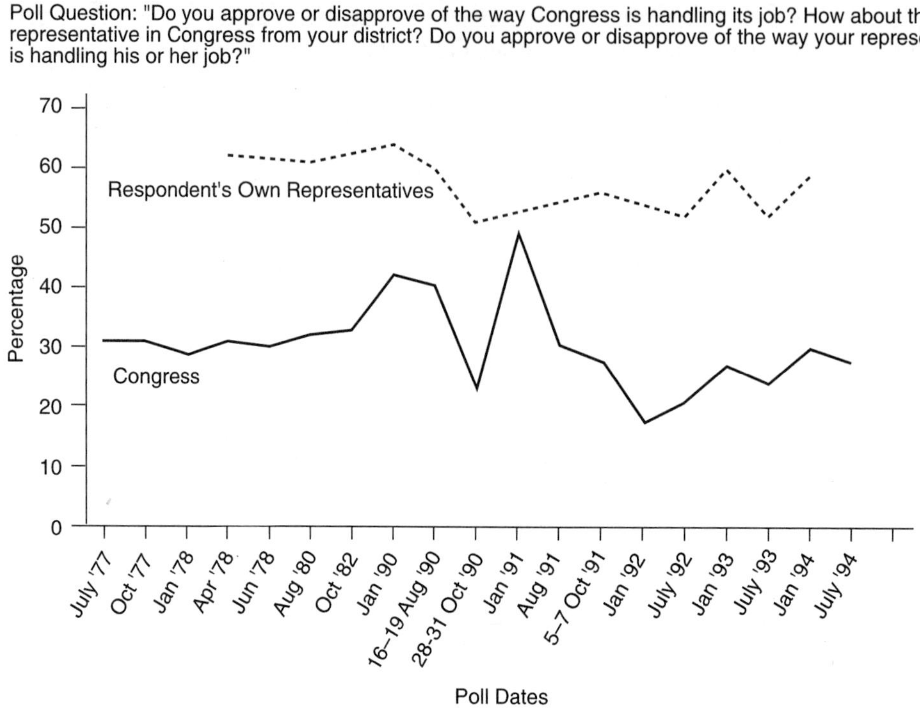

FIGURE 5.3

Public Approval of Congress and Its Individual Members

SOURCE: "Congress, My Congressman," *Public Perspective 3:102* (May/June 1992); July 1992 data from CBS/*New York Times* poll.

Lawmakers have little incentive to defend their institution, but much reason to defend themselves. They actively pursue public support. Political scientist Richard Fenno, a leading scholar of Congress, argues that Members effectively insulate themselves from the public distaste afflicting their institution "because they so ardently sue for our affection" (Fenno 1990, 463).

Many legislators try to present themselves as reliable providers of material rewards for their districts. Pork barrel projects can be brought home. Congressional offices act like small firms with only one product to sell—their Member (Loomis 1979, 52). Legislators actively claim credit for all good news for the district emanating from the federal government. Incumbents also advertise themselves through frequent visits back home and pursue casework aggressively through their district offices (Mayhew 1974a, 44–52). These tactics usually work better for representatives than senators, because House members receive less media scrutiny and have smaller, more manageable districts than do their counterparts in the upper chamber.

Legislators have an occupational imperative to present themselves favorably, and they do so by appearing to run *against* the institution of which they are a part. A good example of a Member who has successfully used this strategy is Senator Phil Gramm (R-TX). In 1981, Gramm conspired with the White House to defeat Democratic budget proposals issuing from the Budget Committee, of which he then was a Democratic member. In 1983, the House Democratic Caucus stripped him of his position on the committee. Gramm responded by resigning and running as a Republican for his House seat in a special election. He claimed in that campaign he had sought to represent east Texas in the House, not the preferences of Speaker O'Neill of Massachusetts. The race became a referendum on Gramm versus the Democratic party in Congress. Gramm won easily, and two years later gained election to the Senate, again as a Republican.

The effectiveness of Members' ability to distance themselves from the institution of which they are a part is dramatic. During the depths of public confidence in Congress, 83 percent of a national poll felt members of the House deliberately bounced checks "because they thought they could get away with it," and 58 percent believed congressional travel allowances were "unjustifiable privileges." Yet in the same poll, only 27 percent of the respondents disapproved of the way their representative was doing his or her job (Rosenbaum 1991, B17).

Media strategies also contribute to our two images of Congress. The national media tend to present a much more negative image of the institution, while the local media have good reason not to offend their representative and to present his or her actions in the most positive light.

One consequence of the distinction we make between Congress and its Members is the high re-election rates for incumbents. In 1993 only 39 percent of the public felt that most members of Congress deserved re-election, while 58 percent felt the same way about their own Member (Gallup Poll). But, "Congress does not run for re-election; its individual members do, and they are more popular than it is" (Wolfinger and Brody 1990, A15).

The general dissatisfaction about Congress clearly undermines the legitimacy of the institution and reduces its power. While members of Congress could react to dissatisfaction with effective internal reforms and renewed effort, other consequences may emerge. Public dissatisfaction has already fueled the attempt to limit congressional terms and "throw the rascals out" (see chapter 10). Several relatively young Members have decided that it is just not worth their efforts to remain in an institution with so many problems and have retired. Public dissatisfaction leads to Member dissatisfaction and does not necessarily mean improvements are forthcoming. "An increasingly miserable Congress may attract increasingly mediocre Members" (Patterson and Caldeira 1990, 42).

CONCLUSION

A well-informed public is critical to both democratic government and the proper functioning of Congress. The media and the Congress play a symbiotic set of games, each needing the other, but each having differing players, goals, and strategies. The president stands in waiting to capture an increasing percentage of media attention. Congress and its Members desire to control their public exposure to present the most positive image possible. The media cover Congress in ways they hope will expand their audience and increase profits. National media tend to present a critical analysis of Congress, while local media seldom take "their" Member to task. Frustration with the media led Congress to develop its own methods of communicating with the public through individual outreach efforts and institutional decisions to harness new technology, such as allowing live television coverage.

The media and outreach efforts result in a mixed public image of Congress. The public generally has a negative image of Congress as an institution, but a much more positive image of their local representative. The nature of the public's evaluation undergirds the electoral success of incumbents while undermining the effectiveness of Congress as an institution.

IN DEPTH

1. Compare your local newspaper's coverage of Congress with one of the national newspapers such as the *New York Times, Washington Post, Christian Science Monitor, Wall Street Journal,* or *Los Angeles Times.* You will need to develop an hypothesis to test and a "coding scheme" for collecting data. You will want to collect data over a number of days (ten or more) in which Congress is in session. The following hypotheses are suggestions on which to build:

A. **Hypothesis:** Congress is more likely to be covered by the national media than by the local media.
Data Collection:
1) Compare the column inches devoted to Congress in each paper, *or*
2) Compare the percentage of the front page in each paper devoted to Congress.

B. **Hypothesis:** The national media is more critical of Congress than is the local media.
Data Collection:
Evaluate the paragraphs about Congress in the local and national papers as "positive," "neutral," or "negative." Determine the percentage of each type of coverage for each type of paper.

2. The rules by which the media selects news are often quite different than we as individuals would apply. If you have access to C-SPAN, you can compare your judgments with that of the media. Follow these steps:

A. Watch an event covered by C-SPAN which seems important enough to be covered by the media (i.e., a major debate on legislation, committee testimony, or a congressional press conference).

B. Write an outline of the story you think should be written about the event. Identify the key pieces of news.

C. Analyze two or three of the following after the event:

- the next network news program
- a major national newspaper
- a local newspaper
- a major news magazine
- a political "trade" magazine such as *Congressional Quarterly* or *National Journal.*

D. Compare the story you would have written with what you find (or don't find) in the media. Analyze the reasons for the variation between the media coverage and the difference between what you would have covered and what the media chose as news.

CHAPTER SIX

THE PUBLIC AND ITS PLAYERS
Organized and Unorganized Citizens

. . . in the great chess board of human society, every single piece has a principle of motion of its own, although different from that which the legislature might wish to impress upon it. If these two principles coincide and act in the same direction, the game of human society will go on easily and harmoniously. . . . If they are opposite or different, the game will go on miserably and the society must be at all times in the highest degree of disorder. (Economist Adam Smith, quoted by Representative Newt Gingrich [R-GA], *Congressional Record,* 30 September 1993, H7354)

But this is the pregame hour of lobbying, the time for posturing, for flaunting popular followings and big budgets. Organizations are being built and gathering momentum in the hope of getting attention. Now is the season of grassroots. (Lobby activities surrounding health care reform, described in Weisskopf 1993, A4)

Some members of the public watch Congress in the same way that a crowd at a sporting event follows the action, analyzing each play and anticipating the next strategy. Others don't watch at all. Interest in and knowledge about Congress varies tremendously in the American public. Many citizens are nowhere near the stadium, remaining totally uninterested in national politics. Others join interest groups that act as players in the contest. Only a tiny fraction of the public, however, recognizes the congressional players as well as most athletic crowds know their favorite teams. Despite the arrival of televised coverage on C-SPAN, Congress does not constitute much of a spectator sport for most Americans.

An absence of public vigilance does not necessarily destroy the possibility of public control over our national legislators. The game of public pressure upon Congress is "a sport of influence," in the words of columnist Elizabeth Drew (1978, 33). **Influence** is the attempt to move another person to a particular course of action. Several methods of influence are possible. One is persuasion, the use of arguments and evidence to change an individual's mind about a course of action. A blunter method involves employing explicit rewards and punishments to influence another person. Effective influence in Congress requires that a person or interest serve as a reliable source of rewards and punishments (Neustadt 1990, 30–32).

The uninvolved mass public and the much smaller elite of informed citizens active in politics each have effective means of influencing legislators to conform to their preferences. The reason lies in the minds of the legislators themselves. Each lawmaker has a strong occupational imperative to identify and be solicitous toward the views of his or her constituents. Members of Congress commonly develop a thorough knowledge of their diverse and often inarticulate voters back home.

READING THE CONSTITUENCY

The simple role definitions of delegate and trustee (see chapter 1) fail to completely capture the complex ways that legislators take constituents into account. The process is interactive. Constituents communicate with their legislators, who in turn assess the communication in terms of its complexity, intensity, and possible political repercussions. Lawmakers must learn to read their constituencies accurately and act on this knowledge in a way that ensures political support and success in the survival game, discussed in chapter 3.

STRATEGIES OF CONSTITUENT COMMUNICATION

Evidence of constituent opinion is not difficult for a legislator to come by. One obvious means is the mail. Though only a small percentage of constituents take the time to write to legislators, congressional offices make answering the mail a matter of high priority (Frantzich 1986, 19). John Kingdon, in his interviews with House members, discovered several consequences of constituent mail. First, it focuses attention on problems that otherwise might be ignored. Second, it offers some indication of what people back home are thinking, and how intense their views are. Third, it can trigger congressional oversight of the bureaucracy as citizens complain about their treatment at the hands of federal administrators (Kingdon 1989, 54–60). Legislators usually receive weekly mail counts and some regular accounting of writers' intensity.

Constituent views also come to Capitol Hill through opinion surveys included in lawmakers' district newsletters. Though the respondents are not scientifically representative of public opinion back home, their answers do help to indicate what more motivated citizens are thinking. The citizens who write letters and answer mail polls are more likely to vote and be active in politics. They ask for attention and receive it.

Another means of information gathering involves regular visits back to the constituency by legislators. Members of Congress, particularly early in their careers, tend to return home often to expand the number of their supporters (Fenno 1978, 172–174). The utility of visits, then, is dual: it helps win votes and sample constituent opinion. As lawmakers remain in office, repeated visits allow them to develop an ever more subtle and complex mental map of the home district or state.

Most congressional election campaigns involve an initial "benchmark" poll of the electorate. Newspapers often publish polls of local opinion. Opinion surveys present legislators and their challengers with a "snapshot" of public opinion, but one that must be approached with caution. First, a poll is a cross-section of the public, including responses by many who have little information about the topic mentioned in the survey. Opinions can be unstable and can vary with how the question is worded. Second, polls seldom measure opinion intensity. Though a majority in an electorate may support gun control, an intense minority of gun owners may be most likely to vote solely on that issue. Thus a legislative vote in favor of the majority opinion could actually prove to be an electoral loser at the polls. Third, "money contributors and volunteer workers often hold unrepresentative opinions and may respond unsympathetically to candidates articulating representative public opinion" (Erikson and Luttbeg 1973, 270).

Out of these various sources, legislators create and refine a mental picture of constituents. Several aspects of constituency opinion receive contemplation: its complexity, intensity on various issues, and likelihood of producing electoral consequences on particular floor votes. If a lawmaker's perceptions are not accurate most of the time, defeat at the polls becomes probable.

CONSTITUENCY COMPLEXITY AND INTENSITY

Representatives and Senators readily identify their constituency in terms of its mass and elite components. Comments such as "it was unpopular back home" mean that the assessment derives from a perception of an undifferentiated mass constituency. Many issues, however, involve parts of an **elite constituency** of citizens who are active, informed, and willing to contact their member of Congress about an issue.

Two types of local elites are particularly significant to legislators. First, there are the policy elites, "those who have a direct expertise or interest in the governmental policy at issue, such as teachers on education funding, farmers on farm policy, bankers on some tax matters . . ." (Kingdon 1989, 33–34). Also evident are process elites, "those such as newspaper editors and party activists . . . who might be important in the more general political process in the district" (Kingdon 1989, 34). Legislators believe process elites have a disproportionately large impact on elections. But not all elites are equal in the minds of lawmakers. Those in the supporting electoral coalition of an incumbent receive much more attention than those that are not. Friendly voters in primary and general elections regularly secure notice and care from incumbents and their offices.

The intensity of constituency opinion about certain issues can weigh heavily in a lawmaker's decision making.[1] Congressional offices estimate individual intensity by the amount of effort a constituent makes to communicate with them. Constituent intensity, however, even on major issues, does not manifest itself that frequently. Even so, legislators are wary of opposing intense views, particularly if they are evident in the supporting electoral coalition. A recent example involves congressional pay raises. Though many Members argue for them in the abstract, when forced to vote on the floor, many bow to the intense constituent hostility to the hikes. As Representative Bill Richardson (D-NM) put it: "I vote against pay raises because I want to be re-elected" (interview with author).

Voters and legislators both evidence intense interest in the economic base of the district. Much of domestic lawmaking involves preserving, protecting, and defending jobs and economic prosperity back home. One tobacco-state representative summed up why the matter was of high intensity for him:

> I've got many, many families in my district who make a living on tobacco. . . . [My thinking] starts with [the constituency] and it ends there. That's all there is to it. If you don't, you aren't going to be around here very long. Not on something like this, where their livelihood is involved. (Kingdon 1989, 64)

FEAR OF ELECTORAL CONSEQUENCES

Carrots and sticks can be quite helpful in winning at the sport of influence. Constituents quietly wield a huge club at incumbent legislators—the prospect of electoral defeat. The weapon's use has grown recently. In 1992, 10 percent of House members lost in either the primary or general election, the highest rate of defeat in several decades. As the electorate grows less reliably partisan and more volatile, even senior lawmakers must increase their efforts to stave off electoral reprisal.

A shrinking electoral margin can alter incumbent behavior. Here is how one legislator recalled handling a demand from a certain part of the constituency: "I won by a razor-thin margin last time. If I had won by a larger margin, frankly, I'd have gone back and told them to stick it. But it's nip and tuck in my case, and on something like this, I'd better be with them" (Kingdon 1989, 64).

Sound reasons exist for incumbents to be careful. R. Douglas Arnold (1993, 401–417) explains why lawmakers remain vigilant about opinions back home even though the broader constituency is inattentive. Citizens may not understand the fine points of policy but they have "outcome preferences" and can turn on incumbents if

---

[1]Political scientists have a hard time analyzing precisely the intensity of constituent opinion. John Kingdon, in his landmark study of House voting decisions, found that those issues that were most politically salient—arousing much interest in and outside of Congress—also seemed to produce the most constituency intensity. The more salient the issue, the more complex the perception of the constituency by the lawmaker. On issues of low salience, lawmakers thought of the constituency only in general, mass terms. Medium salience issues resulted in the active parts of the constituency, various elites, being uppermost in legislators' minds. High salience issues brought a more precise cognition of both elite and mass opinion back home. Regardless of salience, Kingdon found the constituency was a leading influence on roll call voting (see Kingdon 1989, 43).

National lawmakers have strong occupational incentives to understand their constituencies well. Here Representative Nancy Johnson (R-CT) gets acquainted with farmers in her district.

local or national conditions go sour. Voters evaluate the records of incumbents when motivated to do so. Also, elites of district activists serve as the alarm bell about legislator behavior for more passive voters.

In addition, potential electoral rivals are on the watch for votes and actions that they can portray as contrary to district opinion. Negative campaigning can mobilize elites and voters against an incumbent. Fear that opponents will dramatize an incumbent's policy differences with constituents encourages those in office to be responsive to voters (Bernstein 1989, 31). Opponents and activist elites can make all kinds of trouble at election time (Erikson and Luttbeg 1973, 281).

The process of candidate **recruitment** also promotes incumbent responsiveness. Recruitment refers to the means by which a constituency screens and selects candidates to run for office. Most often, the winning congressional candidate in November reflects the dominant attitudes of the constituency. That tends to produce issue congruity between lawmakers and their constituents, as Robert Bernstein noted, "When Members vote their own beliefs, they tend to be voting the beliefs of their constituencies" (Bernstein 1989, 102).

Though most members of the public do not pay attention to their members of Congress, lawmakers behave as if constituents are watching. Recruitment produces a basic conformity of legislators with constituency attitudes. Elites and potential opponents serve as surrogate watchdogs for the largely indifferent mass of voters back home. Incumbents, their potential opponents and various elites all have a sense of "what will play" back in the district. All seek to mobilize the great latent resources of the mass electorate.

INTEREST GROUPS: THE ORGANIZED EXTERNAL PLAYERS

The most notorious practitioners of the sport of influence are interest groups and their thousands of lobbyists—the "influence professionals" of Washington. Powerful groups often engage in highly publicized zero-sum games over the major issues of the day. The game is simpler on more obscure issues, when merely securing the attention of distracted lawmakers may be enough to secure victory. Political scientists Kay Lehman Schlozman and John Tierney note that organized interests command several "means of reward and punishment" when approaching Congress (1986, 312).

The common goal of groups is influence, an actual effect on a legislative outcome. Tracking influence is not an easy task. At times it seems obvious, as in the case of the National Rifle Association's ability to forestall national gun control for many years. In other instances, behind-the-scenes dealings that few ever understand dictate a legislative result. Lobbyists are usually quite discreet about their claims of influence, as if acknowledging it suggests swagger and corruption. They instead talk of **access,** of seeking to "get a hearing" for their viewpoint, as their main goal in approaching Congress. Schlozman and Tierney note, however, that "if access is unequal, it would not be surprising if it were to have consequences for influence" (1986, 165).

LOBBYING RULES AND RESOURCES

The access and influence game proceeds according to loose rules established by Congress. Federal regulation of lobbying activities is found in Title III of the 1946 Legislative Reorganization Act, known as the Federal Regulation of Lobbying Act. It requires registration of lobbyists and reporting of lobbying activities. In 1954 the Supreme Court significantly weakened its provisions, exempting people who spend their own funds to lobby, organizations who claim their "principal purpose" is not to lobby Congress (a wide range of interest groups) and lobbyists who do not contact legislators directly. Enforcement of the act is feeble—its provisions have resulted in the convictions of only two lobbyists.

This does not mean that Washington is awash with sin and corruption spawned by lobbyists. Though some influence peddlers employed "booze and bucks" in the nineteenth and early twentieth centuries, the actual incidence of bribery now is probably quite low. Interest groups instead have found effective, legal means of influence and lawmakers find the electoral risks of payoffs not worth the financial rewards.

The Federal Election Campaign Finance Acts of 1972 and 1974 regulate the flow of money into politics (see chapter 2). Political Action Committees (PACs) must disclose their sources of money and to whom it flows. Further, the amounts PACs can legally give are low—only $5,000 per candidate per election, meaning $10,000 per candidate per election year (for the primary and general elections).

Intrepid PACs found three legal loopholes that allow them to increase their financial influence on campaigns. One method involved **bundling,** when a PAC or interest group leader solicits individual contribution checks from group members, bundles them and gives them to the candidate. Another entailed **independent**

expenditures—PACs that avoid all contact with candidate campaigns in a specific race may spend unlimited amounts of ads and organizational efforts to influence that election outcome.

A third avenue concerned the **soft money** loophole. PACs or individuals could give state parties unlimited funds for "party building activities" such as voter registration and get-out-the-vote drives during an election campaign. Intrepid interest groups channelled money to the state parties, who spent it on behalf of congressional candidates. Such practices, and the entire campaign finance system, came under harsh attack by "public interest groups" such as Common Cause and Ralph Nader's Public Citizen. In response, Congress in 1993 considered banning or restricting the loopholes and tightening lobbying regulations.

Dollars are hardly the sole resource groups use for influence. Lobbyist Rich Roberts argues that money is just one of several tools employed by successful lobbying campaigns:

> Money is one of three key elements of any [lobbying] campaign that must be balanced against the merits of the arguments and attitudes of the voters. The triangle of money, arguments and voters is never equilateral or even isosceles, but however unequal any given leg may be, all three must be present. (Roberts 1987, 377)

Trade unions are strong in all three respects. Business groups fare better at mobilizing money and arguments than voters. The most successful "public interest" groups rely on grassroots voter networks and well-articulated arguments. Resources become effective, however, only if used wisely. Players in the sport of influence employ thrcc proven strategies.

Public Strategies

Some interest groups attempt to win influence in Congress through media campaigns aimed at influencing both public opinion and the views of policymakers. This approach is usually quite costly, involving expensive newspaper and television ads. Business groups with ample monetary resources are particularly apt to pursue this strategy. Less affluent groups sometimes seek to reach the public through protests and demonstrations, often doing so out of desperation. Lacking resources and feeling powerless, they appeal to other citizens via the media to support their demands (Lipsky 1968, 1144–1158).

An ad campaign can involve three strategic approaches: creation of goodwill toward the group and its agenda, offensive campaigns to achieve public policy change, and defensive ads aimed at preventing alteration of the status quo (Hrebnar and Scott 1990, 113–115). More informed voters and policymakers may pay attention, but advertizing is an expensive approach with uncertain results.

Protests and demonstrations produce a highly variable impact. If demonstrations stimulate widespread sympathy, as did the civil rights marches of the 1960s, they can powerfully focus attention in Congress. Generally, protests do not usually engage public opinion. One thorough study of the topic concluded "U.S. citizens have a long history of opposition to demonstrators and protestors, even peaceful

BOX 6.1 Keating and Cranston: Does Money Talk?

The distinction between aiding a campaign contributor and accepting a bribe for services rendered is a fine one, as evident in the actions of Senator Alan Cranston (D-CA) in the "Keating Five" scandal of the late 1980s (see box 3.3). Charles Keating, head of Lincoln Savings and Loan, a major California financial institution, raised a total of $1.5 million in campaign funds for five senators. Keating then repeatedly asked the five for help in avoiding "burdensome" federal banking regulations. All five—Senators Donald Riegle (D-MI), Dennis DeConcini (D-AZ), John Glenn (D-OH), John McCain (R-AZ), and Alan Cranston (D-CA)—attempted to intercede with federal regulators for Keating.

When the controversy first erupted, Keating stated, "One question among the many raised in recent weeks had to do with whether my financial support in any way influenced several political figures to take up my cause. I want to say in the most forceful way I can, I certainly hope so."[a]

The Senate Ethics Committee in November 1989 decided to investigate. The committee finally decided to drop charges against all but Cranston, who would soon retire. The committee found "substantial credible evidence . . . that Senator Cranston engaged in an impermissible pattern of conduct in which fundraising and official activities were substantially linked."[b] Keating had raised some $850,000 for Cranston, most of which went to voter registration groups at Cranston's direction. Shortly after the arrival of each contribution, Cranston did favors for Keating.

The committee found that Cranston's actions looked improper, even though admitting a lack of evidence that the California senator had violated any law. Cranston agreed to a public rebuke by the Senate, but in accepting his punishment argued defiantly in support of the propriety of his actions. In its report on Cranston, the committee claimed the "cardinal principle" for senators is to make decisions "without regard to whether the individual has contributed or promised to contribute."[c] Despite this exhortation, the fine line between assisting supporters and corrupt influence peddling remains blurry.

[a]"Panel Probes Senators' Aid to Keating," *1990 Congressional Quarterly Almanac,* Washington: *Congressional Quarterly,* p. 78.

[b]Phil Kuntz, "Panel Seeks Cranston Sanction That Will Avoid a Floor Fight," *Congressional Quarterly,* 9 September 1991, p. 3264.

[c]Phil Kuntz, "Cranston Case Ends on Floor with a Murky Plea Bargain," *Congressional Quarterly,* 23 November 1991, p. 3436.

ones, and apparently tend not to accept them as credible or legitimate sources of opinion leadership" (Page, Shapiro, and Dempsey 1987, 37). Usually, groups employ demonstrations in tandem with other strategies of influence.

Electoral Strategies

Many groups focus resources on congressional elections to maximize access to incumbents or replace them with legislators more sympathetic to group demands. Many interest groups first seek to assist their friends in office. Incumbents receive about two-thirds of all PAC funds. Business PACs, seeking to maximize influence with the powers that be, give substantial amounts to Democratic incumbents. Those

"Senator, according to this report, you're marked for defeat by the A.D.A., the National Rifle Association, the A.F.L.-C.I.O., the N.A.M., the Sierra Club, Planned Parenthood, the World Student Christian Federation, the Clamshell Alliance . . ."

PACs motivated primarily by liberal or conservative ideology, however, more frequently try to defeat objectionable incumbents (Conway 1991, 207).

Interest groups employ a variety of specific electoral strategies. Several groups construct annual ratings that indicate the percentage of the time each legislator sided with the group on certain "key votes" (see box 6.2). The rating determines whether group support or opposition is forthcoming at election time. Interests as diverse as the Chamber of Commerce of the United States, AFL-CIO, Children's Defense Fund, and National Federation of Independent Businesses employ this strategy. A rating can be used in campaign ads to bolster or discredit a targeted candidate, or employed as a signal to group members as to whom they should vote for.

Groups can also formally endorse a candidate, a practice of varying effectiveness. In the steel country of western Pennsylvania, for example, an AFL-CIO endorsement is essential. Opponents, though, can also strive to picture an endorsed candidate as the "captive" of special interests. For this reason, business groups and corporations in particular seldom endorse candidates.

Perhaps the most widespread group practice in elections involves contributions to candidates. PAC spending now comprises a substantial proportion of incumbents' campaign expenditures. In 1992, 30 percent of funds raised by Senate incumbents came from PACs, up from 23 percent in 1988 and 1990. House incumbents received 44 percent of their funds from PACs in 1992, compared to 49 percent in 1990 and 36.7 percent in 1988 (Donovan and Veron 1993, 723–727). Money is not the only resource that can be donated, however. In-kind contributions involve donating services and volunteers to a campaign. Unions and other grassroots organizations can help candidates greatly by contributing brains and shoe leather. Campaign spending laws place no limits on in-kind contributions.

BOX 6.2 The Rating Game

In addition to serving the strategic needs of interest groups, annual ratings provide a convenient overview of lawmakers' positions on a variety of issues. Groups usually issue ratings annually and calculate them in terms of group support on ten or more floor votes. Ratings vary from zero to 100 percent support.

The Americans for Democratic Action was the first to begin rating legislators, awarding high scores for liberal voting. In 1971, the conservative Americans for Constitutional Action began assigning high ratings for conservative voting. Other prominent ratings now also include those of the AFL-CIO's Committee on Political Education (pro-liberal and labor), The Chamber of Commerce of the United States (pro-business), the League of Conservation Voters (pro-environmental), the American Security Council (pro-defense), and the Consumer Federation of America (pro-consumer).

Why not check out the ratings of your own legislators, those of other lawmakers from your state, or those of congressional leaders? Two major reference sources on Congress, *The Almanac of American Politics* by Michael Barone and Grant Ujifusa (Washington: National Journal) and Congressional Quarterly's *Politics in America* (Washington: Congressional Quarterly) report several group ratings as part of their profiles of each member of Congress. Both are published every two years, and reside in most college libraries. You can quickly learn a lot about lawmakers' issue commitments by examining the results of the rating game.

Institutional Strategies

Public and electoral strategies serve as supplements to the core effort of interest groups toward Congress. Lobbyists in Washington number well over 50,000. A survey of Washington representatives of interest groups found that 89 percent termed Congress a "very important" focus of group activity, while executive agencies ranked a distant second with only 65 percent (Schlozman and Tierney 1986, 272).

Groups play the sport of influence on Capitol Hill according to varying strategies. The first hurdle is access. A group presence in the constituency back home or a campaign contribution can help to provide that. Some "monied interests" use additional means to achieve access. The social lobby refers to the many free receptions and dinners for lawmakers and their staffs that interest groups sponsor on Capitol Hill. Until the House and Senate recently banned them, honoraria for speeches before interest groups also furthered access. Some interests offer lawmakers trips to "conferences" held in vacation spots where the workload is light.

Once groups identify important players and secure access, two sorts of lobbying strategies come to the fore. One is **direct lobbying,** in which the lobbyists present arguments to legislators and their staffs, either through personal contact or by testifying at committee hearings. Schlozman and Tierney (1986, 180) in their survey

BOX 6.3 A Player Speaks: The Five Commandments of Direct Lobbying

Bruce Wolpe, a Washington lawyer and lobbyist, recently outlined the five commandments that lobbyists must follow when directly approaching legislators and their staffs:

1. **Tell the truth.** Lobbying is the political management of information. A lobbyist is only as good as his or her word; your words are your bonds upon which all subsequent judgments are premised. Everyone knows not to lie. Liars are discerned quickly and are never trusted again.
2. **Never promise more than you can deliver.** The success of all tactics depends on an accurate sense of the resources that can be deployed to achieve the objective. Promised resources are effective only when they are in hand.
3. **Know how to listen so that you accurately understand what you are hearing.** When expectations and desire cloud perception, the result inevitably is miscalculation and disappointment.
4. **Staff is there to be worked with and not circumvented.** Winning the confidence of the staff—and maintaining it thereafter—is a prerequisite to an ongoing, successful political relationship with any political office.
5. **Spring no surprises.** Politicians hate the unexpected, and especially any news that is adverse. They want, and need, to have relevant information in a timely fashion and be in a position to act on it, rather than react to it.

SOURCE: Bruce C. Wolpe, *Lobbying Congress: How the System Works,* Congressional Quarterly Press, Inc., 1990, pp. 9–15.

of lobby organizations found that more than 90 percent of lobbyists interviewed acknowledged frequent use of direct lobbying techniques. Experienced lobbyists come to understand the appropriate strategies for direct lobbying, summarized in box 6.3.

Though the direct approach remains important in lobbying Congress, in the last two decades groups developed additional strategies. These involve **indirect lobbying** in that they attempt to influence lawmakers' decisions through the use of third parties, usually constituents and the media (Hrebnar and Scott 1990, chapters 4–5). Indirect strategies include stimulating mail and personal contact between legislators and constituents, mounting "grassroots" issue campaigns in the constituency, and speaking to Congress through national and local media. Groups are also more frequently forming coalitions of like-minded lobbies to better influence legislators, in which the coalition partners play a positive-sum game among themselves. By dividing the effort, all gain some benefit.

Indirect and coalition lobbying strategies arose from changes in technology and congressional structure. Enhanced communication technology encourages coalition formation and facilitates contact with group supporters in constituencies. A more fragmented committee system encourages coalition formation to exploit multiple points of access. Broad-based constituency strategies can effectively influence lawmakers throughout the many power centers of the complex committee system. In all, more groups are employing more lobbying strategies on Capitol Hill than ever before.

WHO ARE THE LOBBYISTS?

Most lobbyists come to their jobs with experience in the federal government (Schlozman and Tierney 1986, 269). The movement from government to the influence community is so frequent that it is known as the "revolving door." Prominent examples of this are numerous. Anne Wexler, assistant for public liaison in the Carter White House, now runs her own lobbying business, as does Jeffrey Bergner, former chief of staff for Senator Richard Lugar (R-IN).

A pointed example of the "revolving door" involves former members of Congress now lobbying their former colleagues. In 1986, the *New York Times* counted more than 200 former lawmakers making their living as lobbyists (23 June 1986, A12). Interest groups seek them out for their political knowledge and direct access to decision makers. Former Representative and current lobbyist Thomas Railsback (R-IL) claims "former members have this advantage. They have an open door and are not treated perfunctorily" (Common Cause 1986, 34). In 1992, Congress passed a law requiring a one-year ban on lobbying for retiring legislators. Nevertheless, 40 percent of retiring lawmakers joined lobbying firms in 1993—not to formally lobby, but as "strategists" (Peters 1994, 5).

The traditional image of a lobbyist suggests a middle-aged white male—perhaps a former legislator—puffing on a cigar while sipping bourbon and branchwater with some legislative cronies. That stereotype is not as accurate as it once was. True, the lobbying community includes former lawmakers and long-established Washington lawyers who have worked the levers of influence for decades, such as Clark Clifford and Tommy Boggs. Hundreds of law firms populate Washington, employing scores of lawyers adept in the ways of traditional, direct lobbying. At the top of this heap are the "superlawyers" like Boggs and Clifford, who have made themselves indispensable to their clients through their ability to provide access.

Lobbying, however, is far more than inside influence anymore. Hedrick Smith identified the "new lobbying game" involving a new breed of Washington professionals (Smith 1988, chapter 9). The new breed includes political consultants, pollsters, and public relations firms, who supplement direct lobbying with many indirect, grassroots efforts. Most major interests now augment direct lobbying with the new indirect, public and constituency-based strategies. Box 6.4 provides an example.

Washington is also home to more than 400 trade associations of kindred businesses that often seek to mobilize their memberships in a grassroots fashion. These associations include all sectors of the economy, from the American Trucking Association to the Association of Dressings and Sauces (the condiment crowd). Another large segment of organizations using the new approaches are the professional associations, such as the American Medical Association and American Bar Association.

Public interest lobbies, whose membership derives not from the drive for economic benefit, but from ideological conviction, pioneered many grassroots approaches. Common Cause, Friends of the Earth, Public Citizen, and the National Taxpayers' Union are examples of such groups. Amidst this cacophony, state and local governments and the White House also pursue influence, usually through direct lobbying.

Indirect lobbying in action. A "boiler room" operated by a coalition of interest groups known as Families USA drums up public support for health care reform in 1994.

BOX 6.4 Catastrophic Health Care: Influence through New Style Lobbying

On July 1, 1988, President Reagan signed into law a bill designed to curb catastrophic health expenses for America's elderly. The bill capped out-of-pocket costs for prescription drugs and acute care and provided for federal payment of the remaining expenses. Less than four months later, Congress repealed the bill. What happened over those months is a textbook example of new style lobbying.

Though many interest groups representing the elderly had supported the bill, reaction from many retirees to its passage was harshly negative. Their objection involved the program's financing. Elderly beneficiaries of the program would pay for its cost, with high-income retirees paying up to 800 dollars a year in additional federal premiums to make the benefits available to the lower-income elderly. A crucial flaw in the law provided for a gradual phase-in of benefits, but an immediate enforcement of higher premiums.

Various groups of elderly citizens employed grassroots strategies to fan the flames of discontent. A leader in the effort was the National Committee to Preserve Social Security and Medicare, headed by James Roosevelt (a son of FDR). Other grassroots organizations sprung up around the issue. One was the United Seniors of America, charging annual dues of fifteen dollars to "help spread the word to get this unfair law changed."[a] Complaining seniors besieged lawmakers—for example, two busloads of seniors appeared and complained at Representative Connie Morella's (R-MD) town meeting on July 31. Congress repealed the program a few months after the grassroots din erupted.

The lesson is a simple one. Higher-income retirees reacted intensely against the law and mobilized in grassroots activity. These citizens were likely to have a strong voice in the next election. They can punish incumbents, certainly an effective means of influence. Congress was forced to relent.

[a]"Catastrophic-Costs Law: A Massive Miscalculation," in *Lobbying Congress: How the System Works*, 1990, Washington: Congressional Quarterly Press Inc., p. 79.

WHO WINS AND WHO LOSES?

What are the results of the influence game? In particular, when are groups most likely to prevail in Congress? Does money dictate victory or defeat? The corrupt use of money in politics was much more possible before the creation of PACs in 1974. Before then, groups could secretly contribute in any amount to legislative candidates. At least now the role of money can come under public scrutiny. Several political scientists have studied the impact of PAC contributions upon roll call voting, with mixed results. Two comprehensive studies, by John Wright and Janet Grenzke, find no evidence of PAC contributions affecting floor voting (Wright 1985, 400–415; Grenzke 1989, 1–24). Wright finds that the local and state committees of organizations direct PAC contributions, not the Washington lobbyists, making coordinated, strategic use of money in lobbying difficult (1985, 414).

This does not mean that money has no effect. Grenzke admits that money does stimulate access, and access does contribute to influence (1989, 22–23). Laura Langbein discovered that House members who reported spending more time in their offices with lobbyists also had received more PAC contributions (Langbein 1986, 1060). Richard Fleisher in a recent study found PACs had a small but significant effect on House defense votes in 1987. Though ideology was by far the strongest determinant of voting, PAC contributions marginally influenced the votes of members, "especially those members with weaker ideological dispositions" (Fleisher 1993, 406).

Standing committees constitute another possible arena of PAC influence. Jeffrey Barry argues that PAC money influences decision making by opening the ears and minds of committee members and staff, long before the role is called on the floor (Barry 1989, 132). Interests manipulate obscure provisions in legislation as a result of PAC contributions:

> Why did Walt Disney Productions and other studios receive a transition rule in the 1986 tax bill giving them a lucrative temporary exemption from a change in the investment tax credit? It's hard to believe that PAC money contributed by the movie industry to selected legislators had nothing to do with it. (Barry 1989, 132)

Recent studies of PAC influence in committees lend some support to Barry's suspicions. Richard Hall and Frank Wayman, in a study of contribution influence upon representatives' activities in committee (such as attendance, speaking, or offering amendments), found that "moneyed interests are able to mobilize legislators already predisposed to support the group's position," but group contributions to potential opponents had either a "negligible or negative" effect on their participation (Hall and Wayman 1990, 814). John Wright found, however, that lobbying contacts, not contributions, proved key in influencing actual voting in committee. Contributions make possible the contacts, which then help to influence voting. He concluded that "money enters the process other than through a direct exchange of favors" (Wright 1990, 433).

Given these varying findings, Grenzke best summarizes the broader situation:

> The public debate about PACs grossly exaggerates their influence because it does not distinguish between a few cases of PAC influence on legislation of relatively minor importance and a general pattern of influence that systematically buys members' votes on major pieces of legislation. (1989, 20)

PAC influence usually does not involve the "great issues of our time," but rather narrow, low-profile issues of great concern to particular PACs. On major issues, the legislator's conscience and the wishes of the supporting electoral coalition back home become most important. Astute groups have discovered this truth and now try to approach legislators through their districts—hence the boom in grassroots lobbying. Cigars, bourbon, and "inside baseball" don't work as they used to.

Schlozman and Tierney point out that groups prevail when they can concentrate sizeable resources, face no opposition, and find an arena sympathetic to their needs. Farm groups target the agriculture committees, for example. The larger the scope of a group demand, the greater the number of opponents, and the more adverse the arena, the less is the likelihood of success (1986, 396–397). Frank Davis studied airline and railroad PAC influence on roll-call votes about transit regulation and found that on such "low visibility issues . . . PAC contributions achieve a significant impact on roll calls" (Davis 1993, 215). To win, the time and place must be right.

In recent years, more complex congressional structure and interest group competition in Washington makes success for individual groups more problematic. A recent major study of Washington interest groups concluded that "on any particular set of policy concerns, groups can seek support in Congress through multiple points of access. But the corollary is that none of the interest groups is likely to carry decisive weight in shaping policy" (Heinz et al. 1993, 388). The electoral security of most incumbents also weakens group power: "As members of Congress find themselves increasingly secure beneficiaries of name recognition and casework, they learn they can afford to stand aloof from many parts of the interest group community" (Heinz 1993, 388). These findings indicate that the public and media often overstate the presence of "raw" interest group power in Congress.

In general, the pluralism of group competition works through a constituent filter before reaching the individual legislator. Groups are more likely to enjoy success with a legislator if a significant number of group members reside in his or her constituency (Kingdon 1989, 174). A Washington team of lobbyists is likely to be more effective when lawmakers view them as playing for the interests of some home team fans. That is as it should be. It is true that the interests of those who are apathetic or of low income or education do not always receive a substantial voice in the chorus of Washington interest groups. On the other hand, congressional votes do not commonly go to the highest bidder. The influence game works best with a constituency connection—in that one can find some reassurance.

CONCLUSION

Both the public and interest groups employ rewards and punishments in playing the influence game in Congress. The aim of the game is first access, then influence. The public, though usually inattentive, does punish lawmakers with electoral defeat if too often ignored or offended. Lawmakers correspondingly take pains to "read" their constituencies carefully. Interest groups pursue three types of strategies, either singly or in combination. The public strategies involve influencing popular and policymaker opinion through such means as advertising or demonstrations. Electoral strategies include mobilizing money and votes to affect who sits in Congress. Institutional strategies concern the effective use of direct lobbying before the legislature. In recent years, many interests began using indirect "grassroots" strategies to augment their direct attempts at influence. They found that a group can most reliably influence lawmakers by demonstrating a presence among their constituents. This "constituent filter" for group demands makes the game of persuading Congress more consistent with the requirements of democratic representation.

IN DEPTH

1. Try examining the status of several different political issues in a given congressional district—such as your home district. Identify the policy elites, process elites, and intensity surrounding each of the issues. Why do these characteristics vary across issues? What overall traits of the district become evident through this investigation?

REFERENCES:

Arnold, R. Douglas. 1990. *The Logic of Congressional Action.* New Haven: Yale University Press.

Cobb, Charles, and James Elder. 1972. *Participation in American Politics: The Dynamics of Agenda-Building.* Boston: Allyn & Bacon.

Kingdon, John. 1989. *Congressmen's Voting Decisions.* Ann Arbor: University of Michigan Press.

Schier, Steven E. 1992. *A Decade of Deficits: Congressional Thought and Fiscal Action.* Albany: State University of New York Press.

2. Identify the reasons for the growing public hostility toward Congress. This requires you to examine polling results on popular attitudes, research recent congressional scandals, and examine others' analysis of the situation.

REFERENCES:

On public opinion:

Ladd, Everett C. 1990. "Public Opinion and the Congress Problem." *The Public Interest* 100 (Summer): 57–67.

Patterson, Samuel C., and Gregory H. Caldeira. 1990. "Standing Up For Congress: Variation in Public Esteem Since the 1960s." *Legislative Studies Quarterly* 15: 25–47.

"A Public Hearing on Congress." 1992. *The American Enterprise* 3, no. 6 (November–December): 82–89.

"The Public's Critique of Congress." 1991. *The American Enterprise 2,* no. 1 (January–February): 82–87.

On recent scandals:

Congressional Quarterly Weekly Report and *National Journal,* both weekly periodicals covering Congress.

Related books:

Bartlett, Donald L., and James B. Steele. 1992. *America: What Went Wrong?* Kansas City: Andrews and McMeel, chapter 10.

Dionne, E. J. 1992. *Why Americans Hate Politics.* New York: Simon and Schuster.

Greider, William. 1992. *Who Will Tell the People? The Breakdown of American Democracy.* New York: Simon and Schuster.

3. Examine the ongoing debate about campaign finance reform in order to stake out your own position. Important issues in this debate include whether PACs should be limited further in their contributions or abolished, whether total spending in congressional races should be limited and how, and whether public financing of campaigns is the best solution—and how this might work.

REFERENCES:

Congressional Quarterly Weekly Report (on recent reform activities in Congress).

Magleby, David B., and Candace J. Nelson. 1990. *The Money Chase.* Washington: Brookings Institution.

Sabato, Larry. 1989. *Paying for Elections.* Twentieth Century Fund.

Sorauf, Frank. 1992. *Inside Campaign Finance.* New Haven: Yale University Press.

4. You can examine interest group politics through one of two lenses: either by examining group behavior surrounding a particular issue in Congress or by assessing the operations of a particular interest group as it seeks influence in the national legislature. Similar questions can be answered in either approach. What are the organizational characteristics and strategies of the group(s)? By what criteria can you assess the effectiveness of the lobby organization(s)? How do the traits of the organization(s) affect policy results?

REFERENCES:

Barry, Jeffrey. 1989. *The Interest Group Society.* Glenview, Ill.: Scott, Foresman.

Heinz, John P., 1993. *The Hollow Core: Private Interests in National Policy Making.* Cambridge: Harvard University Press.

Hrebnar, Ronald J., and Ruth K. Scott. 1990. *Interest Groups in America.* Englewood Cliffs, N.J.: Prentice-Hall.

Schlozman, Kay Lehman, and John Tierney. 1986. *Organized Interests and American Democracy.* New York: Harper & Row.

CHAPTER SEVEN

THE POLICY GAME

The Procedures and Strategies That Determine Winners and Losers

The temper and the integrity with which the political fight is waged is more important for the health of our society than any particular policy. (Theologian Reinhold Niebuhr, quoted in *Congressional Record,* 1 April 1992, p. H2224)

I can't tell you how many people up here I've talked to who say, "Now I know the game. You don't commit yourself until you can see what you can get for it." (Member of Congress Louise Slaughter (D-NY), talking about the bargaining over the North American Free Trade Agreement, *Washington Post,* 18 November 1993)

In politics, as in sports, it does matter how you play the game. The policy game is both about important issues, and also represents how we as a society handle deep and abiding conflicts. The very act of taking up a policy problem represents public recognition of its importance. In a diverse, collective, decision-making body such as Congress the most realistic goal is not to find the "best" solution, but rather a solution that can be sold to a wide variety of Members. To a large degree, Congress can determine which policy problems it will tackle, when it will face them, and how the competing interests will be forged into a winning coalition.

THE EMERGENCE OF POLICY ISSUES: SETTING THE CONGRESSIONAL AGENDA

According to Congress' rules, an issue formally becomes part of Congress' agenda when a Member introduces a piece of legislation. Such a legalistic definition, though, ignores both the parentage and prospects for most legislation. Increasingly Members run for office with clear ideas of the legislation they wish to introduce. These "policy entrepreneurs" arrive in office with a style that "boils down to an emphasis on the individual as captain of his or her own political fate" (Loomis 1988, 234).

Much of the legislation introduced into the congressional process originates in the White House, executive branch agencies, and/or private interest groups to be introduced from drafts suggested by non-congressional sources. Some legislation is crafted within legislative offices[1] based on revelations or suggestions made by the news media. Other large blocs of bills are "dead on arrival," since they were introduced for public relations reasons and have no one to nurture them through the process.

Increasingly, Congress reacts to presidential initiatives from the State of the Union Message and the president's budget proposals. Today we think in terms of the president's "program" and evaluate Congress in terms of its effectiveness in dealing with presidential initiatives. This increased role of the president as "chief legislator" should not mask the fact that a large percentage of the legislation both introduced and passed does not originate in the White House. Much of the president's program is not new. Presidents often serve as "popularizers" of ideas which have been around a long time. Presidents help ideas originated by others, overcome inertia, and get them moving toward enactment (see Peterson 1990, 35–36).

The volume of presidential initiatives is significant. Between 1953 and 1984, Democratic presidents averaged 244 legislative initiatives per year and Republicans 107 (Peterson 1990, 95). More than half of the presidential initiatives survive congressional scrutiny basically intact (Peterson 1990, 96). Since Congress passes about 300 bills per year, and presidential initiatives often account for only part of a bill's content, there are obviously many other factors in congressional agenda setting (see table 7.1).

DEFINING PROBLEMS FOR THE AGENDA

The emergence of issues on the political agenda usually starts with the recognition of a "problem." **Absolute** problems are self-evident to all observers. Major natural disasters and foreign attacks demand congressional response, but the decision to respond does not necessarily lead to consensus on the appropriate *means* to reach the desired end. For example, Iraq's invasion of Kuwait in 1990 led most observers to conclude that the United States had to do something, but we were divided over military involvement versus the use of economic sanctions. Similarly, the devastation of Hurricane Andrew in 1992 and the midwestern floods of 1993 led to a broad chorus of calls for government aid, but there was disagreement over the amount of aid and how much aid should come from the federal government versus state governments.

Other problems do not emerge from absolute standards. They stem from comparisons with past performance or in relation to the performance of some other political systems with which we compare ourselves. A **relative** problem

---

[1]Members of Congress have a nonpartisan Office of Legislative Counsel available, which takes the ideas they suggest and drafts them into proper legislative format. This office also checks to make sure that contrary legislation does not exist and suggests other changes in the legal code required to reach the intended goal.

TABLE 7.1 The Magnitude of the Congressional Agenda

Congress	*No. of bills introduced**		*Bills passed***		*No. of laws passed by both chambers*
	House	**Senate**	**House**	**Senate**	
80th (47–48)	7,611	3,186	1,739	1,670	906
85th (57–58)	14,580	4,532	2,964	2,202	936
90th (67–68)	22,060	4,400	1,213	1,376	640
95th (77–78)	15,587	3,800	1,027	1,970	633
96th (79–80)	9,103	3,480	929	977	613
97th (81–82)	8,094	3,396	704	803	473
98th (83–84)	7,105	3,454	978	936	623
99th (85–86)	6,499	3,386	973	940	664
100th (87–88)	6,263	3,325	1,061	1,002	713
101st (89–90)	6,683	3,669	968	980	650
102nd (91–92)	7,771	4,245	932	947	590

SOURCE: Norman J. Ornstein, Thomas E. Mann, and Michael J. Malbin. *Vital Statistics on Congress, 1993–1994*, pp. 151–156, Congressional Quarterly, Inc.

*Figures based on bills and joint resolutions
**Excludes private bills

emerges when large segments of the population recognize that conditions are not as good as they were in the past (for example, more handgun murders than last year, lower SAT scores than a decade ago) or that our political system is dealing with a problem less effectively than other political systems (for example, infant mortality). There is often more conflict over relative problems, since individuals disagree over both the true nature of the problem and the means by which it might be solved.[2]

Congress plays an important role in setting the agenda of problems to be dealt with and determining the means by which the federal government will deal with them. Both choosing the problems and deciding on the means to solve them involve building coalitions.

KEEPING PROBLEMS OFF THE AGENDA

Keeping problems off the public agenda can be just as important as including them. The decision not to have a federal policy or program to deal with a perceived problem is the goal of many legislators. Conservatives often fight including

[2]Another set of problems have such narrow implications that they fall into the "it's not my problem" category for most Members. Congress deals with unique cases such as immigration or special compensation through private bills that affect only a few individuals.

Cartoon by Draper Hill, © 1991, by *The Detroit News*, reprinted by permission

new government regulations on businesses or limits on freedoms such as the possession of guns. Liberals often oppose including issues such as limiting abortions or free speech on the public agenda.

COALITION BUILDING: THE UNDERLYING STRATEGY OF THE POLICY GAME

Getting an idea onto the legislative agenda is only the first stage in the policy process. The ultimate goal of turning a good idea into the law of the land requires building a winning **coalition,** a group of players agreeing to cooperate by supporting a particular piece of legislation, often for highly different reasons (see Groennings, Kelly, and Leiserson 1970, 7). Coalition building is the key policy process in a collective decision-making body like Congress. Congressional coalitions are generally not permanent alliances, but rather ad hoc groupings of individual Members which come together to take action on a particular bill. The winning coalition on a subsequent piece of legislation will often include only some of the Members of the previous coalition and be augmented by other players. Although alliances are temporary, they may recur in similar form over time as similar legislative proposals come up for consideration.

Coalition managers[3] either within or outside of Congress are constantly activating strategies to garner the fifty-one senators or the 218 House members they need to win final passage on the floor when everyone is present. At other stages in the legislative process, the rules require either larger or smaller winning coalitions.

COALITION BUILDING STRATEGIES

A number of different coalition strategies thrive in Congress. The rules of Congress determine legitimate strategies and the size of the coalition required.

The typical congressional supportive coalition includes two types of players. **Natural** coalition members favor the proposed legislation on its merits; their support requires no further inducement. **Bought** coalition members are willing to trade their support for a piece of legislation in order to receive a specific payoff. Natural and bought coalitions can, of course, also develop in opposition to legislation.

Natural Coalitions

Natural coalitions develop around similarities in constituent interests, party affiliations, and ideological preferences. For example, legislators from farming districts almost automatically support proposals for increased agricultural research, Members of a particular party normally back their party's candidates for chamber leadership positions, and conservatives favor increased defense expenditures more readily than liberals. The task of the natural coalition builder lies in connecting the specific proposal with constituent needs, partisan preferences or ideologies of as many Members as possible. The breakdown of partisan voting and abiding natural coalitions has led to the strategy of using **omnibus** legislation. Introducing legislation that covers many topics increases the chances of pleasing a larger number of Members and encouraging them to join the coalition (see Schneier and Gross 1993, 127–129; and Longley and Oleszek 1989, 67–69). There is also, of course, the possibility that poorly designed omnibus legislation will expand the potential areas for offending large numbers of potential coalition members.

SOME ABIDING COALITIONS Natural coalitions in Congress often lack permanency. The supporters of one piece of legislation might well be locked in total disagreement on another. Building winning natural coalitions one Member at a time would be a daunting task. Fortunately for coalition managers, the building blocs for a winning natural coalition often tend to be identifiable groups of Members sharing partisan, ideological, or constituency interests.

---

[3]There is no official position of "coalition manager" in Congress. The task of building a winning majority on a piece of legislation falls to different people at different times. The president and his staff may try to create a coalition from the outside. Party leaders and committee chairs spend much of their time building coalitions. Individual Members often attempt to build coalitions around interests of great personal or district interest. Particularly in the Senate, but even in the House, staff members often play important roles as coalition managers, serving as extensions of the Members for whom they work (see DeGregorio and Snider 1993, 25–26).

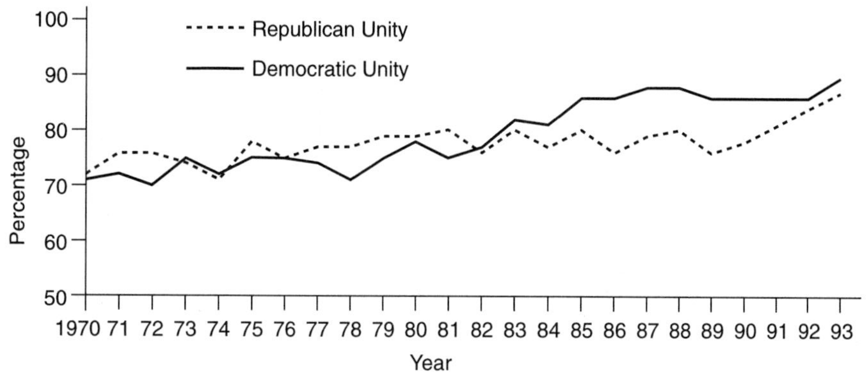

Note: Party votes are defined as roll calls on which a majority of Democrats vote against a majority of Republicans.

FIGURE 7.1

Party Unity Votes in the House

SOURCE: Congressional Quarterly data reported in Norman J. Ornstein, Thomas E. Mann, and Michael E. Malbin, *Vital Statistics on Congress, 1993–1994,* and *Congressional Quarterly Weekly Report,* 18 December 1993, p. 3432.

Partisan building blocs: Partisan attachments serve as one abiding basis for congressional coalitions. As one Member put it,

> After spending thirty years yelling "Republican" at the top of my lungs at campaign rallies or on the floor, I have come to believe that anything with the "Republican" label is somehow better than anything with the "Democrat" label. (author's interview)

Some Members will support an alternative simply because it is the party position. Party members often share ideological outlooks and constituency similarities. Recent years have seen an increase in party-based divisiveness (see figures 7.1 and 7.2).

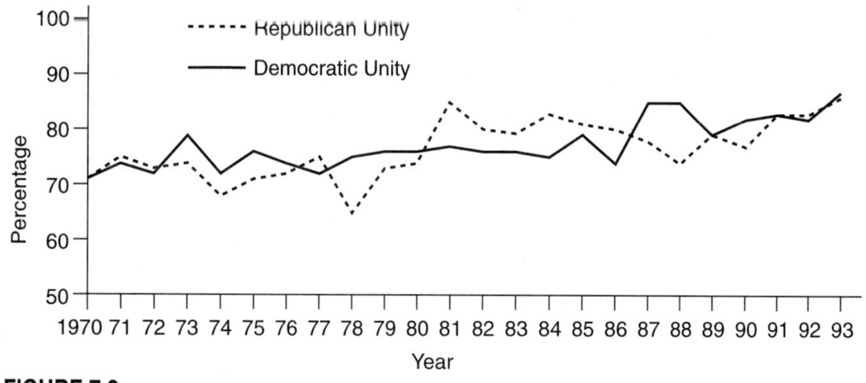

FIGURE 7.2

Party Unity Votes in the Senate

SOURCE: Congressional Quarterly data reported in Norman J. Ornstein, Thomas E. Mann, and Michael E. Malbin, *Vital Statistics on Congress, 1993–1994,* and *Congressional Quarterly Weekly Report,* 18 December 1993, p. 3432.

Identifying something as the "party position" often encourages Members to put aside their objections and join ranks with their teammates. Presidents give clear indications of the "proper" partisan response, and many Members recognize the personal and team embarrassment of not supporting their partisan team captains. Presidential influence on party cohesion across a broad range of issues is somewhat limited, especially in the House. The president's party is significantly more cohesive than the party out of power (see figures 7.1 and 7.2). On key components of the president's program, though, his partisan teammates tend to close ranks.

Party support is not an automatic "knee jerk" reaction in Congress. In fact the level of partisanship and party cohesion is considerably lower in the Congress than in most other national legislatures (Brady and Bullock 1981, 186). Each party team encompasses a relatively wide range of ideological and district backgrounds. Despite limitations, party membership is still the best single predictor of how a Member will vote in Congress, and the utility of party as a predictor has increased in recent years (see figures 7.1 and 7.2). Most congressional decisions begin with a solid bloc of supporters from one party as the core of a natural coalition.

Ideological groupings: The classic example of a natural coalition building bloc is the **Conservative Coalition** which often dominated congressional decision making from the 1930s to the 1980s. This group of Republicans and southern Democrats voted together on as many as one-quarter of the votes and prevailed over two-thirds of the time, especially during the 1940s and 1950s (Brady and Bullock 1981, 191, 198). The coalition did not meet to establish positions nor require formal leadership. It was more of "an understanding between southern Democrats and Republicans about certain issues . . . [who] were already lined up . . . [because they] think more alike" (Members quoted in Brady and Bullock 1981, 188). With partisan realignment in the South allowing conservatives to win as Republicans and the decline of some of the more divisive issues such as race, the natural alliance between southern Democrats and Republicans declined. Even in early 1980s, Ronald Reagan depended heavily on near unanimous Republican voting combined with support for the "Boll Weevils," a group of southern Democrats with a natural affinity for his more conservative economic policies. President Bush's record was less impressive as Republican support of the coalition declined (see Fleisher and Bond 1983, 745–758, and 1992, 525–541; and Bond and Fleisher 1990, 30).

Several other ideological groupings such as the Democratic Study Group and Conservative Opportunity Society (see chapter 4) continue to serve as the basis for natural coalitions. The importance of these groups lies not only in the fact that coalition managers target group members of the natural basis for a coalition, but also members of these groupings tend to interact and share information which frames issues in their minds in conflicting ways. While members of the liberal Democratic Study Group might see Bill Clinton's policies as an "investment in the future," members of the Conservative Opportunity Society might tag it as another round of "tax and spend." Members take voting **cues** from those with whom they interact and those they trust (see Matthews and Stimson 1970, 23), and ideological groupings serve as effective vehicles for these interchanges.

Constituency and personal proclivities: The constituency interests and personal experiences of Members make them susceptible to particular policy positions. Legislation providing crop subsidies has a natural coalition among Members representing farm districts, while backing for pay and benefits packages for federal workers finds support among Members from districts having a large federal work force.

Personal experiences also draw Members toward certain positions on legislation (see box 7.1). Women and minority members of Congress tend to be more supportive of programs aimed at their gender or ethnic group than the average White male member (see Frankovic 1977, 329). Individuals with experience in the military, parochial schools, or unions are most likely to be some of the first to sign on to legislation supporting the interest of those groups.[4]

BOX 7.1 Players Show Their True Colors

Members of Congress are human beings on whom personal experiences leave indelible marks. At times these experiences lead them to champion unexpected issues—for example,

- Senate Majority Robert Dole (R-KN), a conservative who generally opposes federal mandates on business, gave pivotal support to the Americans with Disabilities Act of 1990 which forces industry to accommodate the needs of disabled workers. His experience of losing the use of an arm while serving as an infantry officer in World War II undoubtedly affected his position on the issue.
- Senator Pete Domenici (R-NM) became a strong supporter of mental health legislation after his daughter was diagnosed with mental illness.
- Senator Strom Thurmond (R-SC), usually an opponent of government regulation, expressed support for a bill requiring advertisers to attach safety warnings to liquor commercials after his daughter was killed by a drunk driver.
- Senator Tom Harkin (D-IA) who has lost two sisters to breast cancer and has a deaf brother serves as a champion of more cancer research and expanded civil rights for people with disabilities.

As Representative Joseph Kennedy II (D-MA) sees it,

> Politicians are human beings. When there is a degree of very personal pain one feels toward an issue . . . the commitment level is higher and your willingness to compromise is lower.

SOURCE: Clifford Krauss, "Liquor-Warning Bill Reflects Personal Impact on Public Policy," *New York Times,* May 16, 1993, p. 20.

[4]The exact path of cause and effect is difficult to determine here. A district with a large parochial school population may be more likely to elect a Member who was a product of parochial schools. It is then difficult to determine whether that Member's support for government aid to parochial schools stems from personal experience, constituency interests, or a combination of the two.

Past commitments: Although Ralph Waldo Emerson argued that "a foolish consistency is the hobgoblin of little minds, adored by little statesmen and philosophers and divines" (1903), political activists change their mind at their own political peril. If one wants to know who will support a political alternative next time, see who supported it the last time. While legislative proposals vary considerably in content, Members attempt to simplify the decision-making process by grouping them into relatively fixed categories such as "pro-environment," "empowering of minorities," or "protecting children." They then position themselves toward that category and follow a pattern of decision making which is consistent with their past support or opposition to legislation in that category (see Clausen 1973, 14–21). If a coalition manager can convince a Member that this legislation is "simply the logical extension of the three votes you made last year on related issues," the Member is quite likely to fall naturally in line.

NATURAL COALITIONS IN ACTION If the intrinsic merit of a piece of legislation appeals to a majority of Members from the outset, there is little need to broaden the coalition's membership. Coalition managers, such as the president or party leaders, simply make sure their supporters are present prior to having the measure brought up for a vote—and the initial majority prevails. The "simplicity" of the task may be misleading. The lucky happenstance of a large natural supporting coalition may signal a potential problem. "Overly large coalitions . . . have a tendency to self-destruct" (Schneier and Gross 1993, 149; see also Riker 1962, 66). Individuals knowing that their vote is not really necessary may feel free to abandon the coalition to gain other benefits or may not expend the effort to show up when their vote is needed.

In general, though, coalition managers would prefer a large natural coalition than having to build a winning coalition. For most important legislation, identifying the natural coalition is only the beginning.

"Bought" Coalitions

> **Logrolling:** a game of skill popular among lumberjacks, which calls for two people to cooperatively maintain their balance on a floating log as they spin it with their feet; mutual aid among legislators. (Shafritz 1988, *Dictionary of American Government and Politics,* p. 332)

In order to create the necessary majority, a natural coalition often needs to be augmented through the addition of new Members whose support is "bought" by coalition managers. The process of bargaining and cajoling is often called **logrolling.** The willingness to bargain varies with the commitments and perspectives of the potential bargainers. Four basic conditions must be met for bargaining to take place:

1. *Disagreement:* Bargaining begins with disagreement. If everyone agrees on a course of action from the outset, one has a natural coalition. Bargaining situations array themselves along a continuum from "positive-sum games"[5] in which

[5]At times this end of the continuum might be seen as a "negative-sum game" where everyone loses. In this case, all participants have a stake in losing the least. The common threat between positive-sum and negative-sum games is that the gains and losses do not come at the direct expense of other players. Players can cooperate with each other and mutually pursue gains or protect against losses.

everyone gains something, to "zero-sum games" in which one player's gain is clearly another player's loss. For bargaining situations approaching the positive-sum pole, the disagreement involves determining how much each player gains. Ideally, each player wants to "win it all" and he or she must curb his or her appetite to satisfy some of the interests of other players and not "break the bank" (see upcoming discussion of "pork barrel"). Bargaining is more difficult in situations that approach the zero-sum game pole of the continuum, since the bargainers must give up something to satisfy others. Most bargaining situations fall toward the middle of the continuum and involve a mix of benefits and costs.

2. *Flexibility:* Bargaining requires players who are more interested in reaching a compromise than simply taking a position. Individuals whose moral standards or political needs do not allow them to support anything but one purist position are not good candidates for bargaining. Members of Congress realize that compromise is often viewed as a dirty word and attempt to convince the public that while "compromising a principle sounds wrong, compromising between principles is all right" (Schelling 1984, 9). Members of Congress constantly deal with issues over which reasonable people disagree and compromise is the only way to reach an agreeable consensus.

3. *Mutual Needs:* Bargaining does not occur unless each set of players has something the other players need. For a member of Congress, the ultimate bargaining chip is his or her vote. One of the difficulties in bargaining is the fact that there is no universally accepted measure of value in Congress (Schneier and Gross 1993, 152). Each Member puts his or her own value on items such as amendments, public works projects, and leadership positions. Coalition managers are never completely sure how much they have to deliver to gain a Member's vote.

4. *Trust:* Bargaining is unlikely unless each set of participants trust the other to uphold their end of the bargain.

Bargaining is seldom brute force, but rather subtle manipulation. First you need to know what the other person's goals are and then you attempt to find a way to accommodate them. As masterful congressional bargainer Lyndon Johnson put it,

> You can *tell* a man to go to hell, but you can't *make* him go. . . . Politics is the art and craft of dealing with people. Politics goes beyond the art of the possible. It is the art of making possible what seems impossible (Johnson 1971, 460–461).

Bargaining essentially means "buying" support. Two common methods of buying support are substantially broadening the appeal of the legislation and offering side payments.

BROADENED COALITIONS The support of potential coalition members who have difficulty with the substance of the legislation, can sometimes be "bought" by **compromise** on the legislation's content or the inclusion of desirable provisions. A well-timed amendment or the elimination of a particular provision may bring in new supporters. For example, a Member opposing a new program to aid small businesses, might be supportive if an amendment to help the kinds of businesses in his or her district is included. In the face of reduced foreign threats and the demand to cut defense spending in 1992, House Armed Services Committee Chair, Les Aspin (D-WI) (later Secretary of Defense) broadened his bipartisan coalition by selectively cutting defense programs and locking "in the support of Members whose constituents would keep their jobs because the House bill kept alive the weapons they made" (Kellam 1992, 394–395).

Omnibus legislation which covers a wide range of topics provides the opportunity to buy the support of a wide range of Members, who, while not agreeing with all the components, judge that the overall package provides more benefits than detriments. Building a broadened coalition is more difficult than it seems. Coalition managers must be aware that coalition building strategies **may not be cumulative.** The substantive compromise that encourages some Members to join may simultaneously offend some existing coalition members and force their departure. Potential coalition members also face a daunting task. The exact consequences of most legislative proposals are not clear and there is no assurance that the gains will out measure the losses (see Weingast and Marshall 1988, 138–139).

Laws which include a little bit of something to fit everyone's interests are often called **pork barrel** legislation (see chapter 3). Bills that provide such benefits as highway funds, job training programs, or defense contracts for particular districts make them very appealing to Members whose districts are likely to benefit. The benefits of pork barrel are well known:

> When applied with skill, pork can act as a lubricant to smooth passage of complex or controversial legislation. . . . Whether the projects are meritorious or not, the most time-honored rule of pork-barrelling is that any Member getting a project is duty bound to support the rest of the bill (Congressional Quarterly 1991, 514).

As one key presidential aide put it, "pork buys . . . support" (quoted in Salholz 1992, 23). The exchange among bargainers is relatively clear since all participants get their benefits simultaneously (Weingast and Marshall 1988, 140). Members receiving public works projects are both more likely to support that legislation and to support subsequent legislative initiatives backed by the coalition managers responsible for helping the Member acquire those projects (Evans 1992, i).

SIDE PAYMENTS Expanding a potential coalition is not limited to the substance of the legislation currently at hand. **Side payments,** threats, and/or promises of benefits unrelated to the substance of the current bill, may be offered to obtain the support of potential coalition members. For example, a coalition manager might endorse a Member's campaign for a committee post or promise support on an otherwise unrelated issue. "Pork" is a side payment when used in relation to a bill on a different subject. A coalition manager might promise to back a future public works project such as a highway or postal facility to be located in the Member's district as an inducement to get his or her vote on the pending legislation. Sometimes, the mere expectation of the coalition manager's future good will, the opportunity to say, "Remember when I helped you out? Well now I need some help from you," may well suffice. Bargaining for side payments may involve an explicit "deal," or a very vague agreement (see box 7.2). Congressional bargains

Reprinted with special permission of King Features Syndicate.

based on future rewards are more difficult to strike since it is not always clear whether the person offering a future benefit can deliver (see Weingast and Marshall 1988, 139).

Not all uses of side payments come in the form of rewards; the denial of side payments can also send a signal. In 1990, when Pat Schroeder (D-CO) abandoned the Democratic leadership and cast an embarrassing vote on the franking privilege, the Appropriations Committee refused to fund two Colorado highway and bridge projects in retribution (Hook 1990, 2195). Certain types of potentially effective side payments, such as bribery, are so extraneous to the issue and potentially pernicious they are clearly illegal.

Not all players are comfortable with bargaining based on side payments. Representative Norman Mineta (D-CA) pointed out that President Jimmy Carter "dealt with issues on a vertical plane. He won't say to you 'I need your vote on Mideast arms sales and therefore I will give you the dam you want in your district' " (quoted in Jacobson 1992, 220).

Other coalition managers take a more pragmatic approach, granting the concessions of most importance to Members in exchange for their support.

Coalition Management Strategies

Since bargaining is "expensive" in the sense that it takes time and requires the expenditure of scarce bargaining "chips," coalition managers tend to stop bargaining when they have assembled a **minimum winning coalition,** in most cases a simple majority (see Riker 1962, 40). As one Senate insider put it, "It's a rule of this game

BOX 7.2 Securing a Win with an Assist from the Other Team's Manager

Bill Clinton attempted to build a winning coalition for the North American Free Trade Agreement despite considerable opposition within his own party. A number of Republican supporters whom he desperately needed exacted a political price. They wanted some "cover" from Democratic Party criticism in the 1994 congressional elections and President Clinton sent the Republican supporters in Congress this letter:

THE WHITE HOUSE

WASHINGTON

November 17, 1993

Dear

Please accept my sincere appreciation and great respect for your vote in support of the North American Free Trade Agreement. You and your colleagues who have helped to pass NAFTA may take lasting pride in this momentous vote.

We have come through a difficult debate with many competing pressures. The historic nature of NAFTA and the intense feelings on both sides of the issue and on both sides of the aisle mean it would be best for the House and for our political system if this issue were not re-fought in the 1994 Congressional elections.

Since I have sought the support of all members of the House of Representatives for the NAFTA implementing legislation as a matter of compelling national interest, I will do my utmost to personally encourage a campaign in which anti-NAFTA candidates will not use this issue against pro-NAFTA members, regardless of party, in the coming election. I do not believe that either party should benefit from exploiting the NAFTA issue in electoral politics, and I will personally discourage such NAFTA-related campaigning.

You have my gratitude for having helped achieve this great success.

With best wishes,

Sincerely,

BOX 7.3 Close Calls and No Ties

Members of Congress are paid to make tough choices. Each chamber has provisions which make a tie vote with no side winning or losing impossible. Legislation must receive a majority and a tie is defined as a defeat. The Speaker of the House and the vice president can vote to either make or break a tie. The most closely watched and managed attempts at coalition building often result in very close votes as the following examples indicate:

	For	Against	Needed for Passage
The Panama Canal Treaty (1978)	68	32	67
Highway Bill Veto Override (1987)	67	33	67
Confirmation of John Tower as Secretary of Defense (1989)	47	53	51
Confirmation of Supreme Court Nominee Clarence Thomas (1991)	52	48	51
Clinton Budget Vote (Senate, 1993)	51*	50	51
Clinton Budget Vote (House, 1993)	219	213	217

*with Vice President Al Gore breaking the tie

that when you got the votes, vote; and when you don't, delay" (quoted in Devroy 1991, A6). Many of the most visible votes in Congress were won or lost by a few votes (see box 7.3). Box 7.4 discusses three actual cases of coalition building which illustrate many of the above points.

Not all congressional votes are cliff hangers. At times the natural coalitions overwhelmingly favor one side. Other times it is important to Congress to present a unified front and a unanimous vote or extraordinary majority is desired (see box 7.5). Coalition managers often lack perfect information on the current size of their coalition, making it difficult to determine how many more supporters need to be added (see Gilmour 1989, 2). To be safe, coalition managers often attempt to "pad" their coalitions in case some Members cannot be present or change their minds. Last minute amendments often change the final outcome. Coalitions also can not be "closed" until the final vote is completed. Recognizing that there is comfort in numbers, some Members will join a winning coalition in the last few moments as they see the potential outcome.[6]

[6]This strategy can work in the opposite direction also. Senator Nancy Kassenbaum (R-KN) ended up voting against the nomination of John Tower for Secretary of Defense when she realized that her vote would not have made any difference in saving a nomination made by a president (Bush) from her political party.

BOX 7.4 Assembling Winning Coalitions—Three Cases

A. **The Panama Canal Treaty.** In 1977, after years of negotiation by several presidential administrations, President Jimmy Carter sent a treaty to the Senate, which would, if approved, transfer the ownership of the Panama Canal to the government of Panama by the year 2000. Immediately, two **natural coalitions** emerged. Liberals hailed "democratic self determination" and the end of American imperialism, while conservatives questioned the challenge to American security that would come from losing complete control over the canal. To gain additional votes, President Carter, and eventually the Senate, accepted a compromise in the form of the DeConcini Reservation (named after Democratic Senator Dennis DeConcini of Arizona). This treaty amendment specified that any attempt by Panama to close the canal would justify U.S. military intervention. Its passage broadened the coalition to include a number of senators concerned about the defense implications of the initial treaty. President Carter still did not have the votes needed for passage. Additional support in the Senate was obtained by **side payments** such as public works projects. Senators got side payment commitments for projects, such as Howard Baker (R-TN) got for a federal nuclear research facility. The final vote of sixty-eight to thirty-two just barely reached the two-thirds majority required for passage making it a **minimum winning coalition.**

B. **Speedy Success in Assembling a Winning Coalition.** During the 1974 oil shortage, Congress passed legislation mandating a fifty-five mile per hour speed limit on all federal highways in the interest of energy conservation. As the energy crisis dissipated, opposition to the lower speed limit grew. By 1987, Congress was ready to reassess the situation, and legislation rescinding the fifty-five mile per hour speed limit was included in a highway bill.

Two **natural coalitions** emerged. Members of western states joined with conservatives to support increasing the speed limit and giving drivers more latitude in choosing their speed. Westerners were motivated by inconvenience and cost of travel between their distant population centers, while conservatives objected to federal regulation of what they felt should be a state or local matter. Opponents to an increased speed limit accepted the argument that slower speeds (as opposed to better highways, stiffer drunk driving laws, reduced driving distances, better cars, and other factors) were the primary reason why highway deaths had decreased since 1974.

Members were **bought** into the coalitions through a variety of means. One set of compromises involved the types of highways that were to be allowed a higher speed limit. For example, Members from urban areas wanted their highways to have the fifty-five mile-per-hour limit. In addition, there were a series of **side payments** in the form of specific public works projects slated for a large number of congressional districts. The final bills passed overwhelmingly in each chamber.

This was to be the end of the story, however. President Reagan, philosophically attuned to returning the power to set speed limits to the states, vetoed the bill citing the "budget-busting pork-barrel projects." He attempted to lure budget conscious Members into a coalition to uphold the veto, relying on their ideological commitment to reducing the deficit. In the House, Democratic Speaker Jim Wright (D-TX) favored the override and threatened denial of future **side payments** when he reminded his colleagues that he had a "long memory" and would not forget Members' votes on this issue.

Despite considerable pressure, only one House Democrat switched to the president's side. Among House Republicans, only fifty-five Members came to the president's aid and reversed their votes, while over 100 Republicans rejected his request and voted for the override. Even

BOX 7.4 Continued

Republican Minority Leader Robert Michel (R-IL), lured by the completion of a highway in his district, refused to forfeit this side payment to support President Reagan's cause.

President Reagan needed a minimum of thirty-four votes in the Senate to sustain his veto. With the help of thirty-three Republicans and two Democrats, the initial sixty-five to thirty-five vote looked like a victory for the president. Using a parliamentary maneuver, however, Majority Leader Robert Byrd (D-WV) switched his vote during the final moments to the prevailing side in order to retain the right to call for a reconsideration. The Democrats began to work on freshman Senator Terry Sanford (D-NC), the lone Democratic dissenter. After assuring him that the existing bill provided more highway funds for North Carolina than he had been led to believe, the Democrats successfully convinced him to switch his vote.

President Reagan and his supporters then went to work to convince at least one of the thirteen Republicans supporting the veto override to switch sides. Word went out that "Whatever you want, just tell us, and you can have it," which is about as good a definition of **side payments** as can be imagined (Starobin 1987, 606). Despite a rare personal "vote-hunting" trip to Capitol Hill by President Reagan, the dissenting Republicans stood firm and the veto was overridden with a **minimum winning** coalition vote of sixty-seven to thirty-three.

Few congressional votes end up as the kind of cliff-hangers discussed here, but the extreme cases of coalition building, where every vote counts, offer the best picture of coalition strategies. So when you drive down the highway (legally) at sixty-five miles per hour, enjoy the thrill of speed, but also remember you are experiencing the fruits of coalition building.

C. **Making Up For A Deficit of Supporters.** President Clinton's five-year deficit-reduction package was a prime test of the president's coalition creation capabilities in 1993. At the outset, the president faced a **natural coalition** among Republicans who decided to oppose the budget package unanimously, and thus took themselves out of the bargaining game. Republicans decided early on that they "wanted no fingerprints on a tax-heavy plan that they say will hobble the economy and kill jobs" (Hager and Cloud 1993a, 2122). Most Democrats, on the other had agreed to support their president from the outset. They

> rolled the dice for their own and the party's political future, betting that deficit reduction will now yield lower interest rates that will in turn produce jobs and a healthy economy sometime down the road. If the gamble works, Democrats will get sole credit, because they passed the package without a single Republican vote (Hager and Cloud 1993a, 2122).

Despite strong Democratic support, President Clinton initially lacked the votes to secure passage. He assiduously began using the tried and true tactics of coalition building. His first stop was in the Senate. Attention initially focused on senators who previously supported the plan but now desired specific changes in the substance of the bill. President Clinton **broadened** the coalition by allowing substantive changes. A broadened tax credit of research and development retained the vote of freshman Senator Diane Feinstein (D-CA). Fellow freshman Russell Feingold (D-WI), got a ban on the use of growth hormones for cows (Hager and Cloud 1993a, 2128). Capping increases in the gas tax brought in Senator Kohl (D-WI) (Hook 1993, 2206). Securing previous support was not enough, since Senator Boren (D-OK) had switched to the opposition. Senator DeConcini, a previous opponent, found himself in a key position. He fought for reducing taxes paid on social security income, an issue of great interest to his large constituency of well-off retirees. Senator DeConcini also negotiated a significant **side payment.** Facing a tough re-election fight, he secured a pledge from the Democratic National Committee to help him in any primary fight (Hager and Cloud

Continued on next page

BOX 7.4 Continued

1993a, 2124), a pledge which never had to be repaid after Senator DeConcini decided a month later not to run for re-election. Despite the expansion of support, success in the Senate was still not assured. During the final debate, attention focused on Bob Kerry (D-NE), a 1992 primary opponent of Bill Clinton. Senator Kerry felt the plan did not go far enough and played coy about his voting intentions despite intense White House pressure. As the debate wound down, he expressed his dissatisfaction with the plan directly to President Clinton over television, but concluded that he "could not and should not cast the vote that brings down your presidency" (Hager and Cloud 1993a, 2122). With a tie vote assured, Vice President Al Gore assured the **minimum winning coalition** of fifty-one to fifty with his positive vote.

The prospects for victory in the House were no more assured. President Clinton and his staff initiated almost endless meetings with wavering groups and individuals. Freshmen members of Congress who were once almost ignored by presidents who could count on their party loyalty received regular invitations to meetings with the president since the close vote assured that their support was worth as much as anyone else's (Hook, 1993, 2206). Most of the freshmen gloried in the attention, but had few substantive demands—glorying instead in **side payment** of having attention paid to them. Other groups and individuals had more substantive concerns. The thirty-eight members of the Black Caucus decided to hold their support hostage until the budget proposal was changed to save some of their favored social programs such as earned-income credit for poor families and mandatory immunization for poor children. By acceding to their demands, President Clinton **broadened** the coalition and guaranteed a bloc of thirty-eight votes. Tim Penny (D-MN), speaking for the fiscal conservatives, got a **side payment** in the form of a commitment from President Clinton that he would issue an executive order designed to curb entitlement spending.

As the final vote approached victory was far more assured. The Democratic party organization was hunting votes one at a time. As one of the party whips put it,

> The bad news is that it's a lot like pulling teeth. The good news is that we have a lot of patients in the chair. . . . Some of the undecided folks are really hiding out. Some of the whips are going to their offices for a little face-to-face (Richard J. Durbin [D-IL] quoted in Hager and Cloud 1993a, 2127).

When the electronic voting terminals closed the vote was tied 210 to 210. The Speaker used his power to keep the vote open as the tally see-sawed back and forth. Eventually freshman Marjorie Margolies-Mezvinsky (D-PA), who had been elected in a heavily Republican district and who had earlier that day announced her intention to vote against the plan, was escorted through the chamber "with the terror-struck demeanor of someone being marched to her own hanging" (Hager and Cloud 1993, 2127). Her positive vote created a **minimum winning coalition** of 219 to 213. Representative Margolies-Mezvinsky was long viewed as a "pocket vote" who could be counted on if her vote was absolutely needed to protect the party. She explained her switch more in terms of a **side payment,** touting a commitment she had received from President Clinton to convene a conference on cutting entitlement spending which would be held in her constituency (Hager and Cloud 1993, 2125).

While the president and his party team won the battle, the outcome of the long-term coalition building war remains unclear. The shameless courting of Members could create expectations of similar deference in future battles (Hook 1993, 2206). The "Let's Make A Deal" atmosphere may activate Members who did not put their vote up for sale this time around. Although, Margolies-Mezvinsky's defeat in 1994 might temper such strategy.

BOX 7.5 Staging a Perfect Game

As the defensive initiative of Desert Shield designed to protest Iraq's invasion of Kuwait moved into the more offensive Desert Storm, the Bush administration turned to Congress. It was felt that in order to keep the international coalition intact and to send a message to Iraq's Saddam Hussein, a unanimous congressional vote in support of Operation Desert Storm was necessary. Party leaders worked long and hard to craft a resolution which would imply support without losing the votes of Members continuing to prefer economic sanctions over military invasion. The final resolution was a good case of a **broadened** coalition, as it was worded very carefully to avoid direct support of the president's policy, and specifically to support the troops. The resolution was worded as follows:

> [The U.S. Senate] Commends and supports the efforts and the leadership of the president . . . [and] unequivocally supports the men and women of our armed forces who are carrying out their missions with professional excellence, dedicated patriotism and exemplary bravery (quoted in Dewar and Kenworthy 1991, A29).

The Senate met for a brief and furious debate early one evening in hopes of making a final decision in time for the national evening news programs. Traditionally long winded speeches gave way to an avalanche of short sound bites. From a public relations perspective, the details of the resolution were lost as the media presented the story that the U.S. Congress unanimously supported Operation Desert Storm.

PROCESSING LEGISLATION: HOW A BILL BECOMES A LAW

> The House has taken the whole first half of the game to run one play. (Washington lobbyist quoted in Hager 1990a, 2399)

The legislative process involves a number of stages. Different coalition strategies are applicable at different stages. The legislative process is slow, redundant, and inefficient—and it is intended to be. The founders of the U.S. recognized that Congress would be dealing with issues that impact on some of America's deepest held values. Since the "rightness" or "wrongness" of these value choices can seldom be proven to all interested parties, it is important to develop a value mediating procedure in which Congress' choices would not be attacked on *both* substantive and procedural grounds. The congressional process, with its numerous decision points and opportunities to revisit previous decisions, was established so all parties could have their say on policy options at a number of points (see figure 7.3).

Coalition building in Congress involves a series of **concurrent majorities.** In order to become a law, a bill must receive majority support at each stage of the legislative process. Simply knowing that a bill has majority support at one stage, does not necessarily mean that it will pass all of the hurdles, since each stage consists of coalitions of different Members.

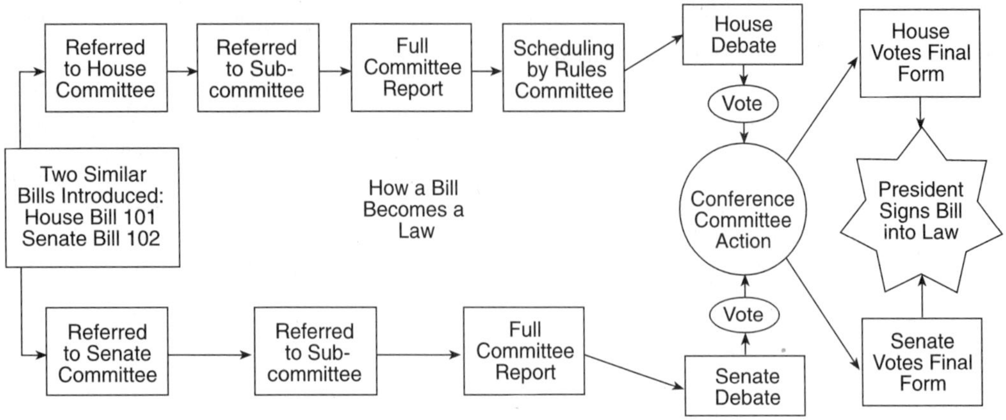

FIGURE 7.3
How a Bill Becomes a Law

INTRODUCING LEGISLATION INTO THE LEGISLATIVE ARENA

Congress does not act on the basis of abstract principles, but rather lines up in support or opposition to specific legislative proposals. The rules outline the legitimate players and what strategies are available to them.

The Rules and Players of Bill Introduction

A bill starts its route to becoming a law when a member of the House or Senate drops a copy in the "hopper" at the front of the legislative chamber. Bills may be introduced in either chamber, with the one constitutional restriction that revenue (tax) bills must originate in the House to keep their contents closer to the people. Motivations for introducing bills include a true desire to see the legislation passed, a response to the demands of the White House and/or interest group, a reaction to a personal experience (see box 7.1), or the desire to send a symbolic signal of one's support for an issue.

Legislation comes in a variety of forms. Most often Members introduce **bills** to deal with broad public policy. Enactment of a bill requires passage of the identical measure by both chambers and the approval of the president. **Resolutions** deal with matters within the prerogative of one chamber and do not require consent of the other chamber or presidential approval. Resolutions lack the force of law and are often used to express the sentiment of the House or Senate or give "advice" to other countries or the executive branch. At times Congress passes **concurrent resolutions** to express the sentiments of both chambers on either substantive or procedural issues (such as fixing the time of adjournment).

The number of bills introduced, especially in the House, has declined in recent years. During the 1970s the average Member introduced about forty bills, but that figure has dropped to thirty for senators and about half that for House members (Ornstein et al. 1992, 151–153). Several factors explain the decline. The House changed its rules in 1978 allowing unlimited **co-sponsorship** (Davidson 1988, 352). This change permitted Members to get public credit for supporting an issue simply by signing onto a bill sponsored by someone else. Since the 1980s, budget constraints have forced Congress to expend much of its efforts refining policy and cutting back on programs as opposed to designing new programs and agencies (Davidson 1988, 352). Finally, Members have become more strategic in how they present and package new legislation.

Bill Introduction Strategies

Legislation is seldom judged on its merits alone. Just introducing a good piece of legislation is not enough. Bills dropped in the hopper and expected to prosper on their own seldom go anywhere. They are like children and must be "nurtured" by their sponsors. Part of the nurturing starts very early at the introduction stage.

PACKAGING FOR SUCCESS How a bill is presented can make a big difference in its eventual success or failure. Both the initial impression and the substance of the bill become factors in a Member's vote.

The naming game: The name given a piece of legislation carries with it a lot of "baggage." Timing the introduction to secure a significant bill number (HR 1, S1776, etc.) establishes a mind set that this piece of legislation is out of the ordinary. Particular bill titles encourage their passage. Few Members could vote against the "Ryan White Care Act" (1990) without implying disrespect for this heroic teenager who died of AIDS. Other proposals such as the "Fair Share Amendment Initiative" proposed by Senator Mack (R-FL) in 1991 to assure more equitable geographic distribution of federal funds, and the 1981 "Economic Recovery Tax Act" have equally appealing titles which often do not reflect the full content or signal the potential for reasonable disagreement about their desirability. A good name can start a bill out with a viable natural coalition of supporters.

Expanding the coalition: For much of Congress' history, most bills had a single purpose and dealt with a narrow range of problems. When one looked at the "Agricultural Subsidy Bill," one could rightfully expect that it dealt entirely with solutions to agricultural problems. Contemporary legislation is more difficult to interpret. Members of Congress have increasingly turned to **omnibus legislation** which bundles together large amounts of often unconnected legislative proposals into one bill (see box 7.6). Members incorporate the legislative desires of other colleagues into their bill and "buy" them into the supporting coalition by broadening its appeal.

Omnibus legislation can also reduce the likelihood that a Member will join the opposing coalition. With such legislation, Members are often forced to "take the bad with the good," and vote for legislation including sections to which they are opposed in order to secure passage of sections which they approve. In a period of expansionary government programs, Members are encouraged to introduce free standing legislation for which they can claim credit (see Mayhew 1974b, 55–61 and chapter 3 of this text). In an era of cutbacks, "blame avoidance" replaces credit claiming, and omnibus legislation facilitates spreading the blame (see Davidson 1988, 354; and Weaver 1987, 43–47).

BOX 7.6 What the Title Doesn't Tell You

A "rose by any other name may still be a rose," but the titles of some recent pieces of legislation often do not tell one much about their additional content:

The Ethics Reform Act of 1989 (Public Law 101–194) included provisions for a congressional pay raise.

The Freedom for Russia and Emerging Eurasian Democracies and Open Markets Support Act of 1992 (Public Law 102–511) had provisions dealing with abortion.

The Termination of the Application of Title IV of the Trade Act of 1974 to Czechoslovakia and Hungary (Public Law 102–182) contained provisions extending unemployment benefits to American workers for an additional thirteen weeks.

The Government Organization and Employees, Title 5 U.S.C., Amendment (Public Law 98–144) included the provisions for the Martin Luther King Holiday.

Evidence of the popularity of omnibus legislation emerges dramatically by looking at the average length of bills passed by Congress. During the 1950s, the average bill was about two pages long. Today bills average over four times that long,[7] with many of the key bills running thousands of pages (see table 7.2).

COOPTING OTHER PLAYERS Giving other Members a stake in your legislation increases their likelihood of supporting it. Junior Members often seek out senior Members—particularly committee chairs—to introduce "their" legislation. Members of the minority party will at times give up their right of sponsorship in favor of getting a Member of the majority to sponsor it.

Seeking out a large and varied list of co-sponsors not only gives them a stake in the outcome, but also sends a signal to the rest of the Members that this legislation already has broad support.

GREASING THE SKIDS Members of Congress realize that one of the first stages in the legislative process is committee consideration. Committees vary in terms of their receptiveness to certain types of legislation. Clever Members write legislation in such a way that it will be assigned to a committee or subcommittee with a record of supporting such legislation. In many cases, the specification of the government agency that will administer a policy determines the committee into whose jurisdiction it will fall. For example, a bill to promote environmental education would go to different committees depending on whether it was to be a program of the Department of Education or the Department of the Interior. Members will often write legislation in such a way that it will go to a committee on which they are serving so

[7]These averages are dramatically diminished by the large number of commemorative resolutions which continue to average just a few pages.

TABLE 7.2 The Average Length of Statutes Passed by Congress

Congress	**Average pages per public bill**
83rd (1953–54)	2.4
85th (1957–58)	2.6
87th (1961–62)	2.3
89th (1965–66)	3.6
91st (1969–70)	4.2
93rd (1973–74)	5.3
95th (1977–78)	8.5
97th (1981–82)	9.2
99th (1985–86)	10.8
101st (1989–90)	8.9
102nd (1991–92)	12.8

SOURCE: Norman J. Ornstein, Thomas E. Mann, and Michael J. Malbin. *Vital Statistics on Congress, 1993–1994,* p. 158, Congressional Quarterly, Inc.

that they can nurture it through the process. Changes in the rules now allow the Speaker or Senate Majority Leader to refer the same bill to more than one committee, creating the potential for healthy competition to process the legislation. With **multiple referrals,** committees often expedite consideration so that "their" bill becomes the one taken up by the chamber (see Young and Cooper 1993, 219).

SURVIVING THE COMMITTEE ARENA

Committees and their subcommittees serve as the graveyard for most legislation. Less than 20 percent of the bills introduced in the House become law and the figures for the Senate are only slightly higher (see Table 7.3). Committees screen out the largest number of bills before they even get to the floor consideration stage. More than 90 percent of the legislation approved by committees eventually becomes law in some form (Strom 1990, 85). Full committees generally do not approve legislation unless it has been approved by the appropriate subcommittee. Committee staff study proposed legislation and prepare for the subcommittee and committee hearings at which it will be discussed (see box 7.7).

Hearings

> Congress has a formal method for receiving expert views; congressional committee hearings. Hearings, however, are generally political undertakings, with witnesses chosen more for the constituency they represent than for the information they can provide committee members. (Stanfield 1990, 552)

TABLE 7.3 Percentage of Introduced Bills Passed by Congress

Congress	***Percentage of Bills Passing House***	***Percentage of Bills Passing Senate***
80th (47–48)	23%	52%
85th (57–58)	14%	49%
90th (67–68)	6%	31%
95th (77–78)	7%	28%
96th (79–80)	10%	28%
97th (81–82)	9%	24%
98th (83–84)	14%	27%
99th (85–86)	15%	28%
100th (87–88)	17%	30%
101st (89–90)	15%	27%
102nd (91–92)	12%	22%

NOTE: Figures are based on bills and joint resolutions, excluding private bills.

SOURCE: Norman J. Ornstein, Thomas E. Mann, and Michael J. Malbin. *Vital Statistics on Congress, 1993–1994,* pp. 153–155, Congressional Quarterly, Inc.

Although designed as neutral information gathering forums, committee and subcommittee hearings often serve quite different purposes. Some hearings are used to publicize an issue, and/or promote the image that Congress is "at least doing something" (see Dutton 1990, B2). Congressional hearings are increasingly public. Until the 1970s, close to 40 percent of committee hearings were closed to the public, while today virtually all are open (Ornstein et al. 1992, 117). C-SPAN airs hundreds of committee meetings each year, gavel-to-gavel. High visibility witnesses from the entertainment or sports industry are often called more for the attention they can generate than for the "expert" information they provide (see box 5.3). Representatives of the executive branch generally view testimony at a congressional committee as a "command performance," although presidents can judiciously use their right of **executive privilege** to deny Congress' access to certain witnesses. Hearings are often "stacked," presenting witnesses who will verify conclusions the majority members have already reached. Witnesses generally submit a prepared written statement and are then questioned by committee members.

Despite their limitations, hearings often help frame issues and provide a forum for their discussion. On occasion new information does emerge which improves the final policy.

Coming to a Committee Decision

Shortly after the hearings, committees or subcommittees schedule a **markup** session in which the final details of the bill are worked out. The committee may either reject the bill, send it forward without recommendation, send it forward as

BOX 7.7 The Players Speak about Committee Hearings

"We write the question. Under the question we write the answer . . . we expect to get on the basis of the staff research that has gone before. The Member who asks the question knows what the witness has told us in weeks and weeks of preparation; and he should get the same information. If he does not get that information, then he has the answer in front of him and he can ad lib the questions that solicit that information or refute it." (committee staff director as quoted in *Workshop on Congressional Oversight and Investigations,* 96th Congress, 1st Session, H. Doc. 96–217, p. 25)

Senate Majority Leader Robert Dole (R-KS) consults with a staff member during a committee meeting.

presented, suggest amendments, or completely rewrite it. Markup sessions are somewhat more likely to be closed to the public to facilitate the compromises necessary to build a winning coalition (see Oleszek 1989, 102). During markup sessions, coalition managers often solicit **proxy** voters for Members unable to attend. After working out details of the legislation, a committee report is sent to the parent chamber. Extensively revised legislation is forwarded as a **clean bill** to be reintroduced with its own number. Without committee support, most legislation is dead, especially in the House. The "gatekeeper" function of committees is less important in the Senate where the rules allow the incorporation of non-germane amendments and even entire bills on the floor (Smith and Deering 1990, 10).

FLOOR CONSIDERATION

All legislation with any possibility of becoming law must go the floor of both chambers for disposition. House and Senate floor procedures differ significantly. The House with its 435 members is much more structured in its consideration of legislation. Strict scheduling, time limits, and constraints on debate prevail. For example, both debates and proposed amendments in the House must be **germane** to the topic under consideration. Such a constraint is not the case in the smaller Senate where rules are much more flexible and scheduling reflects momentary whims of the senators. Majority rule pervades House procedures, while the Senate carefully guards the rights of each individual senator to have his or her own say.

Scheduling

The differing approach to scheduling in the House and Senate reflect the differences between the two chambers in terms of flexibility. Scheduling in the Senate emerges from informal negotiations between the majority and minority party leaders and key committee chairpersons. The majority leader attempts to negotiate a **unanimous consent agreement** which specifies the time at which a bill will be taken up and the approximate length of the debate. A single Member can upset such an agreement, or put a **hold** delaying its consideration. In Senator Simpson's (R-WY) words, "One person can tie this place into a knot. And two can do it even more beautifully" (Greenhouse 1987, B10).

Scheduling important legislation[8] in the House is a two-stage process. After passing the committee stage, most legislation[9] must go to the Rules Committee which considers both its substance and the procedures under which it will be debated. After deciding on the desirability of the legislation, the House Rules Committee suggests a **rule** under which the issue will be debated on the floor. The rule outlines the time allotted for debate and whether or not the proposal can be amended on the floor. Traditionally, most bills came to the floor under **open rules** where amendments are in order, but increasingly limits have been imposed (see table 7.4). The Rules Committee may suggest a **modified open rule** which clearly specifies the types of amendments allowed. More complex rules have created new strategies for affecting legislative outcomes and favoring Members who can master

---

[8]The House has special calendars and procedures for dealing with noncontroversial legislation. The "Consent Calendar" is in order on certain Mondays and each party has three official "objectors" on the floor to make sure that proposals do not contain controversial aspects. A two-thirds majority can bypass the time-consuming amending process by suspending the rules. The Speaker selectively recognizes individuals to offer motions which provide for the adoption of a measure and the amendments included in the motion (Smith 1989, 37). Bills that deal with individuals (extenuating immigration cases, special government reimbursement, etc.) are placed on the "Private Calendar" and dealt with expeditiously (see Oleszek 1989, 111–118).

[9]Some of the committees such as Appropriations, Budget, and Ways and Means have the right to bring certain types of legislation directly to the floor.

TABLE 7.4 The Expanded Use of Restrictive Rules, 1977–1992

Congress	*Total Rules Granted*	*Percent Restrictive*
95th (1977–78)	211	15
96th (1979–80)	214	25
97th (1981–82)	120	25
98th (1983–84)	155	32
99th (1985–86)	115	43
100th (1987–88)	123	46
101st (1989–90)	104	55
102nd (1991–92)	109	66

SOURCE: Barbara Sinclair, "Are Restrictive Rules Leadership Tools?" paper presented at the 1993 annual meeting of the American Political Science Association, Washington D.C.

the rules (see Bach and Smith 1989, passim). The remainder of the legislation is dealt with on a "take it or leave it" basis under a **closed rule.** Since the minority party in Congress has more opportunities for floor success through amending legislation, the increased use of closed rules has raised complaints by the Republicans.

The importance of an entity is often judged by the amount of criticism it engenders. Members of the minority express considerable scorn for the Rules Committee. As one minority member put it,

> Every year, the process breaks down into partisan political haggling with the Republicans accusing the Democrats of stacking the deck and the Democrats accusing the Republicans of not cooperating by playing the game. The no. 1 complaint of the Republican members of Congress is that the referee in the game, the House Rules Committee, is biased. Under the rules of the House of Representatives, which were written and adopted by the Democratic majority, there are nine Democrats and only four Republicans on the Rules Committee. (Rep. Al McCandless [R-CA], *Congressional Record,* 1 July 1990, p. 4822)

The full House of Representatives has the opportunity to debate the proposed rule, before dealing with the legislation per se. Clever strategists often attempt to defeat the rule and thereby kill the legislation. This provides "cover" from criticism from the legislation's supporters, since Members are in a position to say "Oh, I didn't vote against that . . . my objection was to the procedure" (Schneier and Gross 1993, 184).

Debate

The most visible stage in the legislative process is floor debate. Clips of rancorous parliamentary rhetoric often show up on the national news. In reality, floor debate is more for public consumption than to inform the decision-making process. Much debate proceeds with very few Members in the chamber. Debate is more important for justifying a Member's stand to the public and to establish the **legislative intent** which will guide implementing the legislation. At rare, but important junctures, a galvanizing speech, which frames a question in a different way or which provides new information, can change enough votes to determine victory. More often, the floor debate stage is a mine field of potential procedural traps having the potential for delaying or killing a piece of legislation.

THE PLAYERS ON THE FLOOR The visual image of all members of the House and Senate packed on the House floor for a State of the Union Message, or the rare full attendance for a dramatic vote belies the more typical session with a handful of Members speaking to a sparsely populated chamber. Some Members are required to attend by virtue of their party or committee position, while others choose to take part in a particular debate.

The required players: In order to avoid a small clique of unrepresentative Members acting on behalf of their colleagues, legislative bodies establish a legal **quorum** of the minimum number of Members necessary to do business. In the House and Senate, the quorum is set at one-half of the total membership. The constraints of maintaining a quorum are not as significant as it might seem. Although the Constitution requires a quorum to conduct business, a quorum is assumed to exist unless someone questions its absence (Oleszek 1989, 144 and 206). Questioning the presence of a quorum results in a time consuming **quorum call** requiring absent Members to return to the floor to be counted.[10] Such a delaying technique can help a coalition manager "buy time" to get his or her supporters to the floor, or—particularly in the Senate—to work out procedural arrangements (Oleszek 1989, 207). Each party makes sure it has responsible Members on the floor at all times to question the presence of a quorum if the party's interests are being challenged.

Since the House has great difficulty maintaining 218 Members on the floor, it conducts out much of its business in the **Committee of the Whole** with its smaller quorum and more relaxed rules. Any 100 or more Members wishing to stay around for debate constitute a quorum for this ad hoc committee. The committee debates proposed legislation, deals with amendments, and reports back to the entire chamber.

During debate, each side of a legislative battle appoints a **floor manager** to determine the order of speakers, and, especially in the House, to allot exact amounts of time. Most often, floor managers are the committee and/or subcommittee chairs from the committee originating the legislation. Floor management for the opposition is generally taken on by the ranking minority members from the same committees. When amendments are allowed, the majority floor manager negotiates the order of presentation, determines whether the amendments will be accepted by the committee, and presents the majority position.

[10]At times, maintaining a quorum can be difficult. During a rancorous debate on campaign spending laws, the Republicans refused to show up for quorum calls. Senate Majority Leader Robert Byrd and the Democrats voted to have absent senators arrested and brought to the floor. The Senate Sergeant at Arms was sent out to find the absent Republicans and eventually gained a quorum by carrying one Republican senator to the floor bodily (Dewar 1988, A1).

"Pick up" players: The Members who stay on the floor for debate usually have some personal or constituency interest in the legislation. Members present on the chamber floor have an inordinate influence over the final shape of legislation since they vote on the amendments. When it comes to final consideration of a bill, Members absent from debate are given little opportunity to reopen issues already decided upon by Members participating in the debate process.

Floor Rules and Strategies

> Knowing the rules of the game makes it more interesting to watch. . . . It's like a game of chess. To get good at it, you have to watch it played. . . . It's exciting when you see a move and can say, "Oh, I know what the countermove to that should be!" (Congressional Research Service rules expert Ilona Nickels quoted in Harold 1988, 11)

> I am so sick of serving in an institution in which the rules are rigged, the game is stacked, the whole process is patently, consistently, routinely unfair. (Rep. Newt Gingrich [R-GA], *Congressional Record,* 5 June 1992, p. H4322)

Floor rules are ideally designed to facilitate majority rule while protecting minority rights. The differing perspectives on the rules indicated above capture the fact that while only "interesting" to the objective observer, the rules engender passion among those who consistently see their legislative goals thwarted. Members who master the rules are generally much more successful than those who simply master the substance of legislation. The policy game is often won more on the basis of clever strategy than the excellence of the proposal.

THE FILIBUSTER: STALLING THE SENATE The structured rules in the House favor the majority party more than the looser rules in the Senate which allow one, or a few Members to control the flow of legislation (Bach 1991a and 1991b, passim). Probably the major difference between the House and the Senate is the right to **filibuster** in the Senate:

> The right of unlimited debate is one of several peculiarities the Senate has retained from its earliest days to preserve its historic role cooling the majoritarian passions of a democratic government. (Dewar 1991, A15)

Once recognized to speak, a single senator[11]—or more effectively a group of senators—may control the chamber as long as they speak continuously. It takes sixty senators to cut off debate by voting **cloture.** The lack of a requirement for germaneness allows them to speak on any subject. Once used primarily by southern conservatives to block civil rights legislation, the contemporary filibuster serves as a tool for senators of all ideological stripes. While a filibuster stops all other action

---

[11]There is some debate over who has the individual record from filibustering. In 1957, Strom Thurmond (then D-SC) spoke for twenty-four hours and seventeen minutes in a vain attempt to kill civil rights legislation, but he had help from friends who bought him some time off through quorum calls. Wayne Morse (D-OR) singlehandedly held the floor for almost twenty-three hours (Schneier and Gross 1993, 191).

in the Senate, its goal is not necessarily to kill a bill. It may be used as a bargaining ploy to force amendments, or simply to draw attention to an issue. In recent years, about 40 percent of filibusters have been successful in either killing legislation or forcing significant revisions (Smith 1989, 97). In order to reduce the disruptiveness of a filibuster, the Senate has reduced the number of senators needed to impose cloture (from sixty-six to sixty) and instituted a "tracking" system in which the measure under filibuster is set aside temporarily to go on to other business (Smith 1989, 96; and Oleszek 1989, 187). Even after imposing cloture, senators can delay passage through a post-cloture filibuster, where Members use the additional hour allotted to each senator to take up previously introduced amendments or ask for time-consuming roll calls and quorum calls (Oleszek 1989, 226).

AMENDMENT STRATEGIES The most important strategy on the floor of either chamber involves accepting or rejecting amendments. In the House, most amendments are dealt with in the Committee of the Whole, which then recommends its amendments to the entire chamber (Bach 1991a, i). Well-timed amendments can bring votes to a coalition by "sweetening" the measure and making it more palatable (see Enelow 1981, 1062–1089 passim; and Oleszek 1989, 162). In the House, amendments must be germane to the bill under consideration, while in the Senate, nongermane **riders** may be added to the popular bills.

Recognizing the fact that coalitions are often noncumulative, opponents often use the amending process to break up a coalition. In some cases, extreme **killer amendments** are added by the opposition to make the final bill an anathema to a previous supporter. Such strategies are difficult to orchestrate and can be politically dangerous if Members are publically recorded as supporting an amendment unpopular with their constituencies, even if they plan to oppose the final bill (see Schneier and Gross 1993, 135–136). Other crippling amendments may make the bill useless by striking the enacting clause or by tacking on a popular but undesirable feature. For example, in the current era of ill feeling toward Congress, Members may not be able to publicly oppose an up or down vote on an amendment reducing perks, but then turn around and vote down the bill to which the amendment was attached.

The amendment process can be frustrating to supporters of a piece of legislation. After passage of his child-care bill, Senator Dodd (D-CT) bristled at the Republicans' attempt to reopen debate for amendments by saying

> They're playing games with it . . . wanting to play three more innings in a baseball game after nine have been played and one team has already won (Rovner 1990, 1195).

Voting

The final action on a piece of legislation occurs during floor votes in each chamber. Members are faced with more than 700 formal votes each two-year session.[12]

[12]The House tends to vote somewhat more often than the Senate. During the 1980s, the House averaged 865 votes per session and the Senate averaged 763 (Pontious 1991, 12).

LINING UP SUPPORT

> Yogi Berra's famous statement about baseball—"the game ain't over until it's over"—applies to the legislative struggle as well. There are moments of surprise when even the most savvy observers are caught off guard by hidden opponents or last-minute changes of sentiment; as in baseball, however, weak teams are more likely than the strong to be beaten in the late innings. (Schneier and Gross 1993, 183).

The common sports strategy that "the best defense is a good offense" encourages coalition managers to determine the size of their coalition and build on it. Each party has a set of **whips,** tasked with counting votes and assuring that supporters will be on the floor when the votes are needed.[13] In order to expand the "reach" of the whip organization, whip task forces are often created to give more Members a sense of "ownership" in the legislation under consideration. Prior to key votes, party organizations and proponents of legislation station supporters near the entrances to the chamber where they can brief incoming Members on the nature of the vote and the preferred position. Coalition managers meander around the chamber assuring supporters and bargaining with undecided Members.

Coalitions on the floor often do not have to be built one vote at a time. In each chamber there are some "umbrella Members" whose views are respected on specific topics. Coalition leaders look for Members who will be listened to and will take others along with them on key votes (see Wehr 1988, 1919). For example, Senator Mitch McConnell (R-KY) identified Senator Richard Lugar's (R-MO) key role in this sense by commenting, "When he says something on foreign policy, people listen" (Fessler 1992, 1359).

THE ACTUAL VOTE Voting in Congress can be done in a variety of ways. About half the votes are committed orally, with no record kept of the total or how individual Members voted. Voice votes are used for minor issues or when Members find it expeditious not to make a public commitment. If enough Members request,[14] a recorded or **roll call** vote is used. Roll call votes in the Senate are manual, with the clerk reading each name. The House uses an electronic voting system for most of its recorded roll call votes. The presiding officer in each chamber has some control over the length of the voting process. On close votes lacking sufficient support by the majority party, the Speaker of the House often holds the voting terminals open beyond the fifteen-minute limit in hopes of reversing the outcome.[15] In the Senate, the time for a vote is expanded by slowly calling the roll.

---

[13]The whip system is far from perfect. In 1991, Republican Whip Newt Gingrich (R-GA) actually led the opposition to a plan endorsed by President Bush and congressional party leaders. He "took a walk . . . on the toughest vote this Congress—the bipartisan budget-deficit agreement" (Broder 1990, D7).

[14]In the Senate, one-fifth of the senators present can call for a roll call vote. In the House, twenty-five members can call for a recorded vote in the Committee of the Whole, and forty-four in the whole House.

[15]See the unpublished work by Robert X Browning, Purdue University Public Affairs Video Archives.

Members have choices beyond direct support and opposition on a floor vote. Members on opposite sides of an issue may **pair** with each other, thus canceling their votes. This is useful for a Member who must be absent and does not want to be charged with lack of representation of his or her constituents. He or she can simply say, "My vote would not have made a difference." Pairing also provides Members some "cover" on controversial votes, since their name does not come up on the formal list of supporters or opponents. At times, Members simply "take a walk" on issues which trouble their conscience or could give them electoral difficulty. Actually, the only votes which count come from those Members physically in the chamber. Coalition managers must make sure that their team is present to be counted.

If the bills passed by each chamber are identical, they go to the president for signature. Otherwise, two bills with similar components are sent to a conference committee.

RECONCILING DIFFERENCES

Conference committees (see chapter 4) are ad hoc negotiating teams appointed by the leadership of each chamber. Membership is usually drawn from the leadership of the committee from which the legislation originated. At times the chamber will send its conferees to conference with specific instructions as to what they may compromise and what is sacrosanct. As we discussed in chapter 4, the Senate tends to prevail most often in conference committee proceedings (see Longley and Oleszek 1989, 77–78). The report of the conference committee goes back to each chamber and is voted on without amendment.

ACQUIRING PRESIDENTIAL SUPPORT

Congressional actions with the force of law require presidential approval.[16] The president has three basic choices. He can sign the legislation making it law, allow it to become law without his signature, or cast a veto.[17] A presidential veto is a sign that the president has lost in the legislative arena and must confront Congress directly. The *threat* of a veto is a more potent weapon for bringing legislators to the bargaining table than the rather blunt instrument of the veto. Presidents return vetoed legislation to Congress with their rationale and often specific changes they would require before signing the bill. Vetoes can be overridden by a two-thirds vote of *both* chambers—a difficult task. During this century, only about 5 percent of presidential vetoes have been overridden (Clymer 1991, 22; see also chapter 8).

---

[16]Congress does pass various types of resolutions which do not have the force of law. Such resolutions are often used to publicly express Congress' position on an issue, but do not authorize programs or appropriate funds.

[17]When Congress has adjourned, the president has an additional option. If the president does nothing and there is no Congress to return the legislation, a **pocket veto** occurs and the legislation dies.

House and Senate efforts may not create the legislative product desired by the president or the public.

The vast majority of legislation passed by Congress is signed into law. The victorious team gathers in the oval office or some other symbolic location for the bill signing ceremony and are rewarded with both the satisfaction of changing public policy and with a souvenir of the game—a ball point pen.

CONCLUSION

Moving from the identification of a potential problem to the enactment of a public law involves a complex and interrelated set of strategy games. Proposed legislation seldom makes it through the process on the basis of its own self-evident benefits. Like a child, legislation must be nurtured by astute coalition managers.

President Clinton presents James Brady with a pen he used to sign the Brady bill requiring a waiting period for the purchase of handguns. Mr. Brady was wounded in the 1981 attempt on President Reagan's life and has become a key spokesperson for gun control.

The multiple rounds and stages of the legislative process mean that even the most carefully crafted legislative proposal must face numerous potential pitfalls. Successful legislation must ultimately post a win at every stage, while it takes only one defeat to result in failure. Many possible problems never make it to Congress' agenda. Numerous others fail to make it through the subcommittee or committee process. Floor action in the House and Senate involves differing rules and strategies designed to meet the differing needs of the respective chambers and to discourage more than facilitate the passage of a bill. Success in Congress does not necessarily assure the required approval from the presidential arena.

The quantity of legislation passed versus the amount introduced in Congress implies inefficiency, but legislatures should be judged on **quality** not **quantity.** The multiple and interrelated games of the policy process help assure that all legislation is looked at in a variety of different ways, and that bills which pass have the support of many concurrent majorities.

IN DEPTH

1. Follow a piece of legislation through the legislative process facing up to the following questions:

A. Who were the relevant *players* and what motivated them? Who placed the item on the congressional agenda? What problems were supposedly solved by this proposal? Who served as **coalition** managers in support and opposition? What did the initial supporting and opposing **natural coalition** look like? (This can often be determined by looking at the type of "cleavage" the issue represents. Some issues break along ideological lines. Others are more regional.)

B. What were the applicable *rules* under which this legislation was handled? Are there any special rules that apply (i.e., tax legislation must be dealt with by the House first, nominations are dealt with by the Senate alone, etc.)? To what degree did specific rules determine the outcome?

C. What *strategies* were used? Different strategies work at different stages. Assess how the bill was promoted and opposed in committee and on the floor.

D. Who *won* and who *lost?* What did the final vote look like: What was the president's reaction?

REFERENCES: The *Congressional Quarterly Almanac* summarizes major legislation each year. *Congressional Quarterly Weekly Report* analyzes the substance, strategy, and voting on key pieces of legislation. *National Journal* analyzes legislation, especially when it deals with the executive branch. National "newspapers of record" such as the *Washington Post* and the *New York Times* analyze key legislation in great detail. For contemporary issues, don't hesitate to call the office of your local member of Congress. Their office can often provide studies by the Congressional Research Services as well as committee reports and *Congressional Record* excerpts. Most members of Congress have district offices listed under the federal government section of the local telephone book. The main switchboard at the Capitol will connect you with a Member's Washington office (House: 202–225–3121, Senate: 202–224–3121).

CHAPTER EIGHT

CONGRESS AND OTHER WASHINGTON PLAYERS

The President, the Bureaucracy, and the Courts

Politics in Washington is a continuous contest, a constant scramble for points, for power, for influence . . . an olympiad of games, going on simultaneously, all over town. (Smith 1988, xviii–xix)

Congress is hardly the sole player in our nation's capital. Other institutions—the presidency, bureaucracy, and federal courts—also do business there, and the national legislature must establish working relationships with each of them. Richard Neustadt describes our government as one of "separate institutions sharing powers" that out of necessity must establish ways of dealing with each other (Neustadt 1990, 29). Each institution's "team" needs the support of other teams to succeed, but conflict often replaces cooperation between institutions. The competitive norms of the D.C. environment support this behavior.

Three types of games are central to Washington politics. One is the **agenda game**—"to articulate the national purpose; to fix the nation's agenda. Of all the big games at the summit of American politics, the agenda game must be won first" (Smith 1988, 331). Congress and the chief executive compete constantly over the national agenda, while the courts and bureaucracy intervene in the contest on occasion, usually discreetly. The **image game** involves a form of public relations that requires touting a public figure's or institution's personal traits in order to build popular support and policy success. The president has no serious bureaucratic or judicial rivals in this contest. Individual lawmakers, however, carefully cultivate their images back home to preserve their popularity and political independence from the president. That means a popular president cannot be assured of legislative success unless he is also adept at the **coalition game,** the classic contest of "inside baseball" in Congress. Hedrick Smith defines it as "building coalitions and making coalitions work—the heart of our system of government" (Smith 1988, 447). This game consumes the chief executive's time in dealing with lawmakers on Capitol Hill. Bureaucrats' frequent interactions with Congress make them significant participants in coalition contests as well.

The four institutions fend for themselves in these struggles and each brings a distinctive perspective to the competition. Congress usually takes a measured approach to political issues. The federal bureaucracy, like Congress, adopts a measured strategy. Administrators grow attached to their particular programs, and struggle to maintain and gradually expand them. Congress plays a large role in the daily life of the bureaucrats of the executive branch. Legislators pass laws creating and funding government programs, and Congress oversees their ongoing implementation by the executive agencies.

The president and his staff confront Washington from a decidedly different viewpoint. Presidential terms are fixed and time is short. They are only in the game for a few rounds. The president is the national policy initiator, involving leadership of an entrenched Congress and bureaucracy. All presidents encounter frustration in garnering congressional and bureaucratic support. Presidential appointees often advocate bureaucratic perspectives to the White House rather than vice versa. They "go native," adopting the views of their departments. Congress does not do what it is told. The president seeks a quick score, but Congress is content to "grind it out," at times by stalling action to wait out a hostile president.

The Supreme Court and lower federal courts often act as if they are above the Washington political fray. Though the judiciary's daily work brings it into less immediate conflict with other national institutions, the courts are hardly isolated from political currents. The president nominates federal judges. Congress scrutinizes the nominees, determines the structure and jurisdiction of the courts, and approves the compensation of the judges. Court decisions often make wide-ranging policy affecting both the outcome of current political games and how future rounds are played. The Supreme Court is adept at protecting its institutional authority in the way it accepts cases for review and writes opinions (Roche 1955, 759–770). Protecting their own power forms the strategic imperative for the institutions discussed in this chapter.

THE CHANGING RULES OF CONGRESSIONAL-PRESIDENTIAL RELATIONS

The most obvious power shared by the president and national legislature is that of making national law. "The president proposes and the Congress disposes" the old adage states, and each must work with the other in establishing national policy. This relationship involves great stakes, that is, the actual extent of legislative and executive power. Earlier this century power shifted toward the executive, but in the 1970s it moved back toward Congress.

EXECUTIVE POWER AND ITS ASCENDANCY

Two powers lie at the heart of the legislative presidency. The first, stated in Article II, Section 3, is the duty to "advise the Congress on the state of the union" and "recommend to their consideration such measures as [the president] shall judge necessary and expedient." The second is the veto power. These grants of authority establish rules of the game that make the president an integral part of national lawmaking, and produce much power jockeying between the executive and legislature.

Presidential power to propose legislation grew more consequential in the mid-twentieth century as presidents became the dominant players in the agenda game. The onset of the Cold War gave the president preeminent power in crisis decision making. Television consolidated the president's position as the leading political figure in the nation. Presidential power reached new heights in the mid-1960s, under the presidency of Lyndon Baines Johnson. Johnson dominated domestic policy with his sweeping Great Society initiatives and foreign policy with his prosecution of the war in Vietnam. The consequences of the Vietnam war, however, ignited a congressional resurgence in the 1970s.

The resurgence led to many veto battles between the president and Congress. The history of veto use is an uneven one. Andrew Johnson, an obstreperous border state Democrat who faced a hostile Republican Congress during reconstruction, was the first president to wield the veto aggressively. After Johnson, the presidents vetoing most often usually confronted a Congress controlled by the rival party—Grover Cleveland, Harry Truman and Gerald Ford are examples. Congress overrides only a small percentage of vetoes. George Bush's ability to make his vetoes stick (see table 8.1) made the Democratic Congress more responsive to presidential threats. Bill Clinton's veto record is dramatically different. He vetoed no legislation presented to him by the Democratic Congress during his first nineteen months in office.

The actual veto process works as follows. After receiving a bill from Congress, the president has ten days (excluding Sundays) to choose from four options. First, he can sign the bill and it becomes law. This is the fate of most bills. Second, he can return the bill with a veto message to the chamber of Congress where it originated. Third, he can take no action and allow the bill to become law without his signature. The White House seldom exercises this option. It is used for a small category of bills that the president does not oppose strongly enough to veto. Fourth, he can "pocket veto" the bill. If adjournment of Congress prevents the return of the bill, it dies and will not become law without the president's signature. Chief executives use this option to kill bills at the end of a session without having to take the drastic step of a veto.

BOX 8.1 Challenging the Veto Rules in Court

Can a president pocket veto during a brief recess in the middle of a session of Congress, as well as after the final adjournment of the session? President Nixon tried to pocket veto some bills during a brief Christmas recess in 1971. Senator Ted Kennedy challenged the constitutionality of this and won in a 1974 federal court decision, *Kennedy v. Sampson* (511 f.2d430, 437, D.C. Cir. 1974). The Ford administration accepted this decision and did not appeal to the Supreme Court. In November 1983, Ronald Reagan pocket vetoed a bill concerning aid to El Salvador. The 98th Congress had adjourned its first session earlier that month and returned for its second session in January, nine weeks later. Again Congress went to court, and again they prevailed (Fisher 1985a, 154). It now seems clear that pocket vetoes can only occur when a session of Congress adjourns, thanks to congressional challenges of presidential acts.

STRATEGIES OF CONGRESSIONAL RESURGENCE

Public dissatisfaction with Lyndon Johnson's foreign and domestic policies set the stage for the election of Richard Nixon in 1968. Despite a government divided between a Republican White House and Democratic Congress, Nixon sought to extend executive power still further. This produced a dramatic reassertion of authority by Congress. The legislature asserted itself in three major policy domains: war powers, budget and impoundment, and oversight of the executive branch.

War Powers

Before Vietnam, presidents committed troops to military hostilities on more than 250 occasions without congressional consent. During this period, the president asked Congress to declare war only six times. Admittedly, most of the 250 were small-scale engagements, but Vietnam, for which there was no declaration of war, emphatically was not. Revelations in the early 1970s about executive branch deceptions during the early stages of the Vietnam conflict fueled a congressional desire for greater control over America's use of military force.

In 1973, Congress approved, over Nixon's veto, the War Powers Resolution, calling for the "collective judgement" of the Congress and president before troops enter combat. Under this law, the president must (1) consult with Congress before introducing troops into hostilities, (2) report any commitment of troops to Congress within forty-eight hours, and (3) terminate the use of forces within sixty days if Congress does not declare war, or does not extend the period, or is unable to meet.

Since its passage, the War Powers Resolution has received a chilly reception at the White House. The law's machinery depends on a provision of the law that requires an official presidential report on hostilities. Presidents usually do not cite this provision when they inform Congress, making enforcement of the law's other provisions problematic. Still, presidents do at least comply with the spirit of the law by reporting. Congress, for its part, has not stopped troop deployments once conflict began. For example, the popularity of the Grenada invasion in 1983 immediately silenced congressional criticism, and the legislature, although with much breast beating, did approve offensive action to begin the Gulf War without a formal declaration of war. The institutions remain in an uneasy standoff over war powers.

Budget and Impoundments

Presidents have the legal duty to submit to Congress annual budgets for the national government. Richard Nixon aggressively played a spending power game against Congress during his first term; he vetoed spending bills and held the legislature to a spending limit that the White House devised. Congress, at the time, passed each of its fourteen spending bills separately, with no general coordination of spending totals. It proved impossible to override Nixon's spending vetoes, allowing his spending limits to stick.

In response, Congress changed the rules by creating a new budget process designed to impose self-restraint and present a unified front on spending. The process established Budget committees in the House and Senate and gave them the authority to formulate an annual budget resolution providing overall tax totals and spending limits. When the House and Senate agreed to a budget resolution, spending and taxing discipline theoretically would be in place for the next fiscal year. The vehicle for the budget limits was a concurrent resolution, which does not require a presidential signature.

The rudiments of this process remain today. Budget rules allow Congress to speak independently on fiscal policy, but they have not stemmed the rise of large and persistent budget deficits. In the 1980s, presidents Reagan and Bush again confronted Congress on spending by vetoing appropriations bills, and again the legislature had to relent. The budget process remains a resource for greater congressional power over spending but it is one that the legislature often fails to use effectively (see chapter 9).

Congress had more success in creating rules to limit presidential impoundments of spending. An impoundment is a refusal to spend funds appropriated by Congress. The 1974 Budget Act, in addition to setting up the new congressional budget process, defined two types of impoundments: rescissions and deferrals. A rescission calls for cancelling spending on a program. A deferral requests a temporary spending delay (no longer than the duration of the current fiscal year). The act provided that a rescission could go into effect only if both chambers approved it within forty-five days of its proposal by the president. Deferrals went into effect immediately, but by majority vote one chamber could stop a deferral at any time. Since 1974, Congress has accepted most deferrals proposed by the president, but has approved few rescissions.

Oversight

Oversight involves "congressional review of the actions of federal departments, agencies and commissions, and of the programs and policies they administer, including review that takes place during program and policy implementation as well as afterward" (Aberbach 1990, 2). The federal bureaucracy comprises an arena contested between president and Congress because the two branches share constitutional authority over it. Congress passes laws and budgets for the bureaucracy, and can supervise how administrators behave. Oversight is a strategy allowing legislative control of the bureaucracy at presidential expense. Dissatisfaction with an agency's performance can lead to investigations, new policy guidelines, and budget cuts.

Aberbach found that Congress increased oversight activities in the 1970s (1990, 35). A greater willingness to seek power at the expense of the president and the growing size and complexity of government contributed to the increase. Also, a new politics of scarcity as budgets tightened during the 1970s and 1980s enhanced the attractiveness of oversight activities. If the money was not there for new programs, lawmakers could seek power by supervising established ones (Aberbach 1990, 47). Here is how one House member put it in 1979:

> In the 1960s . . . you had to go back to your district and say, "I passed the new Joe Zilch piece of handicapped elephant legislation," something like that, right? And you've got a new bill on the wall, and that was what you wanted. Well, that's not where the returns are now. The political returns are from oversight. (Aberbach 1990, 47)

The tug of war over the bureaucracy now featured a more energetic Congress.

The Legislative Veto

The **legislative veto** is an important strategic resource in congressional oversight. It is a provision in federal law that delays an administrative action, usually for sixty to ninety days, during which time Congress may vote to approve or disapprove the action. In effect, the legislature gives itself final say, or veto power, over certain executive branch activities. Vetoes can take several forms: a one-house veto (by a simple resolution), a two-house veto (by concurrent resolution), committee vetoes, and even committee chair's vetoes. Some legislative vetoes involve further efforts by Congress to gain control over the bureaucracy at the expense of the executive branch. Others are arrangements of convenience between the president and Congress. By the early 1980s, federal law included nearly 200 legislative veto provisions.

Legislative vetoes spawned an inter-institutional power game in the 1980s involving the president, Congress and Supreme Court. The Court weighed in on the issue in a stunning way in its 1983 decision, *Immigration and Naturalization Service v. Chadha* (462 U.S. 919, 1983). Its opinion stated that any action of Congress having the effect of law, as legislative vetoes surely do, could only be valid constitutionally if both chambers and the president approved it. Legislative vetoes gave the president no formal voice in lawmaking, consequently legislative vetoes were unconstitutional.

The decision indicated the limits of the Supreme Court's power, for it must rely on other institutions to actually enforce its decisions. In the sixteen months after *Chadha,* Congress passed fifty additional legislative veto provisions, generally committee vetoes, in eighteen different statutes (Fisher 1985b, 706). The White House initially tried to use the decision to limit congressional power. President Reagan at first challenged some new legislative veto provisions, but soon gave up that effort. The following example helps to explain why.

The appropriations bill for foreign assistance in 1987 included the following veto provision: "None of the funds made available by this Act may be obligated under an appropriation account to which they were not appropriated without the prior written approval of the Committees on Appropriations" (Fisher 1991, 230). James Miller, director of Reagan's Office of Management and Budget, challenged this provision as inconsistent with the *Chadha* decision. In this case, however, Congress had granted the executive branch additional discretion in return for veto authority. The Foreign Operations Subcommittee of the House Appropriations Committee told the Office of Management and Budget (OMB) that it would not only repeal the committee veto but also the ability of OMB to transfer funds to a different account. Miller retreated and apologized for bringing up the subject. Other agencies tried to invoke *Chadha* and then had to back down when Congress threatened to take the executive power away with the veto provision concerning it.

Many legislative veto provisions create positive-sum games for the executive branch and Congress. Administrators get broader discretionary power in return for accepting the legislature's authority to veto their use of discretion. Such arrangements satisfy the power needs of both branches, encouraging them to ignore the *Chadha* decision.

DIVIDED GOVERNMENT: INSTITUTIONAL TEAMS AT ODDS

Since 1968, a single party has controlled both the executive and legislative branches only during the presidencies of Jimmy Carter and Bill Clinton. Two types of **divided government** resulted: either split partisan control of the institutions, with Congress and the White House controlled by different parties, or divided party control in the legislature with a Democratic House arrayed against a Republican Senate and White House (Thurber 1991, 5). James Thurber notes several reasons for the arrival and persistence of divided government (Thurber 1991, 1–9). Different electorates select the president and members of Congress. The chief executive serves a term of different length than do national legislators. Weak political parties do not encourage either the president or Congress to look beyond their own institutional perspectives. Less party voting by the electorate makes divided government more likely.

In divided government, the agenda game can deteriorate into what Hedrick Smith calls the **blame game** when politicians engage in

> maneuvers which have little chance of implementation but which dramatize their side's virtue and the opposition's villainy. . . . In this situation, incentives of the power game reward tactical squeeze plays, finger pointing, damage control and partisan posturing. The temptation for both sides is to protect their sacred cows and gore the other side's oxen (Smith 1988, 645).

A classic example of blame game politics spawned by divided government can be found in the budget politics of the 1980s. Though massive deficits persisted throughout the decade, a Republican president and Democratic Congress continued to point the finger of blame at each other. Presidents Reagan and Bush decried the "tax and spend" policies of Congress as the cause. Democratic legislative leaders assailed bloated Pentagon spending and "irresponsible" tax cuts passed at Reagan's pleading in 1981. Blame was pointed everywhere, but solutions remained elusive.

Even putting partisan differences aside, the challenge of the legislative presidency remains daunting. As the sole elected national leader, a president must wheedle cooperation from lawmakers on Capitol Hill who focus more narrowly on policy

The legislative presidency in action. President Clinton and Vice President Gore meet with House members to muster support for their 1993 economic plan.

and respond to far smaller and less diverse constituencies. All presidents encounter frustration in dealing with Congress. The difference is only one of degree.

PRESIDENTIAL STRATEGIES

Presidential persuasion of Congress operates in a game environment that altered after the resurgence of the legislature in the 1970s. Budget deficits squeezed the fiscal resources of Congress, producing what Roger Davidson terms an era of **cutback politics.** Its characteristics include fewer bills sponsored by individual legislators, a high degree of party-line voting due to budgetary concerns, passage of more noncontroversial resolutions, the creation of "blame avoidance" devices such as commissions to establish congressional pay and close military bases, key policy decisions aggregated into **omnibus bills**, and stronger party leadership (Davidson 1991, 71). Zero and negative-sum outcomes became more likely. The presidential margin for error in legislative relations has grown smaller, requiring more careful strategic planning by the White House when approaching Capitol Hill.

Success at the coalition game in Congress requires a careful appreciation of a president's **strategic position** (Edwards 1989, 213–220). One aspect of this is the perception of the president's last electoral victory. A big electoral triumph can fuel discussion of a popular mandate for the president's policies. Reagan, for example, won by a surprisingly strong margin in 1980, but Jimmy Carter narrowly won after squandering a wide lead in the polls. This gave Reagan more room for maneuver in his first year. Re-elected presidents, constitutionally denied the right to run again, often become "lame ducks" and lose influence, as Reagan discovered in 1985. A second aspect of strategic position involves a president's relations with his party. Carter's fiscal caution caused him trouble with the strong liberal wing of his party, prompting Senator Ted Kennedy to oppose him for renomination in 1980. Reagan, in contrast, remained on good terms with the major factions of his less diverse party. Bill Clinton garnered only 43 percent of the popular vote in 1992, but scored several early legislative successes with his party in Congress.

Public support is a third component of strategic position. Legislators hear opinions about the president back home and are less anxious to confront a popular president. Carter sank steadily in the polls during his term, further weakening his position with the legislature. Though Reagan started modestly in the polls, he added substantially to his popularity over the course of his eight years in office. Bush began as a popular president and reached a 90 percent level of support after victory in the Persian Gulf War. That made Congress less anxious to confront Bush, but did not speed his proposals through to passage. The ensuing deadlock contributed to the precipitous drop in Bush's popularity. Clinton's declining popularity in 1994 encouraged congressional Republicans to repeatedly challenge him.

Finally, the actual agendas and strategies of the White House affect the president's strategic position. The Carter presidency suffered from an overly long initial agenda that failed to set priorities adequately during his crucial first year. In contrast, the Reagan agenda in 1981 tightly focused on a few budget and tax votes on which the president was able to prevail. Reagan and Bush each put forth a less extensive legislative agenda than did Carter or Clinton. Bill Clinton expended significant resources on highly controversial issues such as gays in the military and health care.

In all, strategic position and the expectations and resources comprising the game environment structure the coalition possibilities for a president on Capitol Hill. Cutback politics make it ever more important for presidents to assemble strategic strengths and employ them. Divided government serves to complicate the constructive use of strategic resources.

Presidents use their strategic strengths to play both the image and coalition games. Presidents need to win at these continuous games most of the time. Conveying a favorable image may help with the public and thus sway Congress. The coalition game, however, ultimately reveals the extent of legislative support a president enjoys.

Presidents attempt to win the coalition game through a variety of methods. Assembling a coalition in Congress requires many different strategies because each lawmaker approaches an issue from his or her own position. George C. Edwards identifies six methods presidents use to gain legislative support (Edwards 1989, 189–212). One is bargaining, when the administration either compromises on policy or trades support on two different issues with powerful lawmakers. This time-honored device is a staple of presidential technique, particularly on high-stakes legislation. A second involves personal appeals by the president to fellow partisans in Congress. This tactic, however, often fails because other more potent political forces—such as constituency opinion or a lawmaker's core convictions—run counter to the White House view. Further, the appeals must be infrequent to be effective.

A third method entails consultation with lawmakers about anticipated administration proposals or actions. Such meetings seldom hammer out legislation, however; usually the White House first prepares a proposal and then "consults" with legislators for public relations purposes. Fourth, the president can seek to set priorities in a way to dominate the congressional agenda. Over time, however, events broaden the congressional agenda and dilute presidential influence. Moving fast in the opening months of a new president's term to capitalize on the public popularity of the "honeymoon" period is a fifth approach. This requires a short agenda, such as Reagan proposed in 1981, and must avoid complex policy areas where action is usually slow. Finally, setting the terms of debate by framing issues carefully can be a remarkably efficient approach. Usually this requires a popular mandate that serves to muster congressional attention. Ronald Reagan accomplished this during the budget and tax votes of 1981.

More often, the president must do this one issue at a time, as Bill Clinton has discovered. His administration pulled out a number of narrow victories on major initiatives during his first year, including his deficit reduction plan and approval of the North American Free Trade Agreement. He also happily signed a number of bills stalled by his GOP predecessor, such as those on family medical leave, voter registration reform, and a five-day waiting period for handgun purchases. Congress in 1993 supported Clinton on a dazzling 88 percent of floor votes on which he took a position, and Clinton not once resorted to the veto pen (Hook 1993, 3244). By 1994, however, Clinton's public support fell below 50 percent, suggesting uncertain long-term prospects for his success with Congress.

The president surrounds himself with a variety of staff assistants to aid in strategizing and performing the hard work of the coalition game. The White House Office—particularly his senior and trusted political advisors headed by the president's chief of staff—has a hand in all major legislative strategies. Senior White House staff people often decide which cabinet officials will help with the lobbying and to what degree. Another important advisor is the director of the Office of Management and Budget (OMB), the agency that formulates administration budget proposals and recommends whether to veto legislation. Bill Clinton's initial OMB director and current White House chief of staff, Leon Panetta, is a former chair of the House Budget committee and a knowledgeable and shrewd political operator.

A third important source of staff assistance is the Office of Congressional Liaison (OCL), the president's actual lobbyists on Capitol Hill. Their task is to monitor congressional opinion, attempt to persuade particular legislators, and explain Capitol Hill sentiment to the upper reaches of the administration. Formally established during the Truman presidency, the office expanded in subsequent administrations. Kennedy's head of liaison, Lawrence O'Brien, markedly enhanced the coordination of the lobbying operation. Subsequent presidencies adopted many of O'Brien's techniques. An exception, however, was liaison under the Carter presidency. Headed by Frank Moore, who had no Capitol Hill experience, the OCL got off to a terrible start from which it never recovered. The Reagan and Bush teams, in contrast, included Hill veterans and established a reputation for competence. The Clinton team encountered a rocky start. Their strategy of ignoring the opposition cost the president when Senate Republicans filibustered the administration's economic stimulus package to death. Hill Democrats also complained of inadequate White House consultation with them.

BOX 8.2 White House Versus Congress: The Players Speak

Presidential staff create Capitol Hill strategies for the White House. What follows is a series of quotations from confidential interviews that give us a view from inside this coalition game environment.[a]

One White House assistant for Gerald Ford described the wariness with which an administration approaches Capitol Hill:

> There is an underlying suspicion of Congress. You tell one of them and the others will find out. The first thing they do is go out and tell the press. . . . You want to orchestrate a proposal in the administration, in a way that puts it in the best possible light. You don't want them making the announcement.

Lawmakers and presidents also have very different expectations about what it means to consult with each other, according to an Office of Congressional Liaison (OCL) staffer:

> The rule of thumb on consultation to a member of Congress is spending an hour a week in the Oval Office with the President and having the President accept all he says. Consultation, well it's really something different to Congress than to the President. Far too often, consultation to the Congress means following the wishes of key members of Congress and key members of the staff. Far too often, too, consultation to the President means acquiescing to the President and what he wants to do, and accommodating him.

An aide to President Reagan described the strategy behind submitting legislation to Congress:

> Usually sending up a bill is the initial step in negotiations. And you're not going to want to negotiate away your position right from the start, since you're going to have to negotiate later.

A Washington journalist described how he detected a Reagan administration bargaining strategy:

> That year they had the farm bill, I called [a member of President Reagan's congressional liaison staff]—this was when they were trying to get the boll weevils [conservative southern Democrats] on the budget—I called and said that there were some funny proposals in their farm bill for peanut farmers and sugar. I asked if these were to buy votes, and he started laughing. These are probably put in because that's what they wanted to do, but they also knew they were useful, they were expendable parts of the proposal. They were talking policy on one hand, but also what they had to buy to look around for winners. They could use them for bargaining chips. A lot of times it is that crass.

[a] The quotations are taken from Mark Peterson, 1990, *Legislating Together: The White House and Capitol Hill from Eisenhower to Reagan,* Cambridge: Harvard U. Press, pp. 51, 53, 50 and 63, respectively.

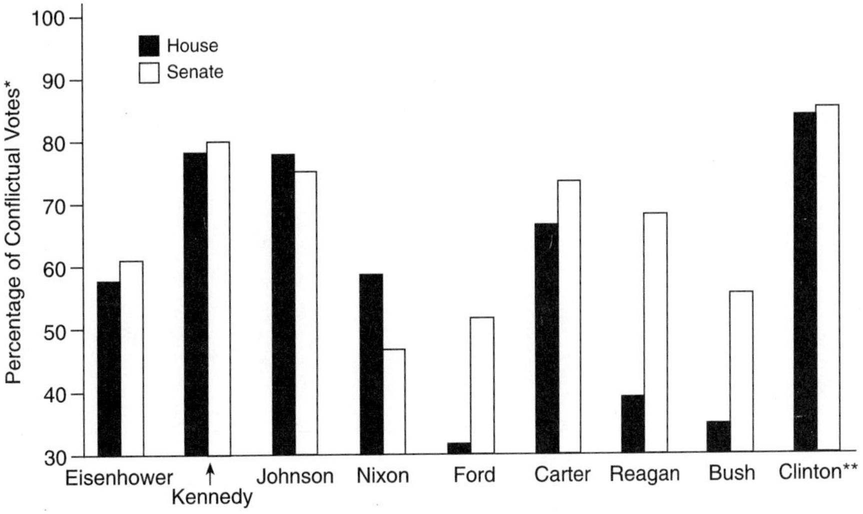

*Percentage of conflictual votes on which the president's position prevailed. Conflictual votes include any vote where the presidential position received less than 80 percent of the floor votes cast. The Eisenhower totals do not include votes from the Republican-controlled 83rd Congress. During that period, Eisenhower prevailed on 76.6 percent of conflictual roll calls in the House and 77.0 percent in the Senate.

** 1993 only

FIGURE 8.1
Presidential Success on Conflictual Roll-Call Votes, 1952–1993

SOURCE: Jon Bond and Richard Fleisher, *The President in the Legislative Arena* (Chicago: University of Chicago Press, 1990). Totals for Bush, Clinton (1993 only), and Reagan (second term) provided by the authors.

PATTERNS OF WINNING AND LOSING

Assessing presidential success in the coalition game with Congress is not a simple task. For decades *Congressional Quarterly* has calculated an annual presidential success score, indicating the percentage of presidential victories in roll-call votes on which the president has announced a position. A more useful measure excludes all roll calls where the president garnered more than 80 percent support in order to assess presidential influence on the "difficult" votes. The number of presidential vetoes and the incidence of veto overrides illustrates presidential conflict with Congress and the degree of White House success in these competitions.

The success of recent presidents on conflictual votes is presented in figure 8.1. Majority presidents—Clinton, Kennedy, Johnson and Carter, who operated with partisan majorities favoring them in each chamber, fared much better on contested votes than did minority presidents—Nixon, Reagan, Ford, and Bush, who faced at least one chamber under the control of the opposition party. Table 8.1 reveals a similar pattern in veto battles. Minority presidents vetoed bills more often and usually suffered overrides more frequently. The coalition game is much more difficult to play when your team lacks adequate players. Divided government clearly costs presidents legislative success. Additional analysis illustrates the dynamics of the problem. Jon Bond and Richard Fleisher found that majority presidents are more likely to win conflictual

TABLE 8.1 Presidential Veto Success, 1952–Present

	Vetoes	*Overridden*	*Percent Overridden*
Clinton (1993–94)*	0	0	0
Bush	45	1	2
Reagan	78	9	12
Carter	31	2	6
Ford	66	12	18
Nixon	43	7	16
Johnson	29	0	0
Kennedy	21	0	0
Eisenhower	188	2	1

*Through August 1994.
SOURCE: Robert J. Spitzer, 1988, *The Presidential Veto,* Albany: State University of New York Press. Update by author. Clinton and Bush totals from *Congressional Quarterly.*

votes if "they take positions that unify their partisans, especially members of their political base, who have the greatest predisposition to agree with the President" (Bond and Fleisher 1990, 113). Conversely, minority presidents won more often if no faction unified in the House or Senate (Bond and Fleisher 1990, 115). A partisan strategy can only work for the president if he has the requisite numbers in Congress.

The "two presidencies" thesis has fascinated scholars for the better part of three decades. This argument holds that "since World War II, Presidents have had much greater success in controlling the nation's defense and foreign policies than in dominating its domestic policies" (Wildavsky 1991, 3). Supposedly the president's large constitutional powers over foreign affairs encourage congressional assent to his foreign policy proposals, while domestic politics remains primarily the domain of legislators, interest groups, and bureaucrats.

Bond and Fleisher found the thesis accurately described Republican administrations, which, since 1954, have confronted hostile Democratic Congresses almost all the time. Democratic presidents didn't have this obstacle and achieved comparable levels of support on domestic and foreign policy votes. It was the much lower Republican presidential success in domestic policy that gives some limited validity to the "two presidencies" thesis (Bond and Fleisher 1990, 158).

Unfortunately, studies relying upon roll-call analysis and *Congressional Quarterly* scores suffer from methodological weaknesses that limit their ability to gauge important but subtle aspects of presidential influence. Support scores and roll-call votes don't reveal whether the president's position was strongly or weakly held, and whether it was essential to his legislative program or chosen merely to enhance the perception of support. The measures also tell us nothing about proposals that failed to reach the floor. They also do not tell us about the significance of a particular vote, for some are more consequential than others (Peterson 1990, 304–305).

Political scientist Mark A. Peterson countered these problems with an innovative approach. He first identified specific domestic policy initiatives articulated by each president from 1953 to 1984, some 5,069 proposals. Peterson then drew a random sample of 299 of these, grouped by year, and prepared an in-depth case study of each (no small task!). Peterson found that only 40 percent of the most innovative presidential initiatives—those involving new and large departures in policy—passed during this time (1990, 271).

Peterson also discovered that the economy affected the playing of the coalition game in Congress. Low GNP growth, large deficits and high inflation all increased conflict between the president and Congress and lessened the amount of the president's program that passed. In general, the proposals of largest scope generated the most conflict in Congress and were the most difficult to enact, but they did get legislative attention. More modest initiatives were more often ignored on the Hill, but once acknowledged, they usually passed (Peterson 1990, 273–274). Congress has a short attention span and normally is unable to handle an extensive, ambitious presidential agenda.

Peterson's conclusions make sound strategic advice for any president attempting to build coalitions in Congress. First, successful leadership requires a *productive* convergence of the president and the political setting. A new president has the best prospects for success with the legislature. Victories in early rounds demoralize the opposition and help promote success in future rounds. Unfortunately, presidential prospects diminish rapidly after an administration's first year and are usually difficult to revive. Second, nothing breeds success for a president like clear priorities. Just as bridge players focus on one suit and monopoly players target their properties, successful politicians choose their words carefully. Take on every problem in the world, and you will accomplish little. Republicans tended to focus better with Congress in this regard than did Democrats, with the starkest contrast being between Carter in 1977 and Reagan in 1981

Frustration may be endemic in White House relations with Capitol Hill, but a shrewd president can seize the moment, utilize public popularity, and build coalitions. The coalition game is difficult work, but a president will be judged a failure if he does not attempt it constantly and earn some success from his labors. The work is always difficult because the political perspectives of the incumbents on each end of Pennsylvania Avenue diverge due to differences in terms, constituencies, and responsibilities.

CONGRESS AND THE BUREAUCRACY

It is impossible for either the president or Congress to carry out the day-to-day operations of government. The federal bureaucracy implements the policies agreed upon by Congress and the president. The constitutionally ambiguous position of the bureaucracy makes the relationship between the three branches complex. Congress creates the executive branch by statute, but the president selects some 4,000 political appointees inhabiting the top policymaking positions in cabinet departments and other important agencies. Congress must approve many of these appointments, and decide annual agency budgets. Both the president and Congress rightfully assert constitutional authority over the bureaucracy.

THE LINE-UP OF THE PLAYERS

Frequently, the bureaucracy joins the legislature in playing a coalition game against the White House. Essential everyday working relationships for agencies of the federal bureaucracy most often involve Congress, not the White House. Congress holds the power of the purse, and works through subcommittees interested specifically in what particular parts of the bureaucracy are doing. White House emissaries often seem merely occasional interlopers in the time-honored relationships between specialized parts of Congress and the bureaucracy. An able administrator carefully orchestrates relationships with relevant members of Congress while simultaneously seeking to give no offense to the White House. Congress must employ several strategies to maintain some control over the bureaucracy.

STRATEGIES OF CONGRESSIONAL CONTROL

Bureaucratic power ultimately results from Congress' delegation of authority to administrators. Delegation occurs for several reasons, according to Louis Fisher,

> Legislators and their staffs may lack the expertise needed to draft specific language for highly specialized subjects. . . . Furthermore, specificity of language may undermine the consensus needed to pass legislation. . . . Congress may also find a responsibility so vexing, so lacking in political rewards, that it tries to shift the chore elsewhere (Fisher 1985a, 105–106).

The necessity of delegation does not absolve Congress of either its responsibility or interest in administrative activities. Lawmakers keep an eye on bureaucrats to guard their constitutional responsibility over public funds, or to respond to constituents' complaints about agency activity. Authorizing and appropriations committees undertake the most aggressive oversight. **Authorizing committees** and their subcommittees produce "authorizing legislation" that establishes in law particular programs and agencies. **Appropriations subcommittees** have the greatest say about the amount of actual dollars given to many agencies for their programs. The line between fulfilling Congress' responsibility and micromanaging is often very thin. Such is the game environment for administrators.

Any skilled political operative in a bureau or agency knows the relevant committees, their members, and staff well. For example, the Agency for International Development, which distributes foreign economic aid, pays careful attention to the remarks and actions of its authorizing committees, House Foreign Affairs and Senate Foreign Relations, and those of the Appropriations subcommittees on Foreign Operations in the Senate and House.

Congress retains considerable means of formal and informal control over administrators. Formally, besides holding the authority to authorize programs and fund them, the legislature regulates personnel policy affecting all federal administrators and conducts oversight of bureaucratic operations. While overseeing, Congress continues to employ legislative vetoes. It also informally guides agency behavior through correspondence, comments at oversight hearings, casework requests, and language in committee reports (Fisher 1981, 82). Frequent interaction between Congress and bureaucracy spawns many informal agreements.

Congress does not simply dominate agency life, however. Bureaucrats have their own resources to employ in their coalition games with the legislature. The merit system provides for nonpolitical hiring of career federal employees and protects them from losing their jobs for political reasons. Bureaucrats' presence in the trenches of policy implementation gives them a day-to-day freedom in policymaking that neither Congress nor the president can consistently circumscribe. Savvy administrators strategically cultivate support from the clients of the programs they administer. A location at the "ground level" of policy execution also furnishes bureaucrats with sole possession of much program information useful to both Congress and the White House. Knowledge and political support provide power, an important game resource.

SUBGOVERNMENTS: GAMES WITHIN GAMES

Despite the complexity of national government, it is possible to generalize about the power relations of agencies, congressional committees, and affected interests in particular policy areas. The ongoing relationships among these players can result in the rise of **subgovernments** (see box 8.3). At times, subgovernments in domestic policy coordinate their activities so thoroughly that they dominate the coalition game in their policy arena. Grant McConnell identified the key players of consensual subgovernments in domestic policy:

> (1) a federal administrative agency within the executive branch; (2) a heavily committed group of congressmen, usually members of a particular committee or subcommittee; (3) a private (or quasi-private) association representing the agency clientele; (4) a quite homogeneous constituency usually composed of local elites (McConnell 1966, 244).

A good example lies in the administration of federal farm price supports. The Agricultural Stabilization and Conservation Service (ASCS), an agency of the Department of Agriculture, administers the several crop support programs. Subgovernments exist for each crop support program. The participants in each are the ASCS, affected interest groups—usually a homogeneous growers association, such as the National Association of Wheat Growers—and the members of a particular commodity subcommittee of the House Agriculture committee. The distinguishing characteristic of an influential subgovernment is consensus on policy goals. Most price support subgovernments have that consensus: "Basically, each commodity subgovernment works to obtain the most favorable support possible for the producers of the commodity" (Ripley and Franklin 1991, 109).

Joel Aberbach aptly summarizes the broader consequences of subgovernments:

> Because subgovernments often have such a powerful influence over policy and administration, and because it is unusually difficult for central authorities—either the President or Congress as a whole—to successfully assert their authority over them, attribution of responsibility for policy and administration is more difficult in the United States than even the formal elements of the system of separate institutions sharing powers would lead one to expect (Aberbach 1990, 12).

BOX 8.3 The Veterans Arena: A Subgovernment at Work

Congressional hearings allow administrators, legislators, and interest groups to share information and jointly influence policy. Hearings in relatively consensual policy areas reveal subgovernments in action. Policy concerning veterans has long been the province of a well-established and relatively consensual group of players. For example, when the House Veterans Affairs committee met on February 19 and 20, 1992, to consider the Fiscal Year 1993 budget for the Department of Veterans Affairs, the players lined up like this:

CONGRESS

Committee chair G. V. (Sonny) Montgomery (D-MS), a retired general in the Army National Guard, presided over the hearings. Of the thirty-one committee members in attendance, a majority—eighteen—were veterans.

EXECUTIVE BRANCH

Testifying were Edward Derwinski, secretary of Veterans Affairs, along with three subordinates in the department. Four regional directors of the department also testified.

INTEREST GROUPS

Representatives of the following groups presented their views: Paralyzed Veterans of America, Disabled American Veterans Auxiliary, Veterans of Foreign Wars, Military Order of the Purple Heart, American Legion, Noncommissioned Officers Association and Blinded Veterans Association.

A subgovernment in action: A veterans' group testifying before the House Veterans' Affairs committee. The chair of the committee shows his solidarity with the group by wearing one of their hats.

It is important not to overstate the presence and importance of subgovernments, however. Not all interactions of groups, lawmakers and bureaucrats create such a consensual game environment. Alongside subgovernments are **issue networks** having "a large number of participants with quite variable degrees of interest, communication, or dependence on others in their environment" (Heclo 1978, 102). Unlike subgovernments, issue networks constantly change as experts in the bureaucracy and interest groups become involved in various issues. On many major issues, the variety of players involved stretches beyond even the definition of issue networks. Recent scholars of Washington interest representation describe these aggregations as "larger concatenations of groups and officials, most of which are too large, too heterogeneous and too unstable in their linkages to qualify even as real networks" (Salisbury et al. 1992, 149). Several important policy areas, such as taxation, health care, and labor and business regulation are fraught with conflict. More conflict brings more players into the game, meaning it is the more likely that policymaking will extend beyond any particular subgovernment to a broader issue network. Greater conflict and more players make the outcome of a coalition game more uncertain.

PATTERNS OF OVERSIGHT

Congressional committee oversight of the bureaucracy grew in the 1970s and 1980s because of a combination of increased governmental complexity and fiscal stringency. When new programs proved too expensive, greater political payoffs existed for lawmakers to oversee existing ones. Aberbach identified the specific stimulants of committee and subcommittee oversight. Committees pursued oversight for five reasons: in reaction to public crises, in response to input from constituents and interest groups about programs, to examine consistently the pattern of policy implementation, to encourage programs they favored, and even because of a growing sense of duty (Aberbach 1990, 120–121).

The earlier conventional wisdom in political science held that oversight was a congressional activity with few rewards and little diligent execution (Ogul 1976, chapter 1). Members of Congress now realize its great impact on policymaking. As one oversight subcommittee chair put it,

> I think the mere fact that our oversight subcommittee is looking at something all of a sudden will make the agency pay a little more attention to that concern every day. . . . I think it's that constant visibility, potential visibility, that you want to keep holding as the stick on an agency to make sure that they are implementing the program as that might have been intended by Congress (Aberbach 1990, 197).

Legislators and bureaucrats try to get along, but oversight ultimately remains a resource for compelling the executive branch careerists to go along with congressional directives. Oversight permits legislators to dominate coalition games played with bureaucrats. It is also a wonderful way for ambitious legislators to portray their commitment to good government. The dutiful prober of a public scandal can reap electoral rewards in the survival game from playing a white knight role. As Congress legislates less, they oversee more.

CONGRESS, THE PRESIDENT, AND THE BUREAUCRACY

None of this is particularly good news for the president. Because of his shorter tenure, greater distance from ongoing policy implementation, and broader perspective, he does not usually become a player in the coalition games of subgovernments. His resources for battling Congress over the bureaucracy include his White House staff, the OMB, and power to reorganize the executive branch. This last authority, though, is subject to legislative veto. Congress is reluctant to approve reorganizations that alter jurisdictions and established relations with agencies. One House committee chair told Richard Nixon, "If by this executive reorganization you affect in a major way the powers of various committees of the Congress, forget it" (Seidman 1975, 823).

The president also controls political appointments in the executive branch, but that power is limited in practice. Lawrence Dodd and Richard Schott argue that "The President's potential for control offered by the power of appointment is seldom fulfilled. . . . Congress, by making certain career officials responsible directly to it, creates substantial gaps in the chain of command (Dodd and Schott 1979, 42). The Office of Management and Budget does prepare the annual budget for submission to Congress. It also exercises legislative clearance in which agencies must receive administration approval before presenting pet policy proposals on the Hill. Congress, however, often ignores OMB requests concerning agency spending and sends its alternative totals to the president in large spending bills that are difficult to veto. Crafty administrators can also get their ideas to Congress by "back channels"—usually via congressional staff—should OMB disapprove.

At "ground level" implementation in many policy arenas, the White House is not a significant player. Below the level of the great national issues, Congress and bureaucracy have developed coalition games that insulate themselves from the encroachments of the president. Congress and the bureaucracy, by sharing power over the ongoing operations of public programs, set many specifics of national governance.

CONGRESS AND THE FEDERAL COURTS

A glance at the Constitution suggests that Congress possesses a surprisingly large amount of control over the operations of the Supreme Court and other federal courts. Article III establishes a Supreme Court and defines its original jurisdiction or cases in which it is the first court of recourse. The appellate jurisdiction of the Court comprises the range of cases on appeal from lower courts. This jurisdiction provides the bulk of the Court's workload and most of its important cases. Congress can alter the appellate jurisdiction should it so desire, but thusfar it has left it unlimited. The legislature also sets the number of justices and decides the structure and duties of all lower federal courts. Congress has established several "legislative courts" for special purposes. Examples include bankruptcy courts and the Court of Military Appeals. Judges in these courts, unlike those in federal district and appeals or Supreme Courts, served fixed terms. All federal court appointments must gain approval by a majority vote in the Senate. Congress can impeach federal judges for misconduct in office, though it does so very rarely.

In this game environment, federal courts protect their authority through sensitivity to Washington power games, especially as they involve Congress. Effective opinions are crafted strategically with an eye toward political circumstances. Only by conserving their authority can courts maintain it. This game is the opposite of the "use it or lose it" approach.

DETERMINING THE JUDICIAL PLAYERS: THE POLITICS

Congress influences the court system most directly through the appointment process. The initiative lies with the president, who nominates appointees to the federal bench. Few lower federal court nominees have trouble getting confirmed by the Senate. The norm of "senatorial courtesy" guides the process. The White House usually accepts the nomination preference of the senator or senators of the president's party from the state where the vacancy exists. If the state's senators are from the opposition party, the administration consults politically powerful members of the president's party from that state—House members, party leaders, and elected officials.

Supreme Court appointments are another matter. Inter-institutional power games at times sink nominees. In recent decades Republican presidents have faced difficulty in the Democratic Senate. Judges Clement Haynesworth and Harold Carswell, nominated by Richard Nixon, and Robert Bork, chosen by Ronald Reagan, suffered defeat on the Senate floor. Clarence Thomas, nominated by George Bush, barely survived a difficult confirmation process to secure appointment by a fifty-two to forty-eight vote. The central legislative players in the appointment game are the members of the Senate Judiciary committee. During confirmation hearings, candidates receive careful scrutiny of their judicial records and philosophy. A chilly reception by the Judiciary committee usually constitutes a kiss of death when the nomination goes to the floor.

Though many senators consider it "inappropriate" to judge a Supreme Court nominee primarily on the basis of his or her political beliefs, outspoken liberals and conservatives on the committee and in the chamber have no such compunction. The debate over Court nominees involves curiously evasive rhetoric. Few senators will say outright that they disapprove of nominees because they disagree with them politically, and instead look for weaknesses in a prospective justice's background to justify their negative verdict. This is a disingenuous strategy. Defenders of the nominee in turn assail opponents for ideological bias in evaluating the nominee. The recent appointments of Robert Bork and Clarence Thomas involved some pitched ideological battles over the nominees (see box 8.4).

THE COURTS AND RULES RELATING TO CONGRESSIONAL POWERS

Though the appointment process entails the most direct interaction of the judicial and legislative branches, federal courts regularly consider questions of congressional powers when making decisions. These questions are of two sorts. First, the constitutionality of the actions of Congress are at times at issue in a particular case. Second, essential in many cases concerning federal law is interpretation of the **legislative intent**—the purpose of the enacted law envisioned by Congress.

BOX 8.4 Image Games: Clarence Thomas and Anita Hill

The nomination of Clarence Thomas to the Supreme Court was a classic example of Washington power politics involving the image and coalition games. The White House and their opponents both fought hard to build coalitions and craft a particular image of the nominee.

Thomas, an outspoken opponent of affirmative action, had served in the Reagan administration as head of the Equal Employment Opportunity Commission. During his confirmation hearings he stressed his humble origins but appeared to back away from some of his earlier controversial statements. He also claimed to have no opinion about the 1973 abortion decision *Roe v. Wade* (410 U.S. 113), causing several committee members to doubt the truthfulness of the image of open-mindedness he put forth.

The Judiciary committee split seven to seven on his confirmation, but it appeared that Thomas had enough support to win on the Senate floor. Thomas' image then came under fierce assault. A few days before the confirmation vote, Anita Hill, a former employee of Thomas at the EEOC, stepped forth to publicly charge Thomas with sexual harassment when she worked for him. Apparently, Democratic committee staff earlier had urged her to give evidence with the assurance of anonymity.

Support for the immediate approval of Thomas quickly collapsed and the Senate instructed the Judiciary Committee to reconvene and investigate the charges. President Bush reiterated his strong support for Thomas. During three days and nights of emotionally-charged, nationally televised hearings, Hill made her charges, Thomas rebutted them. Each side brought forth character witnesses in a game of duelling images. Committee Republicans aggressively questioned Hill's truthfulness. Committee Democrats appeared less energetic in their defense of Hill or questioning of Thomas.

Ultimately, the matter came down to an issue of who had the most trustworthy image and arguments. No conclusive evidence of the alleged incidents turned up. When the Senate finally voted, a coalition of forty-one Republicans and eleven Democrats sided with Thomas. Their argument was that Thomas was "innocent until proven guilty" and that Hill's charges seemed politically motivated. Women's rights activists and other liberals, who had fought hard against the Thomas nomination, reacted with outrage. To them, a Senate dominated by white males had failed to show adequate sensitivity to the serious problem of sexual harassment. In response to these concerns, two women finally gained appointment to the Judiciary Committee in 1993—Senators Diane Feinstein of California and Carol Moseley-Braun of Illinois. The Thomas nomination promised to make future confirmation hearings arenas for harsh partisan conflict over the image and statements of nominees. The nominations of federal judges Ruth Bader Ginsburg in 1993 and Stephen Breyer in 1994, however, sailed through with little fanfare because of their judicial moderation and strong credentials as jurists.

Particularly important sources of legislative intent are the committee reports and floor debates. Committee staffs attempt to explain the meaning of the bill in committee reports. Lawmakers often take pains to enter statements into these reports and in floor debates with an eye to future court interpretations. In determining legislative intent, the judicial norm is that "judges have a subordinate role to play in applying statutory law; their obligation is to help the legislature achieve its goals" (Murphy and Pritchett 1986, 435). Justice Ruth Bader Ginsburg summarized the norm well during her confirmation hearings: "I don't confuse my own predilections with what is the law" ("Ginsburg," 1991). Sound strategy requires that the courts interpret federal law circumspectly. Adventurous decisions invite congressional challenges to judicial authority.

The Supreme Court and lower federal courts earlier in this century changed the rules of the constitutional game by expanding congressional power. In the first decades of the century, the federal courts sanctioned "the use of vague and ill-defined statutory language" in creating regulatory commissions in the federal bureaucracy (Fisher 1985a, 104). In *McGrain v. Daugherty* in 1927, the Supreme Court upheld the right of Congress to conduct investigations (in this case, of the Teapot Dome scandal) as legitimately within the jurisdiction of the legislature (273 U.S. 135, 1927). The Court's endorsement of New Deal legislation in 1937, after its earlier resistance, marked the end of Court efforts to markedly restrict Article I powers.

One strategy the Court employs to avoid political battles with Congress is its doctrine of political questions, which holds that the Court will not deal with political issues if no sufficient statutory or constitutional question is at issue. This is a marvelously vague doctrine that often protects the Court from controversy (Fisher 1985a, xiii). More recently, though, the Court's decisions have stirred controversy in Congress. Congress can overrule a constitutional interpretation of the Court by passing a constitutional amendment. This is difficult because it requires a two-thirds vote by each chamber and majority approval by legislatures in three-fourths of the states. Instead, Congress strategically ignored *Chadha.*

Court decisions about federal law invite another form of defiance. As the Court became steadily more conservative due to the appointment of justices by presidents Reagan and Bush, the judges' interpretations of federal law found little favor in the more liberal Congress. The legislature responded by overturning Court decisions through passing legislation. In doing this, Congress clarifies "legislative intent" in a way to handcuff future Court decisions.

Examples of this strategy abound. A 1982 extension of the Voting Rights Act of 1965 voided Court decisions about racial gerrymandering. President Reagan reluctantly signed the bill into law. Congress in 1988 overrode Reagan's veto on a bill that reversed the Court decision *Grove City College v. Bell,* which limited the ability of the federal government to withhold funds from colleges that discriminate (79 L. Ed. 2nd 516, 1984). In 1991, Congress attempted to negate a Court decision that had allowed administrative regulations that prohibited doctors at federally funded health clinics from discussing abortion with patients. President Bush sided with the Court and vetoed the measure. President Clinton during his first week in office, however, issued an executive order reversing the regulations. A proposed civil rights act in 1991 sought to void Court decisions concerning litigation over job discrimination. President Bush, after vetoing an initial version of the act, finally signed a compromise bill. If constitutional philosophies continue to diverge between the Court and Congress, we can expect more power games between these institutions in the future.

CONCLUSION

Congress competes for power with the other major governmental institutions in Washington. The president possesses an edge in the agenda and image games, but encounters many frustrations in playing the coalition game in Congress. Bureaucratic strategies toward Congress are more subtle than those of the president. The legislature and bureaucracy each possess power resources in this relationship, but the formal lawmaking powers of Congress give it the upper hand. The sort of coalition games played here do not include the president and his White House advisors, often to their frustration. The courts are most removed from the more obvious power games of Washington, but institutional maintenance requires strategic attention to congressional preferences. In recent years, Congress has overturned decisions by a more assertive Supreme Court. Such jostling for power is a staple of the power games between national institutions.

IN DEPTH

1. Did the Supreme Court rule correctly when it declared the legislative veto unconstitutional in *Immigration and Naturalization Service v. Chadha* (462 U.S. 919, 1983)? To explore this, examine the facts of the case and the legal reasoning behind both the decision and the dissenting opinions. Also, investigate the usefulness of legislative veto arrangements for both the legislative and executive branches.

REFERENCES

Craig, Barbara Hinkson. 1988. *Chadha: The Story of an Epic Constitutional Struggle.* Berkeley: University of California Press.

Fisher, Louis. 1985. "Judicial Misjudgments about the Lawmaking Process: The Legislative Veto Case." *Public Administration Review* 45: 705–711.

Fisher, Louis. 1991. *Constitutional Conflicts Between Congress and the President,* 3d ed. Lawrence: University of Kansas Press.

Immigration and Naturalization Service v. Chadha (462 U.S. 919, 1983).

2. Choose a domestic policy area and look for evidence of subgovernments and issue networks. Where are they? How consensual are they? How influential are they? Try to identify their power by examining the subgovernment role in the passage of recent legislation in this policy area.

REFERENCES

Aberbach, Joel. 1990. *Keeping a Watchful Eye: The Politics of Congressional Oversight.* Washington: Brookings Institution.

Ripley, Randall, and Grace A. Franklin. 1991. *Politics, the Bureaucracy and Public Policy.* Pacific Grove, Calif.: Brooks/Cole.

On specific legislation, *Congressional Quarterly Weekly Report* and *National Journal.* Congressional documents, particularly committee hearings and floor debate.

3. What strategies of influence are best pursued by the president in his power game with Congress? A number of political scientists have analyzed presidential legislative success in Congress over the years, each coming to his or her own particular generalizations. What lessons does this literature hold for presidents who seek to increase their influence in Congress? When are presidents most likely to be successful? When are they least likely? Why? What explains the differing success levels among recent administrations?

REFERENCES

Bond, Jon R., and Richard Fleisher. 1990. *The President in the Legislative Arena.* Chicago: University of Chicago Press.

Edwards, George C., III. 1989. *At the Margins: Presidential Leadership of Congress.* New Haven: Yale University Press.

Kerbel, Matthew Robert. 1991. *Beyond Persuasion: Organizational Efficiency and Presidential Power.* Albany: State University of New York Press.

Peterson, Mark A. 1990. *Legislating Together: The White House and Capitol Hill from Eisenhower to Reagan.* Cambridge: Harvard University Press.

4. The institutional resurgence of Congress in the 1970s and its battles with the executive in recent years produced numerous consequences for our political system. What are these? Which consequences are good, and which are bad? On balance, is an aggressive national legislature actively contesting for power in Washington good for our political system? Why or why not?

REFERENCES

Davidson, Roger, ed. 1992. *The Postreform Congress.* New York: Saint Martin's Press.

Ginsberg, Benjamin, and Martin Schefter. 1991. *Politics by Other Means: The Declining Importance of Elections in America.* New York: Basic Books.

Sundquist, James L. 1981. *The Decline and Resurgence of Congress.* Washington: Brookings Institution.

CHAPTER NINE

CONGRESS AND POLICY RESULTS

The substance is important, no doubt about it, for that is what the game is all about. But so is the personal element. . . . The personal is tightly interwoven with the institutional. It is a rare player who can keep the two distinct, much less view both apart from the substance. (Neustadt 1970, 76, 78)

To Washington, Gramm-Rudman is leadership; to the people it is Hillspeak for games. (Bailey 1990, B1)

A game metaphor suggests recreation—relief from the burdens of everyday life. The games of Congress, however, produce consequences far more significant than those resulting from chess or parcheesi. This chapter explores the broader significance of congressional activity by assessing policy results of the many games discussed in previous chapters.

THE POLICY GAME

Chapter 7 explained the moves in the congressional policy game of coalition building. Bargaining, or logrolling, builds coalitions. Through this it is possible to "buy" coalition members who will side with the natural coalition members who favor a measure on its merits. Logrolling involves side payments, often unrelated to the substance of the legislation for which support is sought. The ultimate goal is a minimum winning coalition, the efficient number of votes necessary to carry the day in committee or on the floor.

Scholars often describe the consequences of the policy game as "outputs," a term suggesting the results at the end of a time-bounded competition. The reality of policymaking is a bit more complicated. Contests over what government should do never really stop. Past actions of Congress, along with events and decisions in the national and international political arenas, create the game environment for current policy choices. The struggle over policy in Congress has involved high stakes and often large costs for the losers. Pitched conflict sometimes replaces bargaining in the key plays of policy games.

Two major attributes of the game environment created the heightened sense of policy competition. The first, existing all but two years since 1981, was **divided**

government. In this situation, the distribution of resources among the players complicates the game. Institutional and partisan divisions overlap, at times creating mutual policy jousting between the White House and Congress.

A second characteristic of the game environment since 1980 was a scarcity of monetary resources creating "cutback politics." Fiscal austerity transformed the budget politics from a game of allocating benefits to one of inflicting cuts and slapping tax hikes on parts of the populace. The primary fulcrum moving policy in this direction was the rise of large, recurring budget deficits. Passage of spending programs became much more difficult. Former Senate Majority Leader George Mitchell (D-ME) in 1989 called the deficit dilemma "the whale in the bathtub that leaves no room for anything else" (Dewar 1989, A4). This heated the conflict between president and Congress. Presidents Reagan and Bush shut down the federal government several times by vetoing large spending bills containing funds for programs that they thought the nation could not afford. Bill Clinton had to adjust his initial budget to the realities of cutback politics when Congress pressed him for additional spending cuts.

The red ink created a harshly competitive environment. Since 1980, deficit reduction usually involved a negative-sum game for both president and Congress. No one wanted spending cuts for favored programs or additional taxes, but all had to suffer to lower the deficit. Making the hard choices required bargaining, but most in Congress wanted to avoid bargaining over how to share losses. As Representative Bill Richardson (D-NM) put it in 1986, "This has not been a very fun decade to be a legislator" (Schier 1992, 47).

CONGRESSIONAL POLICY STRATEGIES

Fiscal austerity and perpetual policy conflict in Washington cast many longstanding policymaking strategies of Congress into an unfavorable light. Most of them were of little use in overcoming the problems of divided government and chronic deficits. Congress is above all a collective body that operates by aggregating the votes of separately elected legislators, most of whom stay in office over several terms. Several common strategies flow from this combination of players, rules, and resources.

THE STRATEGY OF LOCALISM

Localism is a survival game strategy by which lawmakers consider policy primarily as it affects the welfare of their districts. All the electoral incentives encourage members of Congress to consider what will benefit their own slice of the nation. Accordingly, they frequently bargain for the best deal they can get. "Legislators prefer . . . rewards for one's district or state. . . . Legislation may include a higher appropriation, lower taxes, or favorable treatment for an industry in a member's district as a price for a positive vote" (Van Horn, Baumer, and Gormley 1989, 138). Local benefits serve as the currency in coalition games. The strategy of localism, however, collides with the need to reduce federal spending and tax breaks, impeding reduction of the deficit. David Stockman, Reagan's budget director, found

Localism in action. Representative Bud Shuster (R-PA) is a senior member of the Appropriations committee's Public Works and Transportation subcommittee. This position allows him to deliver road projects to his district and (not very subtly) claim credit for them.

the negotiations over the administration's tax cut bill in 1981 falling prey to localism over tax preferences: "The last ten to twenty percent of the votes had to be bought, period" (Stockman 1986, 250–251). It is not surprising that the bill as passed cut taxes far too much and further contributed to the deficit.

Localism also plays a role in congressional defense and foreign policymaking. Legislators with substantial ethnic groups back home often try to enact policies that will aid them in the survival game. Irish-American politicians wade into the conflict in Northern Ireland. Representatives of Greek Americans urge the U.S. to support the Greek position regarding Cyprus. Jewish Americans effectively influence legislators concerning support for Israel. Also, as noted later in this chapter, local development interests often take a strong interest in defense procurement decisions. Legislators have long sought to bring military dollars back to the district to provide jobs and win votes. Big battles over the base-closing legislation in the early 1990s resulted because fiscal austerity collided with the imperative of legislative localism.

THE STRATEGY OF FRAGMENTATION

Another strategy in congressional policymaking is **fragmentation,** multiplying the number of players and jurisdictions in major policy areas. Competition over jurisdictions often resembles a simple shoving match. This is the result of the clout-maximizing tendencies of policy entrepreneurs—everybody wants a piece of the action. Individual players seek greater resources. Energy policy is a good example. The authorizing committees for new legislation are the Energy and Natural Resources committee of the Senate and Interstate and Foreign Commerce committee of the House. The House Ways and Means and Senate Finance committees, however preside over energy taxes. If additional spending on energy conservation is necessary, the House and Senate Appropriations committees must recommend the money.

Fragmentation contributes to two important features of policymaking. First, in arenas where fragmentation prevails, disjointed, uncoordinated policy is the likely result. Political scientist Glenn Parker explains:

> The division of congressional authority into islands of legislative power restricts the likelihood that comprehensive policies will emerge from legislative deliberations because decision makers will concern themselves only with those problems directly in their own purview (Parker 1989, 161).

THE STRATEGY OF INCREMENTALISM

Fragmentation also promotes another important congressional policy strategy: **incrementalism.** John Kingdon defines it as follows:

> Instead of beginning consideration of each program or issue afresh, decision makers take what they are currently doing as given, and make small, incremental, marginal adjustments in that current behavior. By taking that tack, they need not canvass formidable numbers of far-reaching changes, they need not spend inordinate time defining their goals, and the comparisons they make between the current state of affairs and the small adjustments to be made in current behavior are entirely manageable. The result is that policy changes very gradually, in small steps (Kingdon 1984, 83–84).

Incrementalism is a long-established strategy in national government because it is so functional for lawmakers and bureaucrats. Small changes entail small risks. Incrementalism traditionally meant an additional small monetary addition to each program each year. The rise of deficits, however, has made decrements, small cuts in funding levels, a more likely fate for federal programs. Fiscal stringency forces **decrementalism** on much of national government.

THE STRATEGY OF SYMBOLISM

An abundance of red ink also compels Congress to pursue a strategy of **symbolism.** Congress can devote time and attention to a problem without actually devoting the necessary resources to solve it. An increasing proportion of annual legislation includes "commemorative resolutions," which costlessly acknowledge a group or problem. In 1986–87, for example, the 99th Congress passed some 307 commemorative bills and joint resolutions expressing a nonbinding "sense of Congress"—46 percent of all public laws during that period![1]

Congress also passes laws with ambitious goals but no realistic means of enforcement. A prime example is the Humphrey-Hawkins Full Employment Act of 1978. The law formally required a reduction in unemployment to 3 percent but provided no funds or jobs programs to reach the goal. In the 1980s and early 1990s, aspirations have continued to outstrip means in many areas of domestic policy.

[1]For more on the implications of political symbolism, see Murray Edelman, *The Symbolic Uses of Politics,* 1964, Urbana: University of Illinois Press.

The broad pattern of congressional policy strategies adds up to a substantial **defensive advantage** for established interests and policies. Those players who have already scored in policy games enjoy a substantial edge over newcomers. The design of Congress does not permit speedy responses for new demands. Fiscal austerity exhausts most funds for innovation. Proponents of major change face daunting odds.

EXCEPTIONS: THE GREAT DEPARTURES

The pattern of play described above does occasionally permit big exceptions. Several of these occurred during the 1980s—the Reagan budget and tax cuts of 1981, the sweeping Social Security overhaul of 1983, and the comprehensive tax reform of 1986. All were large-scale, nonincremental alterations in major areas of governmental activity, occurring despite defensive advantage, divided government or fiscal austerity. How are such big changes possible?

If lawmakers perceive that their constituents favor large-scale change, that such a vote will aid them in the survival game, they are more likely to support it. That was the case with southern Democrats in 1981, the crucial "swing votes" for the Reagan economic plan. Constituency sentiment pushed them to the side of comprehensive reform (Schier 1992, 77). Also, sometimes an idea can seem "right on its merits" though little public and interest group support has coalesced behind it. The 1986 tax reform arose from a widespread belief in Congress and the administration that drastic simplification of federal tax law was long overdue (Conlan, Wrightson, and Beam 1990, chapter 9). Ronald Reagan bought this idea and played upon longstanding public resentment of the tax system to promote the idea of tax simplification.

At times broad change can occur simply by "striking when the iron is hot" by pushing a proposal through to passage when the "policy window," as John Kingdon terms it, is open in Congress (Kingdon 1984, chapter 6). By 1983, many in Washington believed Social Security was in deep fiscal trouble requiring benefit reductions and tax increases. The expectations in the game environment were right for comprehensive reform, if the right people and strategy could combine.

The essential requirement for large-scale policy departures involves a combination of the right strategists and the right time. To win any game, good timing is essential. The Social Security Commission of 1983 bridged partisan differences to craft a comprehensive reform package. Higher taxes upset Republicans; reduced benefits displeased Democrats. Both the president and Democratic leaders in Congress, however, finally embraced the plan. Charles Jones summarized the lesson well: major policy shifts can occur when a well-organized and vocal public unites and demands governmental action or when policy makers reach a temporary consensus around unprecedented proposals (Jones 1974, 462). The game environment does promote major policy innovation—but rarely.

BOX 9.1 Major Policy Change: The Players Speak

The tax reform of 1986 and Social Security revisions of 1983 rank as two of the most stunning policy innovations of the decade. What follows are quotes from the players involved that help us understand how such massive change came about.

In both instances, public attention about the problem grew, along with a desire for something to be done. Addressing the issue became an important strategy in the survival game. In tax reform, President Reagan had played a major role in bringing this about, in effect, raising the stakes for reform. David Brockway, of the Joint Tax Committee staff, recalled,

> In the early 1980s the president began tapping that general public resentment about taxes and saying, "Look, the message is very simple: taxes are too high." Then the members had to respond to the general public. Taxes had become large-scale politics like SALT (Strategic Arms Limitation Treaty) or something. It was a different ballgame.[a]

Former Representative Thomas Downey (D-NY) of the House Ways and Means committee claimed that a partisan blame game over taxation then ensued:

> This was blame avoidance in part when we went into it. . . . If the Republican party turns its back on tax reform . . . Democrats will have the opportunity to beat them about the head and shoulders saying "Your own president wanted it, it was fair, and you were too interested in worrying about big corporations to help the American people." So it is largely a process of dodging political bullets. The party that dodges them best can turn around and use some of those bullets against their adversaries.[b]

Successful coalition-building created a general consensus so the bill could become law. The major players all agreed because the costs of inaction seemed greater to them than the risk of large-scale reform. A similar reform consensus may be forming in the early 1990s on the issue of health care.

A kindred dynamic occurred with Social Security reform. Polls showed great public anxiety over the future of Social Security and a desire for action. One congressional leadership aide recalled that "the public would turn against both parties if nothing was done."[c] In this case, the public apprehension was well justified. David Stockman, Reagan's budget director, in 1981 analyzed the future of Social Security and came to believe that major reform was inevitable, arguing that "by 1983, you will have solvency problems coming out of your ears."[d] This is exactly what happened. The pressure of fiscal danger for the system spawned a bipartisan presidential commission whose report for reform gained the approval of major players in Washington. The chair of the commission, economist Alan Greenspan, attributed its success to the comprehensiveness of its proposed solution:

> We knew in advance that this type of problem is solved by a whole series of initiatives, none of which are desirable politically. Were one to take any of our solutions and put them in front of Congress one by one, all would be voted down by large majorities.[e]

This all-or-nothing strategy proved a winner for Greenspan.

[a] Timothy J. Conlan, Margaret T. Wrightson, and David R. Beam, 1990, *Taxing Choices: The Politics of Tax Reform,* Washington: Congressional Quarterly Press, p. 250.

[b] *Ibid.,* p. 239.

[c] Paul Light, 1985, *Artful Work: The Politics of Social Security Reform,* New York: Random House, p. 193.

[d] William Greider, 1981, "The Education of David Stockman," *The Atlantic* 248 (December): 45.

[e] Light, *Artful Work,* p. 113.

TABLE 9.1 Policy Types and Their Policy Processes

Type	*Primary players*	*Common games*
Domestic distributive policy	congressional subcommittees and committees, executive agencies, small interest groups	positive-sum logrolling
Domestic regulatory policy	congressional subcommittees and committees, full House and Senate, executive agencies, trade associations	bargaining, compromise
Domestic redistributive policy	president and his appointees, committees and/or Congress, large interest groups, liberals and conservatives	zero-sum conflict
Structural foreign policy	congressional subcommittees and committees, executive bureaus, small interest groups	positive-sum logrolling
Strategic foreign policy	executive agencies, president	executive-led compromise
Crisis foreign policy	president and advisers	follow the leader

SOURCE: Adapted from Randall B. Ripley and Grace A. Franklin, 1991, *Congress, the Bureaucracy and Public Policy,* Pacific Grove, Calif.: Brooks/Cole, pp. 18–19.

POLICY TYPES AND POLICY PROCESSES

Policymaking games are seldom as rousing as they are during those infrequent instances of sweeping change. More routine policymaking does, however, have patterns of its own. Those patterns depend primarily on the substance of the policy itself. The type of action requested of government produces a particular set of players, group of working relationships, level of conflict, and sort of policy outcome. Policy substance shapes the policy games played by Congress, creating a political process around that substance (Lowi 1964, 677–715). Political scientists categorize policy types and note the politics that usually surround each type of policy (see table 9.1). The following sections elaborate further, noting how each policy type engenders a different sort of game involving Congress.

DOMESTIC POLICY PATTERNS

A vast range of issues comprise domestic policy. Still, policymaking tends to follow one of three game patterns: distributive policy, redistributive policy, or regulatory policy.

INFLUENCE OF				
President, Presidency and Centralized Bureaucracy	***Executive Agencies***	***Congress as a Whole***	***Congressional Subcommittees***	***Private Sector***
low	high	low	high (supports subcommittees)	high (subsidized groups)
moderately high	moderate	moderately high	moderate	moderately high (regulated interests)
high	low	moderately high	low	moderately high (peak associations representing interest group clusters)
low	high	low	high (supports subcommittees)	high (subsidized groups and corporations)
high	low (often responsive to executive)	high	low	moderate (interest groups, corporations)
high	low	low	low	low

Distributive Policy

Distributive policies "provide subsidies for private activities and convey tangible governmental benefits to the individuals, groups and corporations subsidized" (Ripley and Franklin 1991, 18). The rationale behind this is to encourage private activity—growing business, productive farms—that is good for society and would not occur without governmental support. Highways that increase commerce or schools that educate the labor force are examples of such programs. Government distributes benefits to a small component of the population, while all citizens pay in some tiny part for the subsidy. Because a few win much but many lose only a bit, subgovernments often rule in distributive policy. Congressional committees, interest groups, and bureaucrats work collaboratively to direct benefits through consensus. The president, the rest of Congress, and the media pay little attention to these mutual logrolling games. The common strategy involves reciprocal accommodation—supporting a colleague's pork-barrel project in return for support of your own, or advocating a policy that broadly distributes benefits in many districts.

A good example of distributive politics can be found in farm price supports (see chapter 8) or veterans' benefits. The veterans' subgovernment proved its power over the decades, winning billions in benefits for their interest groups. Admittedly, most Americans see the claim of veterans to governmental benefits as a legitimate one. This has allowed the subgovernment of veterans' groups, Veterans Affairs committees on the Hill and the Veterans Administration (VA) to work collaboratively to increase budgets (see box 8.3). By 1989, the VA had attained cabinet status with an annual budget of more than $30 billion and a quarter of a million employees. Budget cutters in the 1980s scrupulously avoided targeting these popular, consensual programs. Of course, we all pay a small amount to keep these programs operating. As long as voters remain passive, the veterans' subgovernment will continue distributing benefits.

Redistributive Policy

In contrast to the consensual logrolling games played by subgovernments in distributive policy, **redistributive policy** involves highly public, competitive games between the two major parties and uncertain final outcomes. This is because such policies "manipulate the allocation of wealth, property, political or civil rights, or some other valued item among social classes or racial groups" (Ripley and Franklin 1991, 21). Many affected by such actions perceive that benefits one group receives benefits at the direct expense of the other. For example, tax hikes on the rich cause wealthy individuals to view the policy as benefiting other taxpayers at their expense. Some white men view affirmative action as penalizing them in order to benefit women and those of other races.

Major interest groups, the president, and most lawmakers plunge into the competition surrounding redistributive issues. Subgovernments on such issues are not consensual or influential in the policy outcome. Large issue networks commonly arise. The media finds the contest surrounding redistribution irresistible. Instead of logrolling, a strategy of aggressive conflict between sides prevails that resembles a "tug of war"—a competition recognized by the rival players as zero-sum.

A good example of redistributive competition involves the deficit negotiations of 1990 (Schier 1992, 129). Fear of steadily mounting deficits drove the White House and congressional leadership to a series of "summits" in the spring and summer of 1990. Their common strategy sought a bipartisan deficit reduction package of spending cuts and tax hikes totalling almost $500 billion over five years. After they struck a deal and submitted it to Congress in October, backbench Democrats revolted. To them, the package did not raise taxes enough on the rich and penalized those of low and moderate income with spending cuts and tax increases. House Republicans also rebelled at the prospect of an additional $150 billion in new taxes. Many Democrats thrilled at the revival of redistributive politics, believing their position would be more popular than that of the White House. Representative Bob Wise (D-WV) claimed the proposal allowed "the rich to make out like bandits, while my people get hit again" (Hager 1990b, 3187).

The contest over fairness raged throughout the month, commanding headline attention in the national media. A new compromise finally took shape that taxed the rich more and cut benefits in social programs like Medicare less (see box 9.1). The president was an immediate loser as he dropped considerably in the opinion polls. Former Representative Bill Frenzel (R-MN) of the Budget committee stated a strong reason for the decline in Bush's public support: "They beat us to death with this rich and poor thing" (Hager 1991, 3391).

Regulatory Policy

Another controversial sort of domestic policy involves governmental regulation. **Regulatory policies** "are designed to protect the public by setting the conditions under which various private activities can be undertaken" (Ripley and Franklin 1991, 21). Congress prohibits harmful behavior, such as polluting the environment or producing dangerous consumer products. It requires certain activities, like complete disclosure of company financial activities in quarterly stock reports. The goal is to get private entities to "play fair" according to rules set by Congress.

Like redistributive policies, regulatory policies have a broad impact that is more visible to the media and public. Because of the shifting issues and wide range of affected interests, a broad constellation of players, rather than subgovernments, dominate the regulatory policy process. Contests over regulation at times are zero-sum, but bargaining and compromise occur more frequently than in redistributive policy.

An example of regulatory policy and the politics it produces lies in the regulation of federal savings and loan (also known as "thrift") institutions during the 1980s. Lax regulation of savings and loans institutions (S & Ls), the fault of both the White House and Congress, led to huge financial losses by several large thrift institutions by the late 1980s. Some rogue thrifts kept low cash reserves and speculated extensively in risky ventures, leading to big losses. The amount of the red ink required that the Federal Savings and Loan Insurance Corporation (FSLIC), an insurance fund, protect depositors of the failed thrifts. The extent of the problem garnered extensive media attention by 1989.

Congress and the administration initially responded with denial, followed by an ill-informed groping to discover the size of the problem and the cost of a solution. Local thrift institutions at first received sympathetic treatment by lawmakers until enough constituents were up in arms over their compromised savings. The Members' survival game strategy then shifted from defending to attacking thrift institutions. The price tag for rescuing depositors kept growing, from $10 billion in 1987 to well over $100 billion by 1991. After the flurry of attacks on the thrifts, a compromise was reached. To avoid future problems, Congress increased the cash reserve requirement for the thrifts and limited their ability to invest in risky ventures. The cost of the bailout was conveniently moved off-budget, so as not to increase (on paper, at least) the already large budget deficit. This spectacular failure of regulatory policy spawned anger and conflict throughout the political system.

BOX 9.2 Competition over Regulation: The Civil Rights Restoration Act of 1991

Regulatory policy can involve the hot issues of the moment and produce competitive strategies between president and Congress under divided government. A particularly contentious example of regulatory policy concerned a 1991 congressional attempt to revise civil rights law to "correct" nine Supreme Court rulings, five from 1989. The most troublesome of the cases was *Wards Cove Packing v. Atonio* (490 U.S. 642), a 1989 case in which the court changed the rules, making it more difficult to prove discrimination in employment practices. In that case, the court reversed a 1971 standard that put the burden of proof on the employer when charged with discriminatory use of physical tests and educational requirements in job hiring. The *Wards Cove* standard instead placed the burden of proof on the plaintiffs suing the company over discriminatory practices. The 1991 act sought to restore the 1971 standard.

In 1990, President Bush vetoed an initial congressional attempt to reverse the court's decisions on discrimination in business practices. For the first ten months of 1991, the White House continued to voice a strong opposition to the measure, arguing that shifting the burden of proof to employers would require them to adopt job quotas to forestall lawsuits. Republican Senator John Danforth (R-MO), an influential moderate, sharply disagreed with the White House view.

The White House fell back upon a bargaining strategy in October of 1990. Former klansman David Duke's Republican candidacy for the governorship of Louisiana placed a new stigma upon the charge of "quotas." Sexual harassment charges against Supreme Court nominee Clarence Thomas added impetus to efforts to increase the ways that sexual harassment victims could sue for redress. The original 1991 bill had included increased legal penalties for sexual harassment suits. In this more favorable game environment, liberal Democrats played the blame game by accusing the White House of ignoring serious civil rights problems.

All this made the White House and their conservative supporters on Capitol Hill more willing to make a deal. In the end, the posturing on both sides gave way to bargaining and compromise. In return for some language that made the intent of the bill a bit more vague, the White House accepted the other parts of the congressional proposal. Danforth served as the agent of compromise between the administration and Capitol Hill liberals.

FOREIGN POLICY PATTERNS

The broad term "foreign policy" actually includes three distinct types of policies, each with its own set of players and style of play: structural policy, strategic policy, and crisis policy.

Structural Policy

When the Pentagon needs weapons and supplies, it turns to Congress to approve their purchase. **Structural policies** "aim primarily at procuring, deploying, and organizing military personnel and materiel, presumably within the confines and guidelines of previously determined strategic decisions" (Ripley and Franklin 1991, 23). The result is a logrolling game similar to that found in domestic distributive policy. Subgovernments form and hold great influence over the awarding of Pentagon contracts; Congress as a whole usually supports subcommittee recommendations.

The traditional structural policy subgovernment includes Pentagon procurement officials, private contractors, and legislators on Armed Services and Appropriations subcommittees seeking defense monies for their districts. Logs roll and benefits flow to specific parts of the nation. Such arrangements have been in place for many years. When L. Mendel Rivers (D-SC) chaired the House Armed Services committee in the late 1960s, many feared that his coastal district might sink into the ocean under the weight of all the military installations he acquired.

Structural policy draws media and public attention only sporadically. Most procurement decisions receive little interest beyond that of the immediately affected parties. It usually takes a large scandal involving direct payoffs from defense contractors to legislators to interest the media in extensive coverage of a structural issue. Such scandals usually only have great impact on politics in the accused legislator's district. Debate over the massive procurement project of the B-1 bomber drifted in and out of public visibility during its twenty-year history (see box 9.3).

BOX 9.3 The B-1 Bomber: A Successful Waiting Game

We have all played the waiting game, remaining patient but ever ready to seek advantage when events turn in our favor. This describes the successful strategy of procurement for the B-1 bomber, whose supporters prevailed over their opponents in an epic struggle lasting more than twenty years.

The Air Force began lobbying in the early 1960s for a replacement for the aging B-52 bomber, the primary intercontinental nuclear bomber in the U.S. arsenal. The pro-bomber coalition included the Department of Defense, leading members of the Armed Services committees, and a coalition of defense contractors who would build the bomber.

By the mid-1970s, Congress approved development of a prototype plane at the behest of President Nixon. President Ford, in one of his last public acts, authorized production by the defense contractor Rockwell International. His successor, Jimmy Carter, however, preferred development of the cruise missile to an enhancement of the strategic bomber fleet. He prevailed upon Congress to shelve the B-1, but only by promising that the Air Force would not lose any funds due to the bomber's cancellation.

Supporters of the B-1 did not give up hope, however, and pressed the new administration in 1981 to resume construction. Ronald Reagan urged Congress to reverse itself and it agreed to build 100 planes, the last of which Rockwell delivered in 1988. The B-1 had remained a popular option because of its role in the survival game. The district benefits were obvious to many legislators—from 1982 to 1988, 40,000 workers labored in forty-eight states to complete it. As Nick Kotz put it, "Winning or losing a single large contract may determine the fate not only of companies but of communities."[a] With a popular president supporting the project, the votes for the plane could be found.

Consensus, persistence and a savvy concern with the survival game gave this procurement subgovernment the ability to win the waiting game. The strategic combination of congressional localism and the district benefits of structural politics ultimately made the wait worthwhile.

[a] Nick Kotz, 1988, *Wild Blue Yonder: Money, Politics and the B-1 Bomber,* New York: Pantheon Books, p. 237.

In the 1980s, as the defense budget grew, procurement subgovernments experienced the best of times. The 1990s involve greater austerity, since the defense budget will decrease by at least one quarter during the first half of the decade. The common strategy now seeks not to expand facilities, but merely to maintain them. This more frequently negative-sum game environment for structural policies is much more competitive. The traditional subgovernment no longer dominates decisions as effectively as it once did.

Strategic Policy

Strategic policies "are designed to assert and implement the basic military and foreign policy stance of the Untied States toward other nations" (Ripley and Franklin 1991, 23). These involve diplomatic matters—treaty making and ongoing relations with other countries—as well as the broad direction of national military strategy. The game is really between nations, with the president directing our national play. The executive branch dominates the process of strategic policy formulation. Agencies of the defense and state departments compete for influence over the president, who makes final decisions. Congressional involvement in the initial formulation of strategic policies is small. Lawmakers and committees may lobby the executive branch concerning strategic decisions, and at committee hearings executive officials often explain the strategic choices made. The Constitution, however, endows the Senate with authority for treaty ratification, an important power over executive branch policy formulation.

Recent examples of important strategic policies are legion: troop cuts in Europe, reductions in America's nuclear arsenal, aid to the Nicaraguan Contras, the international coalition to carry out the Gulf War, humanitarian aid to Rwanda, and assistance to the changing Soviet Union are merely a few. Congress at times reacts negatively to the president's initiatives by legislating limitations, withholding funds, or rejecting treaties. In all of the above examples, however, the crucible of policymaking remained at the highest levels of the White House. A good example of how president-centered strategic policymaking can be lies in the decision to pursue development of the "Star Wars" missile defense program during the Reagan and Bush presidencies.

In 1983, some officials in the defense department touted the possible use of laser weapons in space to destroy incoming nuclear missiles aimed at the United States. Though such plans were only at an initial stage, Ronald Reagan seized the possibility and made the idea the theme of an important presidential television address in March of 1983. As Robert MacFarlane, the president's national security advisor recalled: "He was terribly excited about that. He wanted to get it out, and he was less worried about the details" (Smith 1988, 600).

The project had its share of skeptics who thought it would require decades of research and too high a cost. Further, Star Wars might destabilize our relations with the Soviets. Congress nevertheless deferred to the president and authorized $1.4 billion for Star Wars research during 1985. The annual amounts grew steadily for five years to about $5 billion annually. Changes in the Soviet Union caused the program to be cut back in the early 1990s, and the Clinton administration persuaded Congress to end major spending on Star Wars. In strategic policy, the usual role of Congress remains secondary and reactionary, and tends toward support of the president.

Crisis Policy

The most president-centered of all decision processes lies in the realm of crisis policy. **Crisis policies** are "responses to immediate problems that are perceived to be serious, that have burst on the policy makers with little or no warning, and that demand immediate action" (Ripley and Franklin 1991, 24). Key players in the crisis game include the president and his top military and diplomatic advisers. The nation—indeed, the world—turns to the president for leadership. For Congress, crises produce a game of "follow the leader." Though crisis decisions are quite visible, Congress usually has little involvement in them and acts in a quiet, supportive way to assist the president. Independent congressional influence is at its lowest in formulating crisis policy.

The Persian Gulf War of 1991 provides an apt example. With the Iraqi invasion of Kuwait on August 3, 1990, a crisis unexpectedly burst upon Washington. After some initial hesitation, President Bush deployed 200,000 American troops to guard against Iraqi territorial encroachments into Saudi Arabia. Most of Bush's energies were directed toward the United Nations Security Council, rather than the Congress, which acquiesced to the president's initiative. The House and Senate passed separately-worded, nonbinding resolutions in support of the initial troop deployment in early October. Though Bush did consult with congressional leaders regularly throughout the crisis, he chiefly focused on coordinating U.N. opposition to the Iraqi regime.

The U.N. Security Council approved an economic embargo of Iraq and in December, passed a resolution allowing the use of force to repel Iraq from Kuwait. By this time American troops in the Gulf numbered more than half a million. Congress had avoided debating the Gulf situation, but after the Security Council action, calls increased for a debate and vote. Just before the U.N. deadline of January 20

ONE VIEW OF CONGRESSIONAL LEADERSHIP ON THE EVE OF THE GULF WAR

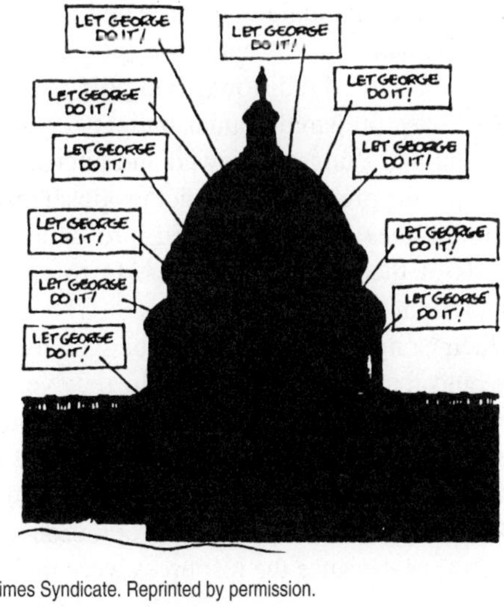

for Iraqi withdrawal, Bush asked the legislature to endorse the Security Council position. The House and, by a mere six-vote margin, the Senate approved the use of troops to expel Iraq from Kuwait. The consequent war and military victory resulted from Bush's actions as crisis leader. Congress avoided the issue and then, reluctantly deferred to the commander in chief at the last minute. At the conclusion of the war, the legislature began after-the-fact oversight of America's diplomatic and military operations in the Gulf. When the dust of a crisis settles, Congress seeks lessons from the experience through investigation.

THE NEW GAME ENVIRONMENT: A DEFICIT ERA

The role of Congress in each of the above types of policy ultimately depends on the perceptions of congressional players. Distributive and structural policies remain noncontroversial if Congress views them as such. The president leads in strategic and crisis policy because lawmakers let him. Few legislators miss weighing in on important regulatory and redistributive issues. The fiscal problems of the last decade, however, altered the strategies and play in foreign and domestic policy arenas.

It is now less possible for distributive and structural policy strategies to produce legislative victories in an era of tight budgets. Benefits to any group in society are now more likely to be seen as coming at the budgetary expense of another. Such initiatives produce more of the zero-sum games that are commonly associated with regulatory and redistributive policies. Deficit reduction efforts produce negative-sum conflict in which all players lose something. As a result, Congress passes fewer laws nowadays, but fights more over its legislative product. To understand why this harsh game environment arose, it is necessary to examine the budget problems that produced it.

TRADITIONAL BUDGETING

The era of traditional budgeting stretched from 1921, when the federal government adopted systematic annual budgeting procedures, to 1974, when major budget reforms became law. Traditional budgeting operated as a consistent, predictable game. Agencies prepared annual budget requests which the president's Office of Management and Budget reviewed and altered in accord with the chief executive's wishes. Once the president's budget proposal arrived on Capitol Hill, the Appropriations committees divided it again into chunks and held subcommittee hearings with heads of the affected agencies. In this way, Congress refigured the budget from the bottom up.

When Congress composed the budget, **incrementalism** reigned. The common strategy held that each agency should receive its base and a "fair share" of additional monies available. From the 1950s to about 1970, increasing revenues poured into the government, allowing appropriators the happy task of awarding increments of additional funds among the agencies (Wildavsky 1988, chapter 3). Congress usually deferred to the decisions of Appropriations subcommittees. Spending gradually nudged upward, because the resources were there to accommodate it.

House Speaker Foley (D-WA) talks strategy on the eve of a crucial 1993 budget vote. Watching are first-term Representative Blanche Lambert (D-AR), then-White House Budget Director Leon Panetta and House Majority Leader Richard Gephardt (D-MO).

BUDGET REFORM

The budgeting game became more conflictual during the presidency of Richard Nixon. As the economy slowed and deficits began to appear, Nixon initiated an inter-institutional competition over the spending power. Several times he successfully vetoed major appropriations bills. He also aggressively impounded spending for programs he opposed. This led Congress to seek new institutional strategies and resources for prevailing in budget battles with the president. The result was a sweeping change in budgeting rules in the Budget and Impoundment Control Act of 1974.[2]

Congress recast the budgeting game. Retained were the powers of the authorizing committees, which formulated specific laws for programs that included a legal maximum for spending, or authorization, for each program under their jurisdiction. The Appropriations committees continued to make specific spending decisions, constrained by the legal maximums of the authorizations. A new layer of committees, the Budget committees, were to formulate budget resolutions to guide authorizing and appropriations committees in their annual work. Budget resolutions set maximum allowable spending in each of nineteen policy categories and specify a minimum amount of taxes for the coming fiscal year. Also created was the Congressional Budget Office, an independent source of budget expertise for Congress. Previously, the president's Office of Management and Budget had dominated the arena of budget analysis.

---

[2] For a discussion of the impoundment provisions of this act, see chapter 8.

It was the job of the Budget committees to get Congress to approve budget resolutions and stick to them, so that the legislature could present a disciplined alternative to presidential spending preferences. The deadline for passage of the first resolution was May 15. The resolution would guide authorizers and appropriators in their summer work, but it was merely advisory, setting targets to aim for. The second resolution was to pass in early September and would be binding—establishing the final totals that Congress had to meet by the beginning of the fiscal year on October 1. If Appropriations or tax committees did not meet the resolution's targets, passage of a reconciliation bill became necessary. The reconciliation bill was to bring authorizations and appropriations in line with the totals included in the second resolution.

Instead of "bottom up" traditional budgeting, the new rules promised a "top down" coordination of the budget by Congress that would give the legislature more autonomy from the White House in spending decisions. The budget game proceeded reasonably smoothly in the late 1970s, mainly because Congress usually passed second resolutions that accepted the totals proposed by spending and tax committees. As a result, deficits began to edge upward. Red ink plus high inflation in 1980 helped to propel Ronald Reagan into the White House. Along with Reagan came some major changes in budgeting, and eventually larger deficits.

THE REAGAN BUDGET REVOLUTION

The sweeping budget changes of 1981—producing less domestic spending, more funds for defense and lower taxes—seemed to many a budget revolution. The changes became possible due to a clever strategy involving the 1974 law's reconciliation provisions. Usually, reconciliation legislation was employed in late September to pare back authorizations and appropriations to conform with the limits of the second budget resolution. However, in 1981, David Stockman, Reagan's budget director, proposed using reconciliation procedures with the first budget resolution in the spring. Changing the rules would change the game. This would allow budget cuts to pass as one big reconciliation bill, rather than bit by bit. Further, by passing cuts in the spring, the mischievous hands of authorizing and Appropriations committees, who wanted to protect their programs, would be tied. Nothing in the budget act prevented this strategy. In fact, congressional Democrats had employed it in 1980.

Why adopt this strategy? Reagan's Republicans had gained control of the Senate, fifty-three to forty-seven, but would have to woo southern Democrats to prevail in the Democratic-controlled House. Requiring a single up-or-down vote on the president's program would maximize support for it. Any number of particular domestic spending cuts would fail if voted upon individually, but the president could effectively sell a broad package.

The strategy proved to be a stunning success. In the spring, Congress passed a reconciliation bill including $35 billion in domestic spending cuts and a $27 billion increase in defense expenditures. In the summer, a similar all-or-nothing strategy produced a huge tax cut that reduced revenues by $750 billion over seven years. Do not assume, however, that the contest always went smoothly for the administration. Success required numerous and complex bargaining games that provided side payments to southern Democrats in the House, the crucial swing votes. Many legislators tried to protect their districts from cuts, in the time-honored tradition of the survival game. In the end, though, a new fiscal era had dawned.

WHY DEFICITS GREW

Budget policy in the 1980s created huge deficits. Formally, a deficit results when the federal government expends more funds in its formal budgetary operations during a fiscal year than it raises in revenue. Deficits are most usefully measured as a percentage of Gross Domestic Product, or GDP. GDP includes the total of the private goods and services produced, private investments made, public funds spent, and exports over imports generated in our national economy each year. Most economists urge that deficits normally be kept under 2 percent of GDP. In 1979, the deficit totalled $40 billion, 1.6 percent of GDP. By 1983, it totalled $221 billion, 6.3 percent of GDP, and persisted at high levels through the remainder of the decade. In 1992, the deficit stood at a whopping $295 billion, 5 percent of GNP.

Sad to say, the $295 billion total understates the size of the deficit problem. Congress moved $77.5 billion in spending for the Savings and Loan bailout to the next fiscal year in order to make the deficit smaller in an election year. The $51 billion "surplus" in revenues raised for the Social Security trust fund actually helped to fund the deficit. Future revenues will be needed to replenish the trust fund. Adding these totals produces an actual deficit of $418.5 billion, 7 percent of GDP for 1992.

Why worry about deficits? The public has found that their short-term economic effects are small indeed. After all, we have had over a decade of federal red ink accompanied usually by economic prosperity. The threat of deficits involves the long term. Persistent federal red ink means that nationally we are spending and borrowing to maintain our living standards. Much of the borrowed money comes from foreign nations, foremost among them Japan. Eventually we must pay back our borrowers with interest. Money to pay for this might otherwise have been used to stimulate our economic growth or pay for necessary governmental programs. In the long term, most economists agree, we will be the poorer for our "great consumption binge" (Courant and Gramlich 1985).

The causes of the deficits of the 1980s and 1990s are several. Throughout the decade the public preferred lower taxes and more federal services. Who wouldn't like something for nothing? National government had structured in increasing spending on entitlement programs—redistributive programs that guarantee certain citizens assistance regardless of budgetary conditions. Major entitlement programs include Social Security, Medicare, and veterans' benefits, and they all increased greatly in size in the 1980s. Also, defense spending mushroomed from 1981 to 1985.

In the mid-1980s, inflation dropped sharply, greatly reducing the flow of income tax revenue to the federal government. Also during that time, interest rates zoomed to historically high rates, raising the cost of borrowing. The substantial economic growth of the decade, however, did not match the increase in government outlays (Schier 1992, chapter 4; Schick 1990, 76–77; White and Wildavsky 1989, chapter 4).

Ultimately, blame for the problem must fall upon the public and their representatives. Since 1980, both Democrats and Republicans in Congress have rated deficit reduction low as a strategic goal. Republicans (including President Reagan) wanted defense spending and opposed tax increases of practically any type. Democrats preferred many types of domestic spending and opposed tax increases on those of modest income. The public complained about the deficits, but did not base their votes on the issue.

Because the costs of deficits are gradual and long term, Congress is particularly ill-equipped to deal with them. By 1985, the legislature had grasped this painful truth, and had devised new budgeting rules, known as Gramm-Rudman-Hollings, that would force the needed budgetary "hard choices." It sought to mobilize a congressional majority for the unpleasant work ahead by imposing a threat of fiscal disaster.

GRAMM-RUDMAN-HOLLINGS AND AFTER

Lawmakers on Capitol Hill don't like to deal with the large-scale, difficult choices that deficit reduction requires. As Randall Ripley writes: "Most members of Congress are happiest when dealing with policies issue by issue" (Ripley 1988, 386). Deficit reduction makes success in the survival game less certain. Serious attention to federal red ink requires overall discipline that legislators find electorally risky and substantively unpleasant. Deficit reduction also was a negative-sum game—all lawmakers would be worse off with programs cut and taxes increased, but some more than others.

Gramm-Rudman-Hollings, passed in 1985, set new rules to force the issue on Congress. The law set deficit-reduction targets for a five-year period. It then required Congress either to make the tough choices that would meet the targets, or to accept brutal, automatic across-the-board spending cuts to reach them. The game here was one of budgetary "chicken"—a battle of nerves to force Congress to get serious about deficit reduction or suffer a fiscal collision.

The Gramm-Rudman-Hollings bill, in effect from 1985 to 1990, did not work, for several reasons. First, the law declared that Congress would get serious about the deficit in the future, without actually producing any deficit reduction itself. Second, if Congress violated the law's budget target after the fiscal year for that target had begun, it then required a majority vote of Congress to enforce the law. No such votes occurred. The legislature would claim to hit a target on paper, and once the fiscal year started, conveniently ignore it. Joseph White and Aaron Wildavsky capture the flawed strategy behind the law: "Gramm-Rudman-Hollings did not really give anything to anybody. Each faction's stake in GRH was negative; it would not help them, but it would hurt others" (White and Wildavsky 1989, 503–504). Democrats and Republicans, facing painful deficit reduction, could each try to place the greater cost on the other side, or they together could evade the whole exercise. Is it any surprise that both sides ducked?

The centrality of deficit reduction made the major work of Congress since 1980 an exercise in **dedistributive policy.** Distributive policy distributes concentrated benefits to a few at a small and diffused cost to many, but dedistribution imposes large and immediate costs on many while providing very diffused and gradual benefits, evident to a relative few. Because dedistributive policy impairs success at the survival game, hard choices dictated policy avoidance. Though Congress cut spending and raised taxes several times during the 1980s, their efforts were not enough to redirect the deficits on a downward track over time.

Finally, in 1990 Congress and the president agreed to a major package of tax increases and spending cuts after months of difficult bargaining. The plan cut the deficit by $496 billion over five years—real progress. Unfortunately, the recession of 1991–92 caused the red ink to flow freely again (see box 9.4). In response, Congress passed another deficit reduction plan at the behest of President Clinton that relied more heavily on taxes than the 1990 agreement. The plan promises to move the deficit downward for four years, after which it will trend higher again. A long-deficit solution remains elusive. Proposals in the GOP's 1994 "Contract with America" recognize defecit problems, but include hard-to-keep promises.

BOX 9.4 1990 Deficit Reduction: The Big Blame Game

In blame game politics, opposing sides are more interested in demonstrating the evil of their opponents than solving the ultimate problem at issue. The deficit reduction of 1990 featured blame game politics as George Bush and the Democratic Congress traded accusations over whose proposals were worse for America.

In early 1990, with future deficit projections surging beyond $300 billion, Bush launched a series of bipartisan talks on deficit reduction between administration officials and congressional leaders. Democrats first won a round of the image game by forcing the President on June 26 to contradict his famous 1988 campaign promise of "Read my lips—no new taxes!" This flip-flop figured in his 1992 defeat. Bush for the first time publicly acknowledged the need for more revenues in a deficit reduction package.

Bipartisan talks wore on until the eve of the 1992 fiscal year, October 1. The final bipartisan package proposed to Congress contained something to offend just about every legislator. The five-year package contained $147 billion in new taxes, enraging many Republicans, and regressive taxes and cuts in Medicare that infuriated many Democrats. Despite the urging of party leaders, the House voted the package down by 179 to 254 on October 5.

Democrats then indulged themselves in an assault on Bush's image. George Bush, they claimed, wanted the middle class and the poor to pay for the deficit that tax cuts to the rich had created. Republicans, for their part, resented any tax increases. On October 16, the House passed a Democratic alternative plan that taxed the rich much more heavily. A representative example of Democratic glee came from Representative Larry Smith (D-FL), who challenged Republicans: "Whether you like it or not, whether the President likes it or not, we are going to have a progressive tax policy that works for America."[a] The White House, in response, blamed the Democrats for being too eager to raise taxes.

Continued on next page

BOX 9.4 Continued

The Senate, meanwhile, passed a bipartisan plan hammered out in the Finance Committee by Senator Lloyd Bentsen (D-TX). The conference committee became a three-way bargaining game involving White House, House and Senate negotiators. Final agreement on a compromise plan came on October 27, less than two weeks before the elections. The margins of approval were narrow: 228 to 200 in the House, fifty-four to forty-five in the Senate. The final package contained $496 billion in deficit reductions over five years. Compared to the original plan, tax increases focused more on high-income individuals, cuts in Medicare were less, and larger defense cuts.

The White House and Congress both perversely succeeded at the blame game, because both suffered in popularity due to the partisan fireworks. President Bush's poll support dropped substantially in October, House members in November saw their re-election margins drop by an average of 5 percent. Bush's violation of his anti-tax pledge contributed to his defeat in 1992.

This blame game cost all of its players, and unfortunately did not do enough to solve the deficit problem. As a result of the 1991 recession, deficit estimates again mushroomed, making another round of tough fiscal decisions inevitable.

[a] George Hager and Pamela Fessler, 1990, "Negotiators Walk Fine Line to Satisfy Both Chambers," *Congressional Quarterly,* (October 20): 3484.

NO EASY ANSWERS

The difficulty of legislating in a period of fiscal austerity led Congress to frequently adopt a strategy of avoiding responsibility for the tough choices. The blame game of 1990 and Gramm-Rudman-Hollings are examples of how treacherous policymaking had become. Dedistributive policy continued to have political costs in 1993. Bill Clinton's popularity dropped as Republicans labelled his deficit reduction plan Democratic "tax and spend."

Inadequate resources create **dedistributive policy games** over deficit reduction, the most dreaded sort of policy challenge that a popularly-elected legislature can confront. Budget conflict also creates competition over legislation that in other times might seem benignly distributive. Water projects, for example, face greater budgetary hurdles than ever before. Those projects now come at the expense of other coveted programs.

In evaluating public policy, we need to find solutions that solve the problem but also are consistent with the actions of a representative republic. To solve the deficit, however, the harsh action necessary seems almost impossible from a representative institution. This is an epic challenge to Congress and president alike. Can our representative republic handle a problem of this magnitude successfully? We shall see.

CONCLUSION

Policy substance shapes the course of policy games in Congress. Distributive and structural policies involve diffuse costs and concentrated benefits, allowing subgovernments important influence over the allocation of such benefits. Redistributive and regulatory domestic policies involve higher costs for more interests and often create major policy competition between president and Congress. Strategic and crisis foreign policy cause Capitol Hill to often defer to White House leadership.

Since 1980, policymaking on Capitol Hill has operated in a difficult game environment. Large deficits and divided government challenged the established policy tendencies of localism, incrementalism, and fragmentation. Deficit reduction is dedistributive policy, with large costs and diffuse, long-term benefits. It creates a negative-sum game in which action on the deficit makes most players worse off. Despite the passage of Gramm-Rudman-Hollings and repeated spending cuts and tax increases, the deficit by the 1990s remains quite large in historical terms. It forms the largest policy challenge facing the president and Congress.

IN DEPTH

1. The deficit problem promises to influence the outcomes of congressional games for years to come. How do deficits alter strategic calculations in Congress? What actions are necessary to reduce the deficit? Would serious deficit reduction require a transformation of the policymaking process in Congress?

REFERENCES

Calleo, David. 1992. *The Bankrupting of America: Funny Money and the Federal Budget Deficit.* New York: Morrow.

Kettl, Donald F. 1992. *Deficit Politics: Public Budgeting in Its Institutional and Historical Context.* New York: Macmillan.

Peterson, Peter G. 1993. "Facing Up." *The Atlantic Monthly* (October 1993) 77–90.

Schier, Steven E. 1992. *A Decade of Deficits: Congressional Thought and Fiscal Action.* Albany: State University of New York Press.

White, Joseph, and Aaron Wildavsky. 1989. *The Deficit and the Public Interest.* Berkeley: University of California Press.

2. Chapter nine identified several policy strategies of Congress: localism, fragmentation, incrementalism, and symbolism. Analyze and evaluate each of these traits in terms of (1) whether they further congressional power in comparison with other Washington powers, and (2) whether they are proper uses of congressional time and resources. How might the operation of Congress be improved by altering its mix of these strategies?

REFERENCES

Arnold, R. Douglas. 1990. *The Logic of Congressional Action.* New Haven: Yale University Press.

Fiorina, Morris. *Congress: Keystone of the Washington Establishment.* New Haven: Yale University Press.

Mayhew, David. 1974. *Congress: The Electoral Connection.* New Haven: Yale University Press.

Parker, Glenn R. 1989. *Characteristics of Congress: Patterns in Congressional Behavior.* Englewood Cliffs, N.J.: Prentice-Hall.

3. Which of the policy types examined in this chapter are relatively easy for Congress to address? Why? What does this tell us about the overall strengths and weaknesses of Congress as an institution?

REFERENCES

Arnold, R. Douglas. 1990. *The Logic of Congressional Action.* New Haven: Yale University Press.

Lowi, Theodore J. 1964. "American Business, Public Policy, Case-Studies and Political Theory." *Journal of Politics* 16: 677–715.

Ripley, Randall B. 1988. *Congress: Process and Policy,* 4th ed. New York: W. W. Norton.

Ripley, Randall B., and Grace A. Franklin. 1991. *Politics, the Bureaucracy and Public Policy.* Pacific Grove, Calif.: Brooks/Cole.

4. Select a major current issue—health care, environmental protection, abortion rights—and analyze it in reference to the policy concepts included in chapter 9. To what extent is it subject to localism, fragmentation, incrementalism, or symbolism? Into which policy category or categories does it fall? What games are played concerning this issue? What does your analysis suggest to you about the ultimate fate and success of the policy?

REFERENCES

Ripley, Randall A., and Grace A. Franklin. 1991. *Congress, the Bureaucracy and Public Policy.* Pacific Grove, Calif.: Brooks/Cole.

On specific policies, *Congressional Quarterly Weekly Report* and *National Journal.*

Congressional documents, especially hearings and floor debate.

CHAPTER TEN

CONGRESS, REFORM, AND THE FUTURE

Games Can Change

Politicians and reformers can tinker with the system, but major changes that affect both policy and the way the game is played also have to come from the grass roots beyond the beltway. When voters straddle, most politicians straddle. (Smith 1988, 713)

The system won't be the system under term limits. Term limits will change the rules of the game. (Political scientist Mark Petracca, quoted in Moore 1992, 2054)

Congress and its games exist in time. The preceding chapters examined the behavior of the national legislature and its Members during the early 1990s. Some changes occur by design, but many do not. The game environment, players, rules, and strategies alter due to forces external to the institution. Reformers hope that the next edition of this book will need extensive revision, because they find much of current congressional practice unacceptable. This chapter examines the forces and strategies for change, proposed reforms of the players and rules, and explores what an ideal Congress might look like.

CHANGE AND REFORM

Though reformers often call themselves "advocates of change," change and reform are not identical concepts. **Change** refers to evolution of any sort, whether intended or unintended. **Reform** involves planning change with a specific goal in mind. The changes resulting from reform may not attain the goal the reformers desired. It is easy to be "for change," for it is inevitable. Successful reform, however, is a much more difficult proposition.

FORCES FOR CHANGE

Congressional evolution results because much legislative work involves continuous games. As the resources, norms, and expectations of the broader game environment alter, so do the contests involving Congress. Several aspects of the changing game environment deserve attention: ever more hostile public opinion, the increasing diversity of public and legislative players, altering technological resources and scarce budgetary resources.

Public opinion alters constantly, and in recent years, that change involved ever harsher public evaluation of all political institutions and Congress in particular (Ladd 1990, 57–58). Public disapproval of Congress recently reached record levels (see chapters 2 and 3). Clearly, the institution no longer commands the resource of public support. Several implications flow from this. First, Members find it increasingly more difficult to distinguish their individual reputations from that of Congress. This suggests that the recent increase in turnover will continue, either through electoral defeat or the retirements of frustrated legislators. Second, hostility toward Congress also compromises efforts to mount more activist government. As cynicism grows, the ability of Members to sell larger programs declines.

A second public trend is literally changing the face of Congress. As Asians, Latinos, and African-Americans steadily become a larger percentage of the American population, they command more resources (votes) in the electoral game. This will produce over time a rise in their numbers in Congress. Further, it is now clear that congressional elections are no longer a "man's game." Recent polls show that the public believes female candidates are more honest, compassionate, and less beholden to special interests than men (Morin 1992b, 36). Public expectations about female candidates suggest a continuing increase in female legislators.

Technological changes have transformed the environment of many congressional games. Improving information technology enhances the dispersion of information and the immediacy of political demands. In recent decades, this encouraged the demise of the role of the Senate as a "cooling saucer." Greater access to information resources altered public expectations about legislative responsiveness and broke down norms that evolved in an earlier time. One casualty was the apprenticeship norm in the Senate. A greater transparency of decision making also resulted from increased technology. More accessible information arms congressional players with increased resources in the policy game. Coalitions of "mixed expectations" become less possible in an information-rich environment.

The rise of new campaign technologies forms a major environmental alteration. Political parties control far fewer campaign resources than they did fifty years ago, leading to a widespread shift in the expectations about candidate behavior. Candidates now routinely create their own independent political operations without party "shoeleather" assistance. As a result, party leaders cannot consistently enforce a "party line." Leaders instead must painstakingly build partisan coalitions vote by vote.

Beyond technological changes, another vast shift in resources continues to affect the game environment. That is the onset of fiscal austerity, producing many changes in congressional behavior well summarized by Roger Davidson as "cutback politics" (Davidson 1991, 71–74). Chapter 9 indicated how an absence of funds increases the number of zero-sum and negative-sum policy games in legislature. The conflictual environment will persist until the deficit shrinks dramatically and the economy surges.

STRATEGIES FOR REFORM

Successful reformers understand the altering game environment and marshal their efforts to harness forces of change moving in their direction. Reform involves planned change and its anticipated and unanticipated consequences. The broad strategic challenge is to convince lawmakers that the anticipated benefits of proposed improvements exceed anticipated costs. An understanding of the general forces for change and a concrete knowledge of strategically important aspects of game situations is indispensable.

Reforms often fall prey to the "magnitude principle" in Congress. Reforms that are too large, like a revamping of the electoral system, or too small, like management improvements for congressional cafeterias, seldom get enacted. The costs of change are too great for large reforms, while the benefits of change from small reforms may be too tiny to fight for. Reform situations often involve a game pitting the "new dogs versus the old dogs." Newcomers to Congress often display impatience with established procedures, but they must contend with more powerful senior Members who benefit from or simply are comfortable with current procedures and oppose reforms. In 1993, the caucus of first-term Democrats in the House called for a 25 percent decrease in the appropriation for House operations, but Speaker Foley informed them that such a "very dramatic" reform was unlikely (Donovan 1993, 809). The astute reformer tries to defang the old dogs before they can bite.

Successful reform depends heavily on strategic timing. Broad changes in national politics can alter the game environment for particular reforms. National political crises surrounding Watergate gave impetus to reforms of campaign finance and House procedures. Similarly, the House bank scandal in 1991–92 increased public dissatisfaction and boosted the hopes for all sorts of reforms, from committee reorganization to ethics (Hook 1992, 1579). Another important strategic resource for reformers concerns the justifications they present. During times of scandal and crisis, such as the middle 1970s and early 1990s, arguments based on the transcendent values of honesty, openness, and democracy hold special sway. Success in reform often depends on the effective use of ethical arguments.

Though elevated, abstract criteria can be effective justifications for reform, it is also strategically helpful to argue for a reform in terms of vague goals. An absence of strict criteria for judging the success of reforms can make them less threatening and more palatable to Members. Another prudent strategy involves buying off opponents. Grandfathering in reform provisions reduces their cost to current Members, making enactment more possible. The 1979 amendments to the Federal

Election Campaign Act are a case in point. The amendments barred conversion of campaign funds for personal use but exempted all House members in office at the time of enactment.[1] Understanding the players and their motives ranks as essential for aspiring reformers and scholars alike.

THE PLAYERS IN CONGRESSIONAL REFORM

The American public is a central but often inattentive player in reform games. In recent years, the inconsistency of public opinion has complicated the task of reform. One example involves attempts to replace incumbent officeholders. Even in the turbulent 1990s, the rate of incumbent re-election in the House and Senate remains high. Congressional scholars have long explained why we love our Congressperson but hate the Congress (Mayhew 1974a, chapter 1; Fenno 1993, 440–447). In recent years, the "fire wall" between public opinion about incumbents and the overall institution has weakened, but does persist.

A similar double standard employed by the public involves the merits of public spending. Congressional boondoggles and parochialism serve the national interest in the minds of the constituents who receive the largess. The demand for more particular spending issues steadily from constituents. Yet the public as a whole believes 46 percent of all spending is waste and demands a balanced budget (Dionne 1992, 11). The message is not lost on lawmakers, each of whom finds delivering benefits a useful survival game strategy. Deficit reduction becomes a formidable task.

Public indignation can erupt over a specific scandal, concerning, for example, the House Bank or Zoe Baird's child care.[2] In such instances, it can be a powerful force promoting a reform agenda. More frequently, the public remains surly and inattentive, complicating the task of Congress through its inconsistency about what government should do.

Other important players include the professional reform lobbies of Washington. Two of the most prominent are Ralph Nader's Public Citizen and Common Cause, headed by Fred Wertheimer. Such groups push hard for reform of Congressional ethics, with particular criticism directed at the relationship between lawmakers and lobbyists. They seek stiffer limits on the amount of money spent to influence Congress. Public financing of campaigns is a long-held goal.

Strategically, such groups must develop a strong sense of timing to capitalize on periodic waves of public indignation toward Congress. Pragmatism in forming

---

[1]After several years of complaints about this by reform groups, Congress did away with the grandfather clause in a November 1989 pay raise bill. The repeal did not go into effect, however, until January 1993. This allowed senior Members several years to decide whether to retire and enjoy their campaign treasuries. See Herbert Alexander, 1992, *Financing Politics: Money, Elections and Political Reform,* Washington: Congressional Quarterly, pp. 42–43.

[2]The scandal over the House Bank in 1991 erupted when the media reported that House members routinely received unlimited, cost-free "overdraft protection" at the bank. Several Members who floated hundreds of "bad checks" retired or failed to win re-election in 1992. Zoe Baird was President Clinton's initial nominee for attorney general in 1993. She was forced to withdraw when the media disclosed that she and her husband had hired illegal aliens to provide child care and had not reported their income to the Internal Revenue Service.

alliances helps as well. For example, in 1989 Nader teamed with conservative activist Paul Weyrich of the Free Congress Foundation to oppose an increase in Congressional pay (*Congressional Quarterly Almanac* 1989, 53). Their effort garnered much publicity as they capitalized on a furor further incited by radio talk-show hosts. Eventually the pay raise went through, but Nader and Weyrich strengthened their organizations through their very public activism. Reform lobbies have arguments at the ready, but need supportive public opinion to prevail.

Reformers face tough sledding in Congress because of the frequently cool reception they receive from the pivotal players in reform games, the lawmakers themselves. The perspective of incumbency shapes reform possibilities on Capitol Hill. Campaign finance reform stalled for years over a difference in perspective between senators and representatives and between Republicans and Democrats. The Senate in recent years has been willing to sharply limit PAC contributions, but the House less so. House members face re-election more frequently and usually are more dependent on PAC contributions. Each of the congressional parties remains suspicious of the reform plans of the other, believing that the rival party's proposals seek to establish partisan advantage in elections. Incumbents are not inclined to surrender their resources for the survival game, despite what reform lobbies demand. Supporting players behind the incumbents are their staffs, who also seek to maintain their own resources—jobs and salaries.

An additional set of players includes the "other" lobbyists, whose activities the reformers seek to curtail or eliminate. Lobbyists don't get far in appealing to public opinion, but can find a more sympathetic audience among incumbents. One strategy they employ in reform contests is to provide arguments and analysis for incumbents who oppose reform. Another is to accept the inevitability or some reforms and find ways to continue their operations under the new rules. Lana Batts, director of the American Financial Services Association, claims that "whenever the rules are changed, the smart lobbyists learn how to work with maximum effectiveness in the new situation" (interview with author).

REFORMS AFFECTING THE PLAYERS

Contests to reform the activities of incumbents and lobbyists involve particularly difficult and complex maneuvers. Three areas for reform have received much attention in recent years: campaign finance, term limits, and congressional ethics.

CAMPAIGN FINANCE REFORM

Congress came steadily closer to comprehensive reform of campaign finance in the early 1990s. A campaign finance bill passed in 1992, but President Bush vetoed it. At the urging of President Clinton, the Senate and House passed bills in 1993. A conference committee finally reported a compromise bill in late September of 1994. The compromise established voluntary campaign spending limits and provided subsidies for candidates accepting them. It also lowered PAC contribution limits and banned the use of bundling and soft money in campaigns. Angry Senate Republicans filibustered the bill to death at the end of the 103rd Congress.

Advocates of reform found many of these provisions inadequate. Common Cause reluctantly supported the reform process but hoped it was merely a stepping stone toward total public finance, the only reform capable in their eyes of making the election game fair (Donovan 1993, 1533). Other reformers objected to anything less than full public financing, arguing that half-measures amounted to little more than an incumbent-protection plan (Donovan 1993b, 1533). Republicans, in contrast, viewed both public financing and any limits on challenger spending as inherently pro-incumbent. They also viewed systems of financial inducements to encourage voluntary acceptance of spending limits as so coercive as to be unconstitutional. President Bush summarized their objections in his 1992 veto message: "There is nothing voluntary about the spending limits in this act. . . . What we do not need is a taxpayer-financed incumbent protection plan" (Bush 1992, 65).

Republicans approached the issue from a partisan perspective, but the professional reformers who want total public financing have their biases as well. David Broder argues,

> Taking money out of politics will clearly reduce the influence of the average union or antiabortion group member, but it won't touch the access the typical Yale Law School or Kennedy School of Government graduate enjoys. So tell me: Which side of this debate represents elitist influence, and which represents populism? (Broder 1993, 6)

A careful examination of the players in campaign finance politics reveals that fair and successful solutions may be more elusive than they initially seem.

TERM LIMITS

Another spirited contest over reform involves proposals to limit the terms of House members and senators. In 1990, Colorado became the first state to pass by referendum twelve-year term limits on representatives and senators. In 1992, similar referenda won in fourteen states. Opponents of the reform raise the issue of its constitutionality. Can a state unilaterally limit the terms of its national legislators, or is a constitutional amendment necessary? In 1994, Speaker Foley successfully challenged in federal district court the constitutionality of newly passed term limits in his home state. Term-limits proponents planned an appeal to the Supreme Court. Foley's suit contributed to his 1994 election defeat.

The argument over term limits primarily concerns the power of incumbency. Proponents of limits make several arguments. Term limits insure more competitive elections by forcing incumbent retirements. Ability, not seniority, would then decide influence in Congress. The quality of candidates would increase because power in Congress would be more accessible to newcomers. Term limits curb the culture of professionalism that increases the distance between governors and the governed (Fund 1992, 225–240). Political scientist Mark Petracca emphasizes this last point: "Extensive experience in government tends to produce legislators who are more interested in defending government than they are in solving serious problems" (Petracca 1990, 8).

Opponents of term limits counter with many arguments of their own. Term limits restrict voters' choices in elections, and will disrupt the congressional norm of seniority. Congress already experiences substantial turnover due to retirements.

The only form of term limitation favored by Congress...
GRANLUND ©1991 MIDDLESEX NEWS.

DAVID E. GRANLUND, Courtesy Middlesex News

Most important, term limits deprive voters of the most competent legislators. Political scientist Nelson Polsby explains:

> . . . in order to take seriously the idea of limiting congressional terms, one must believe that the job of a representative in Congress is relatively simple, and quickly and easily mastered. It is not. . . . Much Congress-bashing these days actually complains about high re-election rates, as though a large population of ill-served constituents would be preferable. (Polsby 1990, 18)

The federal courts form the key arena for this contest. If they permit state-imposed term limits, Congress will alter drastically. The consequences of this reform are far-reaching for the rules, norms, and players.

ETHICS

Now that the House bank has closed and Congress has eliminated many "perks," three issues dominate contests over legislative ethics: regulating lobbying, extending federal civil rights and labor law protection to congressional staff, and devoting more resources to the problem of sexual harassment.

Chapter 6 notes that lobbying regulations receive very weak enforcement. Reformers seek more public disclosure of lobbying expenses and activities and outright bans of certain activities, like flying legislators to resorts for "conferences." Joan Claybrook, president of Public Citizen, claims that "Most of these trips are nothing more than lobbyist-funded vacations for the nation's lawmakers, a form of legalized bribery" (De Witt 1991, A16).

The furious reaction to charges that Senator Robert Packwood (R-OR) had sexually harassed female staff sparked pressure for ethics reform in Congress.

Others argue that restrictions on lobbyists will redistribute influence and access, but not necessarily more fairly. David Broder argues that the interests who hire lobbyists do so because they fear they will not be heard without them. But what of those interests that don't need paid help? They tend to be the peers and friends of lawmakers. He concludes, "In a world without paid lobbyists, access and influence would still exist. But they would be distributed very differently. And the winners . . . would be the elite" (Broder 1993, 6).

The Thomas/Hill confirmation hearings and charges that Senator Robert Packwood (R-OR) made unwelcome advances toward at least ten women, some of whom worked for him, over the course of his career, brought the sexual harassment issue squarely before Congress. Proponents of strong sanctions for sexual harassment argue they are necessary to erase the traditional problem of sexism in Congress. Feminist Naomi Wolf argues that the Thomas confirmation was "a civic betrayal of women" and that sexual harassment is the "culture of the Hill. . . . a legislative body composed only of men is virtually as useless to [women] as would be a straightforward policy of gender apartheid" (Wolf 1991, C2).

"I don't think lobbyists are taking our attempts at ethics reform seriously."

A possible solution entails applying federal civil rights and labor laws to congressional staffs. Both chambers now have fair employment practices offices. The Senate in 1991 applied some sections of civil rights laws to their staffs, but large legal gaps remain. Reformers call Congress "the last plantation" because of the exemption it grants itself to occupational safety and labor laws. Opponents contest the feasibility and constitutionality of such reforms. During the 1991 Senate debate on extended protection, former Senator Warren Rudman (R-NH) claimed that "To submit the employment decisions of this body as it related to our committee staffs or our personal staffs to a review by a judge who is appointed for life tramples any semblance of separation of power" (*Congressional Record,* 29 October 1991, S15376). A bill to broaden the application of federal labor laws to congressional staffs passed the House 427–4 in August 1994. The bill died, however, when the Senate failed to vote on it before adjourning.

The arenas for ethical reform include the House and Senate Ethics committees, which consider charges against individual Members, and the chambers themselves, which set up their ethics enforcement processes and pass rules affecting lobbyists and employees. Controversy over the Senate Ethics committee's handling of the Keating Five and other ethics cases has called into question the operation of congressional ethics enforcement. Senator Dan Coats (R-IN) put it this way: "You would not try an accused person before a jury of his family. But in the eyes of most Americans, that is essentially what the Senate Ethics Committee amounts to." (*Congressional Record,* 7 November 1991, S16242) Still, ethics lapses can be costly. Former Ways and Means chair Dan Rostenkowski (D-IL) lost re-election in 1994 while under multiple indictment for misuse of office funds.

REFORM OF INSTITUTIONAL RULES

Much recent criticism of Congress focused on the rules structuring the legislative process. Lawmakers and observers of Congress complain that the large number of committees has created jumbled jurisdictions. The gradual pace of Senate business and tradition of unlimited debate also seems anachronistic to many in the late twentieth century. Because Congress has handled its spending power poorly in recent years, many proposals exist to strengthen presidential veto authority over spending.

CONGRESSIONAL LAWMAKING

The creation of the Joint Committee on the Reorganization of Congress in 1992 marked another round of attempts to revise the rules of lawmaking. Previous attempts at such reform, in the House in 1974 and Senate in 1977, produced less than resounding success (see box 10.1). A central focus of reform efforts is the structure of the standing committee system. The format of the committee system has not altered since the Legislative Reorganization Act of 1946. Critics argue that since then, the number of committees and subcommittees have grown and jurisdictions now overlap, producing complex bill referrals that slow the legislative process. The complexity produces inefficiency and weaker accountability in lawmaking.

BOX 10.1 Game Theory and Game Reality: Reforming the Committee System

No rules reform in Congress involves greater stakes than the alteration of standing committee jurisdictions. The last major attempts at this occurred in the 1970s. House reformers, at the urging of their staff, relied on the abstract tenets of game theory to prevail in a hostile game environment. Senate reformers operated in a more favorable game environment and proved more flexible on reform specifics. The House effort failed totally; reformers won a limited victory in the Senate. What follows is a tale of two reforms.

In 1973 the House appointed a temporary select committee, headed by Richard Bolling (D-MO), to examine standing committee procedures and proposed reforms. The committee, upon the advice of its ambitious staff, utilized game theory to formulate what they thought were feasible reform goals. According to theory, equalizing committee jurisdictions and eliminating jurisdictional overlap would make the policy game fairer for all players.[a] Each lawmaker would have a more equal standing from which to play the game. Also, according to game theory, a large number of players would approve the new rules because they would increase each other's authority in the committee system.

The Bolling committee proposed a major overhaul of the committee system. For example, Ways and Means would lose all of its nontax jurisdiction, the Education and Labor Committee was to be split into two committees, and other committee jurisdictions would undergo major alteration. Lawmakers would be limited to one major committee assignment each. To increase fairness to all players, proxy voting in committees was to be banned, and Republicans were to receive a more proportional share of committee staff.

The sweeping reforms resulted in much opposition from committees whose jurisdictions came under attack. Ironically, the Bolling plan fell victim to a clever rules manipulation by its opponents. On May 9, 1974, the House Democratic caucus voted ninety-five to eighty-one for

BOX 10.1 Continued

a secret ballot on the reform proposal. This permitted the plan to be derailed anonymously. Then followed a 111 to ninety-five vote to refer the plan to another reform committee, headed by Julia Hansen (D-WA). The Hansen Committee later reported a much less ambitious reform proposal which did not alter committee jurisdictions. It passed the House on October 8, 1974.

Though in the abstract the Bolling plan might have seemed likely to appeal to many lawmakers, its proponents failed to comprehend two aspects of the game environment. First, most House members did not believe the House was in need of drastic committee reordering. Despite the appeal of abstract fairness, most seemed satisfied with current jurisdictions. Second, intense opposition from those lawmakers losing turf, particularly senior Members on established committees, created a strong bulwark of opposition. Players with great resources opposed reform strongly. Leroy Rieselbach summarized the reasons for failure: "The Bolling proposals cut too close to the bone for too many members; they created more losers than winners."[b]

A very different game environment existed at the time the Select Committee to Study the Senate Committee System filed its report on September 30, 1976. Unlike in the House, the demands of the committee system had produced an impossible scheduling situation for senators. From 1946 to 1976, the number of standing committees grew from fifteen to eighteen and subcommittees from ninety-six to 140. The average Senator held fourteen subcommittee assignments and the number of floor votes had increased dramatically over thirty years.[c] The status quo was costly, and reform could make many Members better off. A positive-sum outcome seemed possible.

The Stevenson Committee (named after its chair, Adlai Stevenson, [D-IL]) proposed a number of reforms that appealed to senators. Committee meetings were to be held in the mornings, with no roll calls before 2:00 P.M. Senators would hold only eight committee and subcommittee assignments each. Each senator could chair only one committee and only one subcommittee on the committee he or she chaired. Several committees would be merged and only one select committee would be maintained.

The proposals, like Bolling's, were sweeping, but the reception proved much more friendly. Both the Senate Rules Committee and floor weakened the scale of the committee restructuring. Five committees slated for merger remained intact. Still, the plan the Senate passed dropped the number of committees from thirty-one to twenty-five and created new daily scheduling procedures. Senators limited themselves to eleven committee appointments each. Steven Smith and Christopher Deering summarized the result as evolution "from an innovative restructuring to a moderate, yet significant, realignment of the old committee system."[d] The improved scheduling meant every senator gained from the reform.

Abstract notions of fairness mean little when player resources come under threat from large-scale changes in the rules. Only in a situation where current rules prove costly to players can even moderate reform occur. That was the situation in the Senate, but not in the House. Game theory matters little without an understanding of the realities of the game environment.

[a] Burton D. Sheppard, 1985, *Rethinking Congressional Reform: The Reform Roots of the Special Interest Congress,* Cambridge, Mass.: Schenkman, 127.

[b] Leroy Rieselbach, 1986, *Congressional Reform,* Washington: Congressional Quarterly Press, p. 65.

[c] "Senate Reorganizes its Committees," *1977 CQ Almanac,* p. 781.

[d] Steven S. Smith and Christopher J. Deering, 1990, *Committees in Congress,* Washington: Congressional Quarterly Press, p. 53.

Thomas Mann and Norman Ornstein, in an analysis provided to the Joint Committee on the Reorganization of Congress, argued for abolition of some committees and a more even workload across committees. To them, the current committee system

> . . . has evolved into one in which there is little direct accountability for legislative products and not enough coherence in the manner in which legislative issues are dealt with . . . bills have to pass through so many committees and be vetted by so many individuals that there is frequently no direct responsibility or accountability for the fate of legislation (Mann and Ornstein 1992, 33).

Joint Committee hearings on reform, however, featured many lawmakers defending the existence and jurisdictions of their committees and subcommittees. The committee ultimately did little to challenge existing jurisdictions. Altering jurisdictions means many players will lose resources for playing the policy game. That alone makes major reform of the committee system a long-shot reform strategy.

The "unpredictable and inefficient way in which the Senate often must conduct its business on the floor, despite the best efforts of its Majority Leader" (Bach 1992, 2) also draws criticism from reformers. The rules concerning floor debate and amendments lie at the heart of the difficulty. Unlimited debate occurs until unanimous consent ends it or sixty senators vote for cloture. Senators also can place a "hold" on a bill or resolution, effectively holding it from floor consideration under an implicit threat of a filibuster. Without a cloture vote, amendments can receive indefinite debate and need not be germane to the bill before the floor.

Despite the effects of the debate and amendments rules, senators seem unlikely to alter them soon. Entrepreneurial lawmakers find the rules give individuals greater power over policy than exists in the House. The long tradition of Senate debate earned it (sometimes mockingly) the title of "greatest deliberative body in the world." Senate baron Robert Byrd (D-WV) remains an outspoken proponent of Senate rules: "The fact that we allow for deliberation is an institutional strength" (Byrd 1993). Reform of Senate procedures remains a strategy for the long term.

THE LINE-ITEM VETO

Some in Congress view persistent budget deficits as conclusive evidence that the legislature can't responsibly handle its constitutional spending authority. More venturesome reformers call for a balanced budget amendment to the Constitution. A less expansive reform involves granting item veto authority to the president, which would allow him to veto parts of bills. Forty-three states give their governors some degree of item veto power. Presidents Reagan, Bush, and Clinton asked for the power in some form.

Many lawmakers remain wary of giving the president additional authority of this sort. Senator Mark Hatfield argues that granting such power would have "wide-ranging ramifications on the gamut of decisions made by Congress" because the president would be much more persuasive "if his words were buttressed with a veto stamp over individual projects and activities within our states or districts" (Fisher

1993, 202). Analyst Louis Fisher claims that an item veto would make Congress irresponsible because political posturing would produce extraneous parts of bills that a president had to veto (Fisher 1993, 201). Further, he contends a line-item veto would prove of little use on appropriations bills because they don't itemize spending. Some lawmakers accordingly propose an "enhanced rescission authority" that would strengthen the president even more than the line-item veto. Under this power, the president could veto items in spending bills. Congress could then reject the rescission by a majority vote of both chambers. In return, the president could then veto the rejection, requiring another veto override vote by Congress. The president would prevail unless Congress mustered both simple and two-thirds majorities once each in both chambers.

President Clinton, in a compromise with the House Majority leadership, asked for "expedited rescission authority" in 1993. In this procedure, the president could veto specific parts of spending in an appropriations bill. The rescission would occur only if both chambers subsequently approved it by majority vote. The proposal was withdrawn from the House floor in April 1993 when the Congressional Black Caucus refused to support it. Kweisi Mfume (D-MD), chair of the caucus, explained their position: "We feel very strongly on principled grounds that we should not be ceding power to the executive branch" (Hager 1993, 1008). Many lawmakers share Mfume's skepticism, making future reform at best uncertain.

The strategic prospects for substantial reforms in institutional rules remain dim because all require lawmakers to voluntarily give up important resources: committee jurisdiction, control over the spending power, or individual authority in the Senate. Experienced players understand their personal stakes in rules changes, and don't surrender authority in the midst of high-stakes, continuous games.

THE IDEAL CONGRESS

Reform advocates, in addition to accurately assessing their prospects for success, also need to comprehend the broader goals victory will achieve. A coherent vision of the ideal is the best ground for reform. Many of the above reforms, however, move in opposite directions: committee reorganization might make Congress institutionally stronger, but enhanced rescission authority would weaken it. A lucid set of reform goals aids in picking and choosing among possible innovations. Coherent reform begins with a clear statement of the criteria for reform.

CRITERIA FOR REFORM

The aspiring reformer might base innovation upon a theory of governmental institutions, arguing for executive or congressional supremacy in government, for example. Such theories, however, derive from even more fundamental assumptions about the ends of a legislature. Leroy Rieselbach identified three ends for the "good" legislature: responsibility, responsiveness, and accountability (Rieselbach 1986, 9). Proponents of reform can clarify their aspirations by defining them more concretely in terms of these criteria.

The criterion of **responsibility** concerns the ability of a legislature to solve problems with speed and effectiveness. To Rieselbach, "A responsible institution makes reasonably successful policies that resolve the major issues confronting the country" (Rieselbach 1986, 10). Some hold that incremental reforms can achieve this end, while others argue for a more fundamental transformation of our constitutional system. The public apparently believes Congress has behaved less responsibly in recent decades. A hostile public may make responsibility reform less possible, ironically, because public hostility has fueled more apathy than activism.

The criterion of **responsiveness** deals more with policy process than substance. "To be responsive, Congress must listen to and take account of the ideas and sentiments of those who will be affected by its actions: individual citizens, organized groups, local and state governments, and national executives" (Rieselbach 1986, 11). Responsiveness, however, can slow the legislative pace, impeding responsible policymaking. Gary Jacobson characterizes Congress as a legislature with "responsiveness without responsibility" (Jacobson 1987, 217). The public demand for responsive individual legislators may well obstruct reforms seeking greater responsibility.

Accountability is the third criterion. "Congress should be held accountable for what it does or does not do; that is, its decisions should be evaluated regularly by the citizenry" (Rieselbach 1986, 12). An accountable legislative system provides the public with an adequate opportunity to "throw the bums out." What comprises an adequate opportunity? Proponents of term limits argue the present system so discourages electoral challengers that Congress is now an unaccountable institution. Assessing accountability involves evaluating how incumbents affect the electoral system and whether political parties remain effective agents of accountability in congressional elections.

The above criteria, however, mean little unless joined with an empirical assessment of Congress. For that, it is helpful to return to the concepts of the game environment (norms, expectations, and resources) and game rules. What follows are some questions to aid in formulating a conception of an ideal Congress.

QUESTIONS TO PONDER

The Constitution makes Congress the most independent and powerful legislature in the world. Congressional players gain great authority from the rules. The founders stated many advantages of separated powers. Does legislative autonomy compromise responsibility too greatly? Does the separation of powers unduly weaken the accountability of national government?

A major duty of members of Congress is to represent and to be responsive to constituents. In parliamentary regimes, however, the party loyalty ranks higher on the list of legislators' duties (see box 10.2). The lawmaker serves constituents through the intermediary of a strong national party. This arrangement creates more collective accountability at the expense of responsiveness to local concerns. Is this a trade-off that America should accept? Congressional individualism contributes to incumbent electoral advantage. Is this problem severe enough to require a parliamentary regime in America? Congressional norms and public expectations would require radical transformation with such reform.

Committees in Congress serve as the expert formulators of policy. They also become the major targets for lobbyists seeking to influence legislation, resulting in committee responsiveness to organized interests. The founders did not intend such fragmentation and group concentration within Congress. Further, in parliamentary regimes, committees have little autonomy and receive little group attention (see box 10.2). Does committee power unduly weaken responsibility and accountability in Congress?

Chapter 1 noted how the founders succeeded in creating a slow and inefficient legislative process. Many conservatives hail this as a guarantor of prudent government. For them, responsible government is limited government. Liberals, however, often find congressional procedures obstructive to a properly activist government. When contemplating the ideal Congress, keep in mind that one's institutional preferences about responsiveness, responsibility, and accountability and one's ideological preferences may go hand in hand. It is fair to ask whether they should.

A common temptation exists to propose structural reforms which facilitate short-term success for one's policy preferences, but the damage one does to institutions in making them conform to issue preferences may be great. For example, liberals in the mid-twentieth century long argued for a stronger presidency, but found their dreams becoming nightmares during the Nixon presidency. A person's evaluation of the proper governmental institutions need not simply flow from issue preferences. A liberal may view the separation of powers as institutionally legitimate, despite the fact it often frustrates a liberal policy agenda. Perhaps it is best to argue about institutions and their attributes in terms of the fairest game—in terms of responsiveness, responsibility, and accountability—for all players, regardless of one's personal goals and strategies. This perspective may still lead you to advocate sweeping reforms in the rules and game environment of Congress.

CONGRESS AND THE FUTURE

The widespread public dissatisfaction with Congress comprises a strong force for change in the game environment. Charting the future involves predicting alterations in Congress, and much of it may be dramatic. One way to approach this is to assess the likely congressional response to the many challenges it now faces.

Public expectations are a crucial element in the environment of many congressional games. Reform discussion now occurs in Congress due to widespread public discontent. Campaign finance reform, term limits, and alterations in the committee system and other rules and procedures are all in play. Reforms need great publicity and success to produce dramatic, positive effects upon public opinion. It is difficult to recall a round of reforms that ever satisfied that high standard. Even if reforms do succeed in restoring public confidence, it is likely that the other stiff policy challenges of the 1990s will return the public quickly to its hostile stance. It is difficult to foresee any major alteration of public opinion about Congress.

BOX 10.2 The Differing Rules of Parliamentary Government

Calls for political reform seldom address the underlying constitutional rules that shape Congress. Such parochialism blinds us to the possibility of fundamental transformation of our national rules and game environment. Parliamentary government is the major alternative to the American system. Five characteristics, listed below, distinguish it from the U.S. rules.[a]

PARLIAMENTARY

1. A separate head of state appoints the head of government.
2. The head of government appoints a cabinet that governs.
3. The government rules via majority support in the legislature.
4. The head of government may advise the head of state to dissolve the legislature for elections.
5. The focus of power in the political system is the legislature and government.

SEPARATION OF POWERS (U.S.)

1. The president is head of state and government.
2. The president appoints a cabinet that serves him as subordinates collectively.
3. The president forms the government and is responsible only to the constitution, not legislature.
4. The president can neither dissolve nor coerce the legislature.
5. No central focus of power exists in the political system.

American constitutional rules have hardly become the norm in the world. When Europe democratized in the nineteenth century, its nations disregarded our procedures and instead adopted parliamentary government derived from the British model. Nor have our rules promoted peaceful democracy when applied elsewhere. The thirty-three third world countries that adopted our constitutional structure have suffered many political disruptions and frequent military rule. In contrast, two-thirds of the third world nations adopted parliamentary procedures and have experienced more peaceful and democratic government.[b]

If reformers seek better responsiveness, responsibility, and accountability in government, perhaps they should look to parliamentary-style innovations. Representatives and senators could serve four- and eight-year terms respectively, coinciding with presidential elections. This might encourage voting as an act of a collective government between the legislature and executive. Responsiveness and responsibility might then become more collective, making the party of politicians controlling government more readily accountable to the public.

How might that reform, or a more explicit shift to parliamentary government, alter the players, strategies and game environment of our national legislature? Would this result in greater responsiveness, responsibility, and accountability in government?

[a] Adapted from Douglas V. Verney, "Parliamentary Government and Presidential Government," in Arend Lijphart, ed, *Parliamentary Versus Presidential Government,* 1992, New York: Oxford University Press, pp. 31–47.

[b] Fred W. Riggs, "Presidentialism: A Problematic Regime Type," in Arend Lijphart, *Parliamentary Versus Presidential Government,* 1992, New York: Oxford University Press, pp. 217–222.

Public expectations may become more difficult to satisfy as the public grows more heterogeneous. The legislature will become more diverse in coming decades as the number of female and minority legislators steadily grows. Controversial domestic issues such as affirmative action, gay and lesbian rights, and welfare may become more prominent on the agenda, straining congressional norms of courtesy and reciprocity. Congress in the future may find itself engaged in sharp intergroup competition that consumes much of its time and resources.

Technological change promises to make Congress hyper-responsive to public opinion, and may produce new rules for popular participation that partially displace Congress. Call-in shows on television and radio encourage direct popular participation in policy discussion. Ross Perot's call for "national town meetings" drew a favorable response in 1992. In the future, the public may find additional technological resources allowing them more direct play in the policy game. National town hall meetings and binding referendums may displace legislative deliberation. James Madison no doubt would disapprove. Congress probably would oppose such reforms, but the durability of that opposition is questionable should public demands intensify.

Enhanced information technology means that decision making in Congress will grow ever more transparent. Being "on the scene" will become less important in understanding congressional action. Still, within the population, the motivation to use such resources remains unevenly distributed. The same minority of citizens who press lawmakers now will continue their work in the future. Reforms of lobbying and campaign finance rules will alter the strategic position of interest groups, but their presence will persist on Capitol Hill. Cheap information technology may actually curb the effects of interest group reform if it lowers the cost of group resources and consequently group influence.

Political parties remain the essential teams in Congress, but party leaders will continue to hold their offices through the strategy of following caucus opinion. Legislative individualism will continue its reign unless the national party organizations gain more control over campaign resources—money and media. Incumbent lawmakers frown upon such reforms. As a result, parties probably won't strengthen in the electoral arena. They will persist in the legislative arena, usually operating from the bottom-up, according to Member preferences, rather than top-down by leader direction.

Austerity politics will be with us into the twenty-first century, placing the monetary resources of government at a premium. The increasing burden of health care costs, 14 percent of GDP in 1994 and rising, will continue to encourage popular demands for health care reform and constrain government spending on non-health programs. Baby boomers will begin to retire in the year 2011, placing additional financial burdens on government as the number of retirees swells. Zero-sum and negative-sum spending games promise to afflict Congress in the future.

Congress faces great challenges in the coming years. The environment of legislative games promises to become more conflictual as political resources become more dispersed and financial resources remain constrained. Most congressional games are continuous, so the effects of the changing environment should be gradual. Following the course of the change will continue to depend on a comprehension of the rules, players, strategies, and broader game environment.

CONCLUSION

Public opinion, the increasing diversity of American society, technological innovation, and austerity politics all produce change in the environment of congressional games. A careful understanding of the environment is strategically necessary for those seeking to reform Congress. The players in reform games include the public, legislators and their staffs, and interest groups. Reforms proposed for the players include term limits, new campaign finance rules, and stronger ethics regulations. Institutional rules targeted for reform concern the committee system, Senate floor procedures and the line-item veto. In considering possible improvements, we need first to consider what an ideal Congress might look like. What is best for the institution may not be what best serves our personal ideology. No matter what reforms Congress adopts in the near future, it faces a variety of challenges from changing information technology, a distrustful and more diverse public, and the continuing problem of budget austerity.

IN DEPTH

1. Pick a current reform proposal and develop a strategy for securing its approval. How do aspects of the game environment—norms, expectations, and resources—affect your prospects? Who are the players you must convince, and which arguments are most likely to work with them? How might your reform proposal need to be modified in order to gain approval?

REFERENCES

Oleszek, Walter J. 1988. *Congressional Procedures and the Policy Process* 3d ed. Washington: Congressional Quarterly Press.

Rieselbach, Leroy N. 1994. *Congressional Reform.* Washington: Congressional Quarterly Press.

Sheppard, Burton D. 1985. *Rethinking Congressional Reform.* Cambridge, Mass.: Schneckman.

2. Can you trust the players in Congress to reform themselves? Examine an issue in which they must do so—such as campaign finance or ethics reform—and make an assessment, with particular attention to their past record on the issue.

REFERENCES ON CAMPAIGN FINANCE

Alexander, Herbert E. *Financing Politics: Money, Elections and Political Reform,* 4th ed. 1992. Washington: Congressional Quarterly Press.

Nugent, Margaret Latas, and John R. Johannes, ed. 1990. *Money, Elections and Democracy: Reforming Campaign Finance,* Boulder: Westview Press.

Sabato, Larry. 1984. *PAC Power: Inside the World of Political Action Committees.* New York: Norton, chapter 6.

Sorauf, Frank J. 1992. *Inside Campaign Finance: Myths and Realities.* New Haven: Yale University Press.

REFERENCES ON ETHICS

Congressional Quarterly. 1980. *Congressional Ethics,* 2d ed. Washington: Congressional Quarterly.

Jennings, Bruce, and Daniel Callahan, eds. 1985. *Representation and Responsibility: Exploring Legislative Ethics.* New York: Plenum Press.

Katz, Allan J. 1981. "The Politics of Congressional Ethics," in *The House at Work,* Joseph Cooper and G. Calvin Mackenzie, eds. Austin: University of Texas Press, pp. 97–111.

3. Does our constitutional structure lie at the root of congressional failings? Examine possible constitutional reforms to improve the operation of Congress. How would such rules reforms affect various games in Congress and the accountability, responsiveness, and responsibility of the institution?

REFERENCES

Goldwin, Robert A., and Art Kaufman. 1986. *Separation of Powers: Does it Still Work?* Washington: American Enterprise Institute.

Lijphart, Arend, ed. 1992. *Parliamentary Versus Presidential Government.* New York: Oxford University Press.

Sundquist, James L. 1986. *Constitutional Reform and Effective Government.* Washington: Brookings Institution.

BIBLIOGRAPHY

Aberbach, Joel. 1990. *Keeping a Watchful Eye: The Politics of Congressional Oversight.* Washington: Brookings Institution.

"The Age of Taft." *Time Magazine* XLIX, no. 3 (20 January 1947): 23–26.

Alston, Chuck. 1990. "The Maze of Spending Limits: An Election Field Guide." *Congressional Quarterly Weekly Report* 48, no. 21 (26 May): 1621–1626.

Alston, Chuck. 1991a. "Incumbents Share the Wealth with Redistricting in Mind." *Congressional Quarterly Weekly Report* 49, no. 21 (25 May): 1343.

Alston, Chuck. 1991b. "Members with Cash on Hand Reach out to Help Others." *Congressional Quarterly Weekly Report* 49, no. 39 (28 September): 2763–2765.

Amer, Mildred, and Ilona Nickels. 1989. "The Congress: From Quill to Screen." *CRS Review* (February): 30–32.

American Enterprise Institute. 1991. "The Public's Critique of Congress." *American Enterprise* 2 (Jan.–Feb.): 82–87.

Anderson, Arthur J., and William S. Dahlstrom. 1990. "Technological Gerrymandering: How Computers Can Be Used in the Redistricting Process to Comply with Judicial Criteria." *The Urban Lawyer* 22, no. 1 (Winter): 59–77.

Anderson, Casey. 1992. "Survivors Angle for Seats of Losers, Retirees." States News Service, LEXIS-NEXIS database (13 October).

Anderson, Jack, and Michael Binstein. 1993. "What Makes Byrd Bristle." *The Washington Post* (13 June): C7.

Arkel, Louise. 1988. "Women As Candidates." *Changing Faces* 3 (28 January): 3, 7–8.

Arnold, R. Douglas. 1990. *The Logic of Congressional Action.* New Haven: Yale University Press.

Asher, Herbert. 1973. "The Learning of Legislative Norms." *American Political Science Review* 67 (June): 119–146.

Ayres, Drummond, Jr. 1991. "Senator Who Brings Home the Bacon." *New York Times* (6 September): A16.

Bach, Stanley. 1991a. "The Amending Process in the House of Representatives." Congressional Research Service Report no. 91–605 RCO.

Bach, Stanley. 1991b. "Legislative Floor Process on the House Floor: An Introduction." Congressional Research Service Report no. 91–519 RCO.

Bach, Stanley. 1991c. "Legislative Floor Process on the Senate Floor: An Introduction." Congressional Research Service Report no. 91–520 RCO.

Bach, Stanley. 1992. *The State of the Senate: Conditions, Proposals, and Prospects for Change.* CRS Report for Congress 92–402 S. Washington: Congressional Research Service.

Bach, Stanley, and Steven S. Smith. 1989. *Managing Uncertainty in the House of Representatives: Adaptation and Innovation in Special Rules.* Washington, D.C.: Brookings Institution.

Bailey, Douglas J. 1990. "12 Ideas for a Nation in Search of a Leader." *Washington Post* (8 April): B1.

Baker, Senator Howard. 1983. *Congressional Record* (28 July): 511029.

Baker, John R., and Linda L. M. Bennett. 1991. "The Quest for a Congressional Seat." Paper presented at the 1991 annual meeting of the American Political Science Association, Washington, D.C.

Baker, Richard Allan. 1988. *The Senate of the United States: A Bicentennial History.* Malabar, Fla: Robert E. Krieger Publishing Company.

Baker, Ross K. 1989a. *House and Senate.* New York: W. W. Norton and Co.

Baker, Ross K. 1989b. *The New Fat Cats: Members of Congress as Political Benefactors.* New York: Priority Press Publications.

Balutis, Alan P. 1976. "Congress, the President and the Press." *Journalism Quarterly* (Fall): 509–515.

Barnes, James A. 1989. "Campaign Letter Bombs." *National Journal* 47, no. 43 (25 November): 2881–2887.

Barrett, Marvin, and Zachary Sklar. 1980. *The Eye of the Storm.* New York: Lippincott and Crowell.

Barry, Jeffrey. 1989. *The Interest Group Society.* Glenview, Ill.: Scott, Foresman.

Bates, Stephen, ed. 1987. *The Media and Congress.* Columbus, Ohio: Publishing Horizons.

Benjamin, Gerald, and Michael J. Malbin, eds. 1992. *Limiting Legislative Terms.* Washington, D.C.: Congressional Quarterly Press.

Berke, Richard. 1991. "As Keating Case Comes to a Close, Confusion over Ethics Rules Remains." *New York Times* (24 November): 24.

Bernstein, Robert A. 1986. "Why Are There So Few Women in the House?" *Western Political Quarterly* 39 (March): 156–164.

Bernstein, Robert A. 1989. *Elections, Representation and Congressional Voting Behavior.* Englewood Cliffs, N.J.: Prentice-Hall.

Birnbaum, Jeffrey H. 1991. "The Limits of Constituent Service." *Government Executive* (June): 28.

Bolling, Richard. 1966. *House Out of Order.* New York: E. P. Dutton.

Bond, Jon R., and Fleisher, Richard. 1990. *The President in the Legislative Arena.* Chicago: University of Chicago Press.

Boren, David (D-OK). 1991. "Major Repairs for Congress." *Washington Post* (6 August): A15.

Brady, David W., and Charles S. Bullock. 1981. "Coalition Politics in the House of Representatives." In *Congress Reconsidered,* Lawrence C. Dodd and Bruce I. Oppenheimer, eds. Washington, D.C.: Congressional Quarterly.

Bragdon, Peter. 1990. "Democrat's Ties to Minorities May Be Tested by New Lines." *Congressional Quarterly Weekly Report* 48, no. 22 (2 June): 1739–1742.

Broder, David. 1988. "Three Keys to 'Incumbent Lock.' " *Washington Post* (7 December): A21.

Broder, David. 1990. "Loyalty, Ambition—and Newt Gingrich." *Washington Post* (7 October): D7.

Broder, David. 1991. "A Short Session." *Washington Post* (10 March): D7.

Broder, David. 1992. "Clinton's Prospects Appear Rosy in the House." *Washington Post* (6 December): A9.

Broder, David. 1993. "Beware of the Bandwagon of Political Reform." *Washington Post National Weekly Edition* (3–9 May): 6.

Brown, Lynn P., and Robert L. Peabody. 1984. "Dilemmas of Party Leadership: Majority Whips in the U.S. House of Representatives, 1962–1982." *Congress and the Presidency* 11, no. 2 (Autumn): 179–196.

Brown, Neil. 1993. "Congress Is Looking More Like America." *Congressional Quarterly Weekly Report* 51, no. 31 (14 August): 2246.

Browning, Graeme. 1992. "Strength in Numbers for Hill Group." *National Journal* 24, no. 48 (11 November): 2732.

Bullock, Charles S., III, and David W. Brady. 1983. "Power, Constituency and Roll Call Voting in the U.S. Senate." *Legislative Studies Quarterly* 8 (February): 29–43.

Bullock, Charles S., III, and David England. 1992. "Prescriptive Committee Seats in Congress." *The Midsouth Political Science Journal* 13 (Autumn): 285–308.

Burke, Edmund. 1866. *Works.* Boston: Little, Brown.

Bush, George. 1992. Speech to the National Capital Area Chapter of the American Society for Public Administration, 24 October. LEXIS-NEXIS Database.

Byrd, Robert C. Interview. C-SPAN, 20 July 1993.

Cain, Bruce, John Ferejohn, and Morris Fiorina. 1987. *The Personal Vote: Constituency Service and Electoral Independence.* Cambridge, Mass.: Harvard University Press.

Calmes, Jackie. 1989. *Congressional Quarterly Weekly Report* 47, no. 23 (10 June): 1381.

Cannon, Lou. 1992. "Remap Gives California GOP Chance for Gains, Both Sides Say." *Washington Post* (28 January): A9.

Canon, David. 1990. *Actors, Athletes and Astronauts: Political Amateurs in the United States Congress.* Chicago: University of Chicago Press.

Canon, David. 1993. "The Class of '92: The Year of the Insider." *Extension of Remarks: Legislative Studies Newsletter* (June): 4.

Cantor, Joseph E., and Kevin J. Coleman. 1990. "Expenditures for Campaign Services: A Survey of 1988 Congressional Candidates in Competitive Elections." Congressional Research Service Report 90–457 GOV.

"The Carpetbagging Caucus." 1993. *Roll Call* (22 April): 1.

Cater, Douglas. 1987. "The Fourth Branch, Then and Now." In *The Media and Congress,* Stephen Bates, ed. Columbus, Ohio: Publishing Horizons.

Causey, Mike. 1991. "Sticking up for Staffers." *Washington Post* (7 October): B2.

Cavanaugh, Thomas E. 1979. "The Rational Allocation of Congressional Resources: Member Time and Staff Use in the House." In *Public Policy and Public Choice,* Douglas Rae and Theodore Eismeier, eds. Beverly Hills, Calif.: Sage.

Cavanaugh, Thomas E. 1981. "The Two Arenas of Congress." In *Congress at Work,* Joseph Cooper and G. C. Mackenzie, eds. Austin, Tex.: University of Texas Press.

Clark, Timothy B. 1988 "Budget Lessons from the Director." *Government Executive* (February): 18–23.

Clausen, Aage R. 1973. *How Congressmen Decide.* New York: St. Martin's.

Clymer, Adam. 1991. "Win or Lose, Vetoes by Bush Frustrate Democrats." *New York Times* (29 September): 22.

Clymer, Adam. 1993. "Having a President to Battle with Gives Dole a New Spirit and Verve." *New York Times* (9 April): A1.

Cohen, Richard E. 1990. "Crumbling Committees." *National Journal* 22 (4 August): 1876–1881.

Cohen, Richard E. 1992. "Congress in Distress." *National Journal* 24, no. 3 (18 January): 118–125.

Common Cause Magazine. 1986. (January–February).

Congressional Quarterly. 1976. *Origins and Development of Congress.* Washington, D.C.: Congressional Quarterly, p. 43.

Congressional Quarterly. 1983. *CQ Almanac* 39: 221.

Congressional Quarterly. 1989. "Congress Hikes Pay, Revises Ethics Law." *CQ Almanac* 45: 51–60.

Congressional Quarterly. 1991. *Congressional Quarterly's Guide to the U.S. Congress.* Washington, D.C.: Congressional Quarterly.

Congressional Quarterly. 1993. "Ginsburg Adroit, Amiable But Avoids Specifics." *Congressional Quarterly Weekly Report* 51, no. 30: 1982–1991.

Conlan, Timothy J., Margaret T. Wrightson, and David R. Beam. 1990. *Taxing Choices: The Politics of Tax Reform.* Washington: Congressional Quarterly.

Conway, M. Margaret. 1991. "PACs in the Political Process." In *Interest Group Politics,* Alan J. Cigler and Burdett A. Loomis, eds. Washington: Congressional Quarterly.

Cook, Rhodes. 1989. "Key to Survival for Democrats Lies in Split-Ticket Voting." *Congressional Quarterly Weekly Report* 47, no. 27 (8 July): 1710–1716.

Cook, Rhodes. 1990a. "Foe's Slashing Campaign Gives Representative Murtha a Close Shave." *Congressional Quarterly Weekly Report* 48, no. 2: 1584.

Cook, Rhodes. 1990b. "GOP Plagued by Continued Seat-to-Vote Disparity." *Congressional Quarterly Weekly Report* 48, no. 52 (29 December): 4238–4240.

Cook, Rhodes. 1990c. "Most House Members Survive, But Many Margins Narrow." *Congressional Quarterly Weekly Report* 48, no. 45 (10 November): 3798–3800.

Cook, Timothy E. 1989. *Making Laws and Making News.* Washington, D.C.: The Brookings Institution.

Cooper, Joseph. 1988. *Congress and its Committees.* New York: Garland Publishing Company.

Cooper, Kenneth J. 1993a. "Democrats' House Whips Cut Both Ways on NAFTA." *Washington Post* (5 September): A26.

Cooper, Kenneth J. 1993b. "For Democrats, a New Ballgame." *Washington Post* (30 January): A8.

Cooper, Kenneth J. 1993c. "Future Is Now for House Science Committee." *Washington Post* (26 January): A15.

Cooper, Kenneth J. 1993d. "Hispanic Caucus Shows Its New-Found Clout." *Washington Post* (2 October): A4.

Cooper, Kenneth J., and Helen Dewar. 1992. "Voters Show Incumbents the Door." *Washington Post* (17 September): A16.

Cornwell, Elmer F. 1959. "Presidential News: Expanding the Public Image." *Journalism Quarterly* 39: 275–283.

Costantini, Edmond. 1990. "Political Women and Political Ambition: Closing the Gender Gap." *American Journal of Political Science* 34 (August) 741–770.

Courant, Paul, and Gramlich, Edward. 1985. *Federal Budget Deficits: America's Great Consumption Binge.* Englewood Cliffs, N.J.: Prentice-Hall.

Cover, Albert D. 1980. "Contacting Congressional Constituents: Some Patterns of Perquisite Use." *American Journal of Political Science* 24 (February) 125–135.

Cox, Gary W., and Matthew D. McCubbins. 1993. *Legislative Leviathan: Parties in the U.S. House.* Berkeley: University of California Press.

Cranford, John R. 1991. "Keating and the Five Senators: Putting the Puzzle Together." *Congressional Quarterly Weekly Report* 49, no. 5 (26 January): 221–230.

Cranford, John R., Janet Hook, and Phil Kuntz. 1991. "Decision in Keating Five Case Settles Little for Senate." *Congressional Quarterly Weekly Report* 49, no. 9 (2 March): 517–527.

Cwiklik, Robert. 1992. *House Rules: A Freshman Congressman's Initiation to the Backslapping, Backpedaling, and Backstabbing Ways of Washington.* New York: Villard.

Darcy, R., Susan Welch, and Janet Clark. 1987. *Women, Elections, and Representation.* New York: Longman.

Davidson, Roger H. 1969. *The Role of the Congressman.* Indianapolis: Bobbs-Merrill.

Davidson, Roger H. 1985. "Senate Leaders: Janitors for an Untidy Chamber." In *Congress Reconsidered,* Lawrence Dodd and Bruce Oppenheimer, eds. 3d edition. Washington, D.C.: Congressional Quarterly.

Davidson, Roger H. 1988. "The New Centralization on Capitol Hill." *Review of Politics* 50 (Summer): 345–364.

Davidson, Roger H. 1991. "The Presidency and the Three Eras of the Modern Congress." In *Divided Democracy,* James Thurber, ed. Washington: Congressional Quarterly.

Davidson, Roger, and Walter Oleszek. 1990. *Congress and Its Members.* Washington: Congressional Quarterly.

Davis, Frank L. 1993. "Balancing the Perspective on PAC Contributions: In Search of an Impact on Roll Calls." *American Politics Quarterly* 21 (April): 205–222.

DeGregorio, Christine, and Kevin Snider. 1993. Unpublished paper.

Devroy, Ann. 1991. "Path to Confirmation Became a 'Slippery Slope.' " *Washington Post* (9 October): A6.

Devroy, Ann. 1992. "Among Republicans, Survival Tactics and Signs of Despair." *Washington Post* (14 October): A1.

Dewar, Helen. 1989. "Congress off to Slowest Start in Years." *Washington Post* (13 May): A4.

Dewar, Helen. 1991. "Senate Ploys Curb Majority's Clout." *Washington Post* (13 August): A15.

Dewar, Helen, Retha Hill, Gwen Ifill, Tom Kenworthy, and Michael Weisskopf. 1990. "Military Medical School May Survive." *Washington Post* (27 October): A11.

Dewar, Helen, and Tom Kenworthy. 1991. "Senate Commends Bush, Backs Troops." *Washington Post* (18 January): A29.

De Witt, Karen. 1991. "Consumer Group Criticizes Travel by House Members." *New York Times* (13 September): A16.

Dexter, Lewis A. 1971. "The Representative and His District." In *New Perspectives on the House of Representatives,* Robert L. Peabody and Nelson R. Polsby, eds. Chicago: Rand McNally.

Dionne, E. J. 1992. "For Politicians, The Unkindest Cut." *Washington Post National Weekly Edition* (October 5–12): 11.

Dodd, Lawrence C., and Sean Q. Kelly. 1990. "Electoral Competitiveness and the Presentation of Self." Paper presented at the 1990 meeting of the Midwest Political Science Convention.

Dodd, Lawrence C., and Richard Schott. 1979. *Congress and the Administrative State.* New York: Wiley.

Donovan, Beth. 1991. "Nation Watches as Texas Struggles to Create Minority Districts." *Congressional Quarterly Weekly Report* 49, no. 33 (17 August): 2295.

Donovan, Beth. 1993a. "New Ideas for Reform Slowed by Old Partisan Divisions." *Congressional Quarterly Weekly Report* 51, no. 14 (3 April): 808–809.

Donovan, Beth. 1993b. "Senate Passes Campaign Finance by Gutting Public Funding." *Congressional Quarterly Weekly Report* 51, no. 25 (19 June): 1533–1540.

Donovan, Beth, and Ilyse J. Veron. 1993. "Freshmen Got to Washington with Help of PAC Funds." *Congressional Quarterly Weekly Report* 51, no. 12 (27 March): 723–729.

Drew, Elizabeth. 1978. "A Reporter at Large: Charlie." *New Yorker* 52 (9 January): 32–58.

Duncan, Phil. 1990a. "Cash Is Losing Weight on Election Scales." *Congressional Quarterly Weekly Report* 48, no. 52 (29 December): 4262.

Duncan, Phil. 1990b. "Partisan Remapping Not Cut and Dried." *Congressional Quarterly Weekly Report* 48, no. 46 (17 November): 3902.

Duncan, Phil. 1990c. "Political Redistricting and Zero Deviation." *Congressional Quarterly Weekly Report* 48, no. 41 (13 October): 3462.

Duncan, Phil. 1991a. "How to Make Congress More Representative." *Congressional Quarterly Weekly Report* 49, no. 43 (26 October): 3166.

Duncan, Phil. 1991b. "The Human Element in Hill Politicking." *Congressional Quarterly Weekly Report* 49, no. 27 (6 July): 1862.

Duncan, Phil. 1991c. "The 'Non-Impediment' Approach to Politics." *Congressional Quarterly Weekly Report* 49, no. 32 (10 August): 2274.

Duncan, Phil. 1992a. "GOP's Remap Bounty Likely to Be Modest." *Congressional Quarterly Weekly Report* 50, no. 11 (14 March): 682.

Duncan, Phil. 1992b. "Party Ties Look Strong for House Freshmen." *Congressional Quarterly Weekly Report* 50, no. 45 (19 November): 3656.

Durst, Samantha L., and Ryan W. Rusek. 1993. "Different Genders, Different Votes: An Examination of Voting Behavior in the U.S. House of Representatives." Paper presented at the annual meeting of the American Political Science Association, Washington, D.C.

Dutton, John. 1990. "Congress by Computer." *Washington Post* (6 May): B2.

Edsall, Thomas B. 1992. "Gingrich Gains Narrow Win." *Washington Post* (23 July): A13.

Edwards, George C. 1989. *At the Margins: Presidential Leadership of Congress.* New Haven: Yale University Press.

Ehrenhalt, Alan. 1987. *Politics in America.* Washington, D.C.: Congressional Quarterly Press.

Ehrenhalt, Alan. 1991a. "The Rise of a Political Class: Why Voters Don't Matter." *Washington Post* (21 July): C3.

Ehrenhalt, Alan. 1991b. *The United States of Ambition: Politicians, Power and the Pursuit of Office.* New York: Times Books.

Ellerbee, Linda. 1986. *"And So It Goes": Adventures in Television.* New York: G. P. Putnam's Sons.

Elving, Ronald D. 1989. "Politics of Congress in the Age of TV." *Congressional Quarterly Weekly Report* 47, no. 3 (1 April): 722.

Elving, Ronald D. 1991. "Mosbacher Expected to Ignore Significant Undercount." *Congressional Quarterly Weekly Report* 49, no. 25: 1690–1691.

Elving, Ronald D. 1993. "Era of a Firmer Hand: Foley at the Fore." *Congressional Quarterly Weekly Report* 51, no. 4 (23 January): 194.

Enelow, James M. 1981. "Saving Amendments, Killer Amendments, and an Expected Utility Theory of Sophisticated Voting." *Journal of Politics* 43 (November): 1062–1089.

Erikson, Robert S., and Norman R. Luttbeg. 1973. *American Public Opinion: Its Origins, Content and Impact.* New York: John Wiley.

Evans, C. Lawrence. 1989. "Influence in Congressional Committees: Participation, Manipulation, and Anticipation." In *Congressional Politics,* Christopher J. Deering, ed. Chicago: Dorsey Press.

Evans, C. Lawrence. 1991. *Leadership in a Committee: A Comparative Analysis of Leadership Behavior in the U.S. Senate.* Ann Arbor: University of Michigan Press.

Evans, Diana. 1992. "Policy and Pork: The Use of Pork Barrel Projects in Building Policy Coalitions in the House of Representatives." Paper presented at the Annual Meeting of the Midwest Political Science Association, Chicago.

Evans, Roland, and Robert Novak. 1967. *LBJ: The Exercise of Power.* London: George Allen and Unwin.

Farrand, Max, ed. 1966. *The Records of the Federal Convention of 1787.* New Haven: Yale University Press. Four volumes.

Fenno, Richard. 1973. *Congressmen in Committees.* Boston: Little, Brown.

Fenno, Richard. 1978. *Home Style: House Members in Their Districts.* Boston: Little, Brown.

Fenno, Richard. 1989. "The Senate through a Looking Glass: The Debate over Television." *Legislative Studies Quarterly* 14 (August): 313–349.

Fenno, Richard. 1990. "If, As Ralph Nader Says, Congress is 'The Broken Branch,' How Come We Love Our Congressman So Much?" In *American Government: Readings and Cases,* Peter Woll, ed. Glenview, Ill.: Scott, Foresman.

Fessler, Pamela. 1989. "Florida's Unabashed Liberal Left 41-Year Mark on Hill." *Congressional Quarterly Weekly Report* 47, no. 22 (3 June): 1298–1301.

Fessler, Pamela. 1990. "Quandary for Hill Negotiators: What Role for Committees?" *Congressional Quarterly Weekly Report* 48, no. 27 (7 July): 2127.

Fessler, Pamela. 1992. "Lugar's Low Keyed Persistence." *Congressional Quarterly Weekly Report* 50, no. 20 (16 May): 1359.

Fiorina, Morris. 1977a. "The Case of Vanishing Marginals: The Bureaucracy Did It." *American Political Science Review* 71 (March): 64–71.

Fiorina, Morris. 1977b. *Congress: The Keystone of the Washington Establishment.* New Haven: Yale University Press.

Fisher, Louis. 1981. *The Politics of Shared Power.* Washington: Congressional Quarterly.

Fisher, Louis. 1985a. *Constitutional Conflicts between Congress and the President,* 2nd ed. Princeton: Princeton University Press.

Fisher, Louis. 1985b. "Judicial Misjudgments about the Lawmaking Process: The Legislative Veto Case." *Public Administration Review* 45 (November): 705–711.

Fisher, Louis. 1991. "Congress as Micromanager of the Executive Branch." In *The Managerial Presidency,* James Pfiffner, ed. Pacific Grove, Calif.: Brooks/Cole.

Fisher, Louis. 1993. *The Politics of Shared Power,* 2d ed. Washington, D.C.: Congressional Quarterly.

Fleisher, Richard. 1993. "PAC Contributions and Congressional Voting on National Defense." *Legislative Studies Quarterly* 18 (August): 391–409.

Fleisher, Richard, and Jon R. Bond. 1983. "Assessing Presidential Support in the House: Lessons from Carter and Reagan." *Journal of Politics* 45, no. 3: 745–758.

Fleisher, Richard, and Jon R. Bond. 1992. "Assessing Presidential Support in the House II: Lessons from George Bush." *American Journal of Political Science* 36, no. 2: 525–541.

Foote, Joe S., and Dennis K. Davis. 1987. "Network Visibility of Congressional Leaders, 1969–1985." Paper presented at the Annual Meeting of the International Communication Association, Montreal, Canada.

Fowler, Linda L., and Robert D. McClure. 1989. *Political Ambition.* New Haven: Yale University Press.

Fox, Harrison W., and Susan Webb Hammond. 1977. *Congressional Staffs: The Invisible Force in American Lawmaking.* New York: The Free Press.

Frankovic, Kathleen. 1977. "Sex and Voting in the U.S. House of Representatives, 1961–1975." *American Politics Quarterly* 5 (July): 315–330.

Frantzich, Stephen. 1978. "Opting Out: Retirement from the House of Representatives." *American Politics Quarterly* 6 (July): 251–273.

Frantzich, Stephen. 1982. *Computers in Congress: The Politics of Information.* Beverly Hills, Calif.: Sage Publications.

Frantzich, Stephen. 1986. *Write Your Congressman: Constituent Communications and Representation.* New York: Praeger.

Frantzich, Stephen. 1987. "The Implications of Congressional Computerization." *Bulletin of the American Society for Information Science* (February/March): 13–14.

Frantzich, Stephen. 1989. *Political Parties in the Technological Age.* New York: Longman.

Frantzich, Stephen. 1990. "Legislatures and the Revolution in Communications and Information Processing: Untangling the Linkage Between Technology and Politics." Paper presented at the Annual Meeting of the American Political Science Association, San Francisco.

Frazier, Martin. 1988. "Scholars, Political Analysts are Worried." *Roll Call* (3 April): 3.

Fritz, Sara, and Dwight Morris. 1992. *Handbook of Campaign Spending.* Washington, D.C.: Congressional Quarterly.

Fund, John H. 1992. "Term Limitation: An Idea Whose Time Has Come." In *Limiting Legislative Terms,* Gerald Benjamin and Michael Malbin, eds. Washington, D.C.: Congressional Quarterly.

Gellhorn, Walter. 1966. *When Americans Complain.* Cambridge: Harvard University Press.

Gertzog, Irwin N. 1984. *Congressional Women: Their Recruitment, Treatment and Behavior.* New York: Praeger.

Gilmour, John B. 1989. "Hardball and Softball Politics: A Theory of Coalition Size in Congress." Washington University in St. Louis, political economy working paper.

Gilmour, John B., and Paul Rothstein. 1993. "Early Republican Retirement." *Legislative Studies Quarterly* 28: 345–365.

"Ginsburg Adroit, Amiable but Avoids Specifics." 1993. *Congressional Quarterly Weekly Report* 51, no. 30 (24 July): 1991.

Goldstein, Mark L. 1991. "Our Myopic Legislature." *Government Executive* (January): 10–15.

Graber, Doris. 1980. *Mass Media and American Politics.* Washington, D.C.: Congressional Quarterly.

Greenberg, Daniel S. 1992. "In Defense of Pork-Barrel Science." *Washington Post* (31 March): A17.

Greenfield, Meg. 1992. "From Junta to What?" *Newsweek* (13 April): 72.

Greenhouse, Linda. 1987. "The New, Improved (?) Filibuster in Action." *New York Times* (21 May): B10.

Grenzke, Janet. 1989. "PACs and the Congressional Supermarket: The Currency Is Complex." *American Journal of Political Science* 32 (February): 1–24.

Groennings, Sven, E. W. Kelly, and Michael Leiserson. 1970. *The Study of Coalition Behavior.* New York: Holt, Rinehart & Winston.

Groseclose, Timothy, and Keith Krehbiel. 1994. "Golden Parachutes, Rubber Checks and Strategic Retirements from the 102nd Congress." *American Journal of Political Science* 38 (February): 25.

Gross, Jane. 1992 "State Measures on U.S. Term Limits Gather Momentum." *New York Times* (12 October): A1

Grove, Lloyd. 1992. "House Rivals Tread Fine Line in Race Conscious Mississippi." *Washington Post* (10 February): B1.

Gugliotta, Guy, and Kenneth J. Cooper. 1992. "String of House Scandals Saps Public Confidence." *Washington Post* (11 March): A1.

Hager, George. 1990a. "Conference in Holding Pattern over Clean Air Proposals." *Congressional Quarterly Weekly Report* 48, no. 30 (28 July): 2399–2400.

Hager, George. 1990b. "Defiant House Rebukes Leaders: New Round of Fights Begins." *Congressional Quarterly Weekly Report* (4 October): 3187.

Hager, George. 1991. "Parties Angle for Advantage as White House Falters." *Congressional Quarterly Weekly Report* 48, no. 41 (13 October): 3391.

Hager, George. 1993. "GOP, Black Caucus Force Delay in Line-Item Veto Debate." *Congressional Quarterly Weekly Report* 51, no. 17 (24 April): 1008–1009.

Hager, George, and David S. Cloud. 1993. "Democrats Tie Their Fate to Clinton's Budget Bill." *Congressional Quarterly Weekly Report* 51, no. 32 (7 August): 2122–2131

Hall, Richard L. 1987. "Participation and Purpose in Committee Decision Making." *American Political Science Review* 81 (March): 105–127.

Hall, Richard, and Frank W. Wayman. 1990. "Buying Time: Monied Interests and the Mobilization of Bias in Congressional Committees." *American Political Science Review* 84 (September): 797–820.

Hamilton, Alexander, James Madison, and John Jay. 1961. *The Federalist Papers.* New York: New American Library.

Hammond, Susan Webb. 1989. "Congress Staff Aides As Candidates and As U.S. Representatives." *Social Sciences Journal* 26, no. 3: 277–287.

Hammond, Susan Webb. 1991. "Congressional Caucuses and Party Leaders in the House of Representatives." *Political Science Quarterly* 106 (Summer): 277–294.

Harold, Rosemary. 1988. "Deciphering Rules." *C-SPAN Update* (9 May): 11.

Haskell, Anne. 1992. "Live from Capitol Hill." *Washington Journalism in Review* 4 (November): 48–50.

Heclo, Hugh. 1978. "Issue Networks and the Executive Establishment." In *The New American Political System,* Anthony King, ed. Washington: American Enterprise Institute.

Heinz, John P. 1993. *The Hollow Core: Private Interests in National Policy Making.* Cambridge: Harvard University Press.

Henschen, Beth M., and Edward I. Sidlow. 1986. "The Recruitment and Career Patterns of Congressional Committee Staffs: An Exploration." *Western Political Quarterly* 39 (December): 701–708.

Herrnson, Paul S. 1988. *Party Campaigning in the 1980's.* Cambridge: Harvard University Press.

Herrnson, Paul S. 1991. "Congressional Staff as Congressional Candidates: Some Preliminary Findings." Paper presented at the 1991 meeting of the Midwest Political Science Association.

Hershey, Marjorie Randon. 1984. *Running for Office: The Political Education of Campaigners.* Chatham, N.J.: Chatham House.

Hertzke, Allen D., and Ronald M. Peters, Jr. 1992. *The Atomistic Congress.* Armonk, New York: M. E. Sharp Inc.

Hess, Stephen. 1991a. *Live from Capitol Hill.* Washington, D.C.: Brookings Institution.

Hess, Stephen. 1991b. "Reporters Who Cover Congress." *Society* 28 (January-February): 60–65.

Hibbing, John. 1991. *Congressional Careers: Contours of Life in the U.S. House of Representatives.* Chapel Hill: The University of North Carolina Press.

Hibbing, John. 1993. "The 1992 House Elections and Congressional Careers." *Extension of Remarks, Legislative Studies Newsletter* (June): 2.

Hinds, Michael deCourcy. 1992. "Indictment of Congressman Means Little at Home." *New York Times* (17 May): 28L.

Hook, Janet. 1989a. "101st Congress at Midyear: Overcoming the Tumult." *Congressional Quarterly Weekly Report* 47, no. 32 (12 August): 2093.

Hook, Janet. 1989b. "Rout of Democratic Leaders." *Congressional Quarterly Weekly Report* 47, no. 39 (30 September): 2529.

Hook, Janet. 1989c. "House's New Leadership Brings Next Generation of Power." *Congressional Quarterly Weekly Report* 47, no. 23 (10 June): 1376–1377.

Hook, Janet. 1990. "Some House Democrats Balk at Prospect of Mail Limits." *Congressional Quarterly Weekly Report* 48, no. 28 (14 July): 2195.

Hook, Janet. 1991a. "Gray's Exit Roils Leadership As Party Seeks Stability." *Congressional Quarterly Weekly Report* 49, no. 25 (22 June): 1637–1641.

Hook, Janet. 1991b. "Redrawing West Virginia Map Sets Democrat vs. Democrat." *Congressional Quarterly Weekly Report* 49, no. 19 (7 April): 1035.

Hook, Janet. 1992. "Extensive Reform Proposals Cook on the Front Burner." *Congressional Quarterly Weekly Report* 50, no. 23 (6 June): 1579–1585.

Hook, Janet. 1993. "Clinton's Months of Missteps Give Way to Winning Streak." *Congressional Quarterly Weekly Report* 51, no. 27 (27 November): 3244.

Hornblower, Margot. 1981. "The Master of Gentle Persuasion." *Washington Post* (10 August): A1.

Hrebnar, Ronald J., and Ruth K. Scott. 1990. *Interest Groups in America.* Englewood Cliffs, N.J.: Prentice-Hall.

Huckabee, David C. 1989. "Reelection Rates of House Incumbents: 1790–1988." Congressional Research Service Report 89–173–GOV.

Huckshorn, Robert J., and Robert C. Spencer. 1971. *The Politics of Defeat.* Amherst: The University of Massachusetts Press.

Hunter, Marjorie. 1984. "Senate TV Measure Debated." *New York Times* (8 September): 10.

Ireland, Patricia. 1992. "Address to the International Platform Association." (4 August) Reuter's transcripts.

Jacobson, Gary C. 1987. *The Politics of Congressional Elections,* 2d ed. Boston: Little, Brown.

Jacobson, Gary C. 1991. "The Roots of Divided Government Are Political, Not Structural." *Public Affairs Report* 32 (July): 6–7.

Jacobson, Gary C. 1992. *The Politics of Congressional Elections,* 3d ed. Washington, D.C.: Congressional Quarterly.

Jenkins, Kent Jr. 1988. "Senate Race Keeps Campaigning on Alexandria's Front Burner." *Washington Post* (18 November): B1.

Jenkins, Kent Jr. 1992a. "CIA Cancels Its Divisive W. Va. Move." *Washington Post* (1 April): A1, A14.

Jenkins, Kent Jr. 1992b. "Hoyer Has 'em over a Pork Barrel in Md. 5th." *Washington Post* (5 July): A1.

Jewell, Malcolm, and Chu Chi-Hung. 1974. "Membership Movement and Committee Attractiveness in the U.S. House of Representatives, 1963–1971." *American Journal of Political Science* 18 (May): 433–441.

Johannes, John R. 1983. "Explaining Congressional Casework Styles." *American Journal of Political Science* 27 (Sept./Oct.): 530–547.

Johannes, John R. 1984. *To Serve the People: Congress and Constituency Service.* Lincoln: University of Nebraska Press.

Johnson, Lyndon. 1971. *The Vantage Point.* New York: Holt, Rinehart & Winston.

Jones, Charles O. 1974. "Speculative Argumentation in Federal Air Pollution Policy-Making." *Journal of Politics* 36 (May): 438–464.

Jones, Charles O. 1982. *The U.S. Congress: People, Place and Policy.* Homewood, Ill.: Dorsey Press.

Jordan, Mary. 1992. "For Little College, a Big Helping Hand." *Washington Post* (24 June): A1.

Kahn, Kim Fridkin. 1990. "Senate Elections in the News: Characteristics of Campaign Coverage." Paper presented at the meeting of the Midwest Political Science Association, Chicago.

Kamen, Al. 1993. "Speaking of Gas." *Washington Post* (17 September): A19.

Kazee, Thomas A. 1980. "The Decision to Run for the U.S. Congress: Challenger Attitudes in the 1970s." *Legislative Studies Quarterly* February: 79–100.

Kellam, Susan. 1992. "Defense Policy." *Congressional Quarterly Almanac* XLVII: 394–395.

Kelly, Brian. 1992. *Adventures in Porkland.* New York: Villard.

Kelly, Rita Mae, Michelle Saint-Germain, and Jody Horn. 1991. "Female Public Officials: A Different Voice?" *The Annals of the American Academy* 515 (May): 77–87.

Kenworthy, Tom. 1990a. "House Incumbents Ride the Airwaves." *Washington Post* (17 October): E5.

Kenworthy, Tom. 1990b. "House Members Turn Mailings into Powerful Political Weapon." *Washington Post* (19 June): A4.

Kernell, Samuel. 1977. "Toward Understanding 19th Century Congressional Career: Ambition, Competition, and Rotation." *American Journal of Political Science* 21 (November): 669–693.

Kingdon, John. 1984. *Agendas, Alternatives and Public Policies.* Boston: Little, Brown.

Kingdon, John. 1989. *Congressmen's Voting Decisions,* 3d ed. Ann Arbor: University of Michigan Press.

Kolodny, Robin. 1991. "Leadership and the CCCs: The Congressional Campaign Committees as a Training Ground." Paper prepared for delivery at the Annual Meeting of the Midwest Political Science Association, Chicago.

Kosova, Weston. 1990. "Congress's Mail Prostitution Ring." *Washington Monthly* (22 September): 32–36.

Kosterlitz, Julie. 1992. "Slinging Mud in Oregon's Senate Race." *National Journal* 24, no. 43 (24 October): 2434.

Krauss, Clifford. 1992. "Vying for Committees, Freshmen Mimic Insiders." *New York Times* (30 November): A11.

Krehbiel, Keith. 1991. *Information and Legislative Organization.* Ann Arbor: University of Michigan Press.

Kubik, William J. 1992. "Committee Cohesion and Party Behavior on Roll Call Votes in the House of Representatives." Paper presented at the Annual Meeting of the American Political Science Association, Chicago.

Kuntz, Phil, and George Hager. 1990. "Showdown on Clean Air Bill: Senate Says 'No' to Byrd." *Congressional Quarterly Weekly Report* 48, no. 13 (31 March): 983–987.

Kuntz, Phil, and Janet Hook. 1991. "Even without New Guidelines, Senators Tiptoe to Safe Side." *Congressional Quarterly Weekly Report* 49, no. 9 (2 March): 524–527.

Kurtz, Karl T. 1992. "Is Politics Baseball, or is Baseball Politics?" *Governing* (March): 11.

Ladd, Everett C. 1990. "Public Opinion and the Congress Problem." *The Public Interest* 100 (Summer): 57–67.

Lancaster, John. 1991. "Clearing Up a $10 Million Mystery." *Washington Post* (16 December): A21.

Langbein, Laura J. 1986. "Money and Access: Some Empirical Evidence." *Journal of Politics* 48 (December): 1052–1064.

Larson, Stephanie Greco. 1990. "Information and Learning in a Congressional District: A Social Experiment." *American Journal of Political Science* 34 (November): 1102–1118.

Levush, Ruth, ed. 1991. "Campaign Financing of National Elections in Foreign Countries." Law Library of Congress, Report LL91–8.

Liedl, Mark B. 1990. "Congress's Busywork: 'Constituent Service' Has Replaced Governing." *Washington Post* (28 January): C1, C4.

Light, Paul. 1985. *Artful Work: The Politics of Social Security Reform.* New York: Random House.

Lincoln, Abraham. 1989. *Abraham Lincoln: Speeches and Writings, 1832–1858.* New York: The Library of America.

Lipsky, Michael. 1968. "Protest As a Political Resource." *American Political Science Review* 62 November: 1144–1158.

Longley, Lawrence, and Walter Oleszek. 1989. *Bicameral Politics.* New Haven: Yale University Press.

Loomis, Burdett. 1979. "The Congressional Office As a Small (?) Business: New Members Set Up Shop." *Publius* 9 (Summer): 35–55.

Loomis, Burdett. 1988. *The New American Politician.* New York: Basic Books.

Lowi, Theodore J. 1964. "American Business, Public Policy, Case-Studies and Political Theory." *Journal of Politics* 16 (July): 677–715.

Maisel, Louis Sandy. 1981. "Congressional Information Sources." In *The House at Work,* Joseph Cooper and Calvin Mackenzie, eds. Austin: University of Texas Press.

Malbin, Michael J. 1980. *Unelected Representatives: Congressional Staffs and the Future of Representative Government.* New York: Basic Books.

Mann, Thomas E., and Norman J. Ornstein. 1992. *Renewing Congress: A First Report.* Washington, D.C.: American Enterprises Institute and Brookings Institution.

Mann, Thomas E., and Raymond E. Wolfinger. 1980. "Candidates and Parties in Congressional Elections." *American Political Science Review* 74 (September): 617–632.

Maslow, Abraham. 1954. *Motivation and Personality.* New York: Harper & Row.

Mathias, Senator Charles. 1982. "Congressional Mass Mailing." *Congressional Record.* 97th Congress. 2d Session, vol. 128, no. 120.

Matthews, Donald R., and James A. Stimson. 1970. "Decision-making by U.S. Representatives." In *Political Decision-Making,* Sidney Ulmer, ed. New York: Van Nostrand Reinhold.

Mayhew, David. 1974a. *Congress: The Electoral Connection.* New Haven: Yale University Press.

Mayhew, David. 1974b. "Congressional Elections: The Case of the Vanishing Marginals." *Polity* 6, no. 3: 295–317.

Mayhew, David R. 1991. *Divided We Govern.* New Haven: Yale University Press.

McConnell, Grant. 1966. *Private Power and American Democracy.* New York: Knopf.

Merida, Kevin. 1993a. "On Key Votes, House Whips Start Cracking." *Washington Post* (31 May): A1.

Merida, Kevin. 1993b. "The Whip Lashes Out." *Washington Post* (10 November): C13.

Merry, Robert W. 1991. "The New Commitment to Gerrymandering." *Congressional Quarterly Weekly Report* 49, no. 34 (24 August): 2346.

Mills, Mike. 1991. "House Turns away Attempts to Cut Highway 'Pork.' " *Congressional Quarterly Weekly Report* 49, no. 41 (12 October): 2941.

Mintron, Michael, and Howard Scarrow. 1993. "Do American Voters Favor Divided Government?" Paper presented at the Annual Meeting of the Midwest Political Science Association, Chicago.

Montesquieu, Charles Louis de Secondat. 1964. *The Spirit of the Laws.* New York: Haffner.

Moore, W. John. 1992. "So Long, Mr. Smith." *National Journal* 24, no. 9 (12 September): 2052–2056.

Morgan, Dan. 1990. "Senators Make a Train of Cabooses." *Washington Post* (7 May): A9.

Morin, Richard. 1992a. "The Big 3: Jobs, Deficit, Health Care." *Washington Post* (9 December): A21.

Morin, Richard. 1992b. "Now Is The Time for All Good Women." *Washington Post National Weekly Edition* (23–30 April): 36.

Morin, Richard. 1992c. "Oval Office Odds." *Washington Post* (27 September): C1, C4.

Murphy, Walter F., and C. Herman Pritchett. 1986. *Courts, Judges and Politics,* 3d ed. New York: Random House.

Navasky, Victor. 1991. "People's Frank." *Nation* 14 (October): 438–439.

Neustadt, Richard. 1970. *Alliance Politics.* New York: Columbia University Press.

Neustadt, Richard. 1990. *Presidential Power and the Modern Presidents.* New York: Free Press.

Niemi, Richard G., and Kimball W. Brace. 1993. "Bright Lines, Guidelines and Tradeoffs: The Conflict between Compactness and Minority Representation in the Congressional Districts of the 1990s." Paper presented at the annual meeting of the Midwest Political Science Association, Chicago.

Ogul, Morris S. 1976. *Congress Oversees the Bureaucracy.* Pittsburgh: University of Pittsburgh Press.

Oleszek, Walter J. 1989. *Congressional Procedures and the Policy Process.* Washington, D.C.: Congressional Quarterly Press.

Ornstein, Norman J. 1981. "The House and The Senate in a New Congress." In *The New Congress,* Norman J. Ornstein and Thomas J. Mann, eds. Washington: American Enterprise Institute.

Ornstein, Norman J. 1987. "The Media and the Open Congress." In *The Media and Congress,* Stephen Bates, ed. Columbus, Ohio: Publishing Horizons.

Ornstein, Norman J., Thomas E. Mann, and Michael J. Malbin. 1992. *Vital Statistics on Congress, 1991–1992.* Washington, D.C.: Congressional Quarterly.

Ornstein, Norman J., Thomas E. Mann, and Michael J. Malbin. 1994. *Vital Statistics on Congress, 1993–1994.* Washington, D.C.: Congressional Quarterly.

Ornstein, Norman, and Michael Robinson. 1986. "The Case of the Disappearing Congress." *TV Guide* 34 (11 January): 4–6, 8–10.

Page, Benjamin I., Robert Y. Shapiro, and Glenn R. Dempsey. 1981. "What Moves Public Opinion." *American Political Science Review* 81 (March): 30–46.

Parker, Glenn R. 1980. "The Advantage of Incumbency in House Elections." *American Politics Quarterly* 8, no. 4 (October): 449–464.

Parker, Glenn R. 1989. *Characteristics of Congress: Patterns in Congressional Behavior.* Englewood Cliffs, N.J.: Prentice-Hall.

Parker, Glenn R., and Suzanne L. Parker. 1985. *Factions in House Committees.* Knoxville: University of Tennessee Press.

Patterson, Samuel C. 1993. "Partisanship in the New Congress." *Extension of Remarks: Legislative Studies Newsletter* (June): 7.

Patterson, Samuel C., and Gregory A. Caldeira. 1988. "Party Voting in the United States Congress." *British Journal of Political Science* 17 (January): 111–131.

Patterson, Samuel C., and Gregory A. Caldeira. 1990. "Standing Up for Congress: Variations in Public Esteem Since the 1960s." *Legislative Studies Quarterly* 15 (February): 25–47.

Patterson, Samuel C., and Thomas H. Little. 1992. "The Organization of the Congressional Parties." Paper prepared for delivery at the Annual Meeting of the Midwest Political Science Association.

Peabody, Robert L. 1976. *Leadership in Congress.* Boston: Little, Brown.

Peabody, Robert L. 1981. "Senate Party Leadership: From the 1950's to the 1980's." In *Understanding Congressional Leadership,* Frank H. Mackaman, ed. Washington, D.C.: Congressional Quarterly Press.

Peters, Charles. 1994. "Tilting at Windmills." *The Washington Monthly* 23, no. 3 (March): 4–9.

Peters, Ronald M. 1990. *The American Speakership.* Baltimore: The Johns Hopkins University Press.

Peterson, Mark A. 1990. *Legislating Together: The White House and Capitol Hill from Eisenhower to Reagan.* Cambridge: Harvard University Press.

Petracca, Mark P. 1990. "Term Limits Will Put An End to Permanent Government by Incumbents." *Institute of Governmental Studies Public Affairs Report* 31, no. 6 (November): 8.

Pincus, Walter. 1990. "$65 Million Data Link Approved for Senators." *Washington Post* (14 June): A21.

Platt, Suzy, ed. 1989. *Respectfully Quoted.* Washington, D.C.: Library of Congress.

Polsby, Nelson W. 1990. "Congress-Bashing for Beginners." *The Public Interest* 100 (Summer): 15–23.

Polsby, Nelson W. 1968. "The Institutionalization of the House of Representatives." *American Political Science Review* 26 (March): 144–168.

Pontious, John. 1991. "Congressional Role Call and Other Recorded Votes." Congressional Research Services Report No. 91–571 GOV.

Povich, Elaine S. 1993. "Congressional Rookies Learn Life's More Difficult on Inside." *Chicago Tribune* (18 April): 1.

Public Citizen. 1992. From Civil Rights and Voting Rights to Political and Economic Empowerment. Press release.

Ragsdale, Lynn. 1989. "Do Voters Matter? Democracy in Congressional Elections." In *Congressional Politics,* Christopher J. Deering, ed. Chicago: Dorsey Press.

Ray, Bruce A. 1982. "Research Update: Committee Attractiveness in the U.S. House, 1963–1981." *American Journal of Political Science* 26 (August): 609–613.

Renshon, Stanley. 1974. *Psychological Needs and Political Behavior.* New York: Free Press.

Richardson, Sula P. 1989. "Caucuses and Legislative Service Organizations: Responses to Frequently Asked Questions." Congressional Research Service Report 89–422 GOV.

Richardson, Sula P. 1991. "Caucuses and Legislative Service Organizations of the 102nd Congress." Congressional Research Service Report 91–449 GOV.

Richardson, Sula P. 1992. "Caucuses and Legislative Service Organizations of the 102nd Congress." Congressional Research Service Report No. 92–527 GOV.

Rieselbach, Leroy. 1986. *Congressional Reform.* Washington, D.C.: Congressional Quarterly.

Riker, William. 1962. *The Theory of Political Coalitions.* New Haven: Yale University Press.

Riker, William. 1986. *The Art of Political Manipulation.* New Haven: Yale University Press.

Ripley, Randall. 1988. *Congress: Process and Policy.* New York: W. W. Norton.

Ripley, Randall B., and Franklin, Grace A. 1991. *Congress, the Bureaucracy and Public Policy.* Pacific Grove, Calif.: Brooks/Cole.

Roberts, Rich. 1987. "Politicians, Hired Guns and the Public Interest." In *Congress and Public Policy,* David C. Kozak and John D. Macartney, eds. Chicago: Dorsey Press.

Robinson, Michael J. 1981. "Three Faces of Congressional Media." In *The New Congress,* Thomas Mann and Norman Ornstein, eds. Washington, D.C.: American Enterprise Institute.

Roche, John. 1955. "Judicial Self-Restraint." *American Political Science Review* 49 (September): 759–770.

Roche, John P. 1961. "The Founding Fathers: A Reform Caucus in Action." *American Political Science Review* 55, (December) 799–816.

Rohde, David W. 1988. "Studying Congressional Norms: Concepts and Evidence." *Congress and the Presidency* 15 (Autumn): 139–145.

Rohde, David W. 1991. *Parties and Leaders in the Postreform House.* Chicago: University of Chicago Press.

Rohde, David W., Norman J. Ornstein, and Robert L. Peabody. 1985. "Political Change and Legislative Norms in the U.S. Senate, 1957–1974." In *Studies of Congress,* Glenn R. Parker, ed. Washington, D.C.: Congressional Quarterly Press.

Romano, Lois. 1990. "Women's Place in the House." *Washington Post* (6 March): C1.

Rosenbaum, David E. 1991. "Public in Poll Lambastes Lawmakers on Checks." *New York Times* (10 October): B17.

Rosenbloom, David Lee. 1973. *The Election Men: Professional Campaign Managers and American Democracy.* New York: Quadrangle Books.

Rovner, Julie. 1990. "Child-Care Bill Held Hostage by Senate Republicans." *Congressional Quarterly Weekly Report* 48, no. 16: 1195.

Rule, Wilma. 1992. "Political Dialogue with Some Women Leaders in Moscow and Leningrad." *PS: Political Science and Politics* (June): 308–309.

Rutkus, Denis Steven. 1991. "Newspaper and Television Network News Coverage of Congress during the Summers of 1979 and 1989." U.S. Congress: Congressional Research Service. CRS Report 91–238 GOV.

Sack, Kevin. 1991a. "Albany's New Best Friend: Congress, 7 Near Redistricting." *New York Times* (18 March): A1.

Sack, Kevin. 1991b. "Candidate's Quest: Funds to End Anonymity." *New York Times* (6 June): A1.

Sack, Kevin. 1992. "Albany Getting an Earful over Congressional Map." *New York Times* (10 March): A1.

Safire, William. 1978. *Safire's Political Dictionary.* New York: Random House.

Salholz, Eloise. 1992. "The Hogs on the Hill." *Newsweek* (13 April): 22–23.

Salisbury, Robert H., John P. Heinz, Robert L. Nelson, and Edward O. Laumann. 1992. "Triangles, Networks and Hollow Cores: The Complex Geometry of Washington Interest Representation." In *The Politics of Interests,* Mark P. Petracca, ed. Boulder, Colo.: Westview Press.

Salmore, Stephen, and Barbara Salmore. 1989. *Candidates, Parties and Elections.* Washington, D.C.: Congressional Quarterly Press.

Schelling, Thomas. 1984. *Choices and Consequences.* Cambridge, Mass.: Harvard University Press.

Schick, Allen. 1990. *The Capacity to Budget.* Washington: Urban Institute Press.

Schier, Steven E. 1992. *A Decade of Deficits: Congressional Thought and Fiscal Action.* Albany: State University of New York Press.

Schlozman, Kay Lehman, and John Tierney. 1986. *Organized Interests and American Democracy.* New York: Harper and Row.

Schneier, Edward, and Bertram Gross. 1993. *Legislating Together.* New York: St. Martin's.

Schneier, Edward V. 1988. "Norms and Folkways in Congress: How Much Has Really Changed?" *Congress and the Presidency* 15, (Autumn) 117–137.

Schwartz, Maralee. 1991. "The Gym Rats of the House." *Washington Post* (26 June): A1.

Schwartz, Maralee, and Kenneth J. Cooper. 1992. "Female Candidates Got Major Boost from Contributors." *Washington Post* (8 November): A38.

Seidman, Harold. 1975. "Congressional Committees and Executive Organization." In *Committee Organization in the House.* House Document Number 94–187. 94th Congress, 1st session.

Serra, George. 1992. "Reach Out and Help Someone: The Impact of Casework Solicitation and Word of Mouth Publicity on Member-Constituent Contact." *Southeastern Political Review* 20 (Fall): 231–244.

Serra, George, and Albert Cover. 1992. "The Electoral Consequences of Perquisite Use: The Casework Case." *Legislative Studies Quarterly* (May) 17: 233–246.

Serra, George, Albert D. Cover, Neil Pinney, and Jim Twombly. 1991. "The Changing Shape of Congressional Parties." Paper presented at the Annual Meeting of the American Political Science Association, Washington, D.C.

Shafritz, Jay M. 1988. *Dictionary of American Government and Politics.* Chicago: Dorsey.

Shafritz, Jay. 1993. *The HarperCollins Dictionary of American Government and Politics.* New York: HarperCollins.

Shapiro, Virginia. 1983. *The Political Integration of Women.* Urbana: University of Illinois Press.

Shepsle, Kenneth. 1978. *The Giant Jigsaw Puzzle: Democratic Committee Assignments in the Modern House.* Chicago: University of Chicago Press.

Shepsle, Kenneth A., and Barry R. Weingast. 1987. "The Institutional Foundations of Committee Power." *American Political Science Review* 81, no. 1 (March): 85–104.

Shuman, Howard. 1991. " Lyndon Johnson: Senate Democratic Leader." In *First Among Equals,* Richard A. Baker and Roger H. Davidson, eds. Washington D.C.: Congressional Quarterly, Inc.: 199–235.

Sinclair, Barbara. 1983. *Majority Party Leadership in Congress.* Baltimore: The Johns Hopkins University Press.

Sinclair, Barbara. 1992. "House Majority Party Leadership in an Era of Legislative Constraints." In *The Post Reform Congress,* Robert H. Davidson, ed. New York: St. Martin's Press.

Smith, Hedrick. 1988. *The Power Game: How Washington Works.* New York: Ballentine Books.

Smith, Steven S. 1989. *Call to Order: Floor Politics in the House and Senate.* Washington, D.C.: Brookings Institution.

Smith, Steven S., and Christopher J. Deering. 1990. *Committees in Congress.* Washington, D.C.: CQ Press.

Sorauf, Frank J. 1988. *Money in American Elections.* Glenview, Ill.: Scott, Foresman and Co.

Sovern, Steve. 1991. "Advise and Resent: Mr. Smith Goes to Washington—and Fled the PACs." *Washington Post* (25 August): C1, C4.

Squire, Peverill. 1988. "Who Gets National News Coverage in the U.S. Senate?" *American Politics Quarterly* 16 (April): 139–156.

Squires, Sally. 1990. "Military Med School Targeted in the House." *Washington Post* (12 October): A23.

Stanfield, Rochelle L. 1988. "Plotting Every Move." *National Journal* 20, no. 13 (26 March): 792.

Stanfield, Rochelle L. 1990. "The Golden Rolodex." *National Journal* 22, no. 10 (10 March): 552.

Starobin, Paul. 1987. "Highway Bill Veto Overridden after Close Call in the Senate." *Congressional Quarterly Weekly Report* 45, no. 10 (4 April): 606.

Starobin, Paul. 1991. "Double Trouble." *National Journal* 12, no. 2: 58.

Stencel, Mark. 1993. "Changing Ways That Political Consultants Work." *Washington Post* (business) (8 February): 15.

Stern, Philip. 1988. *The Best Congress Money Can Buy.* New York: Pantheon.

Stockman, David. 1986. *The Triumph of Politics.* New York: Harper & Row.

Strom, Gerald S. 1990. *The Logic of Lawmaking.* Baltimore: Johns Hopkins University.

Sundquist, James L. 1988. "Needed: A Political Theory for the New Era of Coalition Government in the U.S." *Political Science Quarterly* 10 (Winter): 614–630.

Swift, Al (D-WA). 1989. "The 'Permanent Congress' is a Myth." *Washington Post* (19 June): A9.

Thomas, Sue. 1991. "The Impact of Women on State Legislative Policies." *Journal of Politics* 53 (November) 958–976.

Thurber, James. 1991. "The Roots of Divided Democracy." In *Divided Democracy,* James Thurber, ed. Washington, D.C.: Congressional Quarterly.

Thurber, James A. 1981. "The Evolving Role and Effectiveness of the Congressional Research Agencies." In *The House at Work,* Joseph Cooper and Calvin Mackenzie, eds. Austin: University of Texas Press.

U.S. Bureau of the Census. *Statistical Abstract of the U.S.: 1992.* Washington, D.C.

U.S. Congress. House. Commission on Administrative Review. 1977. *Final Report.* H. Doc. 95–272.

U.S. Congress. Office of Technology Assessment. 1988. *Informing the Nation.* Washington, D.C.: Government Printing Office.

Udall, Morris. 1988. *Too Funny to Be President.* New York: Henry Holt.

Uhlaner, Carole Jean, and Kay Lehman Schlozman. 1986. "Candidate Gender and Campaign Receipts." *The Journal of Politics* 48 (February): 30–50.

"Use of the Franking Privilege." 1992. *Washington Post* (22 October): A29.

Uslander, Eric M. 1990. "What Maintains Congressional Norms?" Paper presented at the annual meeting of the American Political Science Association, San Francisco.

Vander Jagt, Representative Guy. 1988. *Congressional Record* (24 May): H3589.

Van Horn, Carl E., Donald C. Baumer, and William T. Gormley, Jr. 1989. *Politics and Public Policy.* Washington, D.C.: Congressional Quarterly.

Vile, M. J. C. 1967. *Constitutionalism and the Separation of Powers.* New York: Oxford University Press.

Vobejda, Barbara. 1991. "Census Puts Undercount in Millions." *Washington Post* (1 April): A17.

Weaver, R. Kent. 1987. "The Politics of Blame." *Journal of Public Policy* 6 (Oct.–Dec.): 371–398.

Wehr, Elizabeth. 1988. "Senate OKs Advance Notice of Plant Closings." *Congressional Quarterly Weekly Report* 46, no. 28 (9 July): 1919.

Weingast, Barry R., and William Marshall. 1988. "The Industrial Organization of Congress." *Journal of Political Economy* 96: 132–163.

Weisskopf, Michael. 1993. "Lining Up Allies in the Health Care Debate." *Washington Post* (3 October): A4.

White, Joseph, and Aaron Wildavsky. 1989. *The Deficit and the Public Interest.* Berkeley: University of California Press.

White, Keith, and Norm Brewer. 1992. "At Least Three New Chairmen Expected in Next Congress." (8 November) Washington, D.C.: Gannet News Service.

Wildavsky, Aaron. 1988. *The New Politics of the Budgetary Process.* Glenview, Ill.: Scott, Foresman.

Wildavsky, Aaron. 1991. "The Two Presidencies." In *The Two Presidencies: A Quarter Century Assessment,* Steven A. Shull, ed. Chicago: Nelson-Hall.

Will, George. 1990. "Is 18 Years on the Hill Enough?" *Washington Post* (7 January): B7.

Will, George. 1991. "One Vote to Limit Terms of Legislators." *Newsday* (3 October): 102.

Will, George. 1992. *Restoration: Congress, Term Limits and the Recovery of Deliberative Democracy.* New York: Free Press.

Wilson, Woodrow. 1885. *Congressional Government.* Boston: Houghton Mifflin (1981 reprint).

Wolf, Naomi. 1991. "Feminism and Intimidation on the Job: Have the Hearings Liberated the Movement?" *Washington Post* (13 October): C1–C2.

Wolf, Richard. 1990. "Losses and Close Calls Give Congress a Chill." *USA TODAY* (8 November): 11a.

Wolfinger, Raymond E., and Richard A. Brody. 1990. "Congress Can't Lose on the Budget Crisis." *Washington Post* (5 November): A15.

Wolfson, Lewis W. 1985. *The Untapped Power of the Press.* New York: Praeger.

Wolpe, Bruce C. 1990. *Lobbying Congress: How the System Works.* Washington, D.C.: Congressional Quarterly Press.

Wood, Gordon. 1969. *The Creation of the American Republic.* Chapel Hill: University of North Carolina Press.

Wright, Gerald C. 1993. "Representation and the Electoral Cycle in the U.S. Senate." Paper presented at the annual meeting of the Midwest Political Science Association.

Wright, John R. 1985. "PACs, Contributions and Roll Calls: An Organizational Perspective." *American Political Science Review* 79 (June): 400–415.

Wright, John R. 1990. "Contributions, Lobbying and Committee Voting in the U.S. House of Representatives." *American Political Science Review* 84 (June): 417–438.

Yeutter, Clayton. 1991. "Incumbents Will Stop at Nothing!" *Washington Post* (9 May): A21.

Yiannakis, Diana E. 1981. "The Grateful Electorate: Casework and Congressional Elections." *American Journal of Political Science* 25 (August): 568–580.

Young, Garry, and Joseph Cooper. 1993. "Multiple Referral and the Transformation of House Decision-Making." In *Congress Reconsidered,* 5th ed., Lawrence E. Dodd and Bruce J. Oppenheimer, eds. Washington, D.C.: Congressional Quarterly.

PHOTO CREDITS

Introduction

BOX I.1: © Marty LaVor; **BOX I.2** and **BOX I.3:** AP/Wide World Photos, Inc.

Chapter 1

p. 2: AP/Wide World Photos, Inc.; **p. 6:** Bettmann Archive; **p. 14L** and **p. 14R:** C-SPAN

Chapter 2

p. 21: Wide World Photos, Inc.; **p. 37:** Bettmann Archive; **BOX 2.6A, BOX 2.6B** and **BOX 2.6C:** Bettmann Archive; **BOX 2.7:** Courtesy Kenneth B. Burkley; **BOX 2.7B:** Sipple: Strategic Communications, Inc./permission of Robert Packwood Campaign Office

Chapter 3

BOX 3.1: Wide World Photos, Inc.; **BOX 3.2:** Bettmann Archive; **BOX 3.3:** © Paul Conklin

Chapter 4

p. 105: © George Tames/NYT Pictures; **BOX 4.2:** AP/Wide World Photos, Inc.; **p. 121:** © Paul Conklin; **p. 124:** Bettmann Archive

Chapter 5

BOX 5.1: Bettmann Archive; **p. 143:** *The People's House,* WQEX(TV) Pittsburgh; **BOX 5.2:** Courtesy Amo Houghton; **p. 147:** © 1993 Nancy Shia/Impact Visuals

Chapter 6

p. 159: © Gale Zucker/Stock Boston; **p. 167:** © Paul Conklin

Chapter 7

BOX 7.2: © Richard A. Bloom 1994; **p. 204:** AP/Wide World Photos, Inc.

Chapter 8

p. 213: AP/Wide World Photos, Inc.; **BOX 8.1:** Courtesy G. V. (Sonny) Montgomery/Committee on Veteran's Affairs

Chapter 9

p. 232: © Scott Goldsmith; **p. 244:** AP/Wide World Photos, Inc.

Chapter 10

p. 260: AP/Wide World Photos, Inc.

INDEX